The Genius of John Ruskin

VICTORIAN LITERATURE AND CULTURE SERIES
Karen Chase, Jerome J. McGann, *and* Herbert Tucker, *Editors*

The Genius of John Ruskin

Selections from His Writings

JOHN D. ROSENBERG, *Editor*

*with a new bibliography by the editor
and a new foreword by* Herbert F. Tucker

University of Virginia Press

Charlottesville and London

University of Virginia Press
Originally published in 1964 by George Braziller, Inc.
© 1998 by the Rector and Visitors of the University of Virginia
All rights reserved

Printed in the United States of America on acid-free paper

9   8   7   6   5

Ruskin, John, 1819–1900.
   The genius of John Ruskin : selections from his writings / John D.
Rosenberg, editor ; with a new bibliography by the editor ; and a new
foreword by Herbert F. Tucker.
      p.   cm. — (Victorian literature and culture series)
   Includes bibliographical references (p.   ).
   ISBN 0-8139-1789-1 (alk. paper)
   I. Rosenberg, John D.   II. Title.   III. Series.
PR5252.R64   1998
828'.809—dc21   97-31013
                                                              CIP

ISBN-13: 978-0-8139-1789-4

CONTENTS

FOREWORD

Teaching anthologies belong to an ephemeral genre, yet among them *The Genius of John Ruskin* has become that rare thing, a classic. With this new Virginia edition of an acclaimed 1963 book that enjoyed wide paperback distribution in 1965, and again in 1979, Rosenberg's Ruskin attains a longevity on the order of Ruskin's own half-century of active publication. Professor Rosenberg now supplies a much expanded bibliography taking into account the wealth of Ruskin scholarship that has appeared during the past three decades. But the rest of the book remains as it was from the first: here are the same judicious representation of texts, culled from a daunting oeuvre and gathered with quiet authority into groupings that are accessible alike to thematic and to chronological study; the same sequence of deft, appreciative introductions; the same admirably spare apparatus and annotation. That so stable an anthology still consorts with a bibliography that has developed so richly, and in such unpredictable directions, attests the classic status of Rosenberg's Ruskin. For, even as subsequent scholars have gone beyond *The Genius* to reconnoiter afresh Ruskin's forty volumes, the canon and career established by this book have furnished consistent points of scholarly departure and return.

It was inevitable that the lapse of time should disconfirm, or at least loosen, certain claims Rosenberg advanced decades ago. His 1963 bets on Hopkins, Dickens, Mill, and Ruskin, as against Arnold, Meredith, Macaulay, and Morris, do look like winners in the hindsight of 1998 or so. Yet the very gesture (p. 11) feels dated, and what it reveals most strikingly today may be how disused a method comparative evaluation has become within a single critical generation— a revelation that may become matter for regret in proportion as we acknowledge that the anthology in our hands results from countless, steady acts of comparative evaluation on Rosenberg's part. A different interest will attach, given the retrenchments of the Clinton epoch, to a later declaration presumably framed on the threshold of a Great Society: that reversing momentum toward the welfare state Ruskin had instrumentally envisioned "would require a revolution" (p. 220). To gauge the double problem in parallax here—between a British sage and an American anthologist, and then between the 1960s' cultural climate and the 1990s'—is to appreciate what interesting changes history can ring on a term like "revolution." But it is also, beyond that, to grasp larger continuities of modern crisis and urgent appeal that, spanning two centuries now, make historical change more than just interesting. Rosenberg reminds us that Ruskin matters and that it was one task of his provoking genius to call out our commitments and refuse us the luxury of sequestering them from our tastes.

As a title, *The Genius of John Ruskin* implies less that Ruskin *was* a genius than that he *had* genius—or, what amounts to much the same thing, that genius had *him*. The fact that Rosenberg made his choice of texts soon after finishing a full-dress study of Ruskin's life and works helped free his anthology of the seductions, and reductions, of mere biographical illustrativeness. Here instead is a book that lets its genius speak and from which there emerges not so much a narrative of personal trial, glory, and pathos as a set of "patterns of thought" (p. 15). Ruskin's kind of genius throve on the possession of insights found rather than created: the critic who early coined the term "the pathetic fallacy" (pp. 61–72) made a point of presenting himself as the draftsman or copyist of truth and not its architect or inventor. The insistent patterns he traced in a carpet or landscape or economy were formidable, recombinant, and yet, with the idiosyncrasy of genius, selfless too—a paradox displayed most fully in *Fors Clavigera* and *Praeterita*, which emerge in Rosenberg's flawless selection as Ruskin's most personal writings and also his least self-conscious. "So passionately disinterested, yet so passionately itself," says Rosenberg about the mind of Ruskin (p. 320); the phrase could serve as well to describe the bold editorial tact that makes this book possible.

With its few notes, lightness of biographical touch, and (boldest tact of all) no pictures, this anthology invites Ruskin's reader to read Ruskin, nothing less. *The Genius of John Ruskin* proposes an undistracted encounter with a mind of great reach and acuteness: a mind quickened always to eloquence, if sometimes to frenzy, by people's failure to attend, to observe the things around them and come to their senses. At our own cultural juncture, as new technologies of simulation and poetics of virtuality sweep into the ascendant, nothing could be more salutary than Ruskin's call to mind. So here it is again.

Herbert F. Tucker

INTRODUCTION

John D. Rosenberg

At the turn of the century a young littérateur in Paris and an Indian lawyer in Johannesburg discovered Ruskin, and in so doing discovered themselves. "He will enable my spirit," Proust wrote in the first fervors of discipleship, "to enter regions to which formerly it had no access, for he is the gate." Gandhi wrote in his autobiography that reading *Unto This Last* had awakened some of his deepest convictions and transformed his life. The list might be extended—William Morris and Ezra Pound, Tolstoy and Clement Attlee, Bernard Shaw and Frank Lloyd Wright—but the additions only heighten one's perplexity that a single mind could so decisively influence such diverse men.

At the age of nine Ruskin began an epic "Poem on the Universe." His subject remained the world, to which he responded with a baffling multiplicity of judgments. In the 1840s he saw in Turner, and taught a visually retarded generation to see, a revolutionary truth to the visible world which had never before been rendered on canvas. But in the 1870s his prejudices blinded him to the achievement of the French impressionists, although they exemplified the very principles he had discovered in Turner thirty years earlier. Modern architects unwittingly borrow his vocabulary—"organic form," harmony of function and design, frank display of structure and materials—and often build upon his principles. Yet he opposed the use of the new materials which have made architecture the most vital of modern arts.* As an economist and social critic, he succeeded more than any other English writer in moderating the barbarisms of nineteenth-century *laissez faire* and persuading his countrymen that starvation in the streets of their prosperous capital was not a "law of nature" but an affront to humanity. Yet he despised parliamentary reforms, ballot boxes, labor unions, indeed the whole egalitarian structure of the Welfare State that he helped bring into being. "I am, and my father was before me, a violent Tory of the old school;— Walter Scott's school, that is to say, and Homer's." So begins *Præterita*, the autobiography of this great nineteenth-century radical who, with equal justice, described himself as "the reddest also of the red." One cannot read Ruskin for very long without a sense of bafflement, perhaps of rage, but always of revelation.

His works are as burdened with contradiction as experience itself. Perhaps that is what Shaw meant when he said that few men have embodied our manifold nature more markedly than Ruskin. Endowed with a great mind yet retaining the emotions of a child, noble and narrow, dogmatic and yielding, immoderate both in delight and despair, arrogant and gentle, self-obsessed and self-sacrificing, compulsively communicative yet solitary, prophetic and blind, Ruskin was always changing and always himself. Even his contradictions have a certain consistency. At different stages of life he reacted differently to the same things; yet each response was absolute in its integrity, reflecting a unity of sensibility rather than of system. Throughout his career his mind was capable of change, and hence of growth; but the change, as he once remarked, was that of a tree, not of a cloud.

During the half century since Ruskin's death in 1900, his

* And also, at times, the most sterile. The blank glitter of the lifeless slab flashed on Ruskin's mind almost a century before it was to rise in reduplicated regularity: "You shall draw out your plates of glass," he predicted, "and beat out your bars of iron till you have encompassed us all . . . with endless perspective of black skeleton and blinding square."

genius lay buried under the bulk of his own words. The standard edition of his *Works* contains thirty-nine oversized volumes; most modern readers are less aware of their contents than of the psychological aberrations of their author. He has never regained the reputation he held among his contemporaries, nor has he attracted the widespread critical attention that has recently illuminated the achievement of Dickens or Hopkins. Ruskin's early critics were for the most part pious eulogists who portrayed him as far tidier and less vital than he is. Between the world wars everything Victorian was so patently repugnant that it was an easy leap to equate the platitudes of the disciples with the perceptions of the master, and to reject them both. At the time of Ruskin's death, few men would have doubted the justice of Tolstoy's praise; until recently few would have believed it: "Ruskin was one of the most remarkable men, not only of England and our time, but of all countries and all times. He was one of those rare men who think with their hearts, and so he thought and said not only what he himself had seen and felt, but what everyone will think and say in the future."

Now that the revaluation of the Victorians is solidly under way, we can recognize their creative exuberance as matched only by that of the Elizabethans. As they recede from us in time, they come closer to us in spirit, until the generation of stern prophets and self-assured dogmatists appears strangely perplexed, less certain of themselves and their world than they cared to admit, and far more like ourselves than we ever suspected. But the rush of reawakened sympathy has lacked true discernment. If we recognize that Gerard Manley Hopkins is a great poet, we have yet to acknowledge that Matthew Arnold is often a bad one. Dickens and Meredith, Mill and Macaulay, Ruskin and Morris are studied in our universities as equal eminences. Thirty years from now such pairings may seem as indiscriminate as those of Shakespeare and Kyd, Blake and Gray.

Of all the Victorians, Ruskin has least found his deserved

place among his contemporaries or in our literature at large. The great Library Edition of his *Works* has served as his monument in a sense unintended by its editors, and the selections available to the general reader have not made resurrection seem especially worthwhile. In our century Ruskin has been read in outdated, truncated fragments in which the sustained sweep, eccentricity, and uniquely personal voice of his genius are altogether obscured. The result has been a popular image of Ruskin at once absurd and contradictory: the arch-aesthete and word-painter who somehow fostered wedding-cake Gothic, Walter Pater, and *l'art pour l'art;* and the puritanical preacher, an effete appendage of Carlyle who overmoralized art and vainly castigated society. Perhaps the present volume will replace the caricature with an authentic portrait. Ideally, it may accomplish for Ruskin what Arnold's edition of Wordsworth did in the late nineteenth century—put in the hands of the educated reader some of the finest work of an author encumbered at his death by uncritical reverence and then eclipsed by undeserved neglect.

Ruskin's genius was a unique fusion of the capacity to see with the amazed eyes of a child and to reason with a mind as swift and penetrating as any that England has produced. He once praised the artist's ability to recover *"innocence of the eye . . .* a sort of childish perception of flat stains of colour, merely as such, without consciousness of what they signify,—as a blind man would see them if suddenly gifted with sight." Anyone who has read Ruskin closely has known that moment when the veil of familiarity abruptly lifts and one feels, as Charlotte Brontë did on first reading *Modern Painters,* that he has been given a new sense—sight. This incapacity to become habituated to the world was the one talent on which all his others depended.

The intensity of Ruskin's perceptions imprisoned him in a private universe where each glance was a revelation but there were no eyes other than his own. In Benjamin Jowett's phrase, "Ruskin never rubbed his mind against others." He had two masters—Turner and Carlyle—and many disciples, but no colleagues. His intellectual isolation was very nearly absolute; to it he owed his occasional arrogance and frequent eccentricity.

Ruskin faltered away from himself only in some of his early prose, which is marred by a self-conscious literary gesticulation. At times the first two volumes of *Modern Painters* bog down in stretches of starchy rhetoric. But the same volumes contain passages which, despite their massed splendor, dazzle the reader less with their magnificence than with their truth. Nonetheless, it was the chief provocation of Ruskin's life to be praised merely for putting words together prettily; since he is best known today for his virtuoso pieces, the illusion persists that he was a fine writer who said foolish things.

Ruskin's style is as varied as his subjects or moods. In youth, when his feeling for physical beauty was keenest, he described nature with an almost audible laughter of delight at his power to make words follow his will. "There is the strong instinct in me," he wrote to his father, "which I cannot analyse—to draw and describe the things I love . . . a sort of instinct like that for eating or drinking." One of his strongest loves was for the "wild, various, fantastic, tameless unity of the sea." For some thirty pages in *Modern Painters* he wrote of the sea with a sustained exaltation unequaled in English, except perhaps for Bunyan's description of the pilgrims crossing the river of death and entering the gates of heaven. The standard excerpts from *Modern Painters* mute the larger rhythms of these prose hymns to nature, destroying the cumulative effect of Ruskin's impassioned precision.

The prose of his middle period gains in subtlety without losing force. The reader still hears sonorous echoes from the King James version of the Bible, but in *Unto This Last* one is less conscious of Ruskin's mastery of the cadenced music of words than of the thrust of his logic and the lucidity of his rage. More and more he revised in order to be concise instead of eloquent. The counterpoint of balanced clauses becomes less conspicuous; assonance predominates over the more obvious effects of alliteration; sound and sense form a single tissue of expression in which the substitution of a word, the alteration of a vowel, distort both music and meaning.

As Ruskin's sense of the mystery and terror of life deepened, his prose became more intimate, achieving the final eloquence of simplicity. He had always felt the need to record all that he had ever seen or thought or felt. But in his later books, above all in *Fors Clavigera*, he wrote less to register his observations than to voice his perplexity and pain, to escape from an enfolding isolation that found him beloved yet incapable of loving, ever in company yet ever alone. As the inner pressures mounted, he brought to bear upon his own psyche the great gifts of penetration and expression that he had previously focused upon external nature. He became his own subject; simultaneously, the tone of his prose shifted. The stately piling up of clauses, perfectly suited to his Alpine descriptions and towering hopes, yielded to a subtler, quieter style which registers the very pulsations of his grief and is as moving as his earlier prose is magnificent.

His late voice is rich in all the nuances of speech, capable almost of physical gesture. We become oblivious of the printed word and follow instead the elusive soliloquy of a mind so habituated to solitude that we seem to overhear it thinking aloud. Nothing else is quite so daringly inconsequent, so immediate, so capable of communicating the music of consciousness itself. Joyce's interior monologues are, by comparison, contrived declamations. The range and inexhaustible vitality of Ruskin's many styles are unsurpassed in English prose.

In his diary Ruskin describes a nightmare in which a skilled surgeon takes a scalpel to his skull and proceeds to dissect himself. Ruskin's self-anatomizing in his books is no less incisive, but the horror is transmuted into a terrible beauty. We may for the moment discount the revolutionary importance of his criticism of the world around him. There remains the world he discovered within himself, a world which he delineated on every page he wrote and which constitutes the most animate record of genius ever preserved in words.

A Note on the Selections

In the selections that follow, I have stressed the five books which most richly display the temper of Ruskin's mind. The first, *Modern Painters*, was begun when Ruskin was in his early twenties. The others—*The Stones of Venice*, *Unto This Last*, *Fors Clavigera*, and *Præterita*—were written in each of the successive decades of his career, *Præterita* marking his end as a writer. The selections are necessarily fragmentary. But they are designed to preserve, within the limits of a single manageable volume, the integrity of Ruskin's most important books in the order in which they were written.

Nothing has been chosen merely because it is felicitous; nothing has been omitted merely because it contains a prejudice offensive to the modern reader. Several selections are anthologized for the first time. They are included less for their novelty than for their illumination of the patterns of thought linking Ruskin's major works. Such light is especially needful because, with few exceptions, Ruskin's books are fragments of a splendid but shattered design which each reader must ultimately compose in his own mind. My purpose has been to present that pattern as fully as possible and with a minimum of distortion.

The text of the selections is that of the authoritative Library Edition of Ruskin's *Works*, published by George Allen (London, 1903–12). Portions of the editor's introductions have previously appeared in *The Darkening Glass: A Portrait of Ruskin's Genius*.

Art

Modern Painters is the first book on art by an English writer of pre-eminent intellectual power; it remains perhaps the finest.

The genesis of *Modern Painters* may be traced to the patterned carpet on Ruskin's nursery floor. His mother, a puritanical Scot, allowed him neither playmates nor playthings. Ruskin passed his childhood in serene but unrelenting solitude, forced to find in his powers of observation the chief pleasures of his being. Alone in the nursery or enclosed in the walled garden of his home at Herne Hill, he examined the patterns of carpet and leaf with the same fanatic fidelity of perception which he later focused on the landscapes of Turner and the jeweled surfaces of Fra Angelico.

On his thirteenth birthday Ruskin was given a copy of Samuel Rogers's *Italy* with illustrations by Turner; the gift initiated him into his life's work, for in Turner's vignettes he discovered the divinity of nature which he was later to celebrate in *Modern Painters*. When he was seventeen, Ruskin wrote a precocious defense of Turner in reply to an attack published in *Blackwood's Magazine*. Turner's reputation had long been established, but the critics denounced the bold and luminous compositions of his great final period. On Turner's advice, Ruskin did not publish the article. But in defending Turner against *Blackwood's'* charge of

ludicrous distortion of nature, he laid the groundwork for
Modern Painters.

Modern Painters would be less perplexing if Ruskin had
known more about art when he began it, or learned less in
the course of its composition. The first volume appeared in
1843, when he was twenty-four and still quite ignorant of
art. The fifth and final volume was published in 1860,
when his interest had shifted from art and nature to society
and man. The point of view remained constant; the range
of vision widened enormously.

Two years after publishing the first volume, Ruskin set
out on one of the most memorable journeys of his life.
Traveling without his parents for the first time, he was
overwhelmed in Italy by a wealth of beauty of which he had
known almost nothing. The tour culminated in Venice, at
the Scuola di San Rocco, where the power of Tintoretto
struck him with the force of a revelation. "I never was so
utterly crushed to the earth before any human intellect,"
he wrote to his father, "as I was to-day—before Tintoret."

Ruskin returned to England in the autumn of 1845. The
second volume of *Modern Painters*, published six months
later, is a testament to his newborn love of Italian art; Tintoretto and Fra Angelico nearly usurp the places of Turner
and nature. The third and fourth volumes did not appear
until 1856, well after Ruskin's visit to the Scuola di San
Rocco had led him to postpone *Modern Painters* and begin
the long digression which produced *The Stones of Venice.*

The temper as well as the direction of Ruskin's thought
was changing. In 1858, two years before completing *Modern
Painters*, he experienced a religious "unconversion" as crucial to the final form of the book as his discovery of Tintoretto or his architectural studies in Venice. One day in
Turin he walked out of a dim Waldensian chapel in disgust at a sermon on the wickedness of the wide world. He
wandered through the festive streets of the "condemned
city" to the Royal Gallery, where, looking at Veronese's
Solomon and the Queen of Sheba glowing in the sunlight,

he abandoned the evangelicalism which had obtruded into the first two volumes of *Modern Painters*. Ruskin's religious and aesthetic responses were complementary aspects of a single emotion; his shutting of the door of the sectarian chapel coincided with his espousal of humanism in the later volumes, with their praise of Veronese, of "The Naturalist Ideal," and of the power and glory of man.

That glory takes on a darker coloring in the last chapters of *Modern Painters,* for Ruskin had become less moved by the beauty of art and nature than by the pathos and terror of life. The tone of the first two volumes is pious and lyrical; that of the later volumes is humanistic and tragic. In *Modern Painters I* and *II* Ruskin looked at mountain peaks and saw God; in *Modern Painters III, IV,* and *V* he looked at their bases and saw shattered rocks and impoverished villages. The face of the Creator gradually withdrew from the creation and in its place man emerged as a tragic figure in the foreground of a still potent, but flawed, nature. With that emergence, Ruskin's interest moved from mountains to men, from art to society.

The selections that follow mirror the evolution of Ruskin's thought during the eighteen-year period in which he wrote *Modern Painters*. In the early chapters he was still very much a Romantic, seeing nature through Turner's eyes and writing of her with a religious fervor akin to Wordsworth's. The invocations to nature throughout *Modern Painters* suggest that the book belongs as much to the history of Romanticism as to the history of art. Turner serves as an artist-priest who interprets the visible world through the divine hieroglyph of art. Ruskin tries to open the eyes of his readers to this new scripture, enlarging their sensibilities and revolutionizing the appreciation of art as Wordsworth and Coleridge had revolutionized the appreciation of poetry. *Modern Painters* is the last great statement of the English Romantic renovation of sensibility, as the *Lyrical Ballads* is the first. Nature is the central term in both, Wordsworth equating it with simplicity in his attack on eighteenth-century poetry, Ruskin with truth in his attack on the "Grand Style" in art.

Almost all of the selections from Volumes I and III are addressed to the great theoretical question of *Modern Painters,* the nature of truth in art. I have omitted Ruskin's extended discussion of "Ideas of Beauty" in Volume II, but I should call the reader's attention to two notable chapters within that volume. One is on "The Imagination Penetrative," a subject to which Ruskin returns conclusively in the anthologized chapter, "Of the Naturalist Ideal." In the other, "The Theoretic Faculty," he distinguishes between *aesthesis,* the mere sensuous pleasure one takes in art, and *theoria,* the response to beauty of one's total moral being. By the end of the century Ruskin's distinction had been forgotten, and the aesthetes became entrapped in the sterile pursuit of art for art's sake. Throughout *Modern Painters* Ruskin opposed the separation of art from life not because he feared what was lovely but because he felt it too important to be divorced from what was good and true.

The closing selections mark the transition from the God-in-Nature of *Modern Painters I* to the Satanic Nature of *The Storm-Cloud of the Nineteenth Century.* Ruskin startlingly juxtaposes the two natures in the final chapters of Volume IV—"The Mountain Gloom" and "The Mountain Glory." The latter is a hymn of praise to the "great cathedrals of the earth," with their gates of rock and vaults of purple. But the chapter on mountain gloom plunges us into a wasteland of blighted Alpine villages where life ebbs away, buildings crumble, and weeds grow in place of flowers.

Turner, the priest of the sacredness of nature in *Modern Painters I,* now exemplifies in his Alpine sketches the unredeemed pathos Ruskin had begun to see everywhere in the nineteenth century. Turner remains the painter of "the loveliness of nature," but a nature "with the worm at its root." This change is most marked in the extraordinary chapter on "The Two Boyhoods" of Giorgione and Turner.

The chapter opens with an ornate description of the shimmering sea-city of marble and gold where Giorgione was born. At the point of excess, Ruskin's prose abruptly modulates to the squalid actuality of the London slums where Turner spent his youth, picking up his first bits of vigorous English around wharves and markets filled with offal. Turner paints nature because he cannot find beauty elsewhere. Of the life of "multitudinous, marred humanity," he paints only labor, sorrow, and death.

The chapter ends with a description of the marred humanity which, during Turner's youth, had died on the battlefields of Europe and in the industrial centers of England, its life "trampled out in the slime of the street, crushed to dust amidst the roaring of the wheel . . . rotted down to forgotten graves through years of ignorant patience, and vain seeking for help from man."

Ruskin published the volume containing "The Two Boyhoods" in the spring of 1860. He had at last completed the long labor of *Modern Painters* and went abroad to Chamonix. There, in the shadow of the same mountains which had inspired the most eloquent passages of *Modern Painters*, he wrote the opening chapter of *Unto This Last*.

—J. D. R.

MODERN PAINTERS

Definition
of Greatness
in Art

Painting, or art generally, as such, with all its technicalities, difficulties, and particular ends, is nothing but a noble and expressive language, invaluable as the vehicle of thought, but by itself nothing. He who has learned what is commonly considered the whole art of painting, that is, the art of representing any natural object faithfully, has as yet only learned the language by which his thoughts are to be expressed. He has done just as much towards being that which we ought to respect as a great painter, as a man who has learnt how to express himself grammatically and melodiously has towards being a great poet. The language is, indeed, more difficult of acquirement in the one case than in the other, and possesses more power of delighting the sense, while it speaks to the intellect; but it is, nevertheless, nothing more than language, and all those excellences which are peculiar to the painter as such, are merely what rhythm, melody, precision, and force are in the words of the orator and the poet, necessary to their greatness, but not the tests of their greatness. It is not by the mode of representing and saying, but by what is represented and said, that the respective greatness either of the painter or the writer is to be finally determined. . . .

If I say that the greatest picture is that which conveys to the mind of the spectator the greatest number of the greatest ideas, I have a definition which will include as subjects of comparison every pleasure which art is capable of conveying. If I were to say, on the contrary, that the best picture was that which most closely imitated nature, I should assume that art could only please by imitating nature; and I should cast out of the pale of criticism those parts of works of art which are not imitative, that is to say, intrinsic beauties of colour and form, and those works of art wholly, which, like the Arabesques of Raffaelle in the Loggias, are not imitative at all. Now, I want a definition of art wide enough to include all its varieties of aim. I do not say, therefore, that the art is greatest which gives most pleasure, because perhaps there is some art whose end is to teach, and not to please. I do not say that the art is greatest which teaches us most, because perhaps there is some art whose end is to please, and not to teach. I do not say that the art is greatest which imitates best, because perhaps there is some art whose end is to create and not to imitate. But I say that the art is greatest which conveys to the mind of the spectator, by any means whatsoever, the greatest number of the greatest ideas; and I call an idea great in proportion as it is received by a higher faculty of the mind, and as it more fully occupies, and in occupying, exercises and exalts, the faculty by which it is received.

If this, then, be the definition of great art, that of a great artist naturally follows. He is the greatest artist who has embodied, in the sum of his works, the greatest number of the greatest ideas. [Vol. I, Part 1, Sec. 1, Chap. 2]

That the Truth of Nature Is Not to Be Discerned by the Uneducated Senses

It is possible for all men, by care and attention, to form a just judgment of the fidelity of artists to nature. To do this no peculiar powers of mind are required, no sympathy with particular feelings, nothing which every man of ordinary intellect does not in some degree possess,—powers, namely,

of observation and intelligence, which by cultivation may
be brought to a high degree of perfection and acuteness. But
until this cultivation has been bestowed, and until the instrument thereby perfected has been employed in a consistent series of careful observations, it is as absurd as it is
audacious to pretend to form any judgment whatsoever respecting the truth of art: and my first business, before going
a step farther, must be to combat the nearly universal error
of belief among the thoughtless and unreflecting, that they
know either what nature is, or what is like her; that they can
discover truth by instinct, and that their minds are such
pure Venice glass as to be shocked by all treachery. I have
to prove to them that there are more things in heaven and
earth than are dreamed of in their philosophy, and that the
truth of nature is a part of the truth of God; to him who
does not search it out, darkness, as it is to him who does,
infinity.

The first great mistake that people make in the matter, is
the supposition that they must *see* a thing if it be before
their eyes. . . . And what is here said, which all must feel by
their own experience to be true, is more remarkably and
necessarily the case with sight than with any other of the
senses, for this reason, that the ear is not accustomed to exercise constantly its functions of hearing; it is accustomed to
stillness, and the occurrence of a sound of any kind whatsoever is apt to awake attention, and be followed with perception, in proportion to the degree of sound; but the eye
during our waking hours, exercises constantly its function
of seeing; it is its constant habit; we always, as far as the
bodily organ is concerned, see something, and we always see
in the same degree; so that the occurrence of sight, as such,
to the eye, is only the continuance of its necessary state of
action, and awakes no attention whatsoever, except by the
particular nature and quality of the sight. And thus, unless
the minds of men are particularly directed to the impressions of sight, objects pass perpetually before the eyes without conveying any impression to the brain at all; and so

pass actually unseen, not merely unnoticed, but in the full clear sense of the word unseen. . . .

With this kind of bodily sensibility to colour and form is intimately connected that higher sensibility which we revere as one of the chief attributes of all noble minds, and as the chief spring of real poetry. I believe this kind of sensibility may be entirely resolved into the acuteness of bodily sense of which I have been speaking, associated with love, love I mean in its infinite and holy functions, as it embraces divine and human and brutal intelligences, and hallows the physical perception of external objects by association, gratitude, veneration, and other pure feelings of our moral nature. And although the discovery of truth is in itself altogether intellectual, and dependent merely on our powers of physical perception and abstract intellect, wholly independent of our moral nature, yet these instruments (perception and judgment) are so sharpened and brightened, and so far more swiftly and effectively used, when they have the energy and passion of our moral nature to bring them into action— perception is so quickened by love, and judgment so tempered by veneration, that, practically, a man of deadened moral sensation is always dull in his perception of truth.

[Vol. I, Part 2, Sec. 1, Chap. 2]

Of Truth of Space

We have seen how indistinctness of individual distances becomes necessary in order to express the adaptation of the eye to one or other of them; we have now to examine that kind of indistinctness which is dependent on real retirement of the object, even when the focus of the eye is fully concentrated upon it. The first kind of indecision is that which belongs to all objects which the eye is not adapted to, whether near or far off: the second is that consequent upon the want of power in the eye to receive a clear image of objects at a great distance from it, however attentively it may regard them.

Draw on a piece of white paper a square and a circle, each about a twelfth or eighth of an inch in diameter, and blacken them so that their forms may be very distinct; place your paper against the wall at the end of the room, and retire from it a greater or less distance accordingly as you have drawn the figures larger or smaller. You will come to a point where, though you can see both the spots with perfect plainness, you cannot tell which is the square and which the circle.

Now this takes place of course with every object in a landscape, in proportion to its distance and size. The definite forms of the leaves of a tree, however sharply and separately they may appear to come against the sky, are quite indistinguishable at fifty yards off, and the form of everything becomes confused before we finally lose sight of it. Now if the character of an object, say the front of a house, be explained by a variety of forms in it, as the shadows in the tops of the windows, the lines of the architraves, the seams of the masonry, etc.; these lesser details, as the object falls into distance, become confused and undecided, each of them losing its definite form, but all being perfectly visible as something, a white or a dark spot or stroke, not lost sight of, observe, but yet so seen that we cannot tell what they are. As the distance increases, the confusion becomes greater, until at last the whole front of the house becomes merely a flat pale space, in which, however, there is still observable a kind of richness and chequering, caused by the details in it, which, though totally merged and lost in the mass, have still an influence on the texture of that mass; until at last the whole house itself becomes a mere light or dark spot which we can plainly see, but cannot tell what it is, nor distinguish it from a stone or any other object.

Now what I particularly wish to insist upon, is the state of vision in which all the details of an object are seen, and yet seen in such confusion and disorder that we cannot in the least tell what they are, or what they mean. It is not mist between us and the object, still less is it shade, still less is it want of character; it is a confusion, a mystery, an interfering of undecided lines with each other, not a diminution of their number; window and door, architrave and frieze, all are there: it is no cold and vacant mass, it is full and rich and abundant, and yet you cannot see a single form so as to know what it is. Observe your friend's face as he is coming up to you. First it is nothing more than a white spot; now it is a face, but you cannot see the two eyes, nor the mouth, even as spots; you see a confusion of lines, a something which you know from experience to be indicative of a face, and yet you cannot tell how it is so. Now he is nearer, and you can see the spots for the eyes and mouth, but they are not blank spots neither; there is detail in them; you cannot see the lips, nor the teeth, nor the brows, and yet you see more than mere spots; it is a mouth and an eye, and there is light and sparkle and expression in them, but nothing distinct. Now he is nearer still, and you can see that he is like your friend, but you cannot tell whether he is, or not; there is a vagueness and indecision of line still. Now you are sure, but even yet there are a thousand things in his face which have their effect in inducing the recognition, but which you cannot see so as to know what they are.

Changes like these, and states of vision corresponding to them, take place with each and all of the objects of nature, and two great principles of truth are deducible from their observation. First, place an object as close to the eye as you like, there is always something in it which you *cannot* see, except in the hinted and mysterious manner above described. You can see the texture of a piece of dress, but you cannot see the individual threads which compose it, though they are all felt, and have each of them influence on the eye. Secondly, place an object as far from the eye as you like, and until it becomes itself a mere spot, there is always something in it which you *can* see, though only in the hinted manner above described. Its shadows and lines and local colours are not lost sight of as it retires; they get mixed and indistinguishable, but they are still there, and there is a difference always perceivable between an object possessing such details and a flat or vacant space. The grass blades of a meadow a mile off, are so far discernible that there will be a marked difference between its appearance and that of a piece of wood painted green. And thus nature is never distinct and never vacant, she is always mysterious, but always abundant; you always see something, but you never see all.

And thus arise that exquisite finish and fulness which God has appointed to be the perpetual source of fresh pleasure to the cultivated and observant eye; a finish which no distance can render invisible, and no nearness comprehensible; which in every stone, every bough, every cloud, and every wave is multiplied around us, for ever presented, and for ever exhaustless. And hence in art, every space or touch in which we can see everything, or in which we can see nothing, is false. Nothing can be true which is either complete or vacant; every touch is false which does not suggest more than it represents, and every space is false which represents nothing.

Now, I would not wish for any more illustrative or marked examples of the total contradiction of these two great principles, than the landscape works of the old masters, taken as a body; the Dutch masters furnishing the cases of seeing everything, and the Italians of seeing nothing. The rule with both is indeed the same, differently applied—"You shall see the bricks in the wall, and be able to count them, or you shall see nothing but a dead flat:" but the Dutch give you the bricks, and the Italians the flat. Nature's rule being the precise reverse—"You shall never be able to count the bricks, but you shall never see a dead space."

Take, for instance, the street in the centre of the really great landscape of Poussin (great in feeling at least) marked 260 in the Dulwich Gallery.* The houses are dead square masses with a light side and a dark side, and black touches

* *A Roman Road,* in the style of Nicolas Poussin.

for windows. There is no suggestion of anything in any of the spaces; the light wall is dead grey, the dark wall dead grey, and the windows dead black. How differently would nature have treated us! She would have let us see the Indian corn hanging on the walls, and the image of the Virgin at the angles, and the sharp, broken, broad shadows of the tiled eaves, and the deep-ribbed tiles with the doves upon them, and the carved Roman capital built into the wall, and the white and blue stripes of the mattresses stuffed out of the windows, and the flapping corners of the mat blinds. All would have been there; not as such, not like the corn, or blinds or tiles, not to be comprehended or understood, but a confusion of yellow and black spots and strokes, carried far too fine for the eye to follow, microscopic in its minuteness, and filling every atom and part of space with mystery, out of which would have arranged itself the general impression of truth and life.

Again, take the distant city on the right bank of the river in Claude's Marriage of Isaac and Rebecca, in the National Gallery. I have seen many cities in my life, and drawn not a few; and I have seen many fortifications, fancy ones included, which frequently supply us with very few ideas indeed, especially in matters of proportion; but I do not remember ever having met with either a city or a fortress *entirely* composed of round towers of various heights and sizes, all facsimiles of each other, and absolutely agreeing in the number of battlements. I have, indeed, some faint recollection of having delineated such a one in the first page of a spelling book when I was four years old; but, somehow or other, the dignity and perfection of the ideal were not appreciated, and the volume was not considered to be increased in value by the frontispiece. Without, however, venturing to doubt the entire sublimity of the same ideal as it occurs in Claude, let us consider how nature, if she had been fortunate enough to originate so perfect a conception, would have managed it in its details. Claude has permitted us to see every battlement, and the first impulse we feel upon looking at the picture is to count how many there are. Nature would have given us a peculiar confused roughness of the upper lines, a multitude of intersections and spots, which we should have known from experience was indicative of battlements, but which we might as well have thought of creating as of counting. Claude has given you the walls below in one dead void of uniform grey. There is nothing to be seen, or felt, or guessed at in it; it is grey paint or grey shade, whichever you may choose to call it, but it is nothing more. Nature would have let you see, nay, would have compelled you to see, thousands of spots and lines, not one to be absolutely understood or accounted for, but yet all characteristic and different from each other; breaking lights on shattered stones, vague shadows from waving vegetation, irregular stains of time and weather, mouldering hollows, sparkling casements; all would have been there; none indeed, seen as such, none comprehensible or like themselves, but all visible; little shadows and sparkles, and scratches, making that whole space of colour a transparent, palpitating, various infinity. . . .

Now it is, indeed, impossible for the painter to follow all this; he cannot come up to the same degree and order of infinity, but he can give us a lesser kind of infinity. He has not one thousandth part of the space to occupy which nature has; but he can, at least, leave no part of that space vacant and unprofitable. If nature carries out her minutiæ over miles, he has no excuse for generalizing in inches. And if he will only give us all he can, if he will give us a fulness as complete and as mysterious as nature's, we will pardon him for its being the fulness of a cup instead of an ocean. . . .

I am somewhat anticipating my subject here, because I can scarcely help answering the objections which I know must arise in the minds of most readers, especially of those who are *partially* artistical, respecting "generalization," "breadth," "effect," etc. It were to be wished that our writers on art would not dwell so frequently on the necessity of breadth, without explaining what it means; and that we had more constant reference made to the principle which I can only remember having seen once clearly explained and insisted on, that breadth is not vacancy. Generalization is unity, not destruction of parts; and composition is not annihilation, but arrangement of materials. The breadth which unites the truths of nature with her harmonies is meritorious and beautiful; but the breadth which annihilates those truths by the million is not painting nature, but painting over her. And so the masses which result from right concords and relations of details are sublime and impressive; but the masses which result from the eclipse of details are contemptible and painful. And we shall show . . . that distances like those of Poussin are mere meaningless tricks of clever execution, which, when once discovered, the artist may repeat over and over again, with mechanical contentment and perfect satisfaction, both to himself and to his superficial admirers, with no more exertion of intellect nor awakening of feeling than any tradesman has in multiplying some ornamental pattern of furniture. . . .

And now, take up one of Turner's distances, it matters not which or of what kind, drawing or painting, small or great, done thirty years ago or for last year's Academy, as you like; say that of the Mercury and Argus; and look if every fact which I have just been pointing out in nature be not carried out in it. Abundant beyond the power of the eye to embrace or follow, vast and various beyond the power of the mind to comprehend, there is yet not one atom in its whole extent and mass which does not suggest more than it represents; nor does it suggest vaguely, but in such a manner as to prove that the conception of each individual inch of that distance is absolutely clear and complete in the master's mind, a separate picture fully worked out: but yet, clearly and fully as the idea is formed, just so much of it is given, and no more, as nature would have allowed us to feel or see; just so much as would enable a spectator of experience and knowledge to understand almost every minute fragment of separate detail, but appears, to the unpractised and careless eye, just what a distance of nature's own would appear, an unintelligible mass. Not one line out of the millions there is without meaning, yet there is not one which is not affected and disguised by the dazzle and indecision of distance. No form is made out, and yet no form is unknown.

[Vol. I, Part 2, Sec. 2, Chap. 5]

Of Water, as Painted by Turner

I believe it is a result of the experience of all artists, that it is the easiest thing in the world to give a certain degree of depth and transparency to water; but that it is next to impossible, to give a full impression of surface. If no reflection be given, a ripple being supposed, the water looks like lead: if reflection be given, it, in nine cases out of ten, looks *morbidly* clear and deep, so that we always go down *into* it, even when the artist most wishes us to glide *over* it. Now, this difficulty arises from the very same circumstance which occasions the frequent failure in effect of the best-drawn foregrounds . . . the change, namely, of focus necessary in the eye in order to receive rays of light coming from different distances. Go to the edge of a pond in a perfectly calm day, at some place where there is duckweed floating on the surface, not thick, but a leaf here and there. Now, you may either see in the water the reflection of the sky, or you may see the duckweed; but you cannot, by any effort, see both together. . . .

Hence it appears, that whenever we see plain reflections of comparatively distant objects, in near water, we cannot possibly see the surface, and *vice versâ;* so that when in a painting we give the reflections with the same clearness with which they are visible in nature, we presuppose the effort of the eye to look under the surface, and, of course, destroy the surface, and induce an effect of clearness which, perhaps, the artist has not particularly wished to attain, but which he has found himself forced into, by his reflections, in spite of himself. And the reason of this effect of clearness appearing preternatural is, that people are not in the habit of looking at water with the distant focus adapted to the reflections, unless by particular effort. We invariably, under ordinary circumstances, use the surface focus; and, in consequence, receive nothing more than a vague and confused impression of the reflected colours and lines. . . . If we take such a piece of water as that in the foreground of Turner's Château of Prince Albert, the first impression from it is, "What a wide *surface!*" We glide over it a quarter of a mile into the picture before we know where we are, and yet the water is as calm and crystalline as a mirror; but we are not allowed to tumble into it, and gasp for breath as we go down, we are kept upon the surface, though that surface is flashing and radiant with every hue of cloud, and sun, and sky, and foliage. But the secret is in the drawing of these reflections. We cannot tell, when we look *at* them and *for* them, what they mean. They have all character, and are evidently reflections of something definite and determined; but yet they are all uncertain and inexplicable; playing colour and palpitating shade, which, though we recognize them in an instant for images of something, and feel that the water is bright, and lovely, and calm, we cannot penetrate nor interpret; we are not allowed to go down to them, and we repose, as we should in nature, upon the lustre of the level surface. It is in this power of saying everything, and yet saying nothing too plainly, that the perfection of art here, as in all other cases, consists. . . .

Be it next observed, that the reflection of all near objects is not an exact copy of the parts of them which we see above the water, but a totally different view and arrangement of them, that which we should get if we were looking at them from beneath. Hence we see the dark sides of leaves hanging over a stream, in their reflection, though we see the light sides above; and all objects and groups of objects are thus seen in the reflection under different lights, and in different positions with respect to each other, from those which they assume above; some which we see on the bank being entirely lost in their reflection, and others which we cannot see on the bank brought into view. Hence nature contrives never to repeat herself, and the surface of water is not a mockery, but a new view of what is above it. And this difference in what is represented, as well as the obscurity of the representation, is one of the chief sources by which the sensation of surface is kept up in the reality. The reflection is not so remarkable, it does not attract the eye in the same degree when it is entirely different from the images above, as when it mocks them and repeats them, and we feel that the space and surface have colour and character of their own, and that the bank is one thing and the water another. It is by not making this change manifest, and giving underneath a mere duplicate of what is seen above, that artists are apt to destroy the essence and substance of water, and to drop us through it.

Now one instance will be sufficient to show the exquisite care of Turner in this respect. On the left-hand side of his Nottingham, the water (a smooth canal) is terminated by a bank fenced up with wood, on which, just at the edge of the water, stands a white sign-post. A quarter of a mile back, the hill on which Nottingham Castle stands rises steeply nearly to the top of the picture. The upper part of this hill is in bright golden light, and the lower in very deep grey shadow, against which the white board of the sign-post is seen entirely in light relief, though, being turned from the light, it is itself in delicate middle tint, illumined only on the edge. But the image of all this in the canal is very different. First, we have the reflection of the piles of the bank sharp and clear, but under this we have not what we see above it, the dark *base* of the hill (for this being a quarter of a mile back, we could not see it over the fence if we were looking from below), but the golden summit of the hill, the shadow of the under part having no record nor place in the reflection. Now this summit, being very distant, cannot be seen clearly by the eye while its focus is adapted to the surface of the water, and accordingly its reflection is entirely vague and confused; you cannot tell what it is meant for, it is mere playing golden light. But the sign-post, being on the bank close to us, will be reflected clearly, and accordingly its distinct image is seen in the midst of this confusion; relieved, however, not now against the dark base, but against the illumined summit of the hill, and appearing therefore, instead of a white space thrown out from the blue shade, a dark grey space thrown out from golden light. I do not know that any more magnificent example could be given of concentrated knowledge, or of the daring statement of most difficult truth. For who but this consummate artist would have had courage, even if he had perceived the laws which required it, to undertake, in a single small space of water, the painting of an entirely new picture, with all its tones and arrangements altered,—what was made above bright by opposition to blue, being underneath made cool and dark by opposition to gold; or would have dared to contradict so boldly the ordinary expectation of the uncultivated eye, to find in the reflection a mockery of the reality? But the reward is immediate, for not only is the change most grateful to the eye, and most exquisite as composition, but the surface of the water in consequence of it is felt to be as spacious as it is clear, and the eye rests not on the inverted image of the material objects, but on the element which receives them. . . .

It will be remembered that it was said above, that Turner was the only painter who had ever represented the surface of calm or the *force* of agitated water. He obtains this expression of force in falling or running water by fearless and full rendering of its forms. He never loses himself and his subject in the splash of the fall, his presence of mind never fails as he goes down; he does not blind us with the spray, or veil the countenance of his fall with its own drapery. A little crumbling white, or lightly rubbed paper, will soon give the effect of indiscriminate foam; but nature gives more than foam, she shows beneath it, and through it, a peculiar character of exquisitely studied form bestowed on every wave and line of fall; and it is this variety of definite character which Turner always aims at, rejecting, as much as possible, everything that conceals or overwhelms it. Thus, in the Upper Fall of the Tees, though the whole basin of the fall is blue and dim with the rising vapour, yet the attention of the spectator is chiefly directed to the concentric zones and delicate curves of the falling water itself; and it is impossible to express with what exquisite accuracy these are given. They are the characteristic of a powerful stream descending without impediment or break, but from a narrow channel, so as to expand as it falls. They are the constant form which such a stream assumes as it descends; and yet I think it would be difficult to point to another instance of their being rendered in art. You will find nothing in the waterfalls even of our best painters, but springing lines of parabolic descent, and splashing shapeless foam; and, in consequence, though they may make you understand the swiftness of the water, they never let you feel the weight of it; the stream in their hands looks *active,* not *supine,* as if it leaped, not as if it fell. Now water will leap a little way, it will leap down a weir or over a stone, but it *tumbles* over a high fall like this; and it is when we have lost the parabolic line, and arrived at the catenary, when we have lost the *spring* of the fall, and arrived at the *plunge* of it, that we begin really to feel its weight and wildness. Where water takes its first leap from the top, it is cool, and collected, and uninteresting, and mathematical; but it is when it finds that it has got into a scrape, and has farther to go than it thought, that its character comes out: it is then that it begins to writhe, and twist, and sweep out, zone after zone, in wilder stretching as it falls; and to send down the rocket-like, lance-pointed, whizzing shafts at its sides, sounding for the bottom. And it is this prostration, this hopeless abandonment of its ponderous power to the air, which is always peculiarly expressed by Turner, and especially in the case before us; while our other artists, keeping to the parabolic line, where they do not lose themselves in smoke and foam, make their cataract look muscular and wiry, and may consider themselves fortunate if they can keep it from stopping. . . .

It is not, however, from the shore that Turner usually studies his sea. Seen from the land, the curl of the breakers, even in nature, is somewhat uniform and monotonous; the size of the waves out at sea is uncomprehended; and those nearer the eye seem to succeed and resemble each other, to move slowly to the beach, and to break in the same lines and forms.

Afloat even twenty yards from the shore, we receive a totally different impression. Every wave around us appears vast, every one different from all the rest; and the breakers present, now that we see them with their backs towards us, the grand, extended, and varied lines of long curvature which are peculiarly expressive both of velocity and power. Recklessness, before unfelt, is manifested in the mad, perpetual, changeful, undirected motion, not of wave after wave, as it appears from the shore, but of the very same water rising and falling. Of waves that successively approach and break, each appears to the mind a separate individual, whose part being performed, it perishes, and is succeeded by another; and there is nothing in this to impress us with the idea of restlessness, any more than in any successive and continuous functions of life and death. But it is when we perceive that it is no succession of wave, but the same water, constantly rising, and crashing, and recoiling, and rolling in again in new forms and with fresh fury, that we perceive the perturbed spirit, and feel the intensity of its unwearied rage. The sensation of power is also trebled; for not only is the vastness of apparent size much increased, but the whole action is different; it is not a passive wave, rolling sleepily forward until it tumbles heavily, prostrated upon the beach; but a sweeping exertion of tremendous and living strength, which does not now appear to *fall*, but to *burst* upon the shore; which never perishes but recoils and recovers.

Aiming at these grand characters of the sea, Turner almost always places the spectator, not on the shore, but twenty or thirty yards from it, beyond the first range of the breakers, as in the Land's End, Fowey, Dunbar, and Laugharne. The latter . . . gives the surge and weight of the ocean in a gale, on a comparatively level shore; but the Land's End, the entire disorder of the surges when every one of them, divided and entangled among promontories as it rolls in, and beaten back part by part from walls of rock on this side and that side, recoils like the defeated division of a great army, throwing all behind it into disorder, breaking up the succeeding waves into vertical ridges, which in their turn, yet more totally shattered upon the shore, retire in more helpless confusion; until the whole surface of the sea becomes one dizzy whirl of rushing, writhing, tortured, undirected rage, bounding, and crashing, and coiling in an anarchy of enormous power; subdivided into myriads of waves, of which every one is not, be it remembered, a separate surge, but part and portion of a vast one, actuated by internal power, and giving in every direction the mighty undulation of impetuous line which glides over the rocks and writhes in the wind, overwhelming the one, and piercing the other with the form, fury, and swiftness of a sheet of lambent fire. And throughout the rendering of all this there is not one false curve given, not one which is not the perfect expression of visible motion; and the forms of the infinite sea are drawn throughout with that utmost mastery of art which, through the deepest study of every line, makes every line appear the wildest child of chance, while yet each is in itself a subject and a picture different from all else around. . . .

Few people, comparatively, have ever seen the effect on the sea of a powerful gale continued without intermission for three or four days and nights; and to those who have not, I believe it must be unimaginable, not from the mere force or size of surge, but from the complete annihilation of the limit between sea and air. The water from its prolonged agitation is beaten, not into mere creaming foam, but into masses of accumulated yeast,* which hang in ropes and wreaths from wave to wave, and, where one curls over to break, form a festoon like a drapery from its edge; these are taken up by the wind, not in dissipating dust, but bodily, in writhing, hanging, coiling masses, which make the air white and thick as with snow, only the flakes are a foot or two long each: the surges themselves are full of foam in their very bodies, underneath, making them white all through, as the water is under a great cataract; and their masses, being thus half water and half air, are torn to pieces by the wind whenever they rise, and carried away in roaring smoke, which chokes and strangles like actual water. Add to this, that when the air has been exhausted of its moisture by long rain, the spray of the sea is caught by it . . . and covers its surface not merely with the smoke of finely divided water, but with boiling mist; imagine also the low rain-clouds brought down to the very level of the sea, as I have often seen them; whirling and flying in rags and fragments from wave to wave; and finally, conceive the surges themselves in their utmost pitch of power, velocity, vastness, and madness, lifting themselves in precipices and peaks, furrowed with their whirl of ascent, through all this chaos; and you will understand that there is indeed no distinction left between the sea and air; that no object, nor horizon, nor any land-

---

* The "yesty waves" of Shakspeare have made the likeness familiar, and probably most readers take the expression as merely equivalent to "foamy;" but Shakspeare knew better. Sea-foam does not, under ordinary circumstances, last a moment after it is formed, but disappears, as above described, in a mere white film. But the foam of a prolonged tempest is altogether different; it is "whipped" foam, thick, permanent, and, in a foul or discoloured sea, very ugly, especially in the way it hangs about the tops of the waves, and gathers into clotted concretions before the driving wind. The sea looks truly working or fermenting. [Ruskin's note.]

mark or natural evidence of position is left; that the heaven is all spray, and the ocean all cloud, and that you can see no farther in any direction than you could see through a cataract. Suppose the effect of the first sunbeam sent from above to show this annihilation to itself, and you have the sea picture of the Academy, 1842, the Snowstorm, one of the very grandest statements of sea-motion, mist, and light, that has ever been put on canvas, even by Turner. Of course it was not understood; his finest works never are: but there was some apology for the public's not comprehending this, for few people have had the opportunity of seeing the sea at such a time, and when they have, cannot face it.* To hold by a mast or a rock, and watch it, is a prolonged endurance of drowning which few people have courage to go through. To those who have, it is one of the noblest lessons of nature.

But, I think, the noblest sea that Turner has ever painted, and, if so, the noblest certainly ever painted by man, is that of the Slave Ship, the chief Academy picture of the Exhibition of 1840. It is a sunset on the Atlantic, after prolonged storm; but the storm is partially lulled, and the torn and streaming rain-clouds are moving in scarlet lines to lose themselves in the hollow of the night. The whole surface of sea included in the picture is divided into two ridges of enormous swell, not high, nor local, but a low broad heaving of the whole ocean, like the lifting of its bosom by deep-drawn breath after the torture of the storm. Between these two ridges the fire of the sunset falls along the trough of the sea, dyeing it with an awful but glorious light, the intense and lurid splendour which burns like gold, and bathes like blood. Along this fiery path and valley, the tossing waves by which the swell of the sea is restlessly divided, lift themselves in dark, indefinite, fantastic forms,

* So that he might better see what he later painted, Turner had himself lashed to the mast of the *Ariel* and for four hours rode out a gale at sea. But the critics, blind to the radical fidelity of his vision, dismissed the *Snowstorm: Steamboat Making Signals* as a "mass of soapsuds and whitewash."

each casting a faint and ghastly shadow behind it along the illumined foam. They do not rise everywhere, but three or four together in wild groups, fitfully and furiously, as the under strength of the swell compels or permits them; leaving between them treacherous spaces of level and whirling water, now lighted with green and lamp-like fire, now flashing back the gold of the declining sun, now fearfully dyed from above with the undistinguishable images of the burning clouds, which fall upon them in flakes of crimson and scarlet, and give to the reckless waves the added motion of their own fiery flying. Purple and blue, the lurid shadows of the hollow breakers are cast upon the mist of night, which gathers cold and low, advancing like the shadow of death upon the guilty* ship as it labours amidst the lightning of the sea, its thin masts written upon the sky in lines of blood, girded with condemnation in that fearful hue which signs the sky with horror, and mixes its flaming flood with the sunlight, and, cast far along the desolate heave of the sepulchral waves, incarnadines the multitudinous sea.

I believe, if I were reduced to rest Turner's immortality upon any single work, I should choose this. Its daring conception, ideal in the highest sense of the word, is based on the purest truth, and wrought out with the concentrated knowledge of a life; its colour is absolutely perfect, not one false or morbid hue in any part or line, and so modulated that every square inch of canvas is a perfect composition; its drawing as accurate as fearless; the ship buoyant, bending, and full of motion; its tones as true as they are wonderful; and the whole picture dedicated to the most sublime of subjects and impressions (completing thus the perfect system of all truth, which we have shown to be formed by Turner's works)—the power, majesty, and deathfulness of the open, deep, illimitable sea.

[Vol. I, Part 2, Sec. 5, Chap. 3]

* She is a slaver, throwing her slaves overboard. The near sea is encumbered with corpses. [Ruskin's note.]

Of the Received Opinions Touching the "Grand Style"

In taking up the clue of an inquiry, now intermitted for nearly ten years, it may be well to do as a traveller would, who had to recommence an interrupted journey in a guideless country; and, ascending, as it were, some little hill beside our road, note how far we have already advanced, and what pleasantest ways we may choose for farther progress.

I endeavoured, in the beginning of the first volume, to divide the sources of pleasure open to us in Art into certain groups, which might conveniently be studied in succession. After some preliminary discussion, it was concluded that these groups were, in the main, three; consisting, first, of the pleasures taken in perceiving simple resemblance to Nature (Ideas of Truth); secondly, of the pleasures taken in the beauty of the things chosen to be painted (Ideas of Beauty); and, lastly, of pleasures taken in the meanings and relations of these things (Ideas of Relation).

The first volume, treating of the Ideas of Truth, was chiefly occupied with an inquiry into the various success with which different artists had represented the facts of Nature,—an inquiry necessarily conducted very imperfectly, owing to the want of pictorial illustration.

The second volume merely opened the inquiry into the nature of ideas of Beauty and Relation, by analysing (as far as I was able to do so) the two faculties of the human mind which mainly seized such ideas; namely, the contemplative and imaginative faculties.

It remains for us to examine the various success of artists, especially of the great landscape-painter whose works have been throughout our principal subject, in addressing these faculties of the human mind, and to consider who among them has conveyed the noblest ideas of beauty, and touched the deepest sources of thought. . . .

I have said that the art is greatest which includes the greatest ideas; but I have not endeavoured to define the nature of this greatness in the ideas themselves. We speak of great truths, of great beauties, great thoughts. What is it which makes one truth greater than another, one thought greater than another? This question is, I repeat, of peculiar importance at the present time; for, during a period now of some hundred and fifty years, all writers on Art who have pretended to eminence, have insisted much on a supposed distinction between what they call the Great and the Low Schools; using the terms "High Art," "Great or Ideal Style," and other such, as descriptive of a certain noble manner of painting, which it was desirable that all students of Art should be early led to reverence and adopt; and character-ising as "vulgar," or "low," or "realist," another manner of painting and conceiving, which it was equally necessary that all students should be taught to avoid.

But lately this established teaching, never very intelligible, has been gravely called in question. The advocates and self-supposed practisers of "High Art" are beginning to be looked upon with doubt, and their peculiar phraseology to be treated with even a certain degree of ridicule. And other forms of Art are partly developed among us, which do not pretend to be high, but rather to be strong, healthy, and humble. This matter of "highness" in Art, therefore, de-serves our most careful consideration. Has it been, or is it, a true highness, a true princeliness, or only a show of it, consisting in courtly manners and robes of state? Is it rocky height or cloudy height, adamant or vapour, on which the sun of praise so long has risen and set? It will be well at once to consider this.

And first, let us get, as quickly as may be, at the exact meaning with which the advocates of "High Art" use that somewhat obscure and figurative term.

I do not know that the principles in question are anywhere more distinctly expressed than in two papers in the
Idler, written by Sir Joshua Reynolds, of course under the
immediate sanction of Johnson; and which may thus be
considered as the utterance of the views then held upon the
subject by the artists of chief skill, and critics of most sense,
arranged in a form so brief and clear, as to admit of their
being brought before the public for a morning's entertainment. I cannot, therefore, it seems to me, do better than
quote these two letters, or at least the important parts of
them, examining the exact meaning of each passage as it
occurs. There are, in all, in the *Idler* three letters on painting, Nos. 76, 79, and 82; of these, the first is directed only
against the impertinences of pretended connoisseurs, and is
as notable for its faithfulness, as for its wit, in the description of the several modes of criticism in an artificial and
ignorant state of society: it is only, therefore, in the two last
papers that we find the expression of the doctrines which it
is our business to examine.

No. 79 (Saturday, Oct. 20th, 1759) begins, after a short
preamble, with the following passage:—

"Amongst the Painters, and the writers on Painting, there
is one maxim universally admitted and continually inculcated. *Imitate nature* is the invariable rule; but I know
none who have explained in what manner this rule is to be
understood; the consequence of which is, that every one
takes it in the most obvious sense—that objects are represented naturally, when they have such relief that they seem
real. It may appear strange, perhaps, to hear this sense of
the rule disputed; but it must be considered, that, if the
excellency of a Painter consisted only in this kind of imitation, Painting must lose its rank, and be no longer considered as a liberal art, and sister to Poetry: this imitation
being merely mechanical, in which the slowest intellect is
always sure to succeed best; for the Painter of genius cannot
stoop to drudgery, in which the understanding has no part;

and what pretence has the Art to claim kindred with Poetry, but by its power over the imagination? To this power the Painter of genius directs him; in this sense he studies Nature, and often arrives at his end, even by being unnatural in the confined sense of the word.

"The grand style of Painting requires this minute attention to be carefully avoided, and must be kept as separate from it as the style of Poetry from that of History. (Poetical ornaments destroy that air of truth and plainness which ought to characterise History; but the very being of Poetry consists in departing from this plain narrative, and adopting every ornament that will warm the imagination.) To desire to see the excellences of each style united—to mingle the Dutch with the Italian school, is to join contrarieties which cannot subsist together, and which destroy the efficacy of each other."

We find, first, from this interesting passage, that the writer considers the Dutch and Italian masters as severally representative of the low and high schools; next, that he considers the Dutch painters as excelling in a mechanical imitation, "in which the slowest intellect is always sure to succeed best;" and, thirdly, that he considers the Italian painters as excelling in a style which corresponds to that of imaginative poetry in literature, and which has an exclusive right to be called the grand style. . . .

We observe, however, farther, that the imitation which Reynolds supposes to be characteristic of the Dutch School is that which gives to objects such relief that they seem real, and that he then speaks of this art of realistic imitation as corresponding to *history* in literature.

Reynolds, therefore, seems to class these dull works of the Dutch School under a general head, to which they are not commonly referred—that of *Historical* painting; while he speaks of the works of the Italian School not as historical, but as *poetical* painting. His next sentence will farther manifest his meaning.

"The Italian attends only to the invariable, the great and general ideas which are fixed and inherent in universal Nature; the Dutch, on the contrary, to literal truth, and a minute exactness in the detail, as I may say, of Nature modified by accident. The attention to these petty peculiarities is the very cause of this naturalness so much admired in the Dutch pictures, which, if we suppose it to be a beauty, is certainly of a lower order, which ought to give place to a beauty of a superior kind, since one cannot be obtained but by departing from the other.

"If my opinion were asked concerning the works of Michael Angelo, whether they would receive any advantage from possessing this mechanical merit, I should not scruple to say, they would not only receive no advantage, but would lose, in a great measure, the effect which they now have on every mind susceptible of great and noble ideas. His works may be said to be all genius and soul; and why should they be loaded with heavy matter, which can only counteract his purpose by retarding the progress of the imagination?"

Examining carefully this and the preceding passage, we find the author's unmistakable meaning to be, that Dutch painting is *history;* attending to literal truth and "minute exactness in the details of nature modified by accident." That Italian painting is *poetry*, attending only to the invariable; and that works which attend only to the invariable are full of genius and soul; but that literal truth and exact detail are "heavy matter which retards the progress of the imagination."

This being then indisputably what Reynolds means to tell us, let us think a little whether he is in all respects right. And first, as he compares his two kinds of painting to history and poetry, let us see how poetry and history themselves differ, in their use of *variable* and *invariable* details. I am writing at a window which commands a view of the head of the Lake of Geneva; and as I look up from my paper, to consider this point, I see, beyond it, a blue breadth of softly moving water, and the outline of the mountains above Chillon, bathed in morning mist. The first verses which naturally come into my mind are—

> *"A thousand feet in depth below*
> *The massy waters meet and flow;*
> *So far the fathom line was sent*
> *From Chillon's snow-white battlement."* *

Let us see in what manner this poetical statement is distinguished from a historical one.

It is distinguished from a truly historical statement, first, in being simply false. The water under the Castle of Chillon is not a thousand feet deep, nor anything like it. Herein, certainly, these lines fulfil Reynolds's first requirement in poetry, "that it should be inattentive to literal truth and minute exactness in detail." In order, however, to make our comparison more closely in other points, let us assume that what is stated is indeed a fact, and that it was to be recorded, first historically, and then poetically.

Historically stating it, then, we should say: "The lake was sounded from the walls of the Castle of Chillon, and found to be a thousand feet deep."

Now, if Reynolds be right in his idea of the difference between history and poetry, we shall find that Byron leaves out of this statement certain *un*necessary details, and retains only the invariable,—that is to say, the points which the Lake of Geneva and Castle of Chillon have in common with all other lakes and castles.

Let us hear, therefore.

> *"A thousand feet in depth below."*

* Ruskin generally quoted from memory, and his memory was phenomenally accurate, ranging at will over the many literatures at his command. Occasionally, as here, in quoting from Byron's "The Prisoner of Chillon," he introduced minor verbal changes which I have let pass uncorrected.

"Below?" Here is, at all events, a word added (instead of anything being taken away); invariable, certainly in the case of lakes, but not absolutely necessary.

"The massy waters meet and flow."

"Massy!" why massy? Because deep water is heavy. The word is a good word, but it is assuredly an added detail, and expresses a character, not which the Lake of Geneva has in common with all other lakes, but which it has in distinction from those which are narrow, or shallow.

"Meet and flow." Why meet and flow? Partly to make up a rhyme; partly to tell us that the waters are forceful as well as massy, and changeful as well as deep. Observe, a farther addition of details, and of details more or less peculiar to the spot, or, according to Reynolds's definition, of "heavy matter, retarding the progress of the imagination."

"So far the fathom line was sent."

Why fathom line? All lines for sounding are not fathom lines. If the lake was ever sounded from Chillon, it was probably sounded in mètres, not fathoms. This is an addition of another particular detail, in which the only compliance with Reynolds's requirement is, that there is some chance of its being an inaccurate one.

"From Chillon's snow-white battlement."

Why snow-white? Because castle battlements are not usually snow-white. This is another added detail, and a detail quite peculiar to Chillon, and therefore exactly the most striking word in the whole passage.

"Battlement!" Why battlement? Because all walls have not battlements, and the addition of the term marks the castle to be not merely a prison, but a fortress.

This is a curious result. Instead of finding, as we expected, the poetry distinguished from the history by the omission of details, we find it consist[s] entirely in the *addition* of details; and instead of being characterised by regard only of the invariable, we find its whole power to consist in the clear expression of what is singular and particular!

The reader may pursue the investigation for himself in other instances. He will find in every case that a poetical is distinguished from a merely historical statement, not by being more vague, but more specific; and it might, therefore, at first appear that our author's comparison should be simply reversed, and that the Dutch School should be called poetical, and the Italian historical. But the term poetical does not appear very applicable to the generality of Dutch painting; and a little reflection will show us, that if the Italians represent only the invariable, they cannot be properly compared even to historians. For that which is incapable of change has no history, and records which state only the invariable need not be written, and could not be read.

It is evident, therefore, that our author has entangled himself in some grave fallacy, by introducing this idea of invariableness as forming a distinction between poetical and historical art. What the fallacy is, we shall discover as we proceed; but as an invading army should not leave an un-taken fortress in its rear, we must not go on with our inquiry into the views of Reynolds until we have settled satisfactorily the question already suggested to us, in what the essence of poetical treatment really consists. For though, as we have seen, it certainly involves the addition of specific details, it cannot be simply that addition which turns the history into poetry. For it is perfectly possible to add any number of details to a historical statement, and to make it more prosaic with every added word. As, for instance, "The lake was sounded out of a flat-bottomed boat, near the crab-tree at the corner of the kitchen-garden, and was found to be a thousand feet nine inches deep, with a muddy bottom." It thus appears that it is not the multiplication of details which constitutes poetry; nor their subtraction which constitutes history, but details themselves, or the method of using them, which invests them with poetical power or historical propriety.

It seems to me, and may seem to the reader, strange that we should need to ask the question, "What is poetry?" Here is a word we have been using all our lives, and, I suppose, with a very distinct idea attached to it; and when I am now called upon to give a definition of this idea, I find myself at a pause. What is more singular, I do not at present recollect hearing the question often asked, though surely it is a very natural one; and I never recollect hearing it answered, or even attempted to be answered. In general, people shelter themselves under metaphors, and while we hear poetry described as an utterance of the soul, an effusion of Divinity, or voice of nature, or in other terms equally elevated and obscure, we never attain anything like a definite explanation of the character which actually distinguishes it from prose.

I come, after some embarrassment, to the conclusion, that poetry is "the suggestion, by the imagination, of noble grounds for the noble emotions." I mean, by the noble emotions, those four principal sacred passions—Love, Veneration, Admiration, and Joy (this latter especially, if unselfish); and their opposites—Hatred, Indignation (or Scorn), Horror, and Grief,—this last, when unselfish, becoming Compassion. These passions in their various combinations constitute what is called "poetical feeling," when they are felt on noble grounds, that is, on great and true grounds. Indignation, for instance, is a poetical feeling, if excited by serious injury; but it is not a poetical feeling if entertained on being cheated out of a small sum of money. It is very possible the manner of the cheat may have been such as to justify considerable indignation; but the feeling is nevertheless not poetical unless the grounds of it be large as well as just. In like manner, energetic admiration may be excited in certain minds by a display of fireworks, or a street of handsome shops; but the feeling is not poetical, because the grounds of it are false, and therefore ignoble. There is in reality nothing to deserve admiration either in the firing of packets of gunpowder, or in the display of the stocks of warehouses. But admiration excited by the budding of a flower is a poetical feeling, because it is impossible that this manifestation of spiritual power and vital beauty can ever be enough admired.

Farther, it is necessary to the existence of poetry that the grounds of these feelings should be *furnished by the imagination.* Poetical feeling, that is to say, mere noble emotion, is not poetry. It is happily inherent in all human nature deserving the name, and is found often to be purest in the least sophisticated. But the power of assembling, by *the help of the imagination,* such images as will excite these feelings, is the power of the poet or literally of the "Maker."

Now this power of exciting the emotions depends of course on the richness of the imagination, and on its choice of those images which, in combination, will be most effective, or, for the particular work to be done, most fit. And it is altogether impossible for a writer not endowed with invention to conceive what tools a true poet will make use of, or in what way he will apply them, or what unexpected results he will bring out by them; so that it is vain to say that the details of poetry ought to possess, or ever do possess, any *definite* character. Generally speaking, poetry runs into finer and more delicate details than prose; but the details are not poetical because they are more delicate, but because they are employed so as to bring out an affecting result. For instance, no one but a true poet would have thought of exciting our pity for a bereaved father by describing his way of locking the door of his house:

> *"Perhaps to himself at that moment he said,*
> *'The key I must take, for my Ellen is dead.'*
> *But of this in my ears not a word did he speak;*
> *And he went to the chase with a tear on his cheek."**

* The final stanza of Wordsworth's "The Childless Father."

In like manner, in painting, it is altogether impossible to say beforehand what details a great painter may make poetical by his use of them to excite noble emotions: and we shall, therefore, find presently that a painting is to be classed in the great or inferior schools, not according to the kind of details which it represents, but according to the uses for which it employs them.

It is only farther to be noticed, that infinite confusion has been introduced into this subject by the careless and illogical custom of opposing painting to poetry, instead of regarding poetry as consisting in a noble use, whether of colours or words. Painting is properly to be opposed to *speaking* or *writing*, but not to *poetry*. Both painting and speaking are methods of expression. Poetry is the employment of either for the noblest purposes.

This question being thus far determined, we may proceed with our paper in the *Idler*.

"It is very difficult to determine the exact degree of enthusiasm that the arts of Painting and Poetry may admit. There may, perhaps, be too great an indulgence as well as too great a restraint of imagination; if the one produces incoherent monsters, the other produces what is full as bad, lifeless insipidity. An intimate knowledge of the passions, and good sense, but not common sense, must at last determine its limits. It has been thought, and I believe with reason, that Michael Angelo sometimes transgressed those limits; and, I think, I have seen figures of him of which it was very difficult to determine whether they were in the highest degree sublime or extremely ridiculous. Such faults may be said to be the ebullitions of genius; but at least he had this merit, that he never was insipid; and whatever passion his works may excite, they will always escape contempt.

"What I have had under consideration is the sublimest style, particularly that of Michael Angelo, the Homer of painting. Other kinds may admit of this naturalness, which of the lowest kind is the chief merit; but in painting, as in poetry, the highest style has the least of common nature."

From this passage we gather three important indications of the supposed nature of the Great Style. That it is the work of men in a state of enthusiasm. That it is like the writing of Homer; and that it has as little as possible of "common nature" in it.

First, it is produced by men in a state of enthusiasm. That is, by men who feel *strongly* and *nobly;* for we do not call a strong feeling of envy, jealousy, or ambition, enthusiasm. That is, therefore, by men who feel poetically. This much we may admit, I think, with perfect safety. Great art is produced by men who feel acutely and nobly; and it is in some sort an expression of this personal feeling. We can easily conceive that there may be a sufficiently marked distinction between such art, and that which is produced by men who do not feel at all, but who reproduce, though ever so accurately, yet coldly, like human mirrors, the scenes which pass before their eyes.

Secondly, Great Art is like the writing of Homer, and this chiefly because it has little of "common nature" in it. We are not clearly informed what is meant by common nature in this passage. Homer seems to describe a great deal of what is common:—cookery, for instance, very carefully in all its processes. I suppose the passage in the *Iliad* which, on the whole, has excited most admiration, is that which describes a wife's sorrow at parting from her husband, and a child's fright at its father's helmet; and I hope, at least, the former feeling may be considered "common nature." But the true greatness of Homer's style is, doubtless, held by our author to consist in his imaginations of things not only uncommon but impossible (such as spirits in brazen armour, or monsters with heads of men and bodies of beasts), and in his occasional delineations of the human character and form in their utmost, or heroic, strength and beauty. We gather then on the whole, that a painter in the Great Style must be enthusiastic, or full of emotion, and must paint the human form in its utmost strength and beauty, and perhaps certain impossible forms besides, liable by persons not in an equally enthusiastic state of mind to be looked upon as in some degree absurd. This I presume to be Reynolds's meaning, and to be all that he intends us to gather from his comparison of the Great Style with the writings of Homer. But if that comparison be a just one in all respects, surely two other corollaries ought to be drawn from it, namely,—first, that these Heroic or Impossible images are to be mingled with others very unheroic and very possible; and, secondly, that in the representation of the Heroic or Impossible forms, the greatest care must be taken in *finishing the details,* so that a painter must not be satisfied with painting well the countenance and the body of his hero, but ought to spend the greatest part of his time (as Homer the greatest number of verses) in elaborating the sculptured pattern on his shield.

Let us, however, proceed with our paper.

"One may very safely recommend a little more enthusiasm to the modern Painters; too much is certainly not the vice of the present age. The Italians seem to have been continually declining in this respect from the time of Michael Angelo to that of Carlo Maratti, and from thence to the very bathos of insipidity to which they are now sunk; so that there is no need of remarking, that where I mentioned the Italian painters in opposition to the Dutch, I mean not the moderns, but the heads of the old Roman and Bolognian Schools; nor did I mean to include, in my idea of an Italian painter, the Venetian school, *which may be said to be the Dutch part of the Italian genius.* I have only to add a word of advice to the Painters,—that, however excellent they may be in painting naturally, they would not flatter themselves very much upon it; and to the Connoisseurs, that when they see a cat or a fiddle painted so finely, that, as the phrase is, it looks as if you could take it up, they would not for that reason immediately compare the Painter to Raffaelle and Michael Angelo."

In this passage there are four points chiefly to be re-marked. The first, that in the year 1759 the Italian painters were, in our author's opinion, sunk in the very bathos of insipidity. The second, that the Venetian painters, *i.e.*, Titian, Tintoret, and Veronese, are, in our author's opinion, to be classed with the Dutch; that is to say, are painters in a style "in which the slowest intellect is always sure to succeed best." Thirdly, that painting naturally is not a difficult thing, nor one on which a painter should pride himself. And, finally, that connoisseurs, seeing a cat or a fiddle suc-cessfully painted, ought not therefore immediately to com-pare the painter to Raphael or Michael Angelo.

Yet Raphael painted fiddles very carefully in the fore-ground of his St. Cecilia,—so carefully, that they quite look as if they might be taken up. So carefully, that I never yet looked at the picture without wishing that somebody *would* take them up, and out of the way. And I am under a very strong persuasion that Raphael did not think painting "naturally" an easy thing.   [Vol. III, Part 4, Chap. 1]

Of the Naturalist Ideal

We now enter on the consideration of that central and highest branch of ideal art which concerns itself simply with things as they ARE, and accepts, in all of them, alike the evil and the good. The question is, therefore, how the art which represents things simply as they are, can be called ideal at all. . . .

In Tintoret's Adoration of the Magi, the Madonna is not an enthroned queen, but a fair girl, full of simplicity and almost childish sweetness. To her are opposed (as Magi) two of the noblest and most thoughtful of the Venetian senators in extreme old age,—the utmost manly dignity, in its de-cline, being set beside the utmost feminine simplicity, in its dawn. The steep foreheads and refined features of the nobles are, again, opposed to the head of a negro servant, and of an Indian; both, however, noble of their kind. On the other side of the picture, the delicacy of the Madonna is farther enhanced by contrast with a largely made farm-servant, leaning on a basket. All these figures are in repose; outside, the troop of the attendants of the Magi is seen coming up at the gallop.

I bring forward this picture, observe, not as an example of the ideal in conception of religious subject, but of the general ideal treatment of the human form; in which the peculiarity is, that the beauty of each figure is displayed to the utmost, while yet, taken separately, the Madonna is an unaltered portrait of a Venetian girl, the Magi are unaltered Venetian senators, and the figure with the basket, an un-altered market-woman of Mestre.

And the greater the master of the ideal, the more per-fectly true in *portraiture* will his individual figures be al-ways found, the more subtle and bold his arts of harmony and contrast. This is a universal principle, common to all great art. Consider, in Shakspere, how Prince Henry is opposed to Falstaff, Falstaff to Shallow, Titania to Bottom, Cordelia to Regan, Imogen to Cloten, and so on; while all the meaner idealists disdain the naturalism, and are shocked at the contrasts. The fact is, a man who can see truth at all, sees it wholly, and neither desires nor dares to mutilate it.

It is evident that *within* this faithful idealism, and as one branch of it only, will arrange itself the representation of the human form and mind in perfection, when this perfec-tion is rationally to be supposed or introduced,—that is to say, in the highest personages of the story. The careless habit of confining the term "ideal" to such representations, and not understanding the imperfect ones to be *equally* ideal in their place, has greatly added to the embarrassment and multiplied the errors of artists. Thersites is just as ideal as Achilles, and Alecto as Helen; and, what is more, all the nobleness of the beautiful ideal depends upon its being just as probable and natural as the ugly one, and having in itself, occasionally or partially, both faults and familiarities.

If the next painter who desires to illustrate the character of Homer's Achilles, would represent him cutting pork chops for Ulysses, he would enable the public to understand the Homeric ideal better than they have done for several centuries. For it is to be kept in mind that the *naturalist ideal* has always in it, to the full, the power expressed by those two words. It is naturalist, because studied from nature, and ideal, because it is mentally arranged in a certain manner. Achilles must be represented cutting pork chops, because that was one of the things which the nature of Achilles involved his doing: he could not be shown wholly as Achilles, if he were not shown doing that. But he shall do it at such time and place as Homer chooses.

Now, therefore, observe the main conclusions which follow from these two conditions, attached always to art of this kind. First, it is to be taken straight from nature: it is to be the plain narration of something the painter or writer saw. Herein is the chief practical difference between the higher and lower artists; a difference which I feel more and more every day that I give to the study of art. All the great men *see* what they paint before they paint it,—see it in a perfectly passive manner,—cannot help seeing it if they would; whether in their mind's eye, or in bodily fact, does not matter; very often the mental vision is, I believe, in men of imagination, clearer than the bodily one; but vision it is, of one kind or another,—the whole scene, character, or incident passing before them as in second sight, whether they will or no, and requiring them to paint it as they see it; they not daring, under the might of its presence, to alter one jot or tittle of it as they write it down or paint it down; it being to them in its own kind and degree always a true vision or Apocalypse, and invariably accompanied in their hearts by a feeling correspondent to the words,—"Write the things *which thou hast seen*, and the things which *are.*"

And the whole power, whether of painter or poet, to describe rightly what we call an ideal thing, depends upon its being thus, to him, not an ideal, but a *real* thing. No man ever did or ever will work well, but either from actual sight or sight of faith; and all that we call ideal in Greek or any other art, because to us it is false and visionary, was, to the makers of it, true and existent. The heroes of Phidias are simply representations of such noble human persons as he every day saw, and the gods of Phidias simply representations of such noble divine persons as he thoroughly believed to exist, and did in mental vision truly behold. Hence I said in the second preface to the *Seven Lamps of Architecture:* "All great art represents something that it sees or believes in;—nothing unseen or uncredited."

And just because it is always something that it sees or believes in, there is the peculiar character above noted, almost unmistakable, in all high and true ideals, of having been as it were studied from the life, and involving pieces of sudden familiarity, and close *specific* painting which never would have been admitted or even thought of, had not the painter drawn either from the bodily life or from the life of faith. For instance, Dante's centaur, Chiron, dividing his beard with his arrow before he can speak, is a thing that no mortal would ever have thought of, if he had not actually seen the centaur do it. They might have composed handsome bodies of men and horses in all possible ways, through a whole life of pseudo-idealism, and yet never dreamed of any such thing. But the real living centaur actually trotted across Dante's brain, and he saw him do it.

And on account of this reality it is, that the great idealists venture into all kinds of what, to the pseudo-idealists, are "vulgarities." Nay, *venturing* is the wrong word; the great men have no choice in the matter; they do not know or care whether the things they describe are vulgarities or not. They *saw* them; they are the facts of the case. If they had merely composed what they describe, they would have had it at their will to refuse this circumstance or add that. But they did not compose it. It came to them ready fashioned; they were too much impressed by it to think what was vulgar or not vulgar in it. It might be a very wrong thing in a centaur to have so much beard; but so it was. And, therefore, among the various ready tests of true greatness there is not any more certain than this daring reference to, or use of, mean and little things—mean and little, that is, to mean and little minds; but, when used by the great men, evidently part of the noble whole which is authoritatively present before them. . . . Thus, in the highest poetry there is no word so familiar but a great man will bring good out of it, or rather, it will bring good to him, and answer some end for which no other word would have done equally well.

A common person, for instance, would be mightily puzzled to apply the word "whelp" to any one, with a view of flattering him. There is a certain freshness and energy in the term, which gives it agreeableness; but it seems difficult, at first hearing, to use it complimentarily. If the person spoken of be a prince, the difficulty seems increased; and when, farther, he is at one and the same moment to be called a "whelp" and contemplated as a hero, it seems that a common idealist might well be brought to a pause. But hear Shakspere do it:—

> *"Awake his warlike spirit,*
> *And your great uncle's, Edward the Black Prince,*
> *Who on the French ground play'd a tragedy,*
> *Making defeat on the full power of France,*
> *While his most mighty father on a hill*
> *Stood smiling, to behold his lion's whelp*
> *Forage in blood of French nobility."**

So a common idealist would have been rather alarmed at the thought of introducing the name of a street in Paris—Straw Street—Rue de Fouarre—into the midst of a description of the highest heavens. Not so Dante. . . .

We may dismiss this matter of vulgarity in plain and few words, at least as far as regards art. There is never vulgarity in a *whole* truth, however commonplace. It may be unimportant or painful. It cannot be vulgar. Vulgarity is only in concealment of truth, or in affectation.

"Well, but," (at this point the reader asks doubtfully,)

* *Henry V*, i, 2.

"if then your great central idealist is to show all truth, low as well as lovely, receiving it in this passive way, what becomes of all your principles of selection, and of setting in the right place, which you were talking about up to the end of your fifth paragraph? How is Homer to enforce upon Achilles the cutting of the pork chops 'only at such time as Homer chooses,' if Homer is to have *no* choice, but merely to see the thing done, and sing it as he sees it?" Why, the choice, as well as the vision, is *manifested* to Homer. The vision comes to him in its chosen order. Chosen *for* him, not *by* him, but yet full of visible and exquisite choice, just as a sweet and perfect dream will come to a sweet and perfect person, so that, in some sense, they may be said to have chosen their dream, or composed it; and yet they could not help dreaming it so, and in no otherwise. Thus, exactly thus, in all results of true inventive power, the whole harmony of the thing done seems as if it had been wrought by the most exquisite rules. But to him who did it, it presented itself so, and his will, and knowledge, and personality, for the moment went for nothing; he became simply a scribe, and wrote what he heard and saw. . . .*

Finally, as far as I can observe, it is a constant law that the greatest men, whether poets or historians, live entirely in their own age, and that the greatest fruits of their work

* In a later chapter on "Turnerian Topography," Ruskin notes how often Turner introduced remembered details, however insignificant, from previous studies. Turner's composition was an arrangement of remembrances, "an act of dream-vision" in which diverse recollections were linked by new and strange laws. The imagination of Dante, Tintoretto, and Turner, he concludes, seems to have consisted not in the voluntary production of new images, but in an involuntary summoning, at precisely the right moment, of things actually seen:

"Imagine all that any of these men had seen or heard in the whole course of their lives, laid up accurately in their memories as in vast storehouses, extending, with the poets, even to the slightest intonations of syllables heard in the beginning of their lives, and with the painters, down to minute folds of drapery, and shapes of leaves or stones; and over all this unindexed and immeasurable mass of treasure, the imagination brooding and wandering, but dream-gifted, so as to summon at any moment exactly such groups of ideas as shall fit each other: this I conceive to be the real nature of the imaginative mind."

are gathered out of their own age. Dante paints Italy in the thirteenth century; Chaucer, England in the fourteenth; Masaccio, Florence in the fifteenth; Tintoret, Venice in the sixteenth; all of them utterly regardless of anachronism and minor error of every kind, but getting always vital truth out of the vital present.

If it be said that Shakspere wrote perfect historical plays on subjects belonging to the preceding centuries, I answer that they *are* perfect plays just because there is no care about centuries in them, but a life which all men recognize for the human life of all time; and this it is, not because Shakspere sought to give universal truth, but because, painting honestly and completely from the men about him, he painted that human nature which is indeed constant enough,—a rogue in the fifteenth century being, *at heart,* what a rogue is in the nineteenth and was in the twelfth; and an honest or a knightly man being, in like manner, very similar to other such at any other time. And the work of these great idealists is, therefore, always universal; not because it is *not portrait,* but because it is *complete* portrait down to the heart, which is the same in all ages; and the work of the mean idealists is *not* universal, not because it is portrait, but because it is *half* portrait,—of the outside, the manners and the dress, not of the heart. Thus Tintoret and Shakspere paint, both of them, simply Venetian and English nature as they saw it in their time, down to the root; and it does for *all* time; but as for any care to cast themselves into the particular ways and tones of thought, or custom, of past time in their historical work, you will find it in neither of them, nor in any other perfectly great man that I know of.   [Vol. III, Part 4, Chap. 7]

Of the Pathetic Fallacy

German dulness, and English affectation, have of late much multiplied among us the use of two of the most objectionable words that were ever coined by the troublesomeness of metaphysicians,—namely, "Objective," and "Subjective."

No words can be more exquisitely, and in all points, useless; and I merely speak of them that I may, at once and for ever, get them out of my way, and out of my reader's. But to get that done, they must be explained.

The word "Blue," say certain philosophers, means the sensation of colour which the human eye receives in looking at the open sky, or at a bell gentian.

Now, say they farther, as this sensation can only be felt when the eye is turned to the object, and as, therefore, no such sensation is produced by the object when nobody looks at it, therefore the thing, when it is not looked at, is not blue; and thus (say they) there are many qualities of things which depend as much on something else as on themselves. To be sweet, a thing must have a taster; it is only sweet while it is being tasted, and if the tongue had not the capacity of taste, then the sugar would not have the quality of sweetness.

And then they agree that the qualities of things which thus depend upon our perception of them, and upon our human nature as affected by them, shall be called Subjective; and the qualities of things which they always have, irrespective of any other nature, as roundness or squareness, shall be called Objective.

From these ingenious views the step is very easy to a farther opinion, that it does not much matter what things are in themselves, but only what they are to us; and that the only real truth of them is their appearance to, or effect upon, us. From which position, with a hearty desire for mystification, and much egotism, selfishness, shallowness, and impertinence, a philosopher may easily go so far as to believe, and say, that everything in the world depends upon his seeing or thinking of it, and that nothing, therefore, exists, but what he sees or thinks of.

Now, to get rid of all these ambiguities and troublesome words at once, be it observed that the word "Blue" does *not* mean the *sensation* caused by a gentian on the human eye; but it means the *power* of producing that sensation: and this power is always there, in the thing, whether we are there to experience it or not, and would remain there though there were not left a man on the face of the earth. Precisely in the same way gunpowder has a power of exploding. It will not explode if you put no match to it. But it has always the power of so exploding, and is therefore called an explosive compound, which it very positively and assuredly is, whatever philosophy may say to the contrary.

In like manner, a gentian does not produce the sensation of blueness, if you don't look at it. But it has always the power of doing so; its particles being everlastingly so arranged by its Maker. And, therefore, the gentian and the sky are always verily blue, whatever philosophy may say to the contrary; and if you do not see them blue when you look at them, it is not their fault, but yours.

Hence I would say to these philosophers: If, instead of using the sonorous phrase, "It is objectively so," you will use the plain old phrase, "It *is* so," and if instead of the sonorous phrase, "It is subjectively so," you will say, in plain old English, "It does so," or "It seems so to me," you will, on the whole, be more intelligible to your fellow-creatures; and besides, if you find that a thing which generally "does so" to other people (as a gentian looks blue to most men), does *not* so to you, on any particular occasion, you will not fall into the impertinence of saying, that the thing is not so, or did not so, but you will say simply (what you will be all the better for speedily finding out), that something is the matter with you. If you find that you cannot explode the gunpowder, you will not declare that all gunpowder is subjective, and all explosion imaginary, but you will simply suspect and declare yourself to be an ill-made match. Which, on the whole, though there may be a distant chance of a mistake about it, is, nevertheless, the wisest conclusion you can come to until further experiment.

Now, therefore, putting these tiresome and absurd words

quite out of our way, we may go on at our ease to examine the point in question,—namely, the difference between the ordinary, proper, and true appearances of things to us; and the extraordinary, or false appearances, when we are under the influence of emotion, or contemplative fancy; false appearances, I say, as being entirely unconnected with any real power or character in the object, and only imputed to it by us.

For instance—

"The spendthrift crocus, bursting through the mould
*Naked and shivering, with his cup of gold."**

This is very beautiful, and yet very untrue. The crocus is not a spendthrift, but a hardy plant; its yellow is not gold, but saffron. How is it that we enjoy so much the having it put into our heads that it is anything else than a plain crocus?

It is an important question. For, throughout our past reasonings about art, we have always found that nothing could be good or useful, or ultimately pleasurable, which was untrue. But here is something pleasurable in written poetry, which is nevertheless *un*true. And what is more, if we think over our favourite poetry, we shall find it full of this kind of fallacy, and that we like it all the more for being so.

It will appear also, on consideration of the matter, that this fallacy is of two principal kinds. Either, as in this case of the crocus, it is the fallacy of wilful fancy, which involves no real expectation that it will be believed; or else it is a fallacy caused by an excited state of the feelings, making us, for the time, more or less irrational. Of the cheating of the fancy we shall have to speak presently; but in this chapter, I want to examine the nature of the other error, that which the mind admits when affected strongly by emotion. Thus, for instance, in *Alton Locke*,—

* From Oliver Wendell Holmes's *Astraea*.

"They rowed her in across the rolling foam—
*The cruel, crawling foam."**

The foam is not cruel, neither does it crawl. The state of
mind which attributes to it these characters of a living
creature is one in which the reason is unhinged by grief.
All violent feelings have the same effect. They produce in
us a falseness in all our impressions of external things,
which I would generally characterize as the "pathetic
fallacy."

Now we are in the habit of considering this fallacy as
eminently a character of poetical description, and the temper of mind in which we allow it, as one eminently poetical,
because passionate. But I believe, if we look well into the
matter, that we shall find the greatest poets do not often
admit this kind of falseness,—that it is only the second order of poets who much delight in it.†

Thus, when Dante describes the spirits falling from the
bank of Acheron "as dead leaves flutter from a bough," he
gives the most perfect image possible of their utter lightness, feebleness, passiveness, and scattering agony of despair,
without, however, for an instant losing his own clear perception that *these* are souls, and *those* are leaves; he makes
no confusion of one with the other. But when Coleridge
speaks of

"The one red leaf, the last of its clan,
That dances as often as dance it can,"‡

he has a morbid, that is to say, a so far false, idea about the
leaf; he fancies a life in it, and will, which there are not;

* From Chapter 26 of Charles Kingsley's novel.
† I admit two orders of poets, but no third; and by these two orders
I mean the creative (Shakspeare, Homer, Dante), and Reflective or
Perceptive (Wordsworth, Keats, Tennyson). But both of these must be
first-rate in their range, though their range is different; and with poetry
second-rate in *quality* no one ought to be allowed to trouble mankind.
[Ruskin's note.]
‡ "Christabel," ll. 49–50.

confuses its powerlessness with choice, its fading death with merriment, and the wind that shakes it with music. Here, however, there is some beauty, even in the morbid passage; but take an instance in Homer and Pope. Without the knowledge of Ulysses, Elpenor, his youngest follower, has fallen from an upper chamber in the Circean palace, and has been left dead, unmissed by his leader or companions, in the haste of their departure. They cross the sea to the Cimmerian land; and Ulysses summons the shades from Tartarus. The first which appears is that of the lost Elpenor. Ulysses, amazed, and in exactly the spirit of bitter and terrified lightness which is seen in Hamlet,* addresses the spirit with the simple, startled words:—

"Elpenor! How camest thou under the shadowy darkness? Hast thou come faster on foot than I in my black ship?"

Which Pope renders thus:—

"O, say, what angry power Elpenor led
To glide in shades, and wander with the dead?
How could thy soul, by realms and seas disjoined,
Outfly the nimble sail, and leave the lagging wind?"

I sincerely hope the reader finds no pleasure here, either in the nimbleness of the sail, or the laziness of the wind! And yet how is it that these conceits are so painful now, when they have been pleasant to us in the other instances? For a very simple reason. They are not a *pathetic* fallacy at all, for they are put into the mouth of the wrong passion —a passion which never could possibly have spoken them— agonized curiosity. Ulysses wants to know the facts of the matter; and the very last thing his mind could do at the moment would be to pause, or suggest in any wise what was *not* a fact. The delay in the first three lines, and conceit in the last, jar upon us instantly like the most frightful discord

* "Well said, old mole! canst work i' the ground so fast?" [Ruskin's note.]

in music. No poet of true imaginative power could possibly have written the passage.

Therefore we see that the spirit of truth must guide us in some sort, even in our enjoyment of fallacy. Coleridge's fallacy has no discord in it, but Pope's has set our teeth on edge. Without farther questioning, I will endeavour to state the main bearings of this matter.

The temperament which admits the pathetic fallacy, is, as I said above, that of a mind and body in some sort too weak to deal fully with what is before them or upon them; borne away, or over-clouded, or over-dazzled by emotion; and it is a more or less noble state, according to the force of the emotion which has induced it. For it is no credit to a man that he is not morbid or inaccurate in his perceptions, when he has no strength of feeling to warp them; and it is in general a sign of higher capacity and stand in the ranks of being, that the emotions should be strong enough to vanquish, partly, the intellect, and make it believe what they choose. But it is still a grander condition when the intellect also rises, till it is strong enough to assert its rule against, or together with, the utmost efforts of the passions; and the whole man stands in an iron glow, white hot, perhaps, but still strong, and in no wise evaporating; even if he melts, losing none of his weight.

So, then, we have the three ranks: the man who perceives rightly, because he does not feel, and to whom the primrose is very accurately the primrose, because he does not love it. Then, secondly, the man who perceives wrongly, because he feels, and to whom the primrose is anything else than a primrose: a star, or a sun, or a fairy's shield, or a forsaken maiden. And then, lastly, there is the man who perceives rightly in spite of his feelings, and to whom the primrose is for ever nothing else than itself—a little flower apprehended in the very plain and leafy fact of it, whatever and how many soever the associations and passions may be that crowd around it. And, in general, these three classes may be rated in comparative order, as the men who are not poets at all, and the poets of the second order, and the poets of the first; only however great a man may be, there are always some subjects which *ought* to throw him off his balance; some, by which his poor human capacity of thought should be conquered, and brought into the inaccurate and vague state of perception, so that the language of the highest inspiration becomes broken, obscure, and wild in metaphor, resembling that of the weaker man, overborne by weaker things.

And thus, in full, there are four classes: the men who feel nothing, and therefore see truly; the men who feel strongly, think weakly, and see untruly (second order of poets); the men who feel strongly, think strongly, and see truly (first order of poets); and the men who, strong as human creatures can be, are yet submitted to influences stronger than they, and see in a sort untruly, because what they see is inconceivably above them. This last is the usual condition of prophetic inspiration. . . .

Dante, in his most intense moods, has entire command of himself, and can look around calmly, at all moments, for the image or the word that will best tell what he sees to the upper or lower world. But Keats and Tennyson, and the poets of the second order, are generally themselves subdued by the feelings under which they write, or, at least, write as choosing to be so; and therefore admit certain expressions and modes of thought which are in some sort diseased or false.

Now so long as we see that the *feeling* is true, we pardon, or are even pleased by, the confessed fallacy of sight which it induces: we are pleased, for instance, with those lines of Kingsley's above quoted, not because they fallaciously describe foam, but because they faithfully describe sorrow. But the moment the mind of the speaker becomes cold, that moment every such expression becomes untrue, as being for ever untrue in the external facts. And there is no greater baseness in literature than the habit of using these metaphorical expressions in cool blood. An inspired writer, in full impetuosity of passion, may speak wisely and truly of "raging waves of the sea foaming out their own shame"; but it is only the basest writer who cannot speak of the sea without talking of "raging waves," "remorseless floods," "ravenous billows," etc.; and it is one of the signs of the highest power in a writer to check all such habits of thought, and to keep his eyes fixed firmly on the *pure fact*, out of which if any feeling comes to him or his reader, he knows it must be a true one. . . .

It may be well, perhaps, to give one or two more instances to show the peculiar dignity possessed by all passages, which thus limit their expression to the pure fact, and leave the hearer to gather what he can from it. Here is a notable one from the *Iliad*. Helen, looking from the Scæan gate of Troy over the Grecian host, and telling Priam the names of its captains, says at last:—

"I see all the other dark-eyed Greeks; but two I cannot see,—Castor and Pollux,—whom one mother bore with me. Have they not followed from fair Lacedæmon, or have they indeed come in their sea-wandering ships, but now will not enter into the battle of men, fearing the shame and the scorn that is in Me?"

Then Homer:—

"So she spoke. But them, already, the life-giving earth possessed, there in Lacedæmon, in the dear fatherland."

Note, here, the high poetical truth carried to the extreme. The poet has to speak of the earth in sadness, but he will not let that sadness affect or change his thoughts of it. No; though Castor and Pollux be dead, yet the earth is our mother still, fruitful, life-giving. These are the facts of the thing. I see nothing else than these. Make what you will of them. . . .

A poet is great, first in proportion to the strength of his passion, and then, that strength being granted, in proportion to his government of it; there being, however, always a point beyond which it would be inhuman and monstrous if he pushed this government, and, therefore, a point at which

all feverish and wild fancy becomes just and true. Thus the
destruction of the kingdom of Assyria cannot be contemplated firmly by a prophet of Israel. The fact is too great,
too wonderful. It overthrows him, dashes him into a confused element of dreams. All the world is, to his stunned
thought, full of strange voices. "Yea, the fir-trees rejoice at
thee, and the cedars of Lebanon, saying, 'Since thou art
gone down to the grave, no feller is come up against us.' "
So, still more, the thought of the presence of Deity cannot
be borne without this great astonishment. "The mountains
and the hills shall break forth before you into singing, and
all the trees of the field shall clap their hands."*

But by how much this feeling is noble when it is justified
by the strength of its cause, by so much it is ignoble when
there is not cause enough for it; and beyond all other ig-
nobleness is the mere affectation of it, in hardness of heart.
Simply bad writing may almost always, as above noticed,
be known by its adoption of these fanciful metaphorical expressions as a sort of current coin; yet there is even a worse,
at least a more harmful condition of writing than this, in
which such expressions are not ignorantly and feelinglessly
caught up, but, by some master, skilful in handling, yet in-
sincere, deliberately wrought out with chill and studied
fancy; as if we should try to make an old lava-stream look
red-hot again, by covering it with dead leaves, or white-hot,
with hoar-frost.

When Young is lost in veneration, as he dwells on the
character of a truly good and holy man, he permits himself
for a moment to be overborne by the feeling so far as to
exclaim—

> "Where shall I find him? angels, tell me where.
> You know him; he is near you; point him out.
> Shall I see glories beaming from his brow,
> Or trace his footsteps by the rising flowers?"†

* Isaiah 14:8; 55:12.
† *Night Thoughts*, ii, 345.

This emotion has a worthy cause, and is thus true and right. But now hear the cold-hearted Pope say to a shepherd girl—

"Where'er you walk, cool gales shall fan the glade;
Trees, where you sit, shall crowd into a shade;
Your praise the birds shall chant in every grove,
And winds shall waft it to the powers above.
But would you sing, and rival Orpheus' strain,
The wondering forests soon should dance again;
The moving mountains hear the powerful call,
And headlong streams hang, listening, in their fall."

This is not, nor could it for a moment be mistaken for, the language of passion. It is simple falsehood, uttered by hypocrisy; definite absurdity, rooted in affectation, and coldly asserted in the teeth of nature and fact. Passion will indeed go far in deceiving itself; but it must be a strong passion, not the simple wish of a lover to tempt his mistress to sing. Compare a very closely parallel passage in Wordsworth, in which the lover has lost his mistress:

"Three years had Barbara in her grave been laid,
When thus his moan he made:—

'Oh, move, thou cottage, from behind yon oak,
  Or let the ancient tree uprooted lie,
That in some other way yon smoke
  May mount into the sky.
If still behind yon pine-tree's ragged bough,
  Headlong, the waterfall must come,
  Oh, let it, then, be dumb—
Be anything, sweet stream, but that which thou art now.' "†

Here is a cottage to be moved, if not a mountain, and a waterfall to be silent, if it is not to hang listening: but with what different relation to the mind that contemplates

---

* *Pastorals,* "Summer," ll. 73–74, 79–84.
† " 'T Is Said That Some Have Died for Love," ll. 11–16, 33–36.

them! Here, in the extremity of its agony, the soul cries out wildly for relief, which at the same moment it partly knows to be impossible, but partly believes possible, in a vague impression that a miracle *might* be wrought to give relief even to a less sore distress,—that nature is kind, and God is kind, and that grief is strong: it knows not well what *is* possible to such grief. To silence a stream, to move a cottage wall,—one might think it could do as much as that!

I believe these instances are enough to illustrate the main point I insist upon respecting the pathetic fallacy,—that so far as it *is* a fallacy, it is always the sign of a morbid state of mind, and comparatively of a weak one.

[Vol. III, Part 4, Chap. 12]

Of Classical Landscape

My reason for asking the reader to give so much of his time to the examination of the pathetic fallacy was, that, whether in literature or in art, he will find it eminently characteristic of the modern mind. . . . For instance, Keats, describing a wave breaking out at sea, says of it—

> *"Down whose green back the short-lived foam, all hoar,*
> *Bursts gradual, with a wayward indolence."*

That is quite perfect, as an example of the modern manner. The idea of the peculiar action with which foam rolls down a long, large wave could not have been given by any other words so well as by this "wayward indolence." But Homer would never have written, never thought of, such words. He could not by any possibility have lost sight of the great fact that the wave, from the beginning to the end of it, do what it might, was still nothing else than salt water; and that salt water could not be either wayward or indolent. He will call the waves "over-roofed," "full-charged," "monstrous," "compact-black," "dark-clear," "violet-coloured,"

* *Endymion,* ii, ll. 349–50.

"wine-coloured," and so on. But every one of these epithets is descriptive of pure physical nature. "Over-roofed" is the term he invariably uses of anything—rock, house, or wave—that nods over at the brow; the other terms need no explanation; they are as accurate and intense in truth as words can be, but they never show the slightest feeling of anything animated in the ocean. Black or clear, monstrous or violet-coloured, cold salt water it is always, and nothing but that.

"Well, but the modern writer, by his admission of the tinge of fallacy, has given an idea of something in the action of the wave which Homer could not, and surely, therefore, has made a step in advance? Also there appears to be a degree of sympathy and feeling in the one writer, which there is not in the other; and as it has been received for a first principle that writers are great in proportion to the intensity of their feelings, and Homer seems to have no feelings about the sea but that it is black and deep, surely in this respect also the modern writer is the greater?"

Stay a moment. Homer *had* some feeling about the sea; a faith in the animation of it much stronger than Keats's. But all this sense of something living in it, he separates in his mind into a great abstract image of a Sea Power. He never says the waves rage, or the waves are idle. But he says there is somewhat in, and greater than, the waves, which rages, and is idle, and *that* he calls a god.

I do not think we ever enough endeavour to enter into what a Greek's real notion of a god was. We are so accustomed to the modern mockeries of the classical religion, so accustomed to hear and see the Greek gods introduced as living personages, or invoked for help, by men who believe neither in them nor in any other gods, that we seem to have infected the Greek ages themselves with the breath, and dimmed them with the shade, of our hypocrisy; and are apt to think that Homer, as we know that Pope, was merely an ingenious fabulist; nay, more than this, that all the nations of past time were ingenious fabulists also, to whom the universe was a lyrical drama, and by whom whatsoever was said about it was merely a witty allegory, or a graceful lie, of which the entire upshot and consummation was a pretty statue in the middle of the court, or at the end of the garden. . . .

What, then, was actually the Greek god? In what way were these two ideas of human form, and divine power, credibly associated in the ancient heart, so as to become a subject of true faith irrespective equally of fable, allegory, superstitious trust in stone, and demoniacal influence?

It seems to me that the Greek had exactly the same instinctive feeling about the elements that we have ourselves; that to Homer, as much as to Casimir de la Vigne,* fire seemed ravenous and pitiless; to Homer, as much as to Keats, the sea-wave appeared wayward or idle, or whatever else it may be to the poetical passion. But then the Greek reasoned upon this sensation, saying to himself: "I can light the fire, and put it out; I can dry this water up, or drink it. It cannot be the fire or the water that rages, or that is wayward. But it must be something *in* this fire and *in* the water, which I cannot destroy by extinguishing the one, or evaporating the other, any more than I destroy myself by cutting off my finger; *I* was *in* my finger,—something of me at least was; I had a power over it and felt pain in it, though I am still as much myself when it is gone. So there may be a power in the water which is not water, but to which the water is as a body;—which can strike with it, move in it, suffer in it, yet not be destroyed with it. This something, this Great Water Spirit, I must not confuse with the waves, which are only its body. *They* may flow hither and thither, increase or diminish. *That* must be indivisible—imperishable—a god. So of fire also; those rays which I can stop, and in the midst of which I cast a shadow, cannot be divine, nor greater than I. They cannot feel, but there may be something in them that feels,—a glorious intelligence, as much nobler and more swift than mine, as these rays, which are its body, are

* Early nineteenth-century poet, dramatist, and member of the French Academy.

nobler and swifter than my flesh;—the spirit of all light, and truth, and melody, and revolving hours."

It was easy to conceive, farther, that such spirits should be able to assume at will a human form, in order to hold intercourse with men, or to perform any act for which their proper body, whether of fire, earth, or air, was unfitted. And it would have been to place them beneath, instead of above, humanity, if, assuming the form of man, they could not also have tasted his pleasures. Hence the easy step to the more or less material ideas of deities, which are apt at first to shock us, but which are indeed only dishonourable so far as they represent the gods as false and unholy. It is not the materialism, but the vice, which degrades the conception; for the materialism itself is never positive, or complete. There is always some sense of exaltation in the spiritual and immortal body; and of a power proceeding from the visible form through all the infinity of the element ruled by the particular god. The precise nature of the idea is well seen in the passage of the *Iliad* which describes the river Scamander defending the Trojans against Achilles. In order to remonstrate with the hero, the god assumes a human form, which nevertheless is in some way or other instantly recognized by Achilles as that of the river-god: it is addressed at once as a river, not as a man; and its voice is the voice of a river "out of the deep whirlpools." Achilles refuses to obey its commands; and from the human form it returns instantly into its natural or divine one, and endeavours to overwhelm him with waves. Vulcan defends Achilles, and sends fire against the river, which suffers in its water-body, till it is able to bear no more. At last even the "nerve of the river," or "strength of the river" (note the expression), feels the fire, and this "strength of the river" addresses Vulcan in supplications for respite. There is in this precisely the idea of a vital part of the river-body, which acted and felt, to which, if the fire reached, it was death, just as would be the case if it touched a vital part of the human body. Throughout the passage the manner of conception is perfectly clear and consistent; and if, in other places, the exact connection between the ruling spirit and the thing ruled is not so manifest, it is only because it is almost impossible for the human mind to dwell long upon such subjects without falling into inconsistencies, and gradually slackening its effort to grasp the entire truth; until the more spiritual part of it slips from its hold, and only the human form of the god is left, to be conceived and described as subject to all the errors of humanity. But I do not believe that the idea ever weakens itself down to mere allegory. When Pallas is said to attack and strike down Mars, it does not mean merely that Wisdom at that moment prevailed against Wrath. It means that there are, indeed, two great spirits, one entrusted to guide the human soul to wisdom and chastity, the other to kindle wrath and prompt to battle. It means that these two spirits, on the spot where, and at the moment when, a great contest was to be decided between all that they each governed in man, then and there (assumed) human form, and human weapons, and did verily and materially strike at each other, until the Spirit of Wrath was crushed. And when Diana is said to hunt with her nymphs in the woods, it does not mean merely, as Wordsworth puts it, that the poet or shepherd saw the moon and stars glancing between the branches of the trees, and wished to say so figuratively. It means that there is a living spirit, to which the light of the moon is a body; which takes delight in glancing between the clouds and following the wild beasts as they wander through the night; and that this spirit sometimes assumes a perfect human form, and in this form, with real arrows, pursues and slays the wild beasts, which with its mere arrows of moonlight it could not slay; retaining, nevertheless, all the while, its power and being in the moonlight, and in all else that it rules.

There is not the smallest inconsistency or unspirituality in this conception. If there were, it would attach equally to the appearance of the angels to Jacob, Abraham, Joshua, or Manoah. In all those instances the highest authority which governs our own faith requires us to conceive divine power clothed with a human form (a form so real that it is recognized for superhuman only by its "doing wondrously"), and retaining, nevertheless, sovereignty and omnipresence in all the world. This is precisely, as I understand it, the heathen idea of a God; and it is impossible to comprehend any single part of the Greek mind until we grasp this faithfully, not endeavouring to explain it away in any wise, but accepting, with frank decision and definition, the tangible existence of its deities:—blue-eyed—white-fleshed—human-hearted,—capable at their choice of meeting man absolutely in his own nature—feasting with him—talking with him—fighting with him, eye to eye, or breast to breast, as Mars with Diomed; or else, dealing with him in a more retired spirituality, as Apollo sending the plague upon the Greeks, when his quiver rattles at his shoulders as he moves, and yet the darts sent forth of it strike not as arrows, but as plague; or, finally, retiring completely into the material universe which they properly inhabit, and dealing with man through that, as Scamander with Achilles, through his waves.

Nor is there anything whatever in the various actions recorded of the gods, however apparently ignoble, to indicate weakness of belief in them. Very frequently things which appear to us ignoble are merely the simplicities of a pure and truthful age. When Juno beats Diana about the ears with her own quiver, for instance, we start at first, as if Homer could not have believed that they were both real goddesses. But what should Juno have done? Killed Diana with a look? Nay, she neither wished to do so, nor could she have done so, by the very faith of Diana's goddess-ship. Diana is as immortal as herself. Frowned Diana into submission? But Diana has come expressly to try conclusions with her, and will by no means be frowned into submission. Wounded her with a celestial lance? That sounds more poetical, but it is in reality partly more savage and partly more absurd, than Homer. More savage, for it makes Juno more cruel, therefore less divine; and more absurd, for it only seems elevated in tone, because we use the word "celestial," which means nothing. What sort of a thing is a "celestial" lance? Not a wooden one. Of what then? Of moonbeams, or clouds, or mist. Well, therefore, Diana's arrows were of mist too; and her quiver, and herself, and Juno, with her lance, and all, vanish into mist. Why not have said at once, if that is all you mean, that two mists met, and one drove the other back? That would have been rational and intelligible, but not to talk of celestial lances. Homer had no such misty fancy; he believed the two goddesses were there in true bodies, with true weapons, on the true earth; and still I ask, what should Juno have done? Not beaten Diana? No; for it is unlady-like. Un-English-lady-like, yes; but by no means un-Greek-lady-like, nor even un-natural-lady-like. If a modern lady does *not* beat her servant or her rival about the ears, it is oftener because she is too weak, or too proud, than because she is of purer mind than Homer's Juno. She will not strike them; but she will overwork the one or slander the other without pity; and Homer would not have thought that one whit more goddess-like than striking them with her open hand.

If, however, the reader likes to suppose that while the two goddesses in personal presence thus fought with arrow and quiver, there was also a broader and vaster contest supposed by Homer between the elements they ruled; and that the goddess of the heavens, as she struck the goddess of the moon on the flushing cheek, was at the same instant exercising omnipresent power in the heavens themselves, and gathering clouds, with which, filled with the moon's own arrows or beams, she was encumbering and concealing the moon; he is welcome to this outcarrying of the idea, provided that he does not pretend to make it an interpretation instead of a mere extension, nor think to explain away my real, running, beautiful beaten Diana, into a moon behind clouds. . . .

Such being their general idea of the gods, we can now easily understand the habitual tone of their feelings towards what was beautiful in nature. With us, observe, the idea of the Divinity is apt to get separated from the life of nature;

and imagining our God upon a cloudy throne, far above the earth, and not in the flowers or waters, we approach those visible things with a theory that they are dead; governed by physical laws, and so forth. But coming to them, we find the theory fail; that they are not dead; that, say what we choose about them, the instinctive sense of their being alive is too strong for us; and in scorn of all physical law, the wilful fountain sings, and the kindly flowers rejoice. And then, puzzled, and yet happy; pleased, and yet ashamed of being so; accepting sympathy from nature, which we do not believe it gives, and giving sympathy to nature, which we do not believe it receives,—mixing, besides, all manner of purposeful play and conceit with these involuntary fellowships,—we fall necessarily into the curious web of hesitating sentiment, pathetic fallacy, and wandering fancy, which form a great part of our modern view of nature. But the Greek never removed his god out of nature at all; never attempted for a moment to contradict his instinctive sense that God was everywhere. "The tree *is* glad," said he, "I know it is; I can cut it down: no matter, there was a nymph in it. The water *does* sing," said he; "I can dry it up; but no matter, there was a naiad in it." But in thus clearly defining his belief, observe, he threw it entirely into a human form, and gave his faith to nothing but the image of his own humanity. What sympathy and fellowship he had, were always for the spirit *in* the stream, not for the stream; always for the dryad *in* the wood, not for the wood. Content with this human sympathy, he approached the actual waves and woody fibres with no sympathy at all. The spirit that ruled them, he received as a plain fact. Them, also, ruled and material, he received as plain facts; they, without their spirit, were dead enough. A rose was good for scent, and a stream for sound and coolness; for the rest, one was no more than leaves, the other no more than water; he could not make anything else of them; and the divine power, which was involved in their existence, having been all distilled away by him into an independent Flora or Thetis, the poor leaves or waves were left, in mere cold corporealness, to make the most of their being discernibly red and soft, clear and wet, and unacknowledged in any other power whatsoever.

Then, observe farther, the Greeks lived in the midst of the most beautiful nature, and were as familiar with blue sea, clear air, and sweet outlines of mountain, as we are with brick walls, black smoke, and level fields. This perfect familiarity rendered all such scenes of natural beauty unexciting, if not indifferent to them, by lulling and overwearying the imagination as far as it was concerned with such things; but there was another kind of beauty which they found it required effort to obtain, and which, when thoroughly obtained, seemed more glorious than any of this wild loveliness —the beauty of the human countenance and form. This, they perceived, could only be reached by continual exercise of virtue; and it was in Heaven's sight, and theirs, all the more beautiful because it needed this self-denial to obtain it. . . .

Farther, the human beauty, which, whether in its bodily being or in imagined divinity, had become, for the reasons we have seen, the principal object of culture and sympathy to these Greeks, was, in its perfection, eminently orderly, symmetrical, and tender. Hence, contemplating it constantly in this state, they could not but feel a proportionate fear of all that was disorderly, unbalanced, and rugged. Having trained their stoutest soldiers into a strength so delicate and lovely, that their white flesh, with their blood upon it, should look like ivory stained with purple; and having always around them, in the motion and majesty of this beauty, enough for the full employment of their imagination, they shrank with dread or hatred from all the ruggedness of lower nature,—from the wrinkled forest bark, the jagged hill-crest, and irregular, inorganic storm of sky; looking to these for the most part as adverse powers, and taking pleasure only in such portions of the lower world as were at once conducive to the rest and health of the human frame, and in harmony with the laws of its gentler beauty.

Thus, as far as I recollect, without a single exception,

every Homeric landscape, intended to be beautiful, is composed of a fountain, a meadow, and a shady grove. This ideal is very interestingly marked, as intended for a perfect one, in the fifth book of the *Odyssey*; when Mercury himself stops for a moment, though on a message, to look at a landscape "which even an immortal might be gladdened to behold." This landscape consists of a cave covered with a running vine, all blooming into grapes, and surrounded by a grove of alder, poplar, and sweet-smelling cypress. Four fountains of white (foaming) water, springing *in succession* (mark the orderliness), and close to one another, flow away in different directions, through a meadow full of violets and parsley (parsley, to mark its moisture, being elsewhere called "marsh-nourished," and associated with the lotus); the air is perfumed not only by these violets, and by the sweet cypress, but by Calypso's fire of finely chopped cedar-wood, which sends a smoke, as of incense, through the island; Calypso herself is singing; and finally, upon the trees are resting, or roosting, owls, hawks, and "long-tongued sea-crows." Whether these last are considered as a part of the ideal landscape, as marine singing birds, I know not; but the approval of Mercury appears to be elicited chiefly by the fountains and violet meadow.

Now the notable things in this description are, first, the evident subservience of the whole landscape to human comfort, to the foot, the taste, or the smell; and, secondly, that throughout the passage there is not a single figurative word expressive of the things being in any wise other than plain grass, fruit, or flower. I have used the term "spring" of the fountains, because, without doubt, Homer means that they sprang forth brightly, having their source at the foot of the rocks (as copious fountains nearly always have); but Homer does not say "spring," he says simply flow, and uses only one word for "growing softly," or "richly," of the tall trees, the vine, and the violets. There is, however, some expression of sympathy with the sea-birds; he speaks of them in precisely the same terms, as in other places of naval nations, saying they "have care of the works of the sea."

If we glance through the references to pleasant landscape which occur in other parts of the *Odyssey*, we shall always be struck by this quiet subjection of their every feature to human service, and by the excessive similarity in the scenes. . . . In all this I cannot too strongly mark the utter absence of any trace of the feeling for what we call the picturesque, and the constant dwelling of the writer's mind on what was available, pleasant, or useful; his ideas respecting all landscape being not uncharacteristically summed, finally, by Pallas herself; when, meeting Ulysses, who after his long wandering does not recognize his own country, and meaning to describe it as politely and soothingly as possible, she says: —"This Ithaca of ours is, indeed, a rough country enough, and not good for driving in; but, still, things might be worse: it has plenty of corn, and good wine, and *always rain*, and soft nourishing dew, and it has good feeding for goats and oxen, and all manner of wood, and springs fit to drink at all the year round."

We shall see presently how the blundering, pseudo-picturesque pseudo-classical minds of Claude and the Renaissance landscape-painters, wholly missing Homer's practical common sense, and equally incapable of feeling the quiet natural grace and sweetness of his asphodel meadows, tender aspen poplars, or running vines,—fastened on his *ports* and *caves*, as the only available features of his scenery; and appointed the type of "classical landscape" thenceforward to consist in a bay of insipid sea, and a rock with a hole through it. . . .

We think of the Greeks as poetical, ideal, imaginative, in a way that a modern poet or novelist is; supposing that their thoughts about their mythology and world were as visionary and artificial as ours are: but I think the passages I have quoted show that it was not so, although it may be difficult for us to apprehend the strange minglings in them of the elements of faith, which, in our days, have been blended with other parts of human nature in a totally different guise. Perhaps the Greek mind may be best imagined by taking, as its groundwork, that of a good, conscientious, but illiterate Scotch Presbyterian Border farmer of a century or two back, having perfect faith in the bodily appearances of Satan and his imps; and in all kelpies, brownies, and fairies. Substitute for the indignant terrors in this man's mind, a general persuasion of the *Divinity*, more or less beneficent, yet faultful, of all these beings; that is to say, take away his belief in the demoniacal malignity of the fallen spiritual world, and lower, in the same degree, his conceptions of the angelical, retaining for him the same firm faith in both; keep his ideas about flowers and beautiful scenery much as they are,—his delight in regular ploughed land and meadows, and a neat garden (only with rows of gooseberry bushes instead of vines), being, in all probability, about accurately representative of the feelings of Ulysses; then, let the military spirit that is in him, glowing against the Border forager, or the foe of old Flodden and Chevy-Chase, be made more principal, with a higher sense of nobleness in soldiership, not as a careless excitement, but a knightly duty; and increased by high cultivation of every personal quality, not of mere shaggy strength, but graceful strength, aided by a softer climate, and educated in all proper harmony of sight and sound; finally, instead of an informed Christian, suppose him to have only the patriarchal Jewish knowledge of the Deity, and even this obscured by tradition, but still thoroughly solemn and faithful, requiring his continual service as a priest of burnt sacrifice and meat offering; and I think we shall get a pretty close approximation to the vital being of a true old Greek.   [Vol. III, Part 4, Chap. 13]

Of Modern Landscape

We turn our eyes, therefore, as boldly and as quickly as may be, from these serene fields and skies of mediæval art, to the most characteristic examples of modern landscape. And, I believe, the first thing that will strike us, or that ought to strike us, is their *cloudiness*.

Out of perfect light and motionless air, we find ourselves on a sudden brought under sombre skies, and into drifting wind: and, with fickle sunbeams flashing in our face, or utterly drenched with sweep of rain, we are reduced to track the changes of the shadows on the grass, or watch the rents of twilight through angry cloud. And we find that whereas all the pleasure of the mediæval was in *stability, definiteness,* and *luminousness,* we are expected to rejoice in darkness, and triumph in mutability; to lay the foundation of happiness in things which momentarily change or fade; and to expect the utmost satisfaction and instruction from what it is impossible to arrest, and difficult to comprehend.

We find, however, together with this general delight in breeze and darkness, much attention to the real form of clouds, and careful drawing of effects of mist; so that the appearance of objects, as seen through it, becomes a subject of science with us; and the faithful representation of that appearance is made of primal importance, under the name of aerial perspective. The aspects of sunset and sunrise, with all their attendant phenomena of cloud and mist, are watchfully delineated; and in ordinary daylight landscape, the sky is considered of so much importance, that a principal mass of foliage, or a whole foreground, is unhesitatingly thrown into shade merely to bring out the form of a white cloud. So that, if a general and characteristic name were needed for modern landscape art, none better could be invented than "the service of clouds."

And this name would, unfortunately, be characteristic of our art in more ways than one. . . . I said that all the Greeks spoke kindly about the clouds, except Aristophanes; and he, I am sorry to say (since his report is so unfavourable), is the only Greek who had studied them attentively. He tells us, first, that they are "great goddesses to idle men"; then, that they are "mistresses of disputings, and logic, and monstrosities, and noisy chattering"; declares that whoso believes in their divinity must first disbelieve in Jupiter, and place supreme power in the hands of an unknown god "Whirlwind"; and, finally, he displays their influence over the mind of one of their disciples, in his sudden desire "to speak ingeniously concerning smoke."

There is, I fear, an infinite truth in this Aristophanic judgment applied to our modern cloud-worship. Assuredly, much of the love of mystery in our romances, our poetry, our art, and, above all, in our metaphysics, must come under that definition so long ago given by the great Greek, "speaking ingeniously concerning smoke." And much of the instinct, which, partially developed in painting, may be now seen throughout every mode of exertion of mind,—the easily encouraged doubt, easily excited curiosity, habitual agitation, and delight in the changing and the marvellous, as opposed to the old quiet serenity of social custom and religious faith,—is again deeply defined in those few words, the "dethroning of Jupiter," the "coronation of the whirlwind." . . .

The next thing that will strike us, after this love of clouds, is the love of liberty. Whereas the mediæval was always shutting himself into castles, and behind fosses, and drawing brickwork neatly, and beds of flowers primly, our painters delight in getting to the open fields and moors, abhor all hedges and moats; never paint anything but free-growing trees, and rivers gliding "at their own sweet will"; eschew formality down to the smallest detail; break and displace the brickwork which the mediæval would have carefully cemented; leave unpruned the thickets he would have delicately trimmed; and, carrying the love of liberty even to license, and the love of wildness even to ruin, take pleasure at last in every aspect of age and desolation which emancipates the objects of nature from the government of men;— on the castle wall displacing its tapestry with ivy, and spreading, through the garden, the bramble for the rose.

Connected with this love of liberty we find a singular manifestation of love of mountains, and see our painters traversing the wildest places of the globe in order to obtain subjects with craggy foregrounds and purple distances. Some few of them remain content with pollards and flat land; but these are always men of third-rate order; and the leading masters, while they do not reject the beauty of the low grounds, reserve their highest powers to paint Alpine peaks or Italian promontories. And it is eminently notice-able, also, that this pleasure in the mountains is never min-gled with fear, or tempered by a spirit of meditation, as with the mediæval; but is always free and fearless, brightly ex-hilarating, and wholly unreflective; so that the painter feels that his mountain foreground may be more consistently ani-mated by a sportsman than a hermit; and our modern society in general goes to the mountains, not to fast, but to feast, and leaves their glaciers covered with chicken-bones and egg-shells.

Connected with this want of any sense of solemnity in mountain scenery, is a general profanity of temper in re-garding all the rest of nature; that is to say, a total absence of faith in the presence of any deity therein. Whereas the mediæval never painted a cloud, but with the purpose of placing an angel in it; and a Greek never entered a wood without expecting to meet a god in it; *we* should think the appearance of an angel in the cloud wholly unnatural, and should be seriously surprised by meeting a god anywhere. Our chief ideas about the wood are connected with poach-ing. We have no belief that the clouds contain more than so many inches of rain or hail, and from our ponds and ditches expect nothing more divine than ducks and water-cresses.

Finally: connected with this profanity of temper is a strong tendency to deny the sacred element of colour, and make our boast in blackness. For though occasionally glar-ing or violent, modern colour is on the whole eminently sombre, tending continually to grey or brown, and by many of our best painters consistently falsified, with a confessed pride in what they call chaste or subdued tints; so that, whereas a mediæval paints his sky bright blue and his foreground bright green, gilds the towers of his castles, and clothes his figures with purple and white, we paint our sky grey, our foreground black, and our foliage brown, and think that enough is sacrificed to the sun in admitting the dangerous brightness of a scarlet cloak or a blue jacket.

These, I believe, are the principal points which would strike us instantly, if we were to be brought suddenly into an exhibition of modern landscapes out of a room filled with mediæval work. It is evident that there are both evil and good in this change; but how much evil, or how much good, we can only estimate by considering, as in the former divisions of our inquiry, what are the real roots of the habits of mind which have caused them.

At first, it is evident that the title "Dark Ages," given to the mediæval centuries, is, respecting art, wholly inapplicable. They were, on the contrary, the bright ages; ours are the dark ones. I do not mean metaphysically, but literally. They were the ages of gold; ours are the ages of umber.

This is partly mere mistake in us; we build brown brick walls, and wear brown coats, because we have been blunderingly taught to do so, and go on doing so mechanically. There is, however, also some cause for the change in our own tempers. On the whole, these are much *sadder* ages than the early ones; not sadder in a noble and deep way, but in a dim wearied way,—the way of ennui, and jaded intellect, and uncomfortableness of soul and body. The Middle Ages had their wars and agonies, but also intense delights. Their gold was dashed with blood; but ours is sprinkled with dust. Their life was inwoven with white and purple: ours is one seamless stuff of brown. Not that we are without apparent festivity, but festivity more or less forced, mistaken, embittered, incomplete—not of the heart. How wonderfully, since Shakspere's time, have we lost the power of laughing at bad jests! The very finish of our wit belies our gaiety.

The profoundest reason of this darkness of heart is, I

believe, our want of faith. There never yet was a generation of men (savage or civilized) who, taken as a body, so wofully fulfilled the words "having no hope, and without God in the world," as the present civilized European race. A Red Indian or Otaheitan savage has more sense of a divine existence round him, or government over him, than the plurality of refined Londoners and Parisians: and those among us who may in some sense be said to believe, are divided almost without exception into two broad classes, Romanist and Puritan; who, but for the interference of the unbelieving portions of society, would, either of them, reduce the other sect as speedily as possible to ashes. . . . Nearly all our powerful men in this age of the world are unbelievers; the best of them in doubt and misery; the worst in reckless defiance; the plurality, in plodding hesitation, doing, as well as they can, what practical work lies ready to their hands. Most of our scientific men are in the last class: our popular authors either set themselves definitely against all religious form, pleading for simple truth and benevolence, (Thackeray, Dickens,) or give themselves up to bitter and fruitless statement of facts, (De Balzac,) or surface-painting, (Scott,) or careless blasphemy, sad or smiling, (Byron, Beranger). Our earnest poets and deepest thinkers are doubtful and indignant, (Tennyson, Carlyle); one or two, anchored, indeed, but anxious or weeping, (Wordsworth, Mrs. Browning); and of these two, the first is not so sure of his anchor, but that now and then it drags with him, even to make him cry out,—

> "Great God, I had rather be
> A Pagan suckled in some creed outworn;
> So might I, standing on this pleasant lea,
> Have glimpses that would make me less forlorn."

In politics, religion is now a name; in art, a hypocrisy or affectation. Over German religious pictures the inscription, "See how Pious I am," can be read at a glance by any clear-sighted person. Over French and English religious pictures the inscription, "See how Impious I am," is equally legible. All sincere and modest art is, among us, profane.

This faithlessness operates among us according to our tempers, producing either sadness or levity, and being the ultimate root alike of our discontents and of our wantonnesses. It is marvellous how full of contradiction it makes us: we are first dull, and seek for wild and lonely places because we have no heart for the garden; presently we recover our spirits, and build an assembly-room among the mountains, because we have no reverence for the desert. I do not know if there be game on Sinai, but I am always expecting to hear of some one's shooting over it.

There is, however, another, and a more innocent root of our delight in wild scenery.

All the Renaissance principles of art tended, as I have before often explained, to the setting Beauty above Truth, and seeking for it always at the expense of truth. And the proper punishment of such pursuit—the punishment which all the laws of the universe rendered inevitable—was, that those who thus pursued beauty should wholly lose sight of beauty. All the thinkers of the age, as we saw previously, declared that it did not exist. The age seconded their efforts, and banished beauty, so far as human effort could succeed in doing so, from the face of the earth, and the form of man. To powder the hair, to patch the cheek, to hoop the body, to buckle the foot, were all part and parcel of the same system which reduced streets to brick walls, and pictures to brown stains. One desert of Ugliness was extended before the eyes of mankind; and their pursuit of the beautiful, so recklessly continued, received unexpected consummation in high-heeled shoes and periwigs—Gower Street, and Gaspar Poussin.

Reaction from this state was inevitable, if any true life was left in the races of mankind; and, accordingly, though still forced, by rule and fashion, to the producing and wearing all that is ugly, men steal out, half-ashamed of themselves for doing so, to the fields and mountains; and, finding among these the colour, and liberty, and variety, and power, which are for ever grateful to them, delight in these to an extent never before known; rejoice in all the wildest shattering of the mountain side, as an opposition to Gower Street, gaze in a rapt manner at sunsets and sunrises, to see there the blue, and gold, and purple, which glow for them no longer on knight's armour or temple porch; and gather with care out of the fields, into their blotted herbaria, the flowers which the five orders of architecture have banished from their doors and casements. . . .

It is not, however, only to existing inanimate nature that our want of beauty in person and dress has driven us. The imagination of it, as it was seen in our ancestors, haunts us continually; and while we yield to the present fashions, or act in accordance with the dullest modern principles of economy and utility, we look fondly back to the manners of the ages of chivalry, and delight in painting, to the fancy, the fashions we pretend to despise, and the splendours we think it wise to abandon. The furniture and personages of our romance are sought, when the writer desires to please most easily, in the centuries which we profess to have surpassed in everything; the art which takes us into the present times is considered as both daring and degraded, and while the weakest words please us, and are regarded as poetry, which recall the manners of our forefathers, or of strangers, it is only as familiar and vulgar that we accept the description of our own.

In this we are wholly different from all the races that preceded us. All other nations have regarded their ancestors with reverence as saints or heroes; but have nevertheless thought their own deeds and ways of life the fitting subjects for their arts of painting or of verse. We, on the contrary, regard our ancestors as foolish and wicked, but yet find our chief artistic pleasure in descriptions of their ways of life.

The Greeks and mediævals honoured, but did not imitate their forefathers; we imitate, but do not honour. . . .

Farther: as the admiration of mankind is found, in our

times, to have in great part passed from men to mountains, and from human emotion to natural phenomena, we may anticipate that the great strength of art will also be warped in this direction; with this notable result for us, that whereas the greatest painters or painter of classical and mediæval periods, being wholly devoted to the representation of humanity, furnished us with but little to examine in landscape, the greatest painters or painter of modern times will in all probability be devoted to landscape principally; and farther, because in representing human emotion words surpass painting, but in representing natural scenery painting surpasses words, we may anticipate also that the painter and poet (for convenience' sake I here use the words in opposition) will somewhat change their relations of rank in illustrating the mind of the age; that the painter will become of more importance, the poet of less; and that the relations between the men who are the types and first-fruits of the age in word and work,—namely, Scott and Turner,—will be, in many curious respects, different from those between Homer and Phidias, or Dante and Giotto. . . .

Then, as touching the kind of work done by these two men, the more I think of it I find this conclusion more impressed upon me,—that the greatest thing a human soul ever does in this world is to *see* something, and tell what it *saw* in a plain way. Hundreds of people can talk for one who can think, but thousands can think for one who can see. To see clearly is poetry, prophecy, and religion,—all in one. [Vol. III, Part 4, Chap. 16]

The Mountain Gloom

I do not know any district possessing a more pure or uninterrupted fulness of mountain character (and that of the highest order), or which appears to have been less disturbed by foreign agencies, than that which borders the course of the Trient between Valorcine and Martigny. The paths which lead to it out of the valley of the Rhone, rising at first in steep circles among the walnut trees, like winding stairs among the pillars of a Gothic tower, retire over the shoulders of the hills into a valley almost unknown, but thickly inhabited by an industrious and patient population. . . .

Green field, and glowing rock, and glancing streamlet, all slope together in the sunshine towards the brows of ravines, where the pines take up their own dominion of saddened shade; and with everlasting roar in the twilight, the stronger torrents thunder down, pale from the glaciers, filling all their chasms with enchanted cold, beating themselves to pieces against the great rocks that they have themselves cast down, and forcing fierce way beneath their ghastly poise.

The mountain paths stoop to these glens in forky zigzags, leading to some grey and narrow arch, all fringed under its shuddering curve with the ferns that fear the light; a cross of rough-hewn pine, iron-bound to its parapet, standing dark against the lurid fury of the foam. Far up the glen, as we pause beside the cross, the sky is seen through the openings in the pines, thin with excess of light; and, in its clear, consuming flame of white space, the summits of the rocky mountains are gathered into solemn crowns and circlets, all flushed in that strange, faint silence of possession by the sunshine which has in it so deep a melancholy; full of power, yet as frail as shadows: lifeless, like the walls of a sepulchre, yet beautiful in tender fall of crimson folds, like the veil of some sea spirit, that lives and dies as the foam flashes; fixed on a perpetual throne, stern against all strength, lifted above all sorrow, and yet effaced and melted utterly into the air by that last sunbeam that has crossed to them from between the two golden clouds.

High above all sorrow: yes; but not unwitnessing to it. The traveller on his happy journey, as his foot springs from the deep turf and strikes the pebbles gaily over the edge of the mountain road, sees with a glance of delight the clusters of nutbrown cottages that nestle among those sloping orchards, and glow beneath the boughs of the pines. Here it may well seem to him, if there be sometimes hardship, there must be at least innocence and peace, and fellowship of the human soul with nature. It is not so. The wild goats that leap along those rocks have as much passion of joy in all that fair work of God as the men that toil among them. Perhaps more. Enter the street of one of those villages, and you will find it foul with that gloomy foulness that is suffered only by torpor, or by anguish of soul. Here, it is torpor—not absolute suffering—not starvation or disease, but darkness of calm enduring; the spring known only as the time of the scythe, and the autumn as the time of the sickle, and the sun only as a warmth, the wind as a chill, and the mountains as a danger. They do not understand so much as the name of beauty, or of knowledge. They understand dimly that of virtue. Love, patience, hospitality, faith, —these things they know. To glean their meadows side by side, so happier; to bear the burden up the breathless mountain flank, unmurmuringly; to bid the stranger drink from their vessel of milk; to see at the foot of their low death-beds a pale figure upon a cross, dying, also patiently;—in this they are different from the cattle and from the stones, but in all this unrewarded as far as concerns the present life. For them, there is neither hope nor passion of spirit; for them neither advance nor exultation. Black bread, rude roof, dark night, laborious day, weary arm at sunset; and life ebbs away. No books, no thoughts, no attainments, no rest; except only sometimes a little sitting in the sun under the church wall, as the bell tolls thin and far in the mountain air; a pattering of a few prayers, not understood, by the altar rails of the dimly gilded chapel, and so back to the sombre home, with the cloud upon them still unbroken— that cloud of rocky gloom, born out of the wild torrents and ruinous stones, and unlightened, even in their religion, except by the vague promise of some better thing unknown, mingled with threatening, and obscured by an unspeakable horror,—a smoke, as it were, of martyrdom, coiling up with the incense, and, amidst the images of tortured bodies and lamenting spirits in hurtling flames, the very cross, for them, dashed more deeply than for others, with gouts of blood.

Do not let this be thought a darkened picture of the life of these mountaineers. It is literal fact. . . . As we penetrate farther among the hills we shall find it becoming very painful. We are walking, perhaps, in a summer afternoon, up the valley of Zermatt (a German valley), the sun shining brightly on grassy knolls and through fringes of pines, the goat leaping happily, and the cattle bells ringing sweetly, and the snowy mountains shining like heavenly castles far above. We see, a little way off, a small white chapel, sheltered behind one of the flowery hillocks of mountain turf; and we approach its little window, thinking to look through it into some quiet home of prayer; but the window is grated with iron, and open to the winds, and when we look through it, behold—a heap of white human bones mouldering into whiter dust!

So also in that same sweet valley, of which I have just been speaking, between Chamouni and the Valais, at every turn of the pleasant pathway, where the scent of the thyme lies richest upon its rock, we shall see a little cross and shrine set under one of them; and go up to it, hoping to receive some happy thought of the Redeemer, by whom all these lovely things were made, and still consist. But when we come near—behold, beneath the cross, a rude picture of souls tormented in red tongues of hell fire, and pierced by demons.

As we pass towards Italy the appearance of this gloom deepens; and when we descend the southern slope of the Alps we shall find this bringing forward of the image of Death associated with an endurance of the most painful aspects of disease; so that conditions of human suffering, which in any other country would be confined in hospitals, are permitted to be openly exhibited by the wayside; and with this exposure of the degraded human form is farther connected an insensibility to ugliness and imperfection in other things; so that the ruined wall, neglected garden, and uncleansed chamber, seem to unite in expressing a gloom of spirit possessing the inhabitants of the whole land. It does not appear to arise from poverty, nor careless contentment with little: there is here nothing of Irish recklessness or humour; but there seems a settled obscurity in the soul, —a chill and plague, as if risen out of a sepulchre, which partly deadens, partly darkens, the eyes and hearts of men, and breathes a leprosy of decay through every breeze, and every stone. "Instead of well-set hair, baldness, and burning instead of beauty." . . .

Of places subjected to such evil influence, none are quite so characteristic as the town of Sion in the Valais. . . . It consists of little more than one main street, winding round the roots of two ridges of crag, and branching, on the side towards the rocks, into a few narrow lanes, on the other, into spaces of waste ground, of which part serve for military exercises, part are enclosed in an uncertain and vague way; a ditch half-filled up, or wall half-broken down, seeming to indicate their belonging, or having been intended to belong, to some of the unfinished houses which are springing up amidst their weeds. But it is difficult to say, in any part of the town, what is garden ground and what is waste; still more, what is new building and what old. The houses have been for the most part built roughly of the coarse limestone of the neighbouring hills, then coated with plaster, and painted, in imitation of Palladian palaces, with grey architraves and pilasters, having draperies from capital to capital. With this false decoration is curiously contrasted a great deal of graceful, honest, and original ironwork, in bulging balconies, and floreted gratings of huge windows, and branching sprays, for any and every purpose of support or guard. The plaster, with its fresco, has in most instances dropped away, leaving the houses peeled and scarred; daubed into uncertain restoration with new mortar, and in the best cases thus left; but commonly fallen also, more or less, into ruin, and either roofed over at the first story when the second has fallen, or hopelessly abandoned;—not pulled down, but left in white and ghastly shells to crumble into heaps of limestone and dust, a pauper or two still inhabiting where inhabitation is possible. The lanes wind among these ruins; the blue sky and mountain grass are seen through the windows of their rooms and over their partitions, on which old gaudy papers flaunt in rags: the weeds gather, and the dogs scratch about their foundations; yet there are no luxuriant weeds, for their ragged leaves are blanched with lime, crushed under perpetually falling fragments, and worn away by listless standing of idle feet. There is always mason's work doing, always some fresh patching and whitening; a dull smell of mortar, mixed with that of stale foulness of every kind, rises with the dust, and defiles every current of air; the corners are filled with accumulations of stones, partly broken, with crusts of cement sticking to them, and blotches of nitre oozing out of their pores. The lichenous rocks and sunburnt slopes of grass stretch themselves hither and thither among the wreck; . . . the grass, in strange sympathy with the inhabitants, will not grow *as* grass, but chokes itself with a network of grey weeds, quite wonderful in their various expression of thorny discontent and savageness; the blue flower of the borage, which mingles with them in quantities, hardly interrupting their character, for the violent black spot in the centre of its blue takes away the tenderness of the flower, and it seems to have grown there in some supernatural mockery of its old renown of being good against melancholy. The rest of the herbage is chiefly composed of the dwarf mallow, the wild succory, the wall-rocket, goose-foot, and milfoil; plants, nearly all of them, jagged in the leaf, broken and dimly clustered in flower, haunters of waste ground and places of outcast refuse. . . .

I know not how far this universal grasp of the sorrowful spirit might be relaxed if sincere energy were directed to amend the ways of life of the Valaisan. But it has always appeared to me that there was, even in more healthy mountain districts, a certain degree of inevitable melancholy; nor

could I ever escape from the feeling that here, where chiefly
the beauty of God's working was manifested to men, warning was also given, and that to the full, of the enduring of
His indignation against sin.

It seems one of the most cunning and frequent of self-
deceptions to turn the heart away from this warning, and
refuse to acknowledge anything in the fair scenes of the
natural creation but beneficence. . . . And in this mountain
gloom, which weighs so strongly upon the human heart that
in all time hitherto, as we have seen, the hill defiles have
been either avoided in terror or inhabited in penance, there
is but the fulfilment of the universal law, that where the
beauty and wisdom of the Divine working are most manifested, there also are manifested most clearly the terror of
God's wrath, and inevitableness of His power.

[Vol. IV, Part 5, Chap. 19]

The Lance of Pallas

All great art is the expression of man's delight in God's
work, not in *his own*. But observe, he is not himself his own
work: he is himself precisely the most wonderful piece of
God's workmanship extant. In this best piece not only he
is bound to take delight, but cannot, in a right state of
thought, take delight in anything else, otherwise than
through himself. Through himself, however, as the sun of
creation, not as *the* creation. In himself, as the light of the
world. Not as being the world. Let him stand in his due
relation to other creatures, and to inanimate things—know
them all and love them, as made for him, and he for them;
—and he becomes himself the greatest and holiest of them.
But let him cast off this relation, despise and forget the less
creation round him, and instead of being the light of the
world, he is a sun in space—a fiery ball, spotted with storm.

All the diseases of mind leading to fatalest ruin consist
primarily in this isolation. They are the concentration of

man upon himself, whether his heavenly interests or his worldly interests, matters not; it is the being *his own* interests which makes the regard of them so mortal. Every form of asceticism on one side, of sensualism on the other, is an isolation of his soul or of his body; the fixing his thoughts upon them alone; while every healthy state of nations and of individual minds consists in the unselfish presence of the human spirit everywhere, energizing over all things; speaking and living through all things.

Man being thus the crowning and ruling work of God, it will follow that all his best art must have something to tell about himself, as the soul of things, and ruler of creatures. It must also make this reference to himself under a true conception of his own nature. Therefore all art which involves no reference to man is inferior or nugatory. And all art which involves misconception of man, or base thought of him, is in that degree false and base.

Now the basest thought possible concerning him is, that he has no spiritual nature; and the foolishest misunderstanding of him possible is, that he has or should have, no animal nature. For his nature is nobly animal, nobly spiritual—coherently and irrevocably so; neither part of it may, but at its peril, expel, despise, or defy the other. All great art confesses and worships both.

The art which, since the writings of Rio and Lord Lindsay,* is specially known as "Christian," erred by pride in its denial of the animal nature of man;—and, in connection with all monkish and fanatical forms of religion, by looking always to another world instead of this. It wasted its strength in visions, and was therefore swept away, notwithstanding all its good and glory, by the strong truth of the naturalist art of the sixteenth century. But that naturalist art erred on the other side; denied at last the spiritual nature of man, and perished in corruption. . . .

* Rio's *De la poésie chrétienne* . . . was published in 1836, Lindsay's *Sketches of the History of Christian Art* in 1847. Ruskin frequently refers to Lindsay's work and learned much from it.

Perhaps an accurate analysis of the schools of art of all time might show us that when the immortality of the soul was practically and completely believed, the elements of decay, danger, and grief in visible things were always disregarded. However this may be, it is assuredly so in the early Christian schools. The ideas of danger or decay seem not merely repugnant, but inconceivable to them; the expression of immortality and perpetuity is alone possible. I do not mean that they take no note of the absolute fact of corruption. This fact the early painters often compel themselves to look fuller in the front than any other men: as in the way they usually paint the Deluge (the raven feeding on the bodies), and in all the various triumphs and processions of the power of Death, which formed one great chapter of religious teaching and painting, from Orcagna's time to the close of the Purist epoch. But I mean that this external fact of corruption is separated in their minds from the main conditions of their work; and its horror enters no more into their general treatment of landscape than the fear of murder or martyrdom, both of which they had nevertheless continually to represent. None of these things appeared to them as affecting the general dealings of the Deity with His world. Death, pain, and decay were simply momentary accidents in the course of immortality, which never ought to exercise any depressing influence over the hearts of men, or in the life of Nature. God, in intense life, peace, and helping power, was always and everywhere. . . .

It may perhaps be thought that this is a very high and right state of mind.

Unfortunately, it appears that the attainment of it is never possible without inducing some form of intellectual weakness.

No painter belonging to the purist religious schools ever mastered his art. Perugino nearly did so; but it was because he was more rational—more a man of the world—than the rest. No literature exists of a high class produced by minds in the pure religious temper. On the contrary, a great deal of literature exists, produced by persons in that temper, which is markedly, and very far, below average literary work. . . . That result indeed follows naturally enough on its habit of assuming that things must be right, or must come right, when, probably, the fact is, that so far as we are concerned, they are entirely wrong; and going wrong: and also on its weak and false way of looking on what these religious persons call "the bright side of things," that is to say, on one side of them only, when God has given them two sides, and intended us to see both.

I was reading but the other day, in a book by a zealous, useful, and able Scotch clergyman, one of these rhapsodies, in which he described a scene in the Highlands to show (he said) the goodness of God. In this Highland scene there was nothing but sunshine, and fresh breezes, and bleating lambs, and clean tartans, and all manner of pleasantness. Now a Highland scene is, beyond dispute, pleasant enough in its own way; but, looked close at, has its shadows. Here, for instance, is the very fact of one, as pretty as I can remember —having seen many. It is a little valley of soft turf, enclosed in its narrow oval by jutting rocks and broad flakes of nodding fern. From one side of it to the other winds, serpentine, a clear brown stream, drooping into quicker ripple as it reaches the end of the oval field, and then, first islanding a purple and white rock with an amber pool, it dashes away into a narrow fall of foam under a thicket of mountain-ash and alder. The autumn sun, low but clear, shines on the scarlet ash-berries and on the golden birch-leaves, which, fallen here and there, when the breeze has not caught them, rest quiet in the crannies of the purple rock. Beside the rock, in the hollow under the thicket, the carcase of a ewe, drowned in the last flood, lies nearly bare to the bone, its white ribs protruding through the skin, raven-torn; and the rags of its wool still flickering from the branches that first stayed it as the stream swept it down. A little lower, the current plunges, roaring, into a circular chasm like a well, surrounded on three sides by a chimney-like hollowness of polished rock, down which the foam slips in detached snow-flakes. Round the edges of the pool beneath, the water circles slowly, like black oil; a little butterfly lies on its back, its wings glued to one of the eddies, its limbs feebly quivering; a fish rises, and it is gone. Lower down the stream, I can just see over a knoll, the green and damp turf roofs of four or five hovels, built at the edge of a morass, which is trodden by the cattle into a black Slough of Despond at their doors, and traversed by a few ill-set stepping-stones, with here and there a flat slab on the tops, where they have sunk out of sight, and at the turn of the brook I see a man fishing, with a boy and a dog—a picturesque and pretty group enough certainly, if they had not been there all day starving. I know them, and I know the dog's ribs also, which are nearly as bare as the dead ewe's; and the child's wasted shoulders, cutting his old tartan jacket through, so sharp are they. . . .

Truly, this Highland and English hill-scenery is fair enough; but has its shadows; and deeper colouring, here and there, than that of heath and rose.

Now, as far as I have watched the main powers of human mind, they have risen first from the resolution to see fearlessly, pitifully, and to its very worst, what these deep colours mean, wheresoever they fall; not by any means to pass on the other side, looking pleasantly up to the sky, but to stoop to the horror, and let the sky, for the present, take care of its own clouds. However this may be in moral matters, with which I have nothing here to do, in my own field of inquiry the fact is so; and all great and beautiful work has come of first gazing without shrinking into the darkness. If, having done so, the human spirit can, by its courage and faith, conquer the evil, it rises into conceptions of victorious and consummated beauty. It is then the spirit of the highest Greek and Venetian Art. If unable to conquer the evil, but remaining in strong though melancholy war with it, not rising into supreme beauty, it is the spirit of the best northern art, typically represented by that of Holbein and Dürer. If, itself conquered by the evil, infected by the dragon breath of it, and at last brought into captivity, so as to take delight in evil for ever, it becomes the spirit of the dark, but still powerful sensualistic art, represented typically by that of Salvator. We must trace this fact briefly through Greek, Venetian, and Düreresque art; we shall then see how the art of decline came of avoiding the evil, and seeking pleasure only; and thus obtain, at last, some power of judging whether the tendency of our own contemplative art be right or ignoble.

The ruling purpose of Greek poetry is the assertion of victory, by heroism, over fate, sin, and death. The terror of these great enemies is dwelt upon chiefly by the tragedians. The victory over them, by Homer.

The adversary chiefly contemplated by the tragedians is Fate, or predestinate misfortune. And that under three principal forms.

(A) Blindness or ignorance; not in itself guilty, but inducing acts which otherwise would have been guilty; and leading, no less than guilt, to destruction.

(B) Visitation upon one person of the sin of another.

(C) Repression by brutal, or tyrannous strength, of a benevolent will.

In all these cases sorrow is much more definitely connected with sin by the Greek tragedians than by Shakspere. The "fate" of Shakspere is, indeed, a form of blindness, but it issues in little more than haste or indiscretion. It is, in the literal sense, "fatal," but hardly criminal.

The "I am fortune's fool" of Romeo, expresses Shakspere's primary idea of tragic circumstance. Often his victims are entirely innocent, swept away by mere current of strong encompassing calamity (Ophelia, Cordelia, Arthur, Queen Katherine). This is rarely so with the Greeks. The victim may indeed be innocent, as Antigone, but is in some way resolutely entangled with crime, and destroyed by it, as if it struck by pollution, no less than participation.

The victory over sin and death is therefore also with the

Greek tragedians more complete than with Shakspere. As the enemy has more direct moral personality,—as it is sinfulness more than mischance, it is met by a higher moral resolve, a greater preparation of heart, a more solemn patience and purposed self-sacrifice. At the close of a Shakspere tragedy, nothing remains but dead march and clothes of burial. At the close of a Greek tragedy there are far-off sounds of a divine triumph, and a glory as of resurrection.*

The Homeric temper is wholly different. Far more tender, more practical, more cheerful; bent chiefly on present things and giving victory now, and here, rather than in hope, and hereafter. The enemies of mankind, in Homer's conception, are more distinctly conquerable; they are ungoverned passions, especially anger, and unreasonable impulse generally ($\dot{\alpha}\tau\eta$). Hence the anger of Achilles, misdirected by pride, but rightly directed by friendship, is the subject of the *Iliad*. The anger of Ulysses ('Οδυσσεὺς, "the angry"), misdirected at first into idle and irregular hostilities, directed at last to execution of sternest justice, is the subject of the *Odyssey*.

Though this is the central idea of the two poems, it is connected with general display of the evil of all unbridled passions, pride, sensuality, indolence, or curiosity. The pride of Atrides, the passion of Paris, the sluggishness of Elpenor, the curiosity of Ulysses himself about the Cyclops, the impatience of his sailors in untying the winds, and all other faults or follies down to that—(evidently no small one in Homer's mind)—of domestic disorderliness, are throughout shown in contrast with conditions of patient affection and household peace.

Also, the wild powers and mysteries of Nature are in the Homeric mind among the enemies of man; so that all the labours of Ulysses are an expression of the contest of manhood, not only with its own passions or with the folly of others, but with the merciless and mysterious powers of the natural world.

* The Alcestis is perhaps the central example of the *idea* of all Greek drama. [Ruskin's note.]

This is perhaps the chief signification of the seven years' stay with Calypso, "the concealer." Not, as vulgarly thought, the concealer of Ulysses, but the great concealer—the hidden power of natural things. She is the daughter of Atlas and the Sea (Atlas, the sustainer of heaven, and the Sea, the disturber of the Earth). She dwells in the island of Ogygia ("the ancient or venerable"). (Whenever Athens, or any other Greek city, is spoken of with any peculiar reverence, it is called "Ogygian.") Escaping from this goddess of secrets, and from other spirits, some of destructive natural force (Scylla), others signifying the enchantment of mere natural beauty (Circe, daughter of the Sun and Sea), he arrives at last at the Phæacian land, whose king is "strength with intellect," and whose queen "virtue." These restore him to his country.

Now observe that in their dealing with all these subjects the Greeks never shrink from horror; down to its uttermost depth, to its most appalling physical detail, they strive to sound the secrets of sorrow. For them there is no passing by on the other side, no turning away the eyes to vanity from pain. Literally, they have not "lifted up their souls unto vanity." Whether there be consolation for them or not, neither apathy nor blindness shall be their saviour; if, for them, thus knowing the facts of the grief of earth, any hope, relief, or triumph may hereafter seem possible,—well; but if not, still hopeless, reliefless, eternal, the sorrow shall be met face to face. This Hector, so righteous, so merciful, so brave, has, nevertheless, to look upon his dearest brother in miserablest death. His own soul passes away in hopeless sobs through the throat-wound of the Grecian spear. That is one aspect of things in this world, a fair world truly, but having, among its other aspects, this one, highly ambiguous.

Meeting it boldly as they may, gazing right into the skeleton face of it, the ambiguity remains; nay, in some sort gains upon them. We trusted in the gods;—we thought that wisdom and courage would save us. Our wisdom and courage themselves deceive us to our death. Athena had the aspect of Deiphobus—terror of the enemy. She has not terrified him, but left us, in our mortal need.*

And beyond that mortality, what hope have we? Nothing is clear to us on that horizon, nor comforting. Funeral honours; perhaps also rest; perhaps a shadowy life—artless, joyless, loveless. No devices in that darkness of the grave, nor daring, nor delight. Neither marrying nor giving in marriage, nor casting of spears, nor rolling of chariots, nor voice of fame. Lapped in pale Elysian mist, chilling the forgetful heart and feeble frame, shall we waste on for ever? Can the dust of earth claim more of immortality than this? Or shall we have even so much as rest? May we, indeed, lie down again in the dust: or have not our sins hidden from us even the things that belong to that peace? May not chance and the whirl of passion govern us there: when there shall be no thought, nor work, nor wisdom, nor breathing of the soul?

Be it so. With no better reward, no brighter hope, we will be men while we may: men, just, and strong, and fearless, and up to our power, perfect. Athena herself, our wisdom and our strength, may betray us:—Phœbus, our sun, smite us with plague, or hide his face from us helpless;—Jove and all the powers of fate oppress us, or give us up to destruction. While we live, we will hold fast our integrity; no weak tears shall blind us, no untimely tremors abate our strength of arm nor swiftness of limb. The gods have given us at least this glorious body and this righteous conscience; these will we keep bright and pure to the end. So may we fall to misery, but not to baseness; so may we sink to sleep, but not to shame.

And herein was conquest. So defied, the betraying and accusing shadows shrank back; the mysterious horror subdued itself to majestic sorrow. Death was swallowed up in victory. Their blood, which seemed to be poured out upon

---

* In the *Iliad*, xxii, Pallas Athena appears to Hector in the guise of his brother, Deiphobus. She treacherously leads him into battle against Achilles, then deserts him, having handed to Achilles the "lance of Pallas" with which he slays Hector.

the ground, rose into hyacinthine flowers. All the beauty of earth opened to them; they had ploughed into its darkness, and they reaped its gold; the gods, in whom they had trusted through all semblance of oppression, came down to love them and be their helpmates. All nature round them became divine,—one harmony of power and peace. The sun hurt them not by day, nor the moon by night; the earth opened no more her jaws into the pit; the sea whitened no more against them the teeth of his devouring waves. Sun, and moon, and earth, and sea,—all melted into grace and love; the fatal arrows rang not now at the shoulders of Apollo, the healer; lord of life, and of the three great spirits of life—Care, Memory, and Melody. Great Artemis guarded their flocks by night; Selene kissed in love the eyes of those who slept. And from all came the help of heaven to body and soul; a strange spirit lifting the lovely limbs; strange light glowing on the golden hair; and strangest comfort filling the trustful heart, so that they could put off their armour, and lie down to sleep,—their work well done, whether at the gates of their temples or of their mountains; accepting the death they once thought terrible, as the gift of Him who knew and granted what was best.

[Vol. V, Part 9, Chap. 2]

The Two Boyhoods

Born half-way between the mountains and the sea—that young George of Castelfranco—of the Brave Castle:—Stout George they called him, George of Georges, so goodly a boy he was—Giorgione.

Have you ever thought what a world his eyes opened on —fair, searching eyes of youth? What a world of mighty life, from those mountain roots to the shore;—of loveliest life, when he went down, yet so young, to the marble city —and became himself as a fiery heart to it?

A city of marble, did I say? nay, rather a golden city,

paved with emerald. For truly, every pinnacle and turret glanced or glowed, overlaid with gold, or bossed with jasper. Beneath, the unsullied sea drew in deep breathing, to and fro, its eddies of green wave. Deep-hearted, majestic, terrible as the sea,—the men of Venice moved in sway of power and war; pure as her pillars of alabaster, stood her mothers and maidens; from foot to brow, all noble, walked her knights; the low bronzed gleaming of sea-rusted armour shot angrily under their blood-red mantle-folds. Fearless, faithful, patient, impenetrable, implacable,—every word a fate—sate her senate. In hope and honour, lulled by flowing of wave around their isles of sacred sand, each with his name written and the cross graved at his side, lay her dead. A wonderful piece of world. Rather, itself a world. It lay along the face of the waters, no larger, as its captains saw it from their masts at evening, than a bar of sunset that could not pass away; but for its power, it must have seemed to them as if they were sailing in the expanse of heaven, and this a great planet, whose orient edge widened through ether. A world from which all ignoble care and petty thoughts were banished, with all the common and poor elements of life. No foulness, nor tumult, in those tremulous streets, that filled, or fell, beneath the moon; but rippled music of majestic change, or thrilling silence. No weak walls could rise above them; no low-roofed cottage, nor straw-built shed. Only the strength as of rock, and the finished setting of stones most precious. And around them, far as the eye could reach, still the soft moving of stainless waters; proudly pure; as not the flower, so neither the thorn nor the thistle, could grow in the glancing fields. Ethereal strength of Alps, dreamlike, vanishing in high procession beyond the Torcellan shore; blue islands of Paduan hills, poised in the golden west. Above, free winds and fiery clouds ranging at their will;— brightness out of the north, and balm from the south, and the stars of the evening and morning clear in the limitless light of arched heaven and circling sea.

Such was Giorgione's school—such Titian's home.

Near the south-west corner of Covent Garden, a square brick pit or well is formed by a close-set block of houses, to the back windows of which it admits a few rays of light. Access to the bottom of it is obtained out of Maiden Lane, through a low archway and an iron gate; and if you stand long enough under the archway to accustom your eyes to the darkness you may see on the left hand a narrow door, which formerly gave quiet access to a respectable barber's shop, of which the front window, looking into Maiden Lane, is still extant, filled, in this year (1860), with a row of bottles, connected, in some defunct manner, with a brewer's business. A more fashionable neighbourhood, it is said, eighty years ago than now—never certainly a cheerful one—wherein a boy being born on St. George's day, 1775, began soon after to take interest in the world of Covent Garden, and put to service such spectacles of life as it afforded.

No knights to be seen there, nor, I imagine, many beautiful ladies; their costume at least disadvantageous, depending much on incumbency of hat and feather, and short waists; the majesty of men founded similarly on shoebuckles and wigs;—impressive enough when Reynolds will do his best for it; but not suggestive of much ideal delight to a boy.

"Bello ovile dov' io dormii agnello";* of things beautiful, besides men and women, dusty sunbeams up or down the street on summer mornings; deep furrowed cabbage-leaves at the greengrocer's; magnificence of oranges in wheelbarrows round the corner; and Thames' shore within three minutes' race.

None of these things very glorious; the best, however, that England, it seems, was then able to provide for a boy of gift: who, such as they are, loves them—never, indeed, forgets them. The short waists modify to the last his visions of Greek ideal. His foregrounds had always a succulent cluster or two of greengrocery at the corners. Enchanted oranges

* Dante's allusion to Florence, *Paradiso*, xxv, 5: "From the fair sheepfold wherein I used to sleep, a lamb."

gleam in Covent Gardens of the Hesperides; and great ships go to pieces in order to scatter chests of them on the waves. That mist of early sunbeams in the London dawn crosses, many and many a time, the clearness of Italian air; and by Thames' shore, with its stranded barges and glidings of red sail, dearer to us than Lucerne lake or Venetian lagoon,— by Thames' shore we will die.

With such circumstance round him in youth, let us note what necessary effects followed upon the boy. I assume him to have had Giorgione's sensibility (and more than Giorgione's, if that be possible) to colour and form. I tell you farther, and this fact you may receive trustfully, that his sensibility to human affection and distress was no less keen than even his sense for natural beauty—heart-sight deep as eyesight.

Consequently, he attaches himself with the faithfullest child-love to everything that bears an image of the place he was born in. No matter how ugly it is,—has it anything about it like Maiden Lane, or like Thames' shore? If so, it shall be painted for their sake. Hence, to the very close of life, Turner could endure ugliness which no one else, of the same sensibility, would have borne with for an instant. Dead brick walls, blank square windows, old clothes, market-womanly types of humanity—anything fishy and muddy, like Billingsgate or Hungerford Market, had great attraction for him; black barges, patched sails, and every possible condition of fog.

You will find these tolerations and affections guiding or sustaining him to the last hour of his life; the notablest of all such endurances being that of dirt. No Venetian ever draws anything foul; but Turner devoted picture after picture to the illustration of effects of dinginess, smoke, soot, dust, and dusty texture; old sides of boats, weedy roadside vegetation, dung-hills, straw-yards, and all the soilings and stains of every common labour.

And more than this, he not only could endure, but enjoyed and looked for *litter*, like Covent Garden wreck after the market. His pictures are often full of it, from side to side; their foregrounds differ from all others in the natural way that things have of lying about in them. Even his richest vegetation, in ideal work, is confused; and he delights in shingle, débris, and heaps of fallen stones. The last words he ever spoke to me about a picture were in gentle exultation about his St. Gothard: "that *litter* of stones which I endeavoured to represent."

The second great result of this Covent Garden training was, understanding of and regard for the poor, whom the Venetians, we saw, despised; whom, contrarily, Turner loved, and more than loved—understood. He got no romantic sight of them, but an infallible one, as he prowled about the end of his lane, watching night effects in the wintry streets; nor sight of the poor alone, but of the poor in direct relations with the rich. He knew, in good and evil, what both classes thought of, and how they dealt with, each other.

Reynolds and Gainsborough, bred in country villages, learned there the country boy's reverential theory of "the squire," and kept it. They painted the squire and the squire's lady as centres of the movements of the universe, to the end of their lives. But Turner perceived the younger squire in other aspects about his lane, occurring prominently in its night scenery, as a dark figure, or one of two, against the moonlight. He saw also the working of city commerce, from endless warehouse, towering over Thames, to the back shop in the lane, with its stale herrings—highly interesting these last; one of his father's best friends, whom he often afterwards visited affectionately at Bristol, being a fishmonger and glue-boiler; which gives us a friendly turn of mind towards herring-fishing, whaling, Calais poissardes, and many other of our choicest subjects in after-life; all this being connected with that mysterious forest below London Bridge on one side; and, on the other, with these masses of human power and national wealth which weigh upon us, at Covent

Garden here, with strange compression, and crush us into narrow Hand Court.

"That mysterious forest below London Bridge" better for the boy than wood of pine, or grove of myrtle. How he must have tormented the watermen, beseeching them to let him crouch anywhere in the bows, quiet as a log, so only that he might get floated down there among the ships, and round and round the ships, and with the ships, and by the ships, and under the ships, staring, and clambering;—these the only quite beautiful things he can see in all the world, except the sky; but these, when the sun is on their sails, filling or falling, endlessly disordered by sway of tide and stress of anchorage, beautiful unspeakably; which ships also are inhabited by glorious creatures—red-faced sailors, with pipes, appearing over the gunwales, true knights, over their castle parapets—the most angelic beings in the whole compass of London world. And Trafalgar happening long before we can draw ships, we, nevertheless, coax all current stories out of the wounded sailors, do our best at present to show Nelson's funeral streaming up the Thames; and vow that Trafalgar shall have its tribute of memory some day. Which, accordingly, is accomplished—once, with all our might, for its death; twice, with all our might, for its victory; thrice, in pensive farewell to the old *Téméraire*, and with it, to that order of things.

Now this fond companying with sailors must have divided his time, it appears to me, pretty equally between Covent Garden and Wapping (allowing for incidental excursions to Chelsea on one side, and Greenwich on the other), which time he would spend pleasantly, but not magnificently, being limited in pocket-money, and leading a kind of "Poor Jack" life on the river.

In some respects, no life could be better for a lad. But it was not calculated to make his ear fine to the niceties of language, nor form his moralities on an entirely regular standard. Picking up his first scraps of vigorous English chiefly at Deptford and in the markets, and his first ideas of female tenderness and beauty among nymphs of the barge and the barrow,—another boy might, perhaps, have become what people usually term "vulgar." But the original make and frame of Turner's mind being not vulgar, but as nearly as possible a combination of the minds of Keats and Dante, joining capricious waywardness, and intense openness to every fine pleasure of sense, and hot defiance of formal precedent, with a quite infinite tenderness, generosity, and desire of justice and truth—this kind of mind did not become vulgar, but very tolerant of vulgarity, even fond of it in some forms; and on the outside, visibly infected by it, deeply enough; the curious result, in its combination of elements, being to most people wholly incomprehensible. It was as if a cable had been woven of blood-crimson silk, and then tarred on the outside. People handled it, and the tar came off on their hands; red gleams were seen through the black underneath, at the places where it had been strained. Was it ochre?—said the world—or red lead?

Schooled thus in manners, literature, and the general moral principles at Chelsea and Wapping, we have finally to inquire concerning the most important point of all. We have seen the principal differences between this boy and Giorgione, as respects sight of the beautiful, understanding of poverty, of commerce, and of order of battle; then follows another cause of difference in our training—not slight, —the aspect of religion, namely, in the neighbourhood of Covent Garden. I say the aspect; for that was all the lad could judge by. Disposed, for the most part, to learn chiefly by his eyes, in this special matter he finds there is really no other way of learning. His father had taught him "to lay one penny upon another." Of Mother's teaching, we hear of none; of parish pastoral teaching, the reader may guess how much.

I chose Giorgione rather than Veronese to help me in carrying out this parallel; because I do not find in Giorgione's work any of the early Venetian monarchist element. He seems to me to have belonged more to an abstract contemplative school. I may be wrong in this; it is no matter;—suppose it were so, and that he came down to Venice somewhat recusant or insentient, concerning the usual priestly doctrines of his day, how would the Venetian religion, from an outer intellectual standing-point, have *looked* to him?

He would have seen it to be a religion indisputably powerful in human affairs; often very harmfully so; sometimes devouring widows' houses, and consuming the strongest and fairest from among the young: freezing into merciless bigotry the policy of the old: also, on the other hand, animating national courage, and raising souls, otherwise sordid, into heroism: on the whole, always a real and great power; served with daily sacrifice of gold, time, and thought; putting forth its claims, if hypocritically, at least in bold hypocrisy, not waiving any atom of them in doubt or fear; and, assuredly, in large measure, sincere, believing in itself, and believed: a goodly system, moreover, in aspect; gorgeous, harmonious, mysterious;—a thing which had either to be obeyed or combated, but could not be scorned. A religion towering over all the city—many-buttressed—luminous in marble stateliness, as the dome of our Lady of Safety shines over the sea; many-voiced, also, giving, over all the eastern seas, to the sentinel his watchword, to the soldier his war-cry; and, on the lips of all who died for Venice, shaping the whisper of death.

I suppose the boy Turner to have regarded the religion of his city also from an external intellectual standing-point.

What did he see in Maiden Lane?

Let not the reader be offended with me: I am willing to let him describe, at his own pleasure, what Turner saw there; but to me, it seems to have been this. A religion maintained occasionally, even the whole length of the lane, at point of constable's staff; but, at other times, placed under the custody of the beadle, within certain black and unstately iron railings of St. Paul's, Covent Garden. Among the wheelbarrows and over the vegetables, no perceptible dominance of religion; in the narrow, disquieted streets, none; in the tongues, deeds, daily ways of Maiden Lane, little. Some honesty, indeed, and English industry, and kindness of heart, and general idea of justice; but faith, of any national kind, shut up from one Sunday to the next, not artistically beautiful even in those Sabbatical exhibitions; its paraphernalia being chiefly of high pews, heavy elocution, and cold grimness of behaviour.

What chiaroscuro belongs to it—(dependent mostly on candlelight),—we will, however, draw, considerately; no goodliness of escutcheon, nor other respectability being omitted, and the best of their results confessed, a meek old woman and a child being let into a pew, for whom the reading by candlelight will be beneficial.*

For the rest, this religion seems to him discreditable—discredited—not believing in itself: putting forth its authority in a cowardly way, watching how far it might be tolerated, continually shrinking, disclaiming, fencing, finessing; divided against itself, not by stormy rents, but by thin fissures, and splittings of plaster from the walls. Not to be either obeyed, or combated, by an ignorant, yet clear-sighted youth! only to be scorned. And scorned not one whit the less, though also the dome dedicated to *it* looms high over distant winding of the Thames; as St. Mark's campanile rose, for goodly landmark, over mirage of lagoon. For St. Mark ruled over life; the Saint of London over death; St. Mark over St. Mark's Place, but St. Paul over St. Paul's Churchyard.

Under these influences pass away the first reflective hours of life, with such conclusion as they can reach. In consequence of a fit of illness, he was taken—I cannot ascertain in what year—to live with an aunt, at Brentford; and here, I believe, received some schooling, which he seems to have

* Liber Studiorum. "Interior of a church." It is worthy of remark that Giorgione and Titian are always delighted to have an opportunity of drawing priests. The English Church may, perhaps, accept it as matter of congratulation that this is the only instance in which Turner drew a clergyman. [Ruskin's note.]

snatched vigorously; getting knowledge, at least by translation, of the more picturesque classical authors, which he
turned presently to use, as we shall see. Hence also, walks
about Putney and Twickenham in the summer time acquainted him with the look of English meadow-ground in
its restricted states of paddock and park; and with some
round-headed appearances of trees, and stately entrances
to houses of mark: the avenue at Bushey, and the iron gates
and carved pillars of Hampton, impressing him apparently
with great awe and admiration; so that in after-life his little
country house is,—of all places in the world,—at Twickenham! Of swans and reedy shores he now learns the soft motion and the green mystery, in a way not to be forgotten.

And at last fortune wills that the lad's true life shall begin; and one summer's evening, after various wonderful
stage-coach experiences on the north road, which gave him
a love of stage-coaches ever after, he finds himself sitting
alone among the Yorkshire hills. For the first time, the
silence of Nature round him, her freedom sealed to him,
her glory opened to him. Peace at last; no roll of cart-wheel,
nor mutter of sullen voices in the back shop; but curlew-cry
in space of heaven, and welling of bell-toned streamlet by
its shadowy rock. Freedom at last. Dead-wall, dark railing,
fenced field, gated garden, all passed away like the dream of
a prisoner; and behold, far as foot or eye can race or range,
the moor, and cloud. Loveliness at last. It is here then,
among these deserted vales! Not among men. Those pale,
poverty-struck, or cruel faces;—that multitudinous, marred
humanity—are not the only things that God has made. Here
is something He has made which no one has marred. Pride
of purple rocks, and river pools of blue, and tender wilderness of glittering trees, and misty lights of evening on immeasurable hills.

Beauty, and freedom, and peace; and yet another teacher,
graver than these. Sound preaching at last here, in Kirkstall
crypt, concerning fate and life. Here, where the dark pool

reflects the chancel pillars, and the cattle lie in unhindered rest, the soft sunshine on their dappled bodies, instead of priests' vestments; their white furry hair ruffled a little, fitfully, by the evening wind deep-scented from the meadow thyme.

Consider deeply the import to him of this, his first sight of ruin, and compare it with the effect of the architecture that was around Giorgione. There were indeed aged buildings, at Venice, in his time, but none in decay. All ruin was removed, and its place filled as quickly as in our London; but filled always by architecture loftier and more wonderful than that whose place it took, the boy himself happy to work upon the walls of it; so that the idea of the passing away of the strength of men and beauty of their works never could occur to him sternly. Brighter and brighter the cities of Italy had been rising and broadening on hill and plain, for three hundred years. He saw only strength and immortality, could not but paint both; conceived the form of man as deathless, calm with power, and fiery with life.

Turner saw the exact reverse of this. In the present work of men, meanness, aimlessness, unsightliness: thin-walled, lath-divided, narrow-garreted houses of clay; booths of a darksome Vanity Fair, busily base.

But on Whitby Hill, and by Bolton Brook, remained traces of other handiwork. Men who could build had been there; and who also had wrought, not merely for their own days. But to what purpose? Strong faith, and steady hands, and patient souls—can this, then, be all you have left? this the sum of your doing on the earth;—a nest whence the night-owl may whimper to the brook, and a ribbed skeleton of consumed arches, looming above the bleak banks of mist, from its cliff to the sea?

As the strength of men to Giorgione, to Turner their weakness and vileness, were alone visible. They themselves, unworthy or ephemeral; their work, despicable, or decayed. In the Venetian's eyes, all beauty depended on man's presence and pride; in Turner's, on the solitude he had left, and the humiliation he had suffered.

And thus the fate and issue of all his work were determined at once. He must be a painter of the strength of nature, there was no beauty elsewhere than in that; he must paint also the labour and sorrow and passing away of men: this was the great human truth visible to him.

Their labour, their sorrow, and their death. Mark the three. Labour; by sea and land, in field and city, at forge and furnace, helm and plough. No pastoral indolence nor classic pride shall stand between him and the troubling of the world; still less between him and the toil of his country,— blind, tormented, unwearied, marvellous England.

Also their Sorrow; Ruin of all their glorious work, passing away of their thoughts and their honour, mirage of pleasure, FALLACY OF HOPE;* gathering of weed on temple step; gaining of wave on deserted strand; weeping of the mother for the children, desolate by her breathless first-born in the streets of the city, desolate by her last sons slain, among the beasts of the field.

And their Death. That old Greek question again;—yet unanswered. The unconquerable spectre still flitting among the forest trees at twilight; rising ribbed out of the sea-sand; —white, a strange Aphrodite,—out of the sea-foam; stretching its gray, cloven wings among the clouds; turning the light of their sunsets into blood. This has to be looked upon, and in a more terrible shape than ever Salvator or Dürer saw it. The wreck of one guilty country does not infer the ruin of all countries, and need not cause general terror respecting the laws of the universe. Neither did the orderly and narrow succession of domestic joy and sorrow in a small German community bring the question in its breadth, or in any

* The title of Turner's manuscript collection of poems, which he often quoted in the catalogue description of his paintings. Ruskin alludes, at the end of this paragraph, to Turner's *Tenth Plague of Egypt* and *Rizpah*.

unresolvable shape, before the mind of Dürer. But the English death—the European death of the nineteenth century —was of another range and power; more terrible a thousand-fold in its merely physical grasp and grief; more terrible, incalculably, in its mystery and shame. What were the robber's casual pang, or the range of the flying skirmish, compared to the work of the axe, and the sword, and the famine, which was done during this man's youth on all the hills and plains of the Christian earth, from Moscow to Gibraltar? He was eighteen years old when Napoleon came down on Arcola. Look on the map of Europe and count the blood-stains on it, between Arcola and Waterloo.

Not alone those blood-stains on the Alpine snow, and the blue of the Lombard plain. The English death was before his eyes also. No decent, calculable, consoled dying; no passing to rest like that of the aged burghers of Nuremberg town. No gentle processions to churchyards among the fields, the bronze crests bossed deep on the memorial tablets, and the skylark singing above them from among the corn. But the life trampled out in the slime of the street, crushed to dust amidst the roaring of the wheel, tossed countlessly away into howling winter wind along five hundred leagues of rock-fanged shore. Or, worst of all, rotted down to forgotten graves through years of ignorant patience, and vain seeking for help from man, for hope in God—infirm, imperfect yearning, as of motherless infants starving at the dawn; oppressed royalties of captive thought, vague ague-fits of bleak, amazed despair.

A goodly landscape this, for the lad to paint, and under a goodly light. Wide enough the light was, and clear; no more Salvator's lurid chasm on jagged horizon, nor Dürer's spotted rest of sunny gleam on hedgerow and field; but light over all the world. Full shone now its awful globe, one pallid charnel-house,—a ball strewn bright with human ashes, glaring in poised sway beneath the sun, all blinding-white with death from pole to pole,—death, not of myriads of poor bodies only, but of will, and mercy, and conscience; death, not once inflicted on the flesh, but daily fastening on the spirit; death, not silent or patient, waiting his appointed hour, but voiceful, venomous; death with the taunting word, and burning grasp, and infixed sting.

"Put ye in the sickle, for the harvest is ripe."* The word is spoken in our ears continually to other reapers than the angels,—to the busy skeletons that never tire for stooping. When the measure of iniquity is full, and it seems that another day might bring repentance and redemption,—"Put ye in the sickle." When the young life has been wasted all away, and the eyes are just opening upon the tracks of ruin, and the faint resolution rising in the heart for nobler things, —"Put ye in the sickle." When the roughest blows of fortune have been borne long and bravely, and the hand is just stretched to grasp its goal,—"Put ye in the sickle." And when there are but a few in the midst of a nation, to save it, or to teach, or to cherish; and all its life is bound up in those few golden ears,—"Put ye in the sickle, pale reapers, and pour hemlock for your feast of harvest home."

This was the sight which opened on the young eyes, this the watchword sounding within the heart of Turner in his youth.

So taught, and prepared for his life's labour, sate the boy at last alone among his fair English hills; and began to paint, with cautious toil, the rocks, and fields, and trickling brooks, and soft white clouds of heaven.   [Vol. V, Part 9, Chap. 9]

Epilogue

. . . All that is involved in these passionate utterances of my youth was first expanded and then concentrated into the aphorism given twenty years afterwards in my inaugural Oxford lectures, "All great Art is Praise"; and on that aphorism, the yet bolder saying founded, "So far from Art's being

* Joel 3:13. The subsequent allusions are to Revelations 14:14–20 and, possibly, to Hosea 10:4.

immoral, in the ultimate power of it, nothing but Art is moral: Life without Industry is sin, and Industry without Art, brutality" (I forget the words, but that is their purport): and now, in writing beneath the cloudless peace of the snows of Chamouni, what must be the really final words of the book which their beauty inspired and their strength guided, I am able, with yet happier and calmer heart than ever heretofore, to enforce its simplest assurance of Faith, that the knowledge of what is beautiful leads on, and is the first step, to the knowledge of the things which are lovely and of good report; and that the laws, the life, and the joy of beauty in the material world of God, are as eternal and sacred parts of His creation as, in the world of spirits, virtue; and in the world of angels, praise.

CHAMOUNI,
   Sunday, September 16th, 1888.

Architecture

Ruskin once complained of having great difficulty preventing the seven lamps of architecture from growing into eight or nine. But he was unusually successful; *The Seven Lamps of Architecture* is one of his briefest and best organized books. He did most of his research in the churches of Normandy in the autumn of 1848, shortly after his marriage to Euphemia Gray. The tensions of their marriage were already apparent, but they were reflected in his writing only in the uncharacteristic dispatch with which he completed the book the following spring.

The Seven Lamps has long been among the most popular of Ruskin's works. Frank Lloyd Wright read it during his early years, and it unquestionably played a formative role, along with *The Stones of Venice,* in shaping his conception of "Organic Architecture." Ruskin is Wright's link to the aesthetic of Nature, that love of "organic forms" which Ruskin saw carved in the weathered capitals of Normandy; Wright has made Ruskin important to an understanding of the architecture of today.

That Ruskin exerted such an influence is surprising in view of his advocacy of Gothic and his hostility to the revolution in building embodied in the plate glass and cast iron of the Crystal Palace. Yet much of what Ruskin says of the architecture of stone holds true for the architecture of steel. More than anyone else in the nineteenth century, he convinced the profession and the public that architecture is not an isolated science of compass and rule, but a vital index of a nation's values. His insistence that a building must be honest if it is to be beautiful, functional and expressive of its materials and locale if it is to merit praise, is echoed less eloquently today. Those who associate his name with wedding-cake Gothic have never read his work. Indeed, in striving to revive Gothic he is to be condemned not for admiring monstrosities but for desiring impossibilities: a revolution in social and economic values which would have made it possible to build permanently and intelligently, instead of throwing up prebuilt slums for quick profit. More than a century ago, in "The Lamp of Memory," he looked upon the first festering signs of suburbia "not merely with the careless disgust of an offended eye, not merely with sorrow for a desecrated landscape, but with a painful foreboding that the roots of our national greatness must be deeply cankered when they are thus loosely struck in their native ground."

The indictment is potent because it refuses to rest on aesthetic grounds alone. Precisely as Ruskin had hoped in *Modern Painters* to make the study of art "an instrument of gigantic moral power," so in *The Seven Lamps* he tried to make architecture a means of enriching the nation's values. His role in the revival of Gothic is merely of historic interest; but he still compels attention as a superbly articulate moralist who could not divorce the science of building from the art of living.

After completing *The Seven Lamps,* Ruskin continued his architectural studies in Venice, where he lived with his wife during much of 1849–52. But he was in fact more wedded to the city than to her. In his letters and diaries of the period we find him strangely oblivious of his wife, but totally absorbed by the great effort of mind through which he deciphered and splendidly re-created Venice's past. The one marriage, never consummated, ended in annulment; the other produced the most elaborate and eloquent monument to a city in our literature.

An almost neurotic sense of urgency drove Ruskin to his labors of research for *The Stones of Venice.* He wrote to his father in 1852 that he had examined piece by piece buildings covering five square miles, read some forty volumes of the city's archives, and made hundreds of architectural drawings—all while unraveling the conflicting chronology of his sources and composing the book. Yet *The Stones of Venice* is even more notable as a work of art than as a work of scholarship. When the book appeared, professional architects condemned Ruskin's perversity in having praised the uncouth St. Mark's in direct opposition to every other architectural critic. His image of Venice was as radically fresh and brilliant as Turner's vision of her sea and sky.

Although Ruskin recounts the history of Venice from its founding through its fall, the unifying theme of the book lies elsewhere. "The relation of the art of Venice to her moral temper," he wrote, "is the chief subject of the book, and that of the life of the workman to his work . . . is the most important practical principle developed in it." Ruskin had touched on both ideas in *The Seven Lamps*. But the last point, almost an irrelevant aside in the earlier book, was the source of the great central chapter of *The Stones of Venice*, "the Nature of Gothic," which William Morris called "one of the very few necessary and inevitable utterances of the century." "The Nature of Gothic" in turn led Ruskin in the 1860s to his radical assault upon the social and economic structure of England.

The actual stones of Venice served Ruskin as touchstones which confirmed the principles of *The Seven Lamps*. His digressiveness was curbed by the orderly flow of Venetian history and by the requirements of a consistently maintained thesis. But in place of the tedious unity of a chronicle, he succeeded in writing a morality drama in which the sequence of doges and styles marks not only moments in Venice's history but also forces contending for the aesthetic and moral integrity of the city itself. *The Stones of Venice* is a Christian epic, magnificent in scope, which in its final volume—*The Fall*—completes the drama of a Gothic paradise lost.

—J. D. R.

THE SEVEN LAMPS
OF ARCHITECTURE

The Lamp of Truth

The violations of truth, which dishonour poetry and painting, are . . . for the most part confined to the treatment
of their subjects. But in architecture another and a less subtle, more contemptible, violation of truth is possible; a direct falsity of assertion respecting the nature of material, or
the quantity of labour. And this is, in the full sense of the
word, wrong; it is as truly deserving of reprobation as any
other moral delinquency; it is unworthy alike of architects
and of nations; and it has been a sign, wherever it has widely
and with toleration existed, of a singular debasement of the
arts. . . . We may not be able to command good, or beautiful,
or inventive, architecture; but we *can* command an honest
architecture: the meagreness of poverty may be pardoned,
the sternness of utility respected; but what is there but scorn
for the meanness of deception?

Architectural Deceits are broadly to be considered under
three heads:—

1st. The suggestion of a mode of structure or support,
other than the true one; as in pendants of late Gothic roofs.

2nd. The painting of surfaces to represent some other material than that of which they actually consist (as in the mar-
bling of wood), or the deceptive representation of sculptured
ornament upon them.

3rd. The use of cast or machine-made ornaments of any
kind.

Now, it may be broadly stated, that architecture will be

noble exactly in the degree in which all these false expedients are avoided. . . .

With deceptive concealments of structure are to be classed, though still more blameable, deceptive assumptions of it,— the introduction of members which should have, or profess to have, a duty, and have none. One of the most general instances of this will be found in the form of the flying buttress in late Gothic. The use of that member is, of course, to convey support from one pier to another when the plan of the building renders it necessary or desirable that the supporting masses should be divided into groups; the most frequent necessity of this kind arising from the intermediate range of chapels or aisles between the nave or choir walls and their supporting piers. The natural, healthy, and beautiful arrangement is that of a steeply sloping bar of stone, sustained by an arch with its spandrel carried farthest down on the lowest side, and dying into the vertical of the outer pier; that pier being, of course, not square, but rather a piece of wall set at right angles to the supported walls, and, if need be, crowned by a pinnacle to give it greater weight. The whole arrangement is exquisitely carried out in the choir of Beauvais. In later Gothic the pinnacle became gradually a decorative member, and was used in all places merely for the sake of its beauty. There is no objection to this; it is just as lawful to build a pinnacle for its beauty as a tower; but also the *buttress* became a decorative member; and was used, first, where it was not wanted, and, secondly, in forms in which it could be of no use, becoming a mere tie, not between the pier and wall, but between the wall and the top of the decorative pinnacle, thus attaching itself to the very point where its thrust, if it made any, could not be resisted. The most flagrant instance of this barbarism that I remember, (though it prevails partially in all the spires of the Netherlands,) is the lantern of St. Ouen at Rouen, where the pierced buttress, having an ogee curve, looks about as much calculated to bear a thrust as a switch of willow; and the pinnacles, huge and richly decorated, have evidently no work to do whatsoever, but stand round the central tower, like four idle servants, as they are—heraldic supporters, that central tower being merely a hollow crown, which needs no more buttressing than a basket does. In fact, I do not know any thing more strange or unwise than the praise lavished upon this lantern; it is one of the basest pieces of Gothic in Europe; its flamboyant traceries being of the last and most degraded forms: and its entire plan and decoration resembling, and deserving little more credit than, the burnt sugar ornaments of elaborate confectionery. . . .

It would be easy to give many instances of the danger of these tricks and vanities; but I shall confine myself to the examination of one which has, as I think, been the cause of the fall of Gothic architecture throughout Europe. I mean the system of intersectional mouldings, which, on account of its great importance, and for the sake of the general reader, I may, perhaps, be pardoned for explaining elementarily. . . .

Tracery arose from the gradual enlargement of the penetrations of the shield of stone which, usually supported by a central pillar, occupied the head of early windows . . . and finally, by thinning out the stony ribs [reached] conditions like that of the glorious typical form of the clerestory of the apse of Beauvais.

Now, it will be noticed that, during the whole of this process, the attention is kept fixed on the forms of the penetrations, that is to say, of the lights as seen from the interior, not of the intermediate stone. All the grace of the window is in the outline of its light; and I have drawn all these traceries as seen from within, in order to show the effect of the light thus treated, at first in far off and separate stars, and then gradually enlarging, approaching, until they come and stand over us, as it were, filling the whole space with their effulgence. And it is in this pause of the star, that we have the great, pure, and perfect form of French Gothic; it was at the instant when the rudeness of the intermediate space had been finally conquered, when the light had expanded to its fullest, and yet had not lost its radiant unity, principality, and visible first causing of the whole, that we have the most exquisite feeling and most faultless judgments in the management alike of the tracery and decorations. . . . That tracery marks a pause between the laying aside of one great ruling principle, and the taking up of another; a pause as marked, as clear, as conspicuous to the distant view of after times, as to the distant glance of the traveller is the culminating ridge of the mountain chain over which he has passed. It was the great watershed of Gothic art. Before it, all had been ascent; after it, all was decline. . . .

The change of which I speak, is expressible in few words; but one more important, more radically influential, could not be. It was the substitution of the *line* for the *mass*, as the element of decoration.

We have seen the mode in which the openings or penetration of the window expanded, until what were, at first, awkward forms of intermediate stone, became delicate lines of tracery; and I have been careful in pointing out the peculiar attention bestowed on the proportion and decoration of the mouldings of the window at Rouen, as compared with earlier mouldings, because that beauty and care are singularly significant. They mark that the traceries had *caught the eye* of the architect. Up to that time, up to the very last instant in which the reduction and thinning of the intervening stone was consummated, his eye had been on the openings only, on the stars of light. He did not care about the stone; a rude border of moulding was all he needed, it was the penetrating shape which he was watching. But when that shape had received its last possible expansion, and when the stone-work became an arrangement of graceful and parallel lines, that arrangement, like some form in a picture, unseen and accidentally developed, struck suddenly, inevitably, on the sight. It had literally not been seen before. It flashed out in an instant, as an independent form. It became a feature of the work. The architect took it under his care, thought over it, and distributed its members as we see.

Now, the great pause was at the moment when the space

and the dividing stone-work were both equally considered. It did not last fifty years. The forms of the tracery were seized with a childish delight in the novel source of beauty; and the intervening space was cast aside, as an element of decoration, for ever. I have confined myself, in following this change, to the window, as the feature in which it is clearest. But the transition is the same in every member of architecture; . . . I pursue here the question of truth, relating to the treatment of the mouldings.

The reader will observe that, up to the last expansion of the penetrations, the stone-work was necessarily considered, as it actually is, *stiff*, and unyielding. It was so, also, during the pause of which I have spoken, when the forms of the tracery were still severe and pure; delicate indeed, but perfectly firm.

At the close of the period of pause, the first sign of serious change was like a low breeze, passing through the emaciated tracery, and making it tremble. It began to undulate like the threads of a cobweb lifted by the wind. It lost its essence as a structure of stone. Reduced to the slenderness of threads, it began to be considered as possessing also their flexibility. The architect was pleased with this his new fancy, and set himself to carry it out; and in a little time, the bars of tracery were caused to appear to the eye as if they had been woven together like a net. This was a change which sacrificed a great principle of truth; it sacrificed the expression of the qualities of the material; and, however delightful its results in their first developments, it was ultimately ruinous.

For, observe the difference between the supposition of ductility, and that of elastic structure noticed above in the resemblance to tree form. That resemblance was not sought, but necessary; it resulted from the natural conditions of strength in the pier or trunk, and slenderness in the ribs or branches, while many of the other suggested conditions of resemblance were perfectly true. A tree branch, though in a certain sense flexible, is not ductile; it is as firm in its own form as the rib of stone; both of them will yield up to certain limits, both of them breaking when those limits are exceeded; while the tree trunk will bend no more than the stone pillar. But when the tracery is assumed to be as yielding as a silken cord; when the whole fragility, elasticity, and weight of the material are to the eye, if not in terms, denied; when all the art of the architect is applied to disprove the first conditions of his working, and the first attributes of his materials; *this* is a deliberate treachery, only redeemed from the charge of direct falsehood by the visibility of the stone surface, and degrading all the traceries it affects exactly in the degree of its presence.

But the declining and morbid taste of the later architects was not satisfied with thus much deception. They were delighted with the subtle charm they had created, and thought only of increasing its power. The next step was to consider and represent the tracery, as not only ductile, but penetrable; and when two mouldings met each other, to manage their intersection, so that one should appear to pass through the other, retaining its independence; or when two ran parallel to each other, to represent the one as partly contained within the other, and partly apparent above it. This form of falsity was that which crushed the art. The flexible traceries were often beautiful, though they were ignoble; but the penetrated traceries, rendered, as they finally were, merely the means of exhibiting the dexterity of the stone-cutter, annihilated both the beauty and dignity of the Gothic types. . . .

It would be too painful a task to follow further the caricatures of form and eccentricities of treatment, which grew out of this single abuse—the flattened arch, the shrunken pillar, the lifeless ornament, the liny moulding, the distorted and extravagant foliation, until the time came when, over these wrecks and remnants, deprived of all unity and principle, rose the foul torrent of the Renaissance, and swept them all away.

So fell the great dynasty of mediæval architecture. It was because it had lost its own strength, and disobeyed its own laws—because its order, and consistency, and organisation, had been broken through—that it could oppose no resistance to the rush of overwhelming innovation. And this, observe, all because it had sacrificed a single truth. From that one surrender of its integrity, from that one endeavour to assume the semblance of what it was not, arose the multitudinous forms of disease and decrepitude, which rotted away the pillars of its supremacy. It was not because its time was come; it was not because it was scorned by the classical Romanist, or dreaded by the faithful Protestant. That scorn and that fear it might have survived, and lived; it would have stood forth in stern comparison with the enervated sensuality of the Renaissance; it would have risen in renewed and purified honour, and with a new soul, from the ashes into which it sank, giving up its glory, as it had received it, for the honour of God—but its own truth was gone, and it sank for ever. There was no wisdom nor strength left in it, to raise it from the dust; and the error of zeal, and the softness of luxury, smote it down and dissolved it away. It is good for us to remember this, as we tread upon the bare ground of its foundations, and stumble over its scattered stones. Those rent skeletons of pierced wall, through which our sea-winds moan and murmur, strewing them joint by joint, and bone by bone, along the bleak promontories on which the Pharos lights came once from houses of prayer —those grey arches and quiet aisles under which the sheep of our valleys feed and rest on the turf that has buried their altars—those shapeless heaps, that are not of the Earth, which lift our fields into strange and sudden banks of flowers, and stay our mountain streams with stones that are not their own, have other thoughts to ask from us than those of mourning for the rage that despoiled, or the fear that forsook them. It was not the robber, not the fanatic, not the blasphemer, who sealed the destruction that they had wrought; the war, the wrath, the terror, might have worked their worst, and the strong walls would have risen, and the slight pillars would have started again, from under the hand of the destroyer. But they could not rise out of the ruins of their own violated truth.

The Lamp of Memory

It is as the centralisation and protectress of this sacred influence [of memory] that Architecture is to be regarded by us
with the most serious thought. We may live without her,
and worship without her, but we cannot remember without
her. How cold is all history, how lifeless all imagery, compared to that which the living nation writes, and the uncor-
rupted marble bears!—how many pages of doubtful record
might we not often spare, for a few stones left one upon another! The ambition of the old Babel builders was well directed for this world: there are but two strong conquerors of
the forgetfulness of men, Poetry and Architecture; and the
latter in some sort includes the former, and is mightier in its
reality: it is well to have, not only what men have thought
and felt, but what their hands have handled, and their
strength wrought, and their eyes beheld, all the days of their
life. The age of Homer is surrounded with darkness, his very
personality with doubt. Not so that of Pericles: and the day
is coming when we shall confess, that we have learned more
of Greece out of the crumbled fragments of her sculpture
than even from her sweet singers or soldier historians. And
if indeed there be any profit in our knowledge of the past,
or any joy in the thought of being remembered hereafter,
which can give strength to present exertion, or patience to
present endurance, there are two duties respecting national
architecture whose importance it is impossible to overrate:
the first, to render the architecture of the day, historical;
and, the second, to preserve, as the most precious of inherit-
ances, that of past ages.

It is in the first of these two directions that Memory may
truly be said to be the Sixth Lamp of Architecture; for it is
in becoming memorial or monumental that a true perfection is attained by civil and domestic buildings; and this
partly as they are, with such a view, built in a more stable
manner, and partly as their decorations are consequently
animated by a metaphorical or historical meaning. . . .

If men lived like men indeed, their houses would be temples—temples which we should hardly dare to injure, and in which it would make us holy to be permitted to live; and there must be a strange dissolution of natural affection, a strange unthankfulness for all that homes have given and parents taught, a strange consciousness that we have been unfaithful to our fathers' honour, or that our own lives are not such as would make our dwellings sacred to our children, when each man would fain build to himself, and build for the little revolution of his own life only. And I look upon those pitiful concretions of lime and clay which spring up, in mildewed forwardness, out of the kneaded fields about our capital—upon those thin, tottering, foundationless shells of splintered wood and imitated stone—upon those gloomy rows of formalised minuteness, alike without difference and without fellowship, as solitary as similar—not merely with the careless disgust of an offended eye, not merely with sorrow for a desecrated landscape, but with a painful foreboding that the roots of our national greatness must be deeply cankered when they are thus loosely struck in their native ground. . . .

Therefore, when we build, let us think that we build for ever. Let it not be for present delight, nor for present use alone; let it be such work as our descendants will thank us for, and let us think, as we lay stone on stone, that a time is to come when those stones will be held sacred because our hands have touched them, and that men will say as they look upon the labour and wrought substance of them, "See! this our fathers did for us." For, indeed, the greatest glory of a building is not in its stones, nor in its gold. Its glory is in its Age, and in that deep sense of voicefulness, of stern watching, of mysterious sympathy, nay, even of approval or condemnation, which we feel in walls that have long been washed by the passing waves of humanity. It is in their lasting witness against men, in their quiet contrast with the transitional character of all things, in the strength which, through the lapse of seasons, and times, and the decline and birth of dynasties, and the changing of the face of the earth, and of the limits of the sea, maintains its sculptured shapeliness for a time insuperable, connects forgotten and following ages with each other, and half constitutes the identity, as it concentrates the sympathy, of nations: it is in that golden stain of time, that we are to look for the real light, and colour, and preciousness of architecture; and it is not until a building has assumed this character, till it has been entrusted with the fame, and hallowed by the deeds of men, till its walls have been witnesses of suffering, and its pillars rise out of the shadows of death, that its existence, more lasting as it is than that of the natural objects of the world around it, can be gifted with even so much as these possess, of language and of life. . . .

In the management of the sculptures of the Parthenon, shadow is frequently employed as a dark field on which the forms are drawn. This is visibly the case in the metopes, and must have been nearly as much so in the pediment. But the use of that shadow is entirely to show the confines of the figures; and it is to *their lines*, and not to the shapes of the shadows behind them, that the art and the eye are addressed. The figures themselves are conceived, as much as possible, in full light, aided by bright reflections; they are drawn exactly as, on vases, white figures on a dark ground; and the sculptors have dispensed with, or even struggled to avoid, all shadows which were not absolutely necessary to the explaining of the form. On the contrary, in Gothic sculpture, the shadow becomes itself a subject of thought. It is considered as a dark colour, to be arranged in certain agreeable masses; the figures are very frequently made even subordinate to the placing of its divisions: and their costume is enriched at the expense of the forms underneath, in order to increase the complexity and variety of the points of shade. There are thus, both in sculpture and painting, two, in some sort, opposite schools, of which the one follows for its subject the essential forms of things, and the other the accidental lights and shades upon them. There are various degrees of their contrariety: middle steps, as in the works of Correggio, and all degrees of nobility and of degradation in the several manners: but the one is always recognised as the pure and the other as the picturesque school. Portions of picturesque treatment will be found in Greek work, and of pure and unpicturesque in Gothic; and in both there are countless instances, as pre-eminently in the works of Michael Angelo, in which shadows become valuable as media of expression, and therefore take rank among essential characteristics. Into these multitudinous distinctions and exceptions I cannot now enter, desiring only to prove the broad applicability of the general definition. . . .

Those styles of architecture which are picturesque in the sense above explained with respect to sculpture, that is to say, whose decoration depends on the arrangement of points of shade rather than on purity of outline, do not suffer, but commonly gain in richness of effect when their details are partly worn away; hence such styles, pre-eminently that of French Gothic, should always be adopted when the materials to be employed are liable to degradation, as brick, sandstone, or soft limestone; and styles in any degree dependent on purity of line, as the Italian Gothic, must be practised altogether in hard and undecomposing materials, granite, serpentine, or crystalline marbles. There can be no doubt that the nature of the accessible materials influenced the formation of both styles; and it should still more authoritatively determine our choice of either.

It does not belong to my present plan to consider at length the second head of duty of which I have above spoken; the preservation of the architecture we possess: but a few words may be forgiven, as especially necessary in modern times. Neither by the public, nor by those who have the care of public monuments, is the true meaning of the word *restoration* understood. It means the most total destruction which a building can suffer: a destruction out of which no remnants can be gathered: a destruction accompanied with false description of the thing destroyed. Do not let us deceive ourselves in this important matter; it is *impossible,* as impossible as to raise the dead, to restore anything that has ever been great or beautiful in architecture. That which I have above insisted upon as the life of the whole, that spirit which is given only by the hand and eye of the workman, can never be recalled.* Another spirit may be given by another time, and it is then a new building; but the spirit of the dead workman cannot be summoned up, and commanded to direct other hands, and other thoughts. And as for direct and simple copying, it is palpably impossible. What copying can there be of surfaces that have been worn half an inch down? The whole finish of the work was in the half inch that is gone; if you attempt to restore that finish, you do it conjecturally; if you copy what is left, granting fidelity to be possible, (and what care, or watchfulness, or cost can secure it,) how is the new work better than the old? There was yet in the old *some* life, some mysterious suggestion of what it had been, and of what it had lost; some sweetness in the gentle lines which rain and sun had wrought. There can be none in the brute hardness of the new carving. . . .

Do not let us talk then of restoration. The thing is a Lie

---

* In Chapter V, "The Lamp of Life," Ruskin had written:

"I believe the right question to ask, respecting all ornament, is simply this: Was it done with enjoyment—was the carver happy while he was about it? It may be the hardest work possible, and the harder because so much pleasure was taken in it; but it must have been happy too, or it will not be living. How much of the stone mason's toil this condition would exclude I hardly venture to consider, but the condition is absolute. There is a Gothic church lately built near Rouen, vile enough, indeed, in its general composition, but excessively rich in detail; many of the details are designed with taste, and all evidently by a man who has studied old work closely. But it is all as dead as leaves in December; there is not one tender touch, not one warm stroke on the whole façade. The men who did it hated it, and were thankful when it was done. And so long as they do so they are merely loading your walls with shapes of clay: the garlands of everlastings in Père la Chaise are more cheerful ornaments. You cannot get the feeling by paying for it—money will not buy life."

from beginning to end. You may make a model of a building as you may of a corpse, and your model may have the
shell of the old walls within it as your cast might have the
skeleton, with what advantage I neither see nor care: but
the old building is destroyed, and that more totally and
mercilessly than if it had sunk into a heap of dust, or melted
into a mass of clay: more has been gleaned out of desolated
Nineveh than ever will be out of re-built Milan. But it is
said, there may come a necessity for restoration! Granted.
Look the necessity full in the face, and understand it on its
own terms. It is a necessity for destruction. Accept it as such,
pull the building down, throw its stones into neglected corners, make ballast of them, or mortar, if you will; but do it
honestly, and do not set up a Lie in their place. And look
that necessity in the face before it comes, and you may prevent it. The principle of modern times, (a principle which,
I believe, at least in France, to be *systematically acted on
by the masons,* in order to find themselves work, as the
abbey of St. Ouen was pulled down by the magistrates of
the town by way of giving work to some vagrants,) is to
neglect buildings first, and restore them afterwards. Take
proper care of your monuments, and you will not need to
restore them. A few sheets of lead put in time upon a roof,
a few dead leaves and sticks swept in time out of a water-
course, will save both roof and walls from ruin. Watch an
old building with an anxious care; guard it as best you may,
and at *any* cost, from every influence of dilapidation. Count
its stones as you would jewels of a crown; set watches about
it as if at the gates of a besieged city; bind it together with
iron where it loosens; stay it with timber where it declines;
do not care about the unsightliness of the aid: better a
crutch than a lost limb; and do this tenderly, and reverently,
and continually, and many a generation will still be born
and pass away beneath its shadow. Its evil day must come at
last; but let it come declaredly and openly, and let no dis-
honouring and false substitute deprive it of the funeral
offices of memory.

Of more wanton or ignorant ravage it is vain to speak; my words will not reach those who commit them, and yet, be it heard or not, I must not leave the truth unstated, that it is again no question of expediency or feeling whether we shall preserve the buildings of past times or not. *We have no right whatever to touch them.* They are not ours. They belong partly to those who built them, and partly to all the generations of mankind who are to follow us. The dead have still their right in them: that which they laboured for, the praise of achievement or the expression of religious feeling, or whatsoever else it might be which in those buildings they intended to be permanent, we have no right to obliterate. What we have ourselves built, we are at liberty to throw down; but what other men gave their strength and wealth and life to accomplish, their right over does not pass away with their death; still less is the right to the use of what they have left vested in us only. It belongs to all their successors. It may hereafter be a subject of sorrow, or a cause of injury, to millions, that we have consulted our present convenience by casting down such buildings as we choose to dispense with. That sorrow, that loss, we have no right to inflict. Did the cathedral of Avranches belong to the mob who destroyed it, any more than it did to us, who walk in sorrow to and fro over its foundation? Neither does any building whatever belong to those mobs who do violence to it. For a mob it is, and must be always; it matters not whether enraged, or in deliberate folly; whether countless, or sitting in committees; the people who destroy anything causelessly are a mob, and Architecture is always destroyed causelessly. A fair building is necessarily worth the ground it stands upon, and will be so until Central Africa and America shall have become as populous as Middlesex: nor is any cause whatever valid as a ground for its destruction. If ever valid, certainly not now, when the place both of the past and future is too much usurped in our minds by the restless and discontented present. The very quietness of nature is gradually withdrawn from us; thousands who once in their necessarily prolonged travel were subjected to an influence, from the silent sky and slumbering fields, more effectual than known or confessed, now bear with them even there the ceaseless fever of their life; and along the iron veins that traverse the frame of our country, beat and flow the fiery pulses of its exertion, hotter and faster every hour. All vitality is concentrated through those throbbing arteries into the central cities; the country is passed over like a green sea by narrow bridges, and we are thrown back in continually closer crowds upon the city gates. The only influence which can in any wise *there* take the place of that of the woods and fields, is the power of ancient Architecture.*

* Ruskin returned to this theme in a remarkable lecture he gave to the Royal Institute of British Architects in 1865. One passage is especially prophetic:

"All lovely architecture was designed for cities in cloudless air; for cities in which piazzas and gardens opened in bright populousness and peace, cities built that men might live happily in them, and take delight daily in each other's presence and powers. But our cities, built in black air which, by its accumulated foulness, first renders all ornament invisible in distance, and then chokes its interstices with soot; cities which are mere crowded masses of store, and warehouse, and counter, and are therefore to the rest of the world what the larder and cellar are to a private house; cities in which the object of men is not life, but labour; and in which all chief magnitude of edifice is to enclose machinery; cities in which the streets are not the avenues for the passing and procession of a happy people, but the drains for the discharge of a tormented mob, in which the only object in reaching any spot is to be transferred to another; in which existence becomes mere transition, and every creature is only one atom in a drift of human dust, and current of interchanging particles, circulating here by tunnels underground, and there by tubes in the air, for a city, or cities, such as this no architecture is possible—nay, no desire of it is possible to their inhabitants." ("The Study of Architecture in Our Schools.")

The Quarry

Since first the dominion of men was asserted over the ocean, three thrones, of mark beyond all others, have been set upon its sands: the thrones of Tyre, Venice, and England. Of the First of these great powers only the memory remains; of the Second, the ruin; the Third, which inherits their greatness, if it forget their example, may be led through prouder eminence to less pitied destruction.

The exaltation, the sin, and the punishment of Tyre have been recorded for us, in perhaps the most touching words ever uttered by the Prophets of Israel against the cities of the stranger. But we read them as a lovely song; and close our ears to the sternness of their warning: for the very depth of the Fall of Tyre has blinded us to its reality, and we forget, as we watch the bleaching of the rocks between the sunshine and the sea, that they were once "as in Eden, the garden of God."

Her successor, like her in perfection of beauty, though less in endurance of dominion, is still left for our beholding in the final period of her decline: a ghost upon the sands of the sea, so weak—so quiet,—so bereft of all but her loveliness, that we might well doubt, as we watched her faint reflection in the mirage of the lagoon, which was the City, and which the Shadow.

I would endeavour to trace the lines of this image before it be for ever lost, and to record, as far as I may, the warning which seems to me to be uttered by every one of the

fast-gaining waves, that beat like passing bells, against the
STONES OF VENICE. . . .

The state of Venice existed Thirteen Hundred and
Seventy-six years, from the first establishment of a consular
government on the island of the Rialto, to the moment
when the General-in-chief of the French army of Italy pronounced the Venetian republic a thing of the past. Of this
period, Two Hundred and Seventy-six years were passed in
a nominal subjection to the cities of old Venetia, especially
to Padua, and in an agitated form of democracy of which
the executive appears to have been entrusted to tribunes,
chosen, one by the inhabitants of each of the principal islands. For six hundred years, during which the power of
Venice was continually on the increase, her government was
an elective monarchy, her King or Doge possessing, in early
times at least, as much independent authority as any other
European sovereign, but an authority gradually subjected
to limitation, and shortened almost daily of its prerogatives,
while it increased in a spectral and incapable magnificence.
The final government of the nobles under the image of a
king, lasted for five hundred years, during which Venice
reaped the fruits of her former energies, consumed them,—
and expired.

Let the reader therefore conceive the existence of the
Venetian states as broadly divided into two periods: the first
of nine hundred, the second of five hundred years, the
separation being marked by what was called the "Serrar del
Consiglio;" that is to say, the final and absolute distinction
of the nobles from the commonalty, and the establishment
of the government in their hands to the exclusion alike of
the influence of the people on the one side, and the authority of the Doge on the other.

Then the first period, of nine hundred years, presents us
with the most interesting spectacle of a people struggling
out of anarchy into order and power; and then governed,
for the most part, by the worthiest and noblest man whom
they could find among them, called their Doge or Leader,

with an aristocracy gradually and resolutely forming itself around him, out of which, and at last by which, he was chosen; an aristocracy owing its origin to the accidental numbers, influence, and wealth of some among the families of the fugitives from the older Venetia, and gradually organising itself, by its unity and heroism, into a separate body.

This first period includes the Rise of Venice, her noblest achievements, and the circumstances which determined her character and position among European powers; and within its range, as might have been anticipated, we find the names of all her hero princes—of Pietro Urseolo, Ordalafo Falier, Domenico Michieli, Sebastiano Ziani, and Enrico Dandolo.

The second period opens with a hundred and twenty years, the most eventful in the career of Venice—the central struggle of her life—stained with her darkest crime, the murder of Carrara—disturbed by her most dangerous internal sedition, the conspiracy of Falier—oppressed by her most fatal war, the war of Chiozza—and distinguished by the glory of her two noblest citizens (for in this period the heroism of her citizens replaces that of her monarchs), Vittor Pisani and Carlo Zeno.

I date the commencement of the Fall of Venice from the death of Carlo Zeno, 8th May 1418; the *visible* commencement from that of another of her noblest and wisest children, the Doge Tomaso Mocenigo, who expired five years later. The reign of Foscari followed, gloomy with pestilence and war; a war in which large acquisitions of territory were made by subtle or fortunate policy in Lombardy, and disgrace, significant as irreparable, sustained in the battles on the Po at Cremona, and in the marshes of Caravaggio. In 1454, Venice, the first of the states of Christendom, humiliated herself to the Turk: in the same year was established the Inquisition of State, and from this period her government takes the perfidious and mysterious form under which it is usually conceived. In 1477, the great Turkish invasion spread terror to the shores of the lagoons; and in 1508 the league of Cambrai marks the period usually assigned as the commencement of the decline of the Venetian power; the commercial prosperity of Venice in the close of the fifteenth century blinding her historians to the previous evidence of the diminution of her internal strength. . . .

The most curious phenomenon in all Venetian history is the vitality of religion in private life, and its deadness in public policy. Amidst the enthusiasm, chivalry, or fanaticism of the other states of Europe, Venice stands, from first to last, like a masked statue; her coldness impenetrable; her exertion only aroused by the touch of a secret spring. That spring was her commercial interest,—this the one motive of all her important political acts, or enduring national animosities. She could forgive insults to her honour, but never rivalship in her commerce; she calculated the glory of her conquests by their value, and estimated their justice by their facility. The fame of success remains, when the motives of attempt are forgotten; and the casual reader of her history may perhaps be surprised to be reminded, that the expedition which was commanded by the noblest of her princes, and whose results added most to her military glory, was one in which, while all Europe around her was wasted by the fire of its devotion, she first calculated the highest price she could exact from its piety for the armament she furnished, and then, for the advancement of her own private interests, at once broke her faith and betrayed her religion.

And yet, in the midst of this national criminality, we shall be struck again and again by the evidences of the most noble individual feeling. . . . We find, on the one hand, a deep and constant tone of individual religion characterising the lives of the citizens of Venice in her greatness; we find this spirit influencing them in all the familiar and immediate concerns of life, giving a peculiar dignity to the conduct even of their commercial transactions. . . . With the fulness of this spirit the prosperity of the state is exactly correspondent, and with its failure her decline, and that with a closeness and precision which it will be one of the collateral objects of the following essay to demonstrate from such accidental evidence as the field of its inquiry presents. . . .

First, receive the witness of Painting.

It will be remembered that I put the commencement of the Fall of Venice as far back as 1418.

Now, John Bellini was born in 1423, and Titian in 1480. John Bellini, and his brother Gentile, two years older than he, close the line of the sacred painters of Venice. But the most solemn spirit of religious faith animates their works to the last. There is no religion in any work of Titian's: there is not even the smallest evidence of religious temper or sympathies either in himself, or in those for whom he painted. His larger sacred subjects are merely themes for the exhibition of pictorial rhetoric,—composition and colour. His minor works are generally made subordinate to purposes of portraiture. The Madonna in the church of the Frari is a mere lay figure, introduced to form a link of connection between the portraits of various members of the Pesaro family who surround her.

Now this is not merely because John Bellini was a religious man and Titian was not. Titian and Bellini are each true representatives of the school of painters contemporary with them; and the difference in their artistic feeling is a consequence not so much of difference in their own natural characters as in their early education: Bellini was brought up in faith; Titian in formalism. Between the years of their births the vital religion of Venice had expired.

The *vital* religion, observe, not the formal. Outward observance was as strict as ever; and Doge and senator still were painted, in almost every important instance, kneeling before the Madonna or St. Mark; a confession of faith made universal by the pure gold of the Venetian sequin. But observe the great picture of Titian's, in the ducal palace, of the Doge Antonio Grimani kneeling before Faith: there is a curious lesson in it. The figure of faith is a coarse portrait of one of Titian's least graceful female models: Faith had become carnal. The eye is first caught by the flash of the Doge's armour: the heart of Venice was in her wars, not in her worship.

The mind of Tintoret, incomparably more deep and serious than that of Titian, casts the solemnity of its own tone over the sacred subjects which it approaches, and sometimes forgets itself into devotion; but the principle of treatment is altogether the same as Titian's: absolute subordination of the religious subject to purposes of decoration or portraiture.

The evidence might be accumulated a thousandfold from the works of Veronese, and of every succeeding painter,— that the fifteenth century had taken away the religious heart of Venice.

Such is the evidence of Painting. To collect that of Architecture will be our task through many a page to come; but I must here give a general idea of its heads. . . .

All European architecture, bad and good, old and new, is derived from Greece through Rome, and coloured and perfected from the East. The history of architecture is nothing but the tracing of the various modes and directions of this derivation. Understand this, once for all: if you hold fast this great connecting clue, you may string all the types of successive architectural invention upon it like so many beads. The Doric and the Corinthian orders are the roots, the one of all Romanesque, massy-capitalled buildings— Norman, Lombard, Byzantine, and what else you can name of the kind; and the Corinthian of all Gothic, Early English, French, German, and Tuscan. Now observe: those old Greeks gave the shaft; Rome gave the arch; the Arabs pointed and foliated the arch. The shaft and arch, the framework and strength of architecture, are from the race of Japheth: the spirituality and sanctity of it from Ismael, Abraham, and Shem. . . .

I have said that the two orders, Doric and Corinthian, are the roots of all European architecture. You have, perhaps, heard of five orders: but there are only two real orders: and there never can be any more until doomsday. On one of these orders the ornament is convex: those are Doric, Norman, and what else you recollect of the kind. On the other the ornament is concave: those are Corinthian, Early English, Decorated, and what else you recollect of that kind. The transitional form, in which the ornamental line is straight, is the centre or root of both. All other orders are varieties of these, or phantasms and grotesques, altogether indefinite in number and species.

This Greek architecture, then, with its two orders, was clumsily copied and varied by the Romans with no particular result, until they began to bring the arch into extensive practical service; except only that the Doric capital was spoiled in endeavours to mend it, and the Corinthian much varied and enriched with fanciful and often very beautiful imagery. And in this state of things came Christianity: seized upon the arch as her own: decorated it, and delighted in it: invented a new Doric capital to replace the spoiled Roman one: and all over the Roman empire set to work, with such materials as were nearest at hand, to express and adorn herself as best she could. This Roman Christian architecture is the exact expression of the Christianity of the time, very fervid and beautiful—but very imperfect; in many respects ignorant, and yet radiant with a strong, childish light of imagination, which flames up under Constantine, illumines all the shores of the Bosphorus and the Ægean and the Adriatic Sea, and then gradually, as the people give themselves up to idolatry, becomes corpse-light. The architecture, like the religion it expressed, sinks into a settled form—a strange, gilded, and embalmed repose; and so would have remained for ever,—so *does* remain, where its languor has been undisturbed. But rough wakening was ordained for it.

This Christian art of the declining empire is divided into two great branches, western and eastern; one centred at Rome, the other at Byzantium, of which the one is the early Christian Romanesque, properly so called, and the other, carried to higher imaginative perfection by Greek workmen, is distinguished from it as Byzantine. . . . Some of the barbaric nations were, of course, not susceptible of this influence; and, when they burst over the Alps, appear like the Huns, as scourges only, or mix, as the Ostrogoths, with the enervated Italians, and give physical strength to the mass with which they mingle, without materially affecting its intellectual character. But others, both south and north of the Empire, had felt its influence, back to the beach of the Indian ocean on the one hand, and to the ice creeks of the North Sea on the other. On the north and west the influence was of the Latins; on the south and east, of the Greeks. Two nations, pre-eminent above all the rest, represent to us the force of derived mind on either side. As the central power is eclipsed, the orbs of reflected light gather into their fulness; and when sensuality and idolatry had done their work, and the religion of the Empire was laid asleep in a glittering sepulchre, the living light rose upon both horizons, and the fierce swords of the Lombard and Arab were shaken over its golden paralysis.

The work of the Lombard was to give hardihood and system to the enervated body and enfeebled mind of Christendom; that of the Arab was to punish idolatry, and to proclaim the spirituality of worship. The Lombard covered every church which he built with the sculptured representations of bodily exercises—hunting and war. The Arab banished all imagination of creature form from his temples, and proclaimed from their minarets, "There is no god but God." Opposite in their character and mission, alike in their magnificence of energy, they came from the North and from the South, the glacier torrent and the lava stream: they met and contended over the wreck of the Roman empire; and the very centre of the struggle, the point of pause of both, the dead water of the opposite eddies, charged with embayed fragments of the Roman wreck, is VENICE.

The Ducal palace of Venice contains the three elements in exactly equal proportions—the Roman, Lombard, and Arab. It is the central building of the world.

The reader will now begin to understand something of the importance of the study of the edifices of a city which concludes, within the circuit of some seven or eight miles, the field of contest between the three pre-eminent architectures of the world:—each architecture expressing a condition of religion; each an erroneous condition, yet necessary to the correction of the others, and corrected by them. . . .

Now observe. The transitional (or especially Arabic) style of the Venetian work is centralised by the date 1180, and is transformed gradually into the Gothic, which extends in its purity from the middle of the thirteenth to the beginning of the fifteenth century; that is to say, over the precise period which I have described as the central epoch of the life of Venice. I dated her decline from the year 1418; Foscari became doge five years later, and in his reign the first marked signs appear in architecture of that mighty change . . . to which London owes St. Paul's, Rome St. Peter's, Venice and Vicenza the edifices commonly supposed to be their noblest, and Europe in general the degradation of every art she has since practised.

This change appears first in a loss of truth and vitality in existing architecture all over the world. (Compare *Seven Lamps,* chap. ii. ["The Lamp of Truth," above].) All the Gothics in existence, southern or northern, were corrupted at once: the German and French lost themselves in every species of extravagance; the English Gothic was confined, in its insanity, by a strait-waistcoat of perpendicular lines; the Italian effloresced on the mainland into the meaningless ornamentation of Certosa of Pavia and the Cathedral of Como (a style sometimes ignorantly called Italian Gothic), and at Venice into the insipid confusion of the Porta della Carta and wild crockets of St. Mark's. This corruption of all architecture, especially ecclesiastical, corresponded with, and marked the state of religion over all Europe,—the peculiar degradation of the Romanist superstition, and of public morality in consequence, which brought about the Reformation.

Against the corrupted papacy arose two great divisions

of adversaries, Protestants in Germany and England; Rationalists in France and Italy; the one requiring the purification of religion, the other its destruction. The Protestant kept the religion, but cast aside the heresies of Rome, and with them her arts, by which last rejection he injured his own character, cramped his intellect in refusing to it one of its noblest exercises, and materially diminished his influence. It may be a serious question how far the Pausing of the Reformation has been a consequence of this error.

The Rationalist kept the arts and cast aside the religion. This rationalistic art is the art commonly called Renaissance, marked by a return to pagan systems, not to adopt them and hallow them for Christianity, but to rank itself under them as an imitator and pupil. In Painting it is headed by Giulio Romano and Nicolo Poussin; in Architecture, by Sansovino and Palladio.

Instant degradation followed in every direction,—a flood of folly and hypocrisy. Mythologies ill understood at first, then perverted into feeble sensualities, take the place of the representations of Christian subjects, which had become blasphemous under the treatment of men like the Caracci. Gods without power, satyrs without rusticity, nymphs without innocence, men without humanity, gather into idiot groups upon the polluted canvas, and scenic affectations encumber the streets with preposterous marble. Lower and lower declines the level of abused intellect; the base school of landscape gradually usurps the place of the historical painting, which had sunk into prurient pedantry,—the Alsatian sublimities of Salvator, the confectionery idealities of Claude, the dull manufacture of Gaspar and Canaletto, south of the Alps, and on the north the patient devotion of besotted lives to delineation of bricks and fogs, fat cattle and ditchwater. And thus, Christianity and morality, courage, and intellect, and art all crumbling together in one wreck, we are hurried on to the fall of Italy, the revolution in France, and the condition of art in England (saved by her Protestantism from severer penalty) in the time of George II.

I have not written in vain if I have heretofore done anything towards diminishing the reputation of the Renaissance landscape painting. But the harm which has been
done by Claude and the Poussins is as nothing when compared to the mischief effected by Palladio, Scamozzi, and
Sansovino. Claude and the Poussins were weak men, and
have had no serious influence on the general mind. There is
little harm in their works being purchased at high prices:
their real influence is very slight, and they may be left without grave indignation to their poor mission of furnishing
drawing-rooms and assisting stranded conversation. Not so
the Renaissance architecture. Raised at once into all the
magnificence of which it was capable by Michael Angelo,
then taken up by men of real intellect and imagination,
such as Scamozzi, Sansovino, Inigo Jones, and Wren, it is
impossible to estimate the extent of its influence on the
European mind; and that the more, because few persons
are concerned with painting, and of those few the larger
number regard it with slight attention; but all men are
concerned with architecture, and have at some time of their
lives serious business with it. It does not much matter that
an individual loses two or three hundred pounds in buying
a bad picture, but it is to be regretted that a nation should
lose two or three hundred thousand in raising a ridiculous
building. Nor is it merely wasted wealth or distempered
conception which we have to regret in this Renaissance
architecture: but we shall find in it partly the root, partly
the expression, of certain dominant evils of modern times—
over-sophistication and ignorant classicalism; the one destroying the healthfulness of general society, the other
rendering our schools and universities useless to a large
number of the men who pass through them.

Now Venice, as she was once the most religious, was in
her fall the most corrupt, of European states; and as she was
in her strength the centre of the pure currents of Christian
architecture, so she is in her decline the source of the Renaissance. It was the originality and splendour of the palaces of

Vicenza and Venice which gave this school its eminence in
the eyes of Europe; and the dying city, magnificent in her
dissipation, and graceful in her follies, obtained wider worship in her decrepitude than in her youth, and sank from
the midst of her admirers into the grave.

It is in Venice, therefore, and in Venice only, that effectual blows can be struck at this pestilent art of the Renaissance. Destroy its claims to admiration there, and it can
assert them nowhere else. This, therefore, will be the final
purpose of the following essay.   [Vol. I, Chap. 1]

The Throne

In the olden days of travelling, now to return no more, in
which distance could not be vanquished without toil, but
in which that toil was rewarded . . . when there was something more to be anticipated and remembered in the first
aspect of each successive halting-place, than a new arrangement of glass roofing and iron girder, there were few moments of which the recollection was more fondly cherished by
the traveller, than that which . . . brought him within sight
of Venice, as his gondola shot into the open lagoon from the
canal of Mestre. Not but that the aspect of the city itself was
generally the source of some slight disappointment, for, seen
in this direction, its buildings are far less characteristic than
those of the other great towns of Italy; but this inferiority
was partly disguised by distance, and more than atoned for
by the strange rising of its walls and towers out of the midst,
as it seemed, of the deep sea, for it was impossible that the
mind or the eye could at once comprehend the shallowness
of the vast sheet of water which stretched away in leagues of
rippling lustre to the north and south, or trace the narrow
line of islets bounding it to the east. The salt breeze, the
white moaning seabirds, the masses of black weed separating
and disappearing gradually, in knots of heaving shoal, under the advance of the steady tide, all proclaimed it to be

indeed the ocean on whose bosom the great city rested so
calmly; not such blue, soft, lake-like ocean as bathes the
Neapolitan promontories, or sleeps beneath the marble
rocks of Genoa, but a sea with the bleak power of our own
northern waves, yet subdued into a strange spacious rest,
and changed from its angry pallor into a field of burnished
gold, as the sun declined behind the belfry tower of the
lonely island church, fitly named "St. George of the Sea-
weed." As the boat drew nearer to the city, the coast which
the traveller had just left sank behind him into one long,
low, sad-coloured line, tufted irregularly with brushwood
and willows: but, at what seemed its northern extremity, the
hills of Arqua rose in a dark cluster of purple pyramids,
balanced on the bright mirage of the lagoon; two or three
smooth surges of inferior hill extended themselves about
their roots, and beyond these, beginning with the craggy
peaks above Vicenza, the chain of the Alps girded the whole
horizon to the north—a wall of jagged blue, here and there
showing through its clefts a wilderness of misty precipices,
fading far back into the recesses of Cadore, and itself rising
and breaking away eastward, where the sun struck opposite
upon its snow, into mighty fragments of peaked light, standing up behind the barred clouds of evening, one after another, countless, the crown of the Adrian Sea, until the eye
turned back from pursuing them, to rest upon the nearer
burning of the campaniles of Murano, and on the great city,
where it magnified itself along the waves, as the quick silent
pacing of the gondola drew nearer and nearer. And at last,
when its walls were reached, and the outmost of its untrod-
den streets was entered, not through towered gate or
guarded rampart, but as a deep inlet between two rocks of
coral in the Indian Sea; when first upon the traveller's sight
opened the long ranges of columned palaces,—each with its
black boat moored at the portal,—each with its image cast
down, beneath its feet, upon that green pavement which
every breeze broke into new fantasies of rich tessellation;
when first, at the extremity of the bright vista, the shadowy

Rialto threw its colossal curve slowly forth from behind the palace of the Camerlenghi; that strange curve, so delicate, so adamantine, strong as a mountain cavern, graceful as a bow just bent; when first, before its moonlike circumference was all risen, the gondolier's cry, "Ah! Stali," struck sharp upon the ear, and the prow turned aside under the mighty cornices that half met over the narrow canal, where the plash of the water followed close and loud, ringing along the marble by the boat's side; and when at last that boat darted forth upon the breadth of silver sea, across which the front of the Ducal Palace, flushed with its sanguine veins, looks to the snowy dome of Our Lady of Salvation, it was no marvel that the mind should be so deeply entranced by the visionary charm of a scene so beautiful and so strange, as to forget the darker truths of its history and its being. Well might it seem that such a city had owed her existence rather to the rod of the enchanter, than the fear of the fugitive; that the waters which encircled her had been chosen for the mirror of her state, rather than the shelter of her nakedness; and that all which in nature was wild or merciless,—Time and Decay, as well as the waves and tempests,—had been won to adorn her instead of to destroy, and might still spare, for ages to come, that beauty which seemed to have fixed for its throne the sands of the hourglass as well as of the sea. . . .

The impotent feelings of romance, so singularly characteristic of this century, may indeed gild, but never save, the remains of those mightier ages to which they are attached like climbing flowers; and they must be torn away from the magnificent fragments, if we would see them as they stood in their own strength. Those feelings, always as fruitless as they are fond, are in Venice not only incapable of protecting, but even of discerning, the objects to which they ought to have been attached. The Venice of modern fiction and drama is a thing of yesterday, a mere efflorescence of decay, a stage dream which the first ray of daylight must dissipate into dust. No prisoner, whose name is worth remembering, or whose sorrow deserved sympathy, ever crossed that "Bridge of Sighs," which is the centre of the Byronic ideal of Venice; no great merchant of Venice ever saw that Rialto under which the traveller now passes with breathless interest: the statue which Byron makes Faliero address as of one of his great ancestors was erected to a soldier of fortune a hundred and fifty years after Faliero's death; and the most conspicuous parts of the city have been so entirely altered in the course of the last three centuries, that if Henry Dandolo or Francis Foscari could be summoned from their tombs, and stood each on the deck of his galley at the entrance of the Grand Canal, that renowned entrance, the painter's favourite subject, the novelist's favourite scene, where the water first narrows by the steps of the Church of La Salute,—the mighty Doges would not know in what part of the world they stood, would literally not recognize one stone of the great city, for whose sake, and by whose ingratitude, their grey hairs had been brought down with bitterness to the grave. The remains of *their* Venice lie hidden behind the cumbrous masses which were the delight of the nation in its dotage; hidden in many a grass-grown court, and silent pathway, and lightless canal, where the slow waves have sapped their foundations for five hundred years, and must soon prevail over them for ever. It must be our task to glean and gather them forth, and restore out of them some faint image of the lost city; more gorgeous a thousandfold than that which now exists, yet not created in the day-dream of the prince, nor by the ostentation of the noble, but built by iron hands and patient hearts, contending against the adversity of nature and the fury of man, so that its wonderfulness cannot be grasped by the indolence of imagination, but only after frank inquiry into the true nature of that wild and solitary scene, whose restless tides and trembling sands did indeed shelter the birth of the city, but long denied her dominion. . . .

In order to know what it was once, let the traveller follow in his boat at evening the windings of some unfrequented channel far into the midst of the melancholy plain; let him remove, in his imagination, the brightness of the great city that still extends itself in the distance, and the walls and towers from the islands that are near; and so wait, until the bright investiture and sweet warmth of the sunset are withdrawn from the waters, and the black desert of their shore lies in its nakedness beneath the night, pathless, comfortless, infirm, lost in dark languor and fearful silence, except where the salt runlets plash into the tireless pools, or the sea-birds flit from their margins with a questioning cry; and he will be enabled to enter in some sort into the horror of heart with which this solitude was anciently chosen by man for his habitation. They little thought, who first drove the stakes into the sand, and strewed the ocean reeds for their rest, that their children were to be the princes of that ocean, and their palaces its pride; and yet, in the great natural laws that rule that sorrowful wilderness, let it be remembered what strange preparation had been made for the things which no human imagination could have foretold, and how the whole existence and fortune of the Venetian nation were anticipated or compelled, by the setting of those bars and doors to the rivers and the sea. Had deeper currents divided their islands, hostile navies would again and again have reduced the rising city into servitude; had stronger surges beaten their shores, all the richness and refinement of the Venetian architecture must have been exchanged for the walls and bulwarks of an ordinary seaport. Had there been no tide, as in other parts of the Mediterranean, the narrow canals of the city would have become noisome, and the marsh in which it was built pestiferous. Had the tide been only a foot or eighteen inches higher in its rise, the water-access to the doors of the palaces would have been impossible: even as it is, there is sometimes a little difficulty, at the ebb, in landing without setting foot upon the lower and slippery steps; and the highest tides sometimes enter the courtyards, and overflow the entrance halls. Eighteen inches more of difference between the level of the flood and ebb would have rendered the doorsteps of every palace, at low water, a treacherous mass of weed and limpets, and the entire system of watercarriage for the higher classes, in their easy and daily intercourse, must have been done away with. The streets of the city would have been widened, its network of canals filled up, and all the peculiar character of the place and the people destroyed.

The reader may perhaps have felt some pain in the contrast between this faithful view of the site of the Venetian Throne, and the romantic conception of it which we ordinarily form: but this pain, if he have felt it, ought to be more than counterbalanced by the value of the instance thus afforded to us at once of the inscrutableness and the wisdom of the ways of God. . . . In the laws which were stretching forth the gloomy margins of those fruitless banks, and feeding the bitter grass among their shallows, there was indeed a preparation, and *the only preparation possible,* for the founding of a city which was to be set like a golden clasp on the girdle of the earth, to write her history on the white scrolls of the sea-surges, and to word it in their thunder, and to gather and give forth, in world-wide pulsation, the glory of the West and of the East, from the burning heart of her Fortitude and Splendour!   [Vol. II, Chap. 1]

Torcello

Seven miles to the north of Venice, the banks of sand, which near the city rise little above low-water mark, attain by degrees a higher level, and knit themselves at last into fields of salt morass, raised here and there into shapeless mounds, and intercepted by narrow creeks of sea. One of the feeblest of these inlets, after winding for some time among buried fragments of masonry, and knots of sunburnt weeds whitened with webs of fucus, stays itself in an utterly stagnant pool beside a plot of greener grass covered with ground ivy and violets. On this mound is built a rude brick campanile, of the commonest Lombardic type, which if we ascend towards evening (and there are none to hinder us, the door of its ruinous staircase swinging idly on its hinges), we may command from it one of the most notable scenes in this wide world of ours. Far as the eye can reach, a waste of wild sea moor, of a lurid ashen grey; not like our northern moors with their jet-black pools and purple heath, but lifeless, the colour of sackcloth, with the corrupted sea-water soaking through the roots of its acrid weeds, and gleaming hither and thither through its snaky channels. No gathering of fantastic mists, nor coursing of clouds across it; but melancholy clearness of space in the warm sunset, oppressive, reaching to the horizon of its level gloom. To the very horizon, on the north-east; but, to the north and west, there is a blue line of higher land along the border of it, and above this, but farther back, a misty band of mountains, touched with snow. To the east, the paleness and roar of the Adriatic, louder at momentary intervals as the surf breaks on the bars of sand; to the south, the widening branches of the calm lagoon, alternately purple and pale green, as they reflect the evening clouds or twilight sky; and almost beneath our feet, on the same field which sustains the tower we gaze from, a group of four buildings, two of them little larger than cottages (though built of stone, and one adorned by a quaint belfry), the third an octagonal chapel, of which we can see but little more than the flat red roof with its rayed tiling, the fourth, a considerable church with nave and aisles, but of which, in like manner, we can see little but the long central ridge and lateral slopes of roof, which the sunlight separates in one glowing mass from the green field beneath and grey moor beyond. There are no living creatures near the buildings, nor any vestige of village or city round about them. They lie like a little company of ships becalmed on a far-away sea.

Then look farther to the south. Beyond the widening branches of the lagoon, and rising out of the bright lake into which they gather, there are a multitude of towers, dark, and scattered among square-set shapes of clustered palaces, a long and irregular line fretting the southern sky.

Mother and daughter, you behold them both in their widowhood,—TORCELLO, AND VENICE.

Thirteen hundred years ago, the grey moorland looked as it does this day, and the purple mountains stood as radiantly in the deep distances of evening; but on the line of the horizon, there were strange fires mixed with the light of sunset, and the lament of many human voices mixed with the fretting of the waves on their ridges of sand. The flames rose from the ruins of Altinum; the lament from the multitude of its people, seeking, like Israel of old, a refuge from the sword in the paths of the sea.

The cattle are feeding and resting upon the site of the city that they left; the mower's scythe swept this day at dawn over the chief street of the city that they built, and the swathes of soft grass are now sending up their scent into the night air, the only incense that fills the temple of their ancient worship. Let us go down into that little space of meadow land.

The inlet which runs nearest to the base of the campanile is not that by which Torcello is commonly approached. Another, somewhat broader, and overhung by alder copse, winds out of the main channel of the lagoon up to the very edge of the little meadow which was once the Piazza of the city, and there, stayed by a few grey stones which present some semblance of a quay, forms its boundary at one extremity. Hardly larger than an ordinary English farmyard, and roughly enclosed on each side by broken palings and hedges of honeysuckle and briar, the narrow field retires from the water's edge, traversed by a scarcely traceable footpath, for some forty or fifty paces, and then expanding into the form of a small square, with buildings on three sides of it, the fourth being that which opens to the water. . . . The first strong impression which the spectator receives from the whole scene is, that whatever sin it may have been which has on this spot been visited with so utter a desolation, it could not at least have been ambition. Nor will this impression be diminished as we approach, or enter, the larger church, to which the whole group of building is subordinate. It has evidently been built by men in flight and distress, who sought in the hurried erection of their island church such a shelter for their earnest and sorrowful worship as, on the one hand, could not attract the eyes of their enemies by its splendour, and yet, on the other, might not awaken too bitter feelings by its contrast with the churches which they had seen destroyed. There is visible everywhere a simple and tender effort to recover some of the form of the temples which they had loved, and to do honour to God by that which they were erecting, while distress and humiliation prevented the desire, and prudence precluded the admission, either of luxury or ornament or magnificence of plan. The exterior is absolutely devoid of decoration, with the exception only of the western entrance and the lateral door, of which the former has carved sideposts and architrave, and the latter, crosses of rich sculpture; while the massy stone shutters of the windows, turning on huge rings of stone, which answer the double purpose of stanchions and brackets, cause the whole building rather to resemble a refuge from Alpine storm than the cathedral of a populous city; and, internally, the two solemn mosaics of the eastern and western extremities,—one representing the Last Judgment, the other the Madonna, her tears falling as her hands are raised to bless,—and the noble range of pillars which enclose the space between, terminated by the high throne for the pastor and the semicircular raised seats for the superior clergy, are expressive at once of the deep sorrow and the sacred courage of men who had no home left them upon earth, but who looked for one to come, of men "persecuted but not forsaken, cast down but not destroyed." . . .

Let us consider a little . . . what is very peculiar to this church, its luminousness. This perhaps strikes the traveller more from its contrast with the excessive gloom of the Church of St. Mark's; but it is remarkable when we compare the Cathedral of Torcello with any of the contemporary basilicas in South Italy or Lombardic churches in the North. St. Ambrogio at Milan, St. Michele at Pavia, St. Zeno at Verona, St. Frediano at Lucca, St. Miniato at Florence, are all like sepulchral caverns compared with Torcello, where the slightest details of the sculptures and mosaics are visible, even when twilight is deepening. And there is something especially touching in our finding the sunshine thus freely admitted into a church built by men in sorrow. They did not need the darkness; they could not perhaps bear it. There was fear and depression upon them enough, without a material gloom. They sought for comfort in their religion, for tangible hopes and promises, not for threatenings or mysteries; and though the subjects chosen for the mosaics on the walls are of the most solemn character, there are no artificial shadows cast upon them, nor dark colours used in them: all is fair and bright, and intended evidently to be regarded in hopefulness and not with terror. . . .

The severity which is so marked in the pulpit at Torcello is still more striking in the raised seats and episcopal throne which occupy the curve of the apse. The arrangement at first somewhat recalls to the mind that of the Roman amphitheatres; the flight of steps which lead up to the central throne divides the curve of the continuous steps or seats (it appears in the first three ranges questionable which were intended, for they seem too high for the one, and too low and close for the other), exactly as in an amphitheatre the stairs for access intersect the sweeping ranges of seats. But in the very rudeness of this arrangement, and especially in the want of all appliances of comfort (for the whole is of marble, and the arms of the central throne are not for convenience, but for distinction, and to separate it more conspicuously from the undivided seats), there is a dignity which no furniture of stalls nor carving of canopies ever could attain, and well worth the contemplation of the Protestant, both as sternly significative of an episcopal authority which in the early days of the Church was never disputed, and as dependent for all its impressiveness on the utter absence of any expression either of pride or self-indulgence.

But there is one more circumstance which we ought to remember as giving peculiar significance to the position which the episcopal throne occupies in this island church, namely, that in the minds of all early Christians the Church itself was most frequently symbolised under the image of a ship, of which the bishop was the pilot. Consider the force which this symbol would assume in the imaginations of men to whom the spiritual Church had become an ark of refuge in the midst of a destruction hardly less terrible than that from which the eight souls were saved of old, I Peter iii. 20, a destruction in which the wrath of man had become as broad as the earth and as merciless as the sea, and who saw the actual and literal edifice of the Church raised up, itself like an ark in the midst of the waters. No marvel if with the surf of the Adriatic rolling between them and the shores of their birth, from which they were separated for ever, they should have looked upon each other as the disciples did when the storm came down on the Tiberias Lake, and have yielded ready and loving obedience to those who ruled them in His name, who had there rebuked the winds and commanded stillness to the sea. And if the stranger would yet learn in what spirit it was that the dominion of Venice was begun, and in what strength she went forth conquering and to conquer, let him not seek to estimate the wealth of her arsenals or number of her armies, nor look upon the pageantry of her palaces, nor enter into the secrets of her councils; but let him ascend the highest tier of the stern ledges that sweep round the altar of Torcello, and then, looking as the pilot did of old along the marble ribs of the goodly temple-ship, let him re-people its veined deck with the shadows of its dead mariners, and strive to feel in himself the strength of heart that was kindled within them, when first, after the pillars of it had settled in the sand, and the roof of it had been closed against the angry sky that was still

reddened by the fires of their homesteads,—first, within the
shelter of its knitted walls, amidst the murmur of the waste
of waves and the beating of the wings of the sea-birds round
the rock that was strange to them,—rose that ancient hymn,
in the power of their gathered voices:

> THE SEA IS HIS, AND HE MADE IT;
> AND HIS HANDS PREPARED THE DRY LAND.

[Vol. II, Chap. 2]

St. Mark's

"And so Barnabas took Mark, and sailed unto Cyprus." If
as the shores of Asia lessened upon his sight, the spirit of
prophecy had entered into the heart of the weak disciple
who had turned back when his hand was on the plough,
and who had been judged, by the chiefest of Christ's captains, unworthy thenceforward to go forth with him to the
work, how wonderful would he have thought it, that by the
lion symbol in future ages he was to be represented among
men! how woful, that the war-cry of his name should so
often reanimate the rage of the soldier, on those very plains
where he himself had failed in the courage of the Christian,
and so often dye with fruitless blood that very Cypriot Sea,
over whose waves, in repentance and shame, he was following the Son of Consolation!

That the Venetians possessed themselves of his body in
the ninth century, there appears no sufficient reason to
doubt, nor that it was principally in consequence of their
having done so, that they chose him for their patron saint.
There exists, however, a tradition that before he went into
Egypt he had founded the church at Aquileia, and was thus
in some sort the first bishop of the Venetian isles and people. . . . But whether St. Mark was first bishop of Aquileia
or not, St. Theodore was the first patron of the city; nor can
he yet be considered as having entirely abdicated his early

right, as his statue, standing on a crocodile, still companions the winged lion on the opposing pillar of the piazzetta. A church erected to this Saint is said to have occupied, before the ninth century, the site of St. Mark's; and the traveller, dazzled by the brilliancy of the great square, ought not to leave it without endeavouring to imagine its aspect in that early time, when it was a green field, cloister-like and quiet, divided by a small canal, with a line of trees on each side; and extending between the two churches of St. Theodore and St. Geminian, as the little piazza of Torcello lies between its "palazzo" and cathedral.

But in the year 813, when the seat of government was finally removed to Rialto, a Ducal Palace, built on the spot where the present one stands, with a Ducal Chapel beside it, gave a very different character to the Square of St. Mark; and fifteen years later, the acquisition of the body of the Saint, and its deposition in the Ducal Chapel, perhaps not yet completed, occasioned the investiture of that Chapel with all possible splendour. St. Theodore was deposed from his patronship, and his church destroyed, to make room for the aggrandizement of the one attached to the Ducal Palace, and thenceforward known as "St. Mark's."

This first church was however destroyed by fire, when the Ducal Palace was burned in the revolt against Candiano, in 976. It was partly rebuilt by his successor, Pietro Orseolo, on a larger scale; and, with the assistance of Byzantine architects, the fabric was carried on under successive Doges for nearly a hundred years; the main building being completed in 1071, but its incrustation with marble not till considerably later. It was consecrated on the 8th of October, 1085, according to Sansovino and the author of the "Chiesa Ducale di S. Marco," in 1094 according to Lazari, but certainly between 1084 and 1096, those years being the limits of the reign of Vital Falier; I incline to the supposition that it was soon after his accession to the throne in 1085, though Sansovino writes, by mistake, Ordelafo instead of Vital Falier. But, at all events, before the close of the eleventh century the great consecration of the church took place. It was again injured by fire in 1106, but repaired; and from that time to the fall of Venice there was probably no Doge who did not in some slight degree embellish or alter the fabric, so that few parts of it can be pronounced boldly to be of any given date. Two periods of interference are, however, notable above the rest: the first, that in which the Gothic school had superseded the Byzantine towards the close of the fourteenth century, when the pinnacles, upper archivolts, and window traceries were added to the exterior, and the great screen, with various chapels and tabernacle-work, to the interior; the second, when the Renaissance school superseded the Gothic, and the pupils of Titian and Tintoret substituted, over one half of the church, their own compositions for the Greek mosaics with which it was originally decorated; happily, though with no good-will, having left enough to enable us to imagine and lament what they destroyed. . . .

And now I wish that the reader, before I bring him into St. Mark's Place, would imagine himself for a little time in a quiet English cathedral town, and walk with me to the west front of its cathedral. Let us go together up the more retired street, at the end of which we can see the pinnacles of one of the towers, and then through the low grey gateway, with its battlemented top and small latticed window in the centre, into the inner private-looking road or close, where nothing goes in but the carts of the tradesmen who supply the bishop and the chapter, and where there are little shaven grass-plots, fenced in by neat rails, before old-fashioned groups of somewhat diminutive and excessively trim houses, with little oriel and bay windows jutting out here and there, and deep wooden cornices and eaves painted cream colour and white, and small porches to their doors in the shape of cockleshells, or little, crooked, thick, indescribable wooden gables warped a little on one side; and so forward till we come to larger houses, also old-fashioned, but of red brick, and with garden behind them, and fruit walls, which show here and there, among the nectarines, the vestiges of an old cloister arch or shaft, and looking in front on the cathedral square itself, laid out in rigid divisions of smooth grass and gravel walk, yet not uncheerful, especially on the sunny side, where the canon's children are walking with their nurserymaids. And so, taking care not to tread on the grass, we will go along the straight walk to the west front, and there stand for a time, looking up at its deep-pointed porches and the dark places between their pillars where there were statues once, and where the fragments, here and there, of a stately figure are still left, which has in it the likeness of a king, perhaps indeed a king on earth, perhaps a saintly king long ago in heaven; and so higher and higher up to the great mouldering wall of rugged sculpture and confused arcades, shattered, and grey, and grisly with heads of dragons and mocking fiends, worn by the rain and swirling winds into yet unseemlier shape, and coloured on their stony scales by the deep russet-orange lichen, melancholy gold; and so, higher still, to the bleak towers, so far above that the eye loses itself among the bosses of their traceries, though they are rude and strong, and only sees like a drift of eddying black points, now closing, now scattering, and now settling suddenly into visible places among the bosses and flowers, the crowd of restless birds that fill the whole square with that strange clangour of theirs, so harsh and yet so soothing, like the cries of birds on a solitary coast between the cliffs and sea.

Think for a little while of that scene, and the meaning of all its small formalisms, mixed with its serene sublimity. Estimate its secluded, continuous, drowsy felicities, and its evidence of the sense and steady performance of such kind of duties as can be regulated by the cathedral clock; and weigh the influence of those dark towers on all who have passed through the lonely square at their feet for centuries, and on all who have seen them rising far away over the wooded plain, or catching on their square masses the last rays of the sunset, when the city at their feet was indicated only by the mist at the bend of the river. And then let us quickly recollect that we are in Venice, and land at the extremity of the Calle Lunga San Moisè, which may be considered as there answering to the secluded street that led us to our English cathedral gateway.

We find ourselves in a paved alley, some seven feet wide where it is widest, full of people, and resonant with cries of itinerant salesmen,—a shriek in their beginning, and dying away into a kind of brazen ringing, all the worse for its confinement between the high houses of the passage along which we have to make our way. Overhead, an inextricable confusion of rugged shutters, and iron balconies and chimney flues, pushed out on brackets to save room, and arched windows with projecting sills of Istrian stone, and gleams of green leaves here and there where a fig-tree branch escapes over a lower wall from some inner cortile, leading the eye up to the narrow stream of blue sky high over all. On each side, a row of shops, as densely set as may be, occupying, in fact, intervals between the square stone shafts, about eight feet high, which carry the first floors: intervals of which one is narrow and serves as a door; the other is, in the more respectable shops, wainscotted to the height of the counter and glazed above, but in those of the poorer tradesmen left open to the ground, and the wares laid on benches and tables in the open air, the light in all cases entering at the front only, and fading away in a few feet from the threshold into a gloom which the eye from without cannot penetrate, but which is generally broken by a ray or two from a feeble lamp at the back of the shop, suspended before a print of the Virgin. . . . But a few steps farther on, at the regular wine-shop of the calle, where we are offered "Vino Nostrani a Soldi 28·32," the Madonna is in great glory, enthroned above ten or a dozen large red casks of three-year-old vintage, and flanked by goodly ranks of bottles of Maraschino, and two crimson lamps; and for the evening, when the gondoliers will come to drink out, under her auspices, the money they have gained during the day, she will have a whole chandelier.

A yard or two farther, we pass the hostelry of the Black Eagle, and glancing as we pass through the square door of marble, deeply moulded, in the outer wall, we see the shadows of its pergola of vines resting on an ancient well, with a pointed shield carved on its side; and so presently emerge on the bridge and Campo San Moisè, whence to the entrance into St. Mark's Place, called the Bocca di Piazza (mouth of the square), the Venetian character is nearly destroyed, first by the frightful façade of San Moisè, which we will pause at another time to examine, and then by the modernizing of the shops as they near the piazza, and the mingling with the lower Venetian populace of lounging groups of English and Austrians. We will push fast through them into the shadow of the pillars at the end of the "Bocca di Piazza," and then we forget them all; for between those pillars there opens a great light, and, in the midst of it, as we advance slowly, the vast tower of St. Mark seems to lift itself visibly forth from the level field of chequered stones; and, on each side, the countless arches prolong themselves into ranged symmetry, as if the rugged and irregular houses that pressed together above us in the dark alley had been struck back into sudden obedience and lovely order, and all their rude casements and broken walls had been transformed into arches charged with goodly sculpture, and fluted shafts of delicate stone.

And well may they fall back, for beyond those troops of ordered arches there rises a vision out of the earth, and all the great square seems to have opened from it in a kind of awe, that we may see it far away;—a multitude of pillars and white domes, clustered into a long low pyramid of coloured light; a treasure-heap, it seems, partly of gold, and partly of opal and mother-of-pearl, hollowed beneath into five great vaulted porches, ceiled with fair mosaic, and beset with sculpture of alabaster, clear as amber and delicate as ivory,—sculpture fantastic and involved, of palm leaves and lilies, and grapes and pomegranates, and birds clinging and fluttering among the branches all twined together into an endless network of buds and plumes; and in the midst of it, the solemn forms of angels, sceptred, and robed to the feet, and leaning to each other across the gates, their figures indistinct among the gleaming of the golden ground through the leaves beside them, interrupted and dim, like the morning light as it faded back among the branches of Eden, when first its gates were angel-guarded long ago. And round the walls of the porches there are set pillars of variegated stones, jasper and porphyry, and deep-green serpentine spotted with flakes of snow, and marbles, that half refuse and half yield to the sunshine, Cleopatra-like, "their bluest veins to kiss"—the shadow, as it steals back from them, revealing line after line of azure undulation, as a receding tide leaves the waved sand; their capitals rich with interwoven tracery, rooted knots of herbage, and drifting leaves of acanthus and vine, and mystical signs, all beginning and ending in the Cross; and above them, in the broad archivolts, a continuous chain of language and of life—angels, and the signs of heaven, and the labours of men, each in its appointed season upon the earth; and above these, another range of glittering pinnacles, mixed with white arches edged with scarlet flowers,—a confusion of delight, amidst which the breasts of the Greek horses are seen blazing in their breadth of golden strength, and the St. Mark's lion, lifted on a blue field covered with stars, until at last, as if in ecstasy, the crests of the arches break into a marble foam, and toss themselves far into the blue sky in flashes and wreaths of sculptured spray, as if the breakers on the Lido shore had been frost-bound before they fell, and the sea-nymphs had inlaid them with coral and amethyst.

Between that grim cathedral of England and this, what an interval! There is a type of it in the very birds that haunt them; for, instead of the restless crowd, hoarse-voiced and sable-winged, drifting on the bleak upper air, the St. Mark's porches are full of doves, that nestle among the marble foliage, and mingle the soft iridescence of their living plumes, changing at every motion, with the tints, hardly less lovely, that have stood unchanged for seven hundred years.

And what effect has this splendour on those who pass beneath it? You may walk from sunrise to sunset, to and fro, before the gateway of St. Mark's, and you will not see an eye lifted to it, nor a countenance brightened by it. Priest and layman, soldier and civilian, rich and poor, pass by it alike regardlessly. Up to the very recesses of the porches, the meanest tradesmen of the city push their counters; nay, the foundations of its pillars are themselves the seats—not "of them that sell doves"* for sacrifice, but of the vendors of toys and caricatures. Round the whole square in front of the church there is almost a continuous line of cafés, where the idle Venetians of the middle classes lounge, and read empty journals; in its centre the Austrian bands play during the time of vespers, their martial music jarring with the organ notes,—the march drowning the miserere, and the sullen crowd thickening round them,—a crowd, which if it had its will, would stiletto every soldier that pipes to it.† And in the recesses of the porches, all day long, knots of men of the lowest classes, unemployed and listless, lie basking in the sun like lizards; and unregarded children,—every heavy glance of their young eyes full of desperation and stony depravity, and their throats hoarse with cursing,—gamble, and fight, and snarl, and sleep, hour after hour, clashing their bruised centesimi upon the marble ledges of the church porch. And the images of Christ and His angels look down upon it continually. . . .

Let us enter the church itself. It is lost in still deeper twilight, to which the eye must be accustomed for some moments before the form of the building can be traced; and then there opens before us a vast cave, hewn out into the

* "And Jesus went into the temple of God . . . and overthrew the tables of the moneychangers, and the seats of them that sold doves" (Matt. 21:12).
† Venice was under Austrian occupation when Ruskin wrote this passage.

form of a Cross, and divided into shadowy aisles by many
pillars. Round the domes of its roof the light enters only
through narrow apertures like large stars; and here and
there a ray or two from some far-away casement wanders
into the darkness, and casts a narrow phosphoric stream
upon the waves of marble that heave and fall in a thousand
colours along the floor. What else there is of light is from
torches, or silver lamps, burning ceaselessly in the recesses
of the chapels; the roof sheeted with gold, and the polished
walls covered with alabaster, give back at every curve and
angle some feeble gleaming to the flames; and the glories
round the heads of the sculptured saints flash out upon us
as we pass them, and sink again into the gloom. Under foot
and over head, a continual succession of crowded imagery,
one picture passing into another, as in a dream; forms
beautiful and terrible mixed together; dragons and serpents,
and ravening beasts of prey, and graceful birds that in the
midst of them drink from running fountains and feed from
vases of crystal; the passions and the pleasures of human life
symbolized together, and the mystery of its redemption; for
the mazes of interwoven lines and changeful pictures lead
always at last to the Cross, lifted and carved in every place
and upon every stone; sometimes with the serpent of eternity wrapt round it, sometimes with doves beneath its arms,
and sweet herbage growing forth from its feet; but conspicuous most of all on the great rood that crosses the church
before the altar, raised in bright blazonry against the shadow
of the apse. And although in the recesses of the aisles and
chapels, when the mist of the incense hangs heavily, we may
see continually a figure traced in faint lines upon their marble, a woman standing with her eyes raised to heaven, and
the inscription above her, "Mother of God," she is not here
the presiding deity. It is the Cross that is first seen, and always, burning in the centre of the temple; and every dome
and hollow of its roof has the figure of Christ in the utmost
height of it, raised in power, or returning in judgment.

[Vol. II, Chap. 4]

The Nature of Gothic

We are now about to enter upon the examination of that school of Venetian architecture which forms an intermediate step between the Byzantine and Gothic forms; but which I find may be conveniently considered in its connexion with the latter style. In order that we may discern the tendency of each step of this change, it will be wise in the outset to endeavour to form some general idea of its final result. We know already what the Byzantine architecture is from which the transition was made, but we ought to know something of the Gothic architecture into which it led. I shall endeavour therefore to give the reader in this chapter an idea, at once broad and definite, of the true nature of *Gothic* architecture, properly so called; not of that of Venice only, but of universal Gothic: for it will be one of the most interesting parts of our subsequent inquiry to find out how far Venetian architecture reached the universal or perfect type of Gothic, and how far it either fell short of it, or assumed foreign and independent forms.

The principal difficulty in doing this arises from the fact that every building of the Gothic period differs in some important respect from every other; and many include features which, if they occurred in other buildings, would not be considered Gothic at all; so that all we have to reason upon is merely, if I may be allowed so to express it, a greater or less degree of *Gothicness* in each building we examine. And it is this Gothicness,—the character which, according as it is found more or less in a building, makes it more or less Gothic,—of which I want to define the nature. . . . That is to say, pointed arches do not constitute Gothic, nor vaulted roofs, nor flying buttresses, nor grotesque sculptures; but all or some of these things, and many other things with them, when they come together so as to have life. . . .

We have, then, the Gothic character submitted to our analysis, just as the rough mineral is submitted to that of the chemist, entangled with many other foreign substances, itself perhaps in no place pure, or ever to be obtained or seen in purity for more than an instant; but nevertheless a thing of definite and separate nature, however inextricable or confused in appearance. Now observe: the chemist defines his mineral by two separate kinds of character; one external, its crystalline form, hardness, lustre, etc.; the other internal, the proportions and nature of its constituent atoms. Exactly in the same manner, we shall find that Gothic architecture has external forms and internal elements. Its elements are certain mental tendencies of the builders, legibly expressed in it; as fancifulness, love of variety, love of richness, and such others. Its external forms are pointed arches, vaulted roofs, etc. And unless both the elements and the forms are there, we have no right to call the style Gothic. It is not enough that it has the Form, if it have not also the power and life. It is not enough that it has the Power, if it have not the form. We must therefore inquire into each of these characters successively; and determine first, what is the Mental Expression, and secondly, what the Material Form of Gothic architecture, properly so called. . . .

I believe, then, that the characteristic or moral elements of Gothic are the following, placed in the order of their importance:

1. Savageness.	4. Grotesqueness.
2. Changefulness.	5. Rigidity.
3. Naturalism.	6. Redundance.

These characters are here expressed as belonging to the building; as belonging to the builder, they would be expressed thus:—1. Savageness or Rudeness. 2. Love of Change. 3. Love of Nature. 4. Disturbed Imagination. 5. Obstinacy. 6. Generosity. And I repeat, that the withdrawal of any one, or any two, will not at once destroy the Gothic character of a building, but the removal of a majority of them will. I shall proceed to examine them in their order.

(1.) SAVAGENESS. I am not sure when the word "Gothic" was first generically applied to the architecture of the North; but I presume that, whatever the date of its original usage, it was intended to imply reproach, and express the barbaric character of the nations among whom that architecture arose. It never implied that they were literally of Gothic lineage, far less that their architecture had been originally invented by the Goths themselves; but it did imply that they and their buildings together exhibited a degree of sternness and rudeness, which, in contradistinction to the character of Southern and Eastern nations, appeared like a perpetual reflection of the contrast between the Goth and the Roman in their first encounter. And when that fallen Roman, in the utmost impotence of his luxury, and insolence of his guilt, became the model for the imitation of civilized Europe, at the close of the so-called Dark ages, the word Gothic became a term of unmitigated contempt, not unmixed with aversion. From that contempt, by the exertion of the antiquaries and architects of this century, Gothic architecture has been sufficiently vindicated; and perhaps some among us, in our admiration of the magnificent science of its structure, and sacredness of its expression, might desire that the term of ancient reproach should be withdrawn, and some other, of more apparent honourableness, adopted in its place. There is no chance, as there is no need, of such a substitution. As far as the epithet was used scornfully, it was used falsely; but there is no reproach in the word, rightly understood; on the contrary, there is a profound truth, which the instinct of mankind almost unconsciously recognizes. It is true, greatly and deeply true, that the architecture of the North is rude and wild; but it is not true, that, for this reason, we are to condemn it, or despise. Far otherwise: I believe it is in this very character that it deserves our profoundest reverence.

The charts of the world which have been drawn up by modern science have thrown into a narrow space the expression of a vast amount of knowledge, but I have never

yet seen any one pictorial enough to enable the spectator
to imagine the kind of contrast in physical character which
exists between Northern and Southern countries. We know
the differences in detail, but we have not that broad glance
and grasp which would enable us to feel them in their
fulness. We know that gentians grow on the Alps, and
olives on the Apennines; but we do not enough conceive
for ourselves that variegated mosaic of the world's surface
which a bird sees in its migration, that difference between
the district of the gentian and of the olive which the stork
and the swallow see far off, as they lean upon the sirocco
wind. Let us, for a moment, try to raise ourselves even
above the level of their flight, and imagine the Mediterranean lying beneath us like an irregular lake, and all its
ancient promontories sleeping in the sun: here and there
an angry spot of thunder, a grey stain of storm, moving
upon the burning field; and here and there a fixed wreath
of white volcano smoke, surrounded by its circle of ashes;
but for the most part a great peacefulness of light, Syria
and Greece, Italy and Spain, laid like pieces of a golden
pavement into the sea-blue, chased, as we stoop nearer to
them, with bossy beaten work of mountain chains, and
glowing softly with terraced gardens, and flowers heavy
with frankincense, mixed among masses of laurel, and
orange, and plumy palm, that abate with their grey-green
shadows the burning of the marble rocks, and of the ledges
of porphyry sloping under lucent sand. Then let us pass
farther towards the north, until we see the orient colours
change gradually into a vast belt of rainy green, where the
pastures of Switzerland, and poplar valleys of France, and
dark forests of the Danube and Carpathians stretch from the
mouths of the Loire to those of the Volga, seen through
clefts in grey swirls of rain-cloud and flaky veils of the mist
of the brooks, spreading low along the pasture lands: and
then, farther north still, to see the earth heave into mighty
masses of leaden rock and heathy moor, bordering with a
broad waste of gloomy purple that belt of field and wood,

and splintering into irregular and grisly islands amidst the northern seas, beaten by storm, and chilled by ice-drift, and tormented by furious pulses of contending tide, until the roots of the last forests fail from among the hill ravines, and the hunger of the north wind bites their peaks into barrenness; and, at last, the wall of ice, durable like iron, sets, deathlike, its white teeth against us out of the polar twilight. And, having once traversed in thought this gradation of the zoned iris of the earth in all its material vastness, let us go down nearer to it, and watch the parallel change in the belt of animal life; the multitudes of swift and brilliant creatures that glance in the air and sea, or tread the sands of the southern zone; striped zebras and spotted leopards, glistening serpents, and birds arrayed in purple and scarlet. Let us contrast their delicacy and brilliancy of colour, and swiftness of motion, with the frost-cramped strength, and shaggy covering, and dusky plumage of the northern tribes; contrast the Arabian horse with the Shetland, the tiger and leopard with the wolf and bear, the antelope with the elk, the bird of paradise with the osprey; and then, submissively acknowledging the great laws by which the earth and all that it bears are ruled throughout their being, let us not condemn, but rejoice in the expression by man of his own rest in the statutes of the lands that gave him birth. Let us watch him with reverence as he sets side by side the burning gems, and smooths with soft sculpture the jasper pillars, that are to reflect a ceaseless sunshine, and rise into a cloudless sky: but not with less reverence let us stand by him, when, with rough strength and hurried stroke, he smites an uncouth animation out of the rocks which he has torn from among the moss of the moorland, and heaves into the darkened air the pile of iron buttress and rugged wall, instinct with work of an imagination as wild and wayward as the northern sea; creatures of ungainly shape and rigid limb, but full of wolfish life; fierce as the wind that beat, and changeful as the clouds that shade them.

There is, I repeat, no degradation, no reproach in this,

but all dignity and honourableness: and we should err grievously in refusing either to recognize as an essential character of the existing architecture of the North, or to admit as a desirable character in that which it yet may be, this wildness of thought, and roughness of work; this look of mountain brotherhood between the cathedral and the Alp; this magnificence of sturdy power, put forth only the more energetically because the fine finger-touch was chilled away by the frosty wind, and the eye dimmed by the moor-mist, or blinded by the hail; this out-speaking of the strong spirit of men who may not gather redundant fruitage from the earth, nor bask in dreamy benignity of sunshine, but must break the rock for bread, and cleave the forest for fire, and show, even in what they did for their delight, some of the hard habits of the arm and heart that grew on them as they swung the axe or pressed the plough.

If, however, the savageness of Gothic architecture, merely as an expression of its origin among Northern nations, may be considered, in some sort, a noble character, it possesses a higher nobility still, when considered as an index, not of climate, but of religious principle.

In the 13th and 14th paragraphs of Chapter XXI. of the first volume of this work, it was noticed that the systems of architectural ornament, properly so called, might be divided into three:—1. Servile ornament, in which the execution or power of the inferior workman is entirely subjected to the intellect of the higher;—2. Constitutional ornament, in which the executive inferior power is, to a certain point, emancipated and independent, having a will of its own, yet confessing its inferiority and rendering obedience to higher powers;—and 3. Revolutionary ornament, in which no executive inferiority is admitted at all. I must here explain the nature of these divisions at somewhat greater length.

Of Servile ornament, the principal schools are the Greek, Ninevite, and Egyptian; but their servility is of different kinds. The Greek master-workman was far advanced in knowledge and power above the Assyrian or Egyptian. Neither he nor those for whom he worked could endure the appearance of imperfection in anything; and, therefore, what ornament he appointed to be done by those beneath him was composed of mere geometrical forms,—balls, ridges, and perfectly symmetrical foliage,—which could be executed with absolute precision by line and rule, and were as perfect in their way, when completed, as his own figure sculpture. The Assyrian and Egyptian, on the contrary, less cognisant of accurate form in anything, were content to allow their figure sculpture to be executed by inferior workmen, but lowered the method of its treatment to a standard which every workman could reach, and then trained him by discipline so rigid, that there was no chance of his falling beneath the standard appointed. The Greek gave to the lower workman no subject which he could not perfectly execute. The Assyrian gave him subjects which he could only execute imperfectly, but fixed a legal standard for his imperfection. The workman was, in both systems, a slave.

But in the mediæval, or especially Christian, system of ornament, this slavery is done away with altogether; Christianity having recognized, in small things as well as great, the individual value of every soul. But it not only recognizes its value; it confesses its imperfection, in only bestowing dignity upon the acknowledgment of unworthiness. That admission of lost power and fallen nature, which the Greek or Ninevite felt to be intensely painful, and, as far as might be, altogether refused, the Christian makes daily and hourly, contemplating the fact of it without fear, as tending, in the end, to God's greater glory. Therefore, to every spirit which Christianity summons to her service, her exhortation is: Do what you can, and confess frankly what you are unable to do; neither let your effort be shortened for fear of failure, nor your confession silenced for fear of shame. And it is, perhaps, the principal admirableness of the Gothic schools of architecture, that they thus receive the results of the labour of inferior minds; and out of fragments full of imperfection, and betraying that imperfection in every touch, indulgently raise up a stately and unaccusable whole.

But the modern English mind has this much in common with that of the Greek, that it intensely desires, in all things, the utmost completion or perfection compatible with their nature. This is a noble character in the abstract, but becomes ignoble when it causes us to forget the relative dignities of that nature itself, and to prefer the perfectness of the lower nature to the imperfection of the higher; not considering that as, judged by such a rule, all the brute animals would be preferable to man, because more perfect in their functions and kind. . . . And therefore, while in all things that we see or do, we are to desire perfection, and strive for it, we are nevertheless not to set the meaner thing, in its narrow accomplishment, above the nobler thing, in its mighty progress; not to esteem smooth minuteness above shattered majesty; not to prefer mean victory to honourable defeat; not to lower the level of our aim, that we may the more surely enjoy the complacency of success. But, above all, in our dealings with the souls of other men, we are to take care how we check, by severe requirement or narrow caution, efforts which might otherwise lead to a noble issue. . . .

And observe, you are put to stern choice in this matter. You must either make a tool of the creature, or a man of him. You cannot make both. Men were not intended to work with the accuracy of tools, to be precise and perfect in all their actions. If you will have that precision out of them, and make their fingers measure degrees like cogwheels, and their arms strike curves like compasses, you must unhumanize them. All the energy of their spirits must be given to make cogs and compasses of themselves. All their attention and strength must go to the accomplishment of the mean act. The eye of the soul must be bent upon the finger-point, and the soul's force must fill all the invisible nerves that guide it, ten hours a day, that it may not err from its steely precision, and so soul and sight be worn away, and the whole human being be lost at last—a heap of sawdust, so far as its intellectual work in this world is concerned: saved only by its Heart, which cannot go into the form of cogs and compasses, but expands, after the ten hours are over, into fireside humanity. On the other hand, if you will make a man of the working creature, you cannot make a tool. Let him but begin to imagine, to think, to try to do anything worth doing; and the engine-turned precision is lost at once. Out come all his roughness, all his dulness, all his incapability; shame upon shame, failure upon failure, pause after pause: but out comes the whole majesty of him also; and we know the height of it only when we see the clouds settling upon him. And, whether the clouds be bright or dark, there will be transfiguration behind and within them.

And now, reader, look round this English room of yours, about which you have been proud so often, because the work of it was so good and strong, and the ornaments of it so finished. Examine again all those accurate mouldings, and perfect polishings, and unerring adjustments of the seasoned wood and tempered steel. Many a time you have exulted over them, and thought how great England was, because her slightest work was done so thoroughly. Alas! if read rightly, these perfectnesses are signs of a slavery in our England a thousand times more bitter and more degrading than that of the scourged African, or helot Greek. Men may be beaten, chained, tormented, yoked like cattle, slaughtered like summer flies, and yet remain in one sense, and the best sense, free. But to smother their souls with them, to blight and hew into rotting pollards the suckling branches of their human intelligence, to make the flesh and skin which, after the worm's work on it, is to see God, into leathern thongs to yoke machinery with,—this is to be slave-masters indeed; and there might be more freedom in England, though her feudal lords' lightest words were worth men's lives, and though the blood of the vexed husband-man dropped in the furrows of her fields, than there is while the animation of her multitudes is sent like fuel to feed the factory smoke, and the strength of them is given daily to be wasted into the fineness of a web, or racked into the exactness of a line.

And, on the other hand, go forth again to gaze upon the old cathedral front, where you have smiled so often at the fantastic ignorance of the old sculptors: examine once more those ugly goblins, and formless monsters, and stern statues, anatomiless and rigid; but do not mock at them, for they are signs of the life and liberty of every workman who struck the stone; a freedom of thought, and rank in scale of being, such as no laws, no charters, no charities can secure; but which it must be the first aim of all Europe at this day to regain for her children.

Let me not be thought to speak wildly or extravagantly. It is verily this degradation of the operative into a machine, which, more than any other evil of the times, is leading the mass of the nations everywhere into vain, incoherent, destructive struggling for a freedom of which they cannot explain the nature to themselves. Their universal outcry against wealth, and against nobility, is not forced from them either by the pressure of famine, or the sting of mortified pride. These do much, and have done much in all ages; but the foundations of society were never yet shaken as they are at this day. It is not that men are ill fed, but that they have no pleasure in the work by which they make their bread, and therefore look to wealth as the only means of pleasure. It is not that men are pained by the scorn of the upper classes, but they cannot endure their own; for they feel that the kind of labour to which they are condemned is verily a degrading one, and makes them less than men. Never had the upper classes so much sympathy with the lower, or charity for them, as they have at this day, and yet never were they so much hated by them: for, of old, the separation between the noble and the poor was merely a wall built by law; now it is a veritable difference in level of standing, a precipice between upper and lower grounds in the field of humanity, and there is pestilential air at the bottom of it. . . .

We have much studied and much perfected, of late, the great civilized invention of the division of labour; only we give it a false name. It is not, truly speaking, the labour that is divided; but the men:—Divided into mere segments of men—broken into small fragments and crumbs of life; so that all the little piece of intelligence that is left in a man is not enough to make a pin, or a nail, but exhausts itself in making the point of a pin or the head of a nail. Now it is a good and desirable thing, truly, to make many pins in a day; but if we could only see with what crystal sand their points were polished,—sand of human soul, much to be magnified before it can be discerned for what it is—we should think there might be some loss in it also. And the great cry that rises from all our manufacturing cities, louder than their furnace blast, is all in very deed for this,—that we manufacture everything there except men; we blanch cotton, and strengthen steel, and refine sugar, and shape pottery; but to brighten, to strengthen, to refine, or to form a single living spirit, never enters into our estimate of advantages. And all the evil to which that cry is urging our myriads can be met only in one way: not by teaching nor preaching, for to teach them is but to show them their misery, and to preach to them, if we do nothing more than preach, is to mock at it. It can be met only by a right understanding, on the part of all classes, of what kinds of labour are good for men, raising them, and making them happy; by a determined sacrifice of such convenience, or beauty, or cheapness as is to be got only by the degradation of the workman; and by equally determined demand for the products and results of healthy and ennobling labour.

And how, it will be asked, are these products to be recognized, and this demand to be regulated? Easily: by the observance of three broad and simple rules:

1. Never encourage the manufacture of any article not absolutely necessary, in the production of which *Invention* has no share.

2. Never demand an exact finish for its own sake, but only for some practical or noble end.

3. Never encourage imitation or copying of any kind, except for the sake of preserving records of great works.

The second of these principles is the only one which directly rises out of the consideration of our immediate subject; but I shall briefly explain the meaning and extent of the first also, reserving the enforcement of the third for another place.

1. Never encourage the manufacture of anything not necessary, in the production of which invention has no share.

For instance. Glass beads are utterly unnecessary, and there is no design or thought employed in their manufacture. They are formed by first drawing out the glass into rods; these rods are chopped up into fragments of the size of beads by the human hand, and the fragments are then rounded in the furnace. The men who chop up the rods sit at their work all day, their hands vibrating with a perpetual and exquisitely timed palsy, and the beads dropping beneath their vibration like hail. Neither they, nor the men who draw out the rods or fuse the fragments, have the smallest occasion for the use of any single human faculty; and every young lady, therefore, who buys glass beads is engaged in the slave-trade, and in a much more cruel one than that which we have so long been endeavouring to put down.

But glass cups and vessels may become the subjects of exquisite invention; and if in buying these we pay for the invention, that is to say, for the beautiful form, or colour, or engraving, and not for mere finish of execution, we are doing good to humanity. . . .

On a large scale, and in work determinable by line and rule, it is indeed both possible and necessary that the thoughts of one man should be carried out by the labour of others; in this sense I have already defined the best architecture to be the expression of the mind of manhood by the hands of childhood. But on a smaller scale, and in a design which cannot be mathematically defined, one man's thoughts can never be expressed by another: and the dif-

ference between the spirit of touch of the man who is in-
venting, and of the man who is obeying directions, is often
all the difference between a great and a common work of
art. How wide the separation is between original and
second-hand execution, I shall endeavour to show elsewhere; it is not so much to our purpose here as to mark the
other and more fatal error of despising manual labour
when governed by intellect; for it is no less fatal an error
to despise it when thus regulated by intellect, than to value
it for its own sake. We are always in these days endeavouring
to separate the two; we want one man to be always thinking, and another to be always working, and we call one a
gentleman, and the other an operative; whereas the workman ought often to be thinking, and the thinker often to be
working, and both should be gentlemen, in the best sense.
As it is, we make both ungentle, the one envying, the other
despising, his brother; and the mass of society is made up
of morbid thinkers, and miserable workers. Now it is only
by labour that thought can be made healthy, and only by
thought that labour can be made happy, and the two cannot
be separated with impunity. . . .

I should be led far from the matter in hand, if I were
to pursue this interesting subject. Enough, I trust, has been
said to show the reader that the rudeness or imperfection
which at first rendered the term "Gothic" one of reproach
is indeed, when rightly understood, one of the most noble
characters of Christian architecture, and not only a noble
but an *essential* one. It seems a fantastic paradox, but it is
nevertheless a most important truth, that no architecture
can be truly noble which is *not* imperfect. And this is easily
demonstrable. For since the architect, whom we will suppose capable of doing all in perfection, cannot execute the
whole with his own hands, he must either make slaves of his
workmen in the old Greek, and present English fashion, and
level his work to a slave's capacities, which is to degrade it;
or else he must take his workmen as he finds them, and let
them show their weaknesses together with their strength,

which will involve the Gothic imperfection, but render the whole work as noble as the intellect of the age can make it.

But the principle may be stated more broadly still. I have confined the illustration of it to architecture, but I must not leave it as if true of architecture only. Hitherto I have used the words imperfect and perfect merely to distinguish between work grossly unskilful, and work executed with average precision and science; and I have been pleading that any degree of unskilfulness should be admitted, so only that the labourer's mind had room for expression. But, accurately speaking, no good work whatever can be perfect, and *the demand for perfection is always a sign of a misunderstanding of the ends of art.*

This for two reasons, both based on everlasting laws. The first, that no great man ever stops working till he has reached his point of failure: that is to say, his mind is always far in advance of his powers of execution, and the latter will now and then give way in trying to follow it; besides that he will always give to the inferior portions of his work only such inferior attention as they require; and according to his greatness he becomes so accustomed to the feeling of dissatisfaction with the best he can do, that in moments of lassitude or anger with himself he will not care though the beholder be dissatisfied also. I believe there has only been one man who would not acknowledge this necessity, and strove always to reach perfection, Leonardo; the end of his vain effort being merely that he would take ten years to a picture and leave it unfinished. And therefore, if we are to have great men working at all, or less men doing their best, the work will be imperfect, however beautiful. Of human work none but what is bad can be perfect, in its own bad way.*

The second reason is, that imperfection is in some sort

* The Elgin marbles are supposed by many persons to be "perfect." In the most important portions they indeed approach perfection, but only there. The draperies are unfinished, the hair and wool of the animals are unfinished, and the entire bas-reliefs of the frieze are roughly cut. [Ruskin's note.]

essential to all that we know of life. It is the sign of life in a mortal body, that is to say, of a state of progress and change. Nothing that lives is, or can be, rigidly perfect; part of it is decaying, part nascent. The foxglove blossom,—a third part bud, a third part past, a third part in full bloom, —is a type of the life of this world. And in all things that live there are certain irregularities and deficiencies which are not only signs of life, but sources of beauty. No human face is exactly the same in its lines on each side, no leaf perfect in its lobes, no branch in its symmetry. All admit irregularity as they imply change; and to banish imperfection is to destroy expression, to check exertion, to paralyze vitality. All things are literally better, lovelier, and more beloved for the imperfections which have been divinely appointed, that the law of human life may be Effort, and the law of human judgment, Mercy.

Accept this then for a universal law, that neither architecture nor any other noble work of man can be good unless it be imperfect; and let us be prepared for the otherwise strange fact, which we shall discern clearly as we approach the period of the Renaissance, that the first cause of the fall of the arts of Europe was a relentless requirement of perfection, incapable alike either of being silenced by veneration for greatness, or softened into forgiveness of simplicity.

Thus far then of the Rudeness or Savageness, which is the first mental element of Gothic architecture. It is an element in many other healthy architectures also, as the Byzantine and Romanesque; but true Gothic cannot exist without it.

The second mental element above named was CHANGE-FULNESS, or Variety.

I have already enforced the allowing independent operation to the inferior workman, simply as a duty *to him*, and as ennobling the architecture by rendering it more Christian. We have now to consider what reward we obtain for the performance of this duty, namely, the perpetual variety of every feature of the building.

Wherever the workman is utterly enslaved, the parts of the building must of course be absolutely like each other; for the perfection of his execution can only be reached by exercising him in doing one thing, and giving him nothing else to do. The degree in which the workman is degraded may be thus known at a glance, by observing whether the several parts of the building are similar or not; and if, as in Greek work, all the capitals are alike, and all the mouldings unvaried, then the degradation is complete; if, as in Egyptian or Ninevite work, though the manner of executing certain figures is always the same, the order of design is perpetually varied, the degradation is less total; if, as in Gothic work, there is perpetual change both in design and execution, the workman must have been altogether set free.

How much the beholder gains from the liberty of the labourer may perhaps be questioned in England, where one of the strongest instincts in nearly every mind is that Love of Order which makes us desire that our house windows should pair like our carriage horses, and allows us to yield our faith unhesitatingly to architectural theories which fix a form for everything, and forbid variation from it. I would not impeach love of order: it is one of the most useful elements of the English mind; it helps us in our commerce and in all purely practical matters; and it is in many cases one of the foundation stones of morality. Only do not let us suppose that love of order is love of art. It is true that order, in its highest sense, is one of the necessities of art, just as time is a necessity of music; but love of order has no more to do with our right enjoyment of architecture or painting, than love of punctuality with the appreciation of an opera. Experience, I fear, teaches us that accurate and methodical habits in daily life are seldom characteristic of those who either quickly perceive, or richly possess, the creative powers of art; there is, however, nothing inconsistent between the two instincts, and nothing to hinder us from retaining our business habits, and yet fully allowing and enjoying the noblest gifts of Invention. We already do so, in every other branch of art except architecture, and we only do *not* so there because we have been taught that it would be wrong. Our architects gravely inform us that, as there are four rules of arithmetic, there are five orders of architecture; we, in our simplicity, think that this sounds consistent, and believe them. They inform us also that there is one proper form for Corinthian capitals, another for Doric, and another for Ionic. We, considering that there is also a proper form for the letters A, B, and C, think that this also sounds consistent, and accept the proposition. Understanding, therefore, that one form of the said capitals is proper, and no other, and having a conscientious horror of all impropriety, we allow the architect to provide us with the said capitals, of the proper form, in such and such a quantity, and in all other points to take care that the legal forms are observed; which having done, we rest in forced confidence that we are well housed.

But our higher instincts are not deceived. We take no pleasure in the building provided for us, resembling that which we take in a new book or a new picture. We may be proud of its size, complacent in its correctness, and happy in its convenience. We may take the same pleasure in its symmetry and workmanship as in a well-ordered room, or a skilful piece of manufacture. And this we suppose to be all the pleasure that architecture was ever intended to give us. The idea of reading a building as we would read Milton or Dante, and getting the same kind of delight out of the stones as out of the stanzas, never enters our mind for a moment. And for good reason;—There is indeed rhythm in the verses, quite as strict as the symmetries or rhythm of the architecture, and a thousand times more beautiful, but there is something else than rhythm. The verses were neither made to order, nor to match, as the capitals were; and we have therefore a kind of pleasure in them other than a sense of propriety. But it requires a strong effort of common sense to shake ourselves quit of all that we have been taught for the last two centuries, and wake to the perception of a truth just as simple and certain as it is new: that great art, whether expressing itself in words, colours, or stones, does *not* say the same thing over and over again; that the merit of architectural, as of every other art, consists in its saying new and different things; that to repeat itself is no more a characteristic of genius in marble than it is of genius in print; and that we may, without offending any laws of good taste, require of an architect, as we do of a novelist, that he should be not only correct, but entertaining. . . .

And this we confess in deeds, though not in words. All the pleasure which the people of the nineteenth century take in art, is in pictures, sculpture, minor objects of virtù, or mediæval architecture, which we enjoy under the term picturesque: no pleasure is taken anywhere in modern buildings, and we find all men of true feeling delighting to escape out of modern cities into natural scenery: hence, as I shall hereafter show, that peculiar love of landscape, which is characteristic of the age. It would be well, if in all other matters, we were as ready to put up with what we dislike, for the sake of compliance with established law, as we are in architecture.

How so debased a law came to be established, we shall see when we come to describe the Renaissance schools; here we have only to note, as a second most essential element of the Gothic spirit, that it broke through that law wherever it found it in existence; it not only dared, but delighted in, the infringement of every servile principle; and invented a series of forms of which the merit was, not merely that they were new, but that they were *capable of perpetual novelty*. The pointed arch was not merely a bold variation from the round, but it admitted of millions of variations in itself; for the proportions of a pointed arch are changeable to infinity, while a circular arch is always the same. The grouped shaft was not merely a bold variation from the single one, but it admitted of millions of variations in its grouping, and in the proportions resultant from its grouping. The introduction of tracery was not only a startling change in the treatment of window lights, but admitted endless changes in the interlacement of the tracery bars themselves. So that, while in all living Christian architecture the love of variety exists, the Gothic schools exhibited that love in culminating energy; and their influence, wherever it extended itself, may be sooner and farther traced by this character than by any other; the tendency to the adoption of Gothic types being always first shown by greater irregularity, and richer variation in the forms of architecture it is about to supersede, long before the appearance of the pointed arch or of any other recognizable *outward* sign of the Gothic mind. . . .

From these facts we may gather generally that monotony is, and ought to be, in itself painful to us, just as darkness is; that an architecture which is altogether monotonous is a dark or dead architecture; and of those who love it, it may be truly said, "they love darkness rather than light." But monotony in certain measure, used in order to give value to change, and above all, that *transparent* monotony, which, like the shadows of a great painter, suffers all manner of dimly suggested form to be seen through the body of it, is an essential in architectural as in all other composition; and the endurance of monotony has about the same place in a healthy mind that the endurance of darkness has: that is to say, as a strong intellect will have pleasure in the solemnities of storm and twilight, and in the broken and mysterious lights that gleam among them, rather than in mere brilliancy and glare, while a frivolous mind will dread the shadow and the storm; and as a great man will be ready to endure much darkness of fortune in order to reach greater eminence of power or felicity, while an inferior man will not pay the price; exactly in like manner a great mind will accept, or even delight in, monotony which would be wearisome to an inferior intellect, because it has more patience and power of expectation, and is ready to pay the full price for the great future pleasure of change. But in all cases it is not that the noble nature loves monotony, any more than it loves darkness or pain. But it can bear with it, and receive a high pleasure in the endurance or patience, a pleasure necessary to the well-being of this world; while those who will not submit to the temporary sameness, but rush from one change to another, gradually dull the edge of change itself, and bring a shadow and weariness over the whole world from which there is no more escape.

From these general uses of variety in the economy of the world, we may at once understand its use and abuse in architecture. The variety of the Gothic schools is the more healthy and beautiful, because in many cases it is entirely unstudied, and results, not from mere love of change, but from practical necessities. For in one point of view Gothic is not only the best, but the *only rational* architecture, as being that which can fit itself most easily to all services, vulgar or noble. Undefined in its slope of roof, height of shaft, breadth of arch, or disposition of ground plan, it can shrink into a turret, expand into a hall, coil into a staircase, or spring into a spire, with undegraded grace and unexhausted energy; and whenever it finds occasion for change in its form or purpose, it submits to it without the slightest sense of loss either to its unity or majesty,—subtle and flexible like a fiery serpent, but ever attentive to the voice of the charmer. And it is one of the chief virtues of the Gothic builders, that they never suffered ideas of outside symmetries and consistencies to interfere with the real use and value of what they did. If they wanted a window, they opened one; a room, they added one; a buttress, they built one; utterly regardless of any established conventionalities of external appearance, knowing (as indeed it always happened) that such daring interruptions of the formal plan would rather give additional interest to its symmetry than injure it. So that, in the best times of Gothic, a useless window would rather have been opened in an unexpected place for the sake of the surprise, than a useful one forbidden for the sake of symmetry. Every successive architect, employed upon a great work, built the pieces he added in his own way, utterly regardless of the style adopted by his pred-

ecessors; and if two towers were raised in nominal correspondence at the sides of a cathedral front, one was nearly
sure to be different from the other, and in each the style
at the top to be different from the style at the bottom. . . .

A picture or poem is often little more than a feeble utterance of man's admiration of something out of himself; but
architecture approaches more to a creation of his own, born
of his necessities, and expressive of his nature. It is also, in
some sort, the work of the whole race, while the picture or
statue is the work of one only, in most cases more highly
gifted than his fellows. And therefore we may expect that
the first two elements of good architecture should be expressive of some great truths commonly belonging to the
whole race, and necessary to be understood or felt by them
in all their work that they do under the sun. And observe
what they are: the confession of Imperfection, and the confession of Desire of Change. The building of the bird and
the bee needs not express anything like this. It is perfect
and unchanging. But just because we are something better
than birds or bees, our building must confess that we have
not reached the perfection we can imagine, and cannot rest
in the condition we have attained. If we pretend to have
reached either perfection or satisfaction, we have degraded
ourselves and our work. God's work only may express that;
but ours may never have that sentence written upon it,—
"And behold, it was very good." And, observe again, it is not
merely as it renders the edifice a book of various knowledge,
or a mine of precious thought, that variety is essential to its
nobleness. The vital principle is not the love of *Knowledge,*
but the love of *Change.* It is that strange *disquietude* of the
Gothic spirit that is its greatness; that restlessness of the
dreaming mind, that wanders hither and thither among
the niches, and flickers feverishly around the pinnacles, and
frets and fades in labyrinthine knots and shadows along
wall and roof, and yet is not satisfied, nor shall be satisfied.
The Greek could stay in his triglyph furrow, and be at
peace; but the work of the Gothic heart is fretwork still,

and it can neither rest in, nor from, its labour, but must pass on, sleeplessly, until its love of change shall be pacified for ever in the change that must come alike on them that wake and them that sleep.

The third constituent element of the Gothic mind was stated to be NATURALISM; that is to say, the love of natural objects for their own sake, and the effort to represent them frankly, unconstrained by artistical laws.

This characteristic of the style partly follows in necessary connection with those named above. For, so soon as the workman is left free to represent what subjects he chooses, he must look to the nature that is round him for material, and will endeavour to represent it as he sees it, with more or less accuracy according to the skill he possesses, and with much play of fancy, but with small respect for law. There is, however, a marked distinction between the imaginations of the Western and Eastern races, even when both are left free; the Western, or Gothic, delighting most in the representation of facts, and the Eastern (Arabian, Persian, and Chinese) in the harmony of colours and forms. Each of these intellectual dispositions has its particular forms of error and abuse. . . .

Of the various forms of resultant mischief it is not here the place to speak; the reader may already be somewhat wearied with a statement which has led us apparently so far from our immediate subject. But the digression was necessary, in order that I might clearly define the sense in which I use the word Naturalism when I state it to be the third most essential characteristic of Gothic architecture. I mean that the Gothic builders belong to the central or greatest rank in *both* the classifications of artists which we have just made; that considering all artists as either men of design, men of facts, or men of both, the Gothic builders were men of both; and that again, considering all artists as either Purists, Naturalists, or Sensualists, the Gothic builders were Naturalists.

I say first, that the Gothic builders were of that central

class which unites fact with design; but that the part of the work which was more especially their own was the truthfulness. Their power of artistical invention or arrangement was not greater than that of Romanesque and Byzantine workmen: by those workmen they were taught the principles, and from them received their models, of design; but to the ornamental feeling and rich fancy of the Byzantine the Gothic builder added a love of *fact* which is never found in the South. Both Greek and Roman used conventional foliage in their ornament, passing into something that was not foliage at all, knotting itself into strange cup-like buds or clusters, and growing out of lifeless rods instead of stems; the Gothic sculptor received these types, at first, as things that ought to be, just as we have a second time received them; but he could not rest in them. He saw there was no veracity in them, no knowledge, no vitality. Do what he would, he could not help liking the true leaves better; and cautiously, a little at a time, he put more of nature into his work, until at last it was all true, retaining, nevertheless, every valuable character of the original well-disciplined and designed arrangement. . . .

There is, however, one direction in which the Naturalism of the Gothic workmen is peculiarly manifested; and this direction is even more characteristic of the school than the Naturalism itself; I mean their peculiar fondness for the forms of Vegetation. . . . I have before alluded to the strange and vain supposition, that the original conception of Gothic architecture had been derived from vegetation,— from the symmetry of avenues, and the interlacing of branches. It is a supposition which never could have existed for a moment in the mind of any person acquainted with early Gothic; but, however idle as a theory, it is most valuable as a testimony to the character of the perfected style. It is precisely because the reverse of this theory is the fact, because the Gothic did not arise out of, but develope itself into, a resemblance to vegetation, that this resemblance is so instructive as an indication of the temper of the builders. It was no chance suggestion of the form of an arch from the bending of a bough, but a gradual and continual discovery of a beauty in natural forms which could be more and more perfectly transferred into those of stone, that influenced at once the heart of the people, and the form of the edifice. The Gothic architecture arose in massy and mountainous strength, axe-hewn, and iron-bound, block heaved upon block by the monk's enthusiasm and the soldier's force; and cramped and stanchioned into such weight of grisly wall, as might bury the anchoret in darkness, and beat back the utmost storm of battle, suffering but by the same narrow crosslet the passing of the sunbeam, or of the arrow. Gradually, as that monkish enthusiasm became more thoughtful, and as the sound of war became more and more intermittent beyond the gates of the convent or the keep, the stony pillar grew slender and the vaulted roof grew light, till they had wreathed themselves into the semblance of the summer woods at their fairest, and of the dead field-flowers, long trodden down in blood, sweet monumental statues were set to bloom for ever, beneath the porch of the temple, or the canopy of the tomb. . . .

The fourth essential element of the Gothic mind was above stated to be the sense of the GROTESQUE; but I shall defer the endeavour to define this most curious and subtle character until we have occasion to examine one of the divisions of the Renaissance schools, which was morbidly influenced by it (Vol. III. Chap. III. ["Grotesque Renaissance"]). It is the less necessary to insist upon it here, because every reader familiar with Gothic architecture must understand what I mean, and will, I believe, have no hesitation in admitting, that the tendency to delight in fantastic and ludicrous, as well as in sublime, images, is a universal instinct of the Gothic imagination.

The fifth element above named was RIGIDITY; and this character I must endeavour carefully to define, for neither the word I have used, nor any other that I can think of, will express it accurately. For I mean, not merely stable, but *active* rigidity; the peculiar energy which gives tension to movement, and stiffness to resistance, which makes the fiercest lightning forked rather than curved, and the stoutest oak-branch angular rather than bending, and is as much seen in the quivering of the lance as in the glittering of the icicle.

I have before had occasion . . . to note some manifestations of this energy or fixedness; but it must be still more attentively considered here, as it shows itself throughout the whole structure and decoration of Gothic work. Egyptian and Greek buildings stand, for the most part, by their own weight and mass, one stone passively incumbent on another; but in the Gothic vaults and traceries there is a stiffness analogous to that of the bones of a limb, or fibres of a tree; an elastic tension and communication of force from part to part, and also a studious expression of this throughout every visible line of the building. And, in like manner, the Greek and Egyptian ornament is either mere surface engraving, as if the face of the wall had been stamped with a seal, or its lines are flowing, lithe, and luxuriant; in either case, there is no expression of energy in the framework of the ornament itself. But the Gothic ornament stands out in prickly independence, and frosty fortitude, jutting into crockets, and freezing into pinnacles; here starting up into a monster, there germinating into a blossom, anon knitting itself into a branch, alternately thorny, bossy, and bristly, or writhed into every form of nervous entanglement; but, even when most graceful, never for an instant languid, always quickset: erring, if at all, ever on the side of brusquerie. . . .

Last, because the least essential, of the constituent elements of this noble school, was placed that of REDUNDANCE, —the uncalculating bestowal of the wealth of its labour. There is, indeed, much Gothic, and that of the best period, in which this element is hardly traceable, and which depends for its effect almost exclusively on loveliness of simple design and grace of uninvolved proportion: still, in the most characteristic buildings, a certain portion of their effect depends upon accumulation of ornament; and many of those which have most influence on the minds of men, have attained it by means of this attribute alone. And although, by careful study of the school, it is possible to arrive at a condition of taste which shall be better contented by a few perfect lines than by a whole façade covered with fretwork, the building which only satisfies such a taste is not to be considered the best. For the very first requirement of Gothic architecture being, as we saw above, that it shall both admit the aid, and appeal to the admiration, of the rudest as well as the most refined minds, the richness of the work is, paradoxical as the statement may appear, a part of its humility. No architecture is so haughty as that which is simple: which refuses to address the eye, except in a few clear and forceful lines; which implies, in offering so little to our regards, that all it has offered is perfect; and disdains, either by the complexity or the attractiveness of its features, to embarrass our investigation, or betray us into delight. That humility, which is the very life of the Gothic school, is shown not only in the imperfection, but in the accumulation, of ornament. The inferior rank of the workman is often shown as much in the richness, as the roughness, of his work; and if the co-operation of every hand, and the sympathy of every heart, are to be received, we must be content to allow the redundance which disguises the failure of the feeble, and wins the regard of the inattentive. There are, however, far nobler interests mingling, in the Gothic heart, with the rude love of decorative accumulation: a magnificent enthusiasm, which feels as if it never could do enough to reach the fulness of its ideal; an unselfishness of sacrifice, which would rather cast fruitless labour before the altar than stand idle in the market; and, finally, a profound sympathy with the fulness and wealth of the material universe, rising out of that Naturalism whose operation we have already endeavoured to define. The sculptor who sought for his models among the forest leaves, could not but quickly and deeply feel that complexity need not involve the loss of grace, nor richness that of repose; and every hour which he spent in the study of the minute and various work of Nature, made him feel more forcibly the barrenness of what was best in that of man: nor is it to be wondered at, that, seeing her perfect and exquisite creations poured forth in a profusion which conception could not grasp nor calculation sum, he should think that it ill became him to be niggardly of his own rude craftsmanship; and where he saw throughout the universe a faultless beauty lavished on measureless spaces of broidered field and blooming mountain, to grudge his poor and imperfect labour to the few stones that he had raised one upon another, for habitation or memorial. The years of his life passed away before his task was accomplished; but generation succeeded generation with unwearied enthusiasm, and the cathedral front was at last lost in the tapestry of its traceries, like a rock among the thickets and herbage of spring.

We have now, I believe, obtained a view approaching to completeness of the various moral or imaginative elements which composed the inner spirit of Gothic architecture.

[Vol. II, Chap. 6]

Roman Renaissance

Unhappy and childish pride in knowledge . . . was the first constituent element of the Renaissance mind, and it was enough, of itself, to have cast it into swift decline: but it was aided by another form of pride, which was above called the Pride of State; and which we have next to examine.

It was noticed, in the second volume of *Modern Painters,* that the principle which had most power in retarding the modern school of portraiture was its constant expression of individual vanity and pride. And the reader cannot fail to have observed that one of the readiest and commonest ways in which the painter ministers to this vanity is by introducing the pedestal or shaft of a column, or some fragment, however simple, of Renaissance architecture, in the background of the portrait. And this is not merely because such architecture is bolder or grander than, in general, that of the apartments of a private house. No other architecture would produce the same effect in the same degree. The

richest Gothic, the most massive Norman, would not produce the same sense of exaltation as the simple and meagre
lines of the Renaissance.

And if we think over this matter a little, we shall soon
feel that in those meagre lines there is indeed an expression
of aristocracy in its worst characters; coldness, perfectness of
training, incapability of emotion, want of sympathy with
the weakness of lower men, blank, hopeless, haughty self-
sufficiency. All these characters are written in the Renaissance architecture as plainly as if they were graven on it in
words. For, observe, all other architectures have something
in them that common men can enjoy; some concession to the
simplicities of humanity, some daily bread for the hunger
of the multitude. Quaint fancy, rich ornament, bright
colour, something that shows a sympathy with men of
ordinary minds and hearts; and this wrought out, at least
in the Gothic, with a rudeness showing that the workman
did not mind exposing his own ignorance if he could please
others. But the Renaissance is exactly the contrary of all
this. It is rigid, cold, inhuman; incapable of glowing, of
stooping, of conceding for an instant. Whatever excellence
it has is refined, high-trained, and deeply erudite; a kind
which the architect well knows no common mind can taste.
He proclaims it to us aloud. "You cannot feel my work
unless you study Vitruvius. I will give you no gay colour, no
pleasant sculpture, nothing to make you happy; for I am a
learned man. All the pleasure you can have in anything I
do is in its proud breeding, its rigid formalism, its perfect
finish, its cold tranquility. I do not work for the vulgar, only
for the men of the academy and the court." . . .

While the older workman lavished his labour on the
minute niche and narrow casement, on the doorways no
higher than the head, and the contracted angles of the tur-
reted chamber, the Renaissance builder spared such cost and
toil in his detail, that he might spend it in bringing larger
stones from a distance; and restricted himself to rustication
and five orders, that he might load the ground with colossal
piers, and raise an ambitious barrenness of architecture, as

inanimate as it was gigantic, above the feasts and follies of
the powerful or the rich. The Titanic insanity extended
itself also into ecclesiastical design: the principal church in
Italy was built with little idea of any other admirableness
than that which was to result from its being huge; and the
religious impressions of those who enter it are to this day
supposed to be dependent, in a great degree, on their dis-
covering that they cannot span the thumbs of the statues
which sustain the vessels for holy water. . . .

But of all the evidence bearing upon this subject presented by the various art of the fifteenth century, none is
so interesting or so conclusive as that deduced from its
tombs. For, exactly in proportion as the pride of life became
more insolent, the fear of death became more servile; and
the difference in the manner in which the men of early and
later days adorned the sepulchre, confesses a still greater
difference in their manner of regarding death. To those he
came as the comforter and the friend, rest in his right hand,
hope in his left; to these as the humiliator, the spoiler, and
the avenger. And, therefore, we find the early tombs at once
simple and lovely in adornment, severe and solemn in their
expression; confessing the power, and accepting the peace, of
death, openly and joyfully; and in all their symbols marking
that the hope of resurrection lay only in Christ's righteousness; signed always with this simple utterance of the dead,
"I will lay me down in peace, and take my rest; for it is
thou, Lord, only that makest me dwell in safety." But the
tombs of the later ages are a ghastly struggle of mean pride
and miserable terror: the one mustering the statues of the
Virtues about the tomb, disguising the sarcophagus with
delicate sculpture, polishing the false periods of the elaborate epitaph, and filling with strained animation the features of the portrait statue; and the other summoning
underneath, out of the niche or from behind the curtain,
the frowning skull, or scythed skeleton, or some other more
terrible image of the enemy in whose defiance the whiteness
of the sepulchre had been set to shine above the whiteness
of the ashes. . . .

Tomaso Mocenigo was succeeded by the renowned Doge, Francesco Foscari, under whom, it will be remembered, the last additions were made to the Gothic Ducal Palace; additions which in form only, not in spirit, correspond to the older portions; since, during his reign, the transition took place which permits us no longer to consider the Venetian architecture as Gothic at all. He died in 1457, and his tomb is the first important example of Renaissance art.

Not, however, a good characteristic example. It is remarkable chiefly as introducing all the faults of the Renaissance at an early period, when its merits, such as they were, were yet undeveloped. Its claim to be rated as a classical composition is altogether destroyed by the remnants of Gothic feeling which cling to it here and there in their last forms of degradation; and of which, now that we find them thus corrupted, the sooner we are rid the better. Thus the sarcophagus is supported by a species of trefoiled arches; the bases of the shafts have still their spurs; and the whole tomb is covered by a pediment, with crockets and a pinnacle. We shall find that the perfect Renaissance is at least pure in its insipidity, and subtile in its vice; but this monument is remarkable as showing the refuse of one style encumbering the embryo of another, and all principles of life entangled either in the swaddling clothes or the shroud.

With respect to our present purpose, however, it is a monument of enormous importance. We have to trace, be it remembered, the pride of state in its gradual intrusion upon the sepulchre; and the consequent and correlative vanishing of the expressions of religious feeling and heavenly hope, together with the more and more arrogant setting forth of the virtues of the dead. Now this tomb is the largest and most costly we have yet seen; but its means of religious expression are limited to a single statue of Christ, small, and used merely as a pinnacle at the top. The rest of the composition is as curious as it is vulgar. The conceit, so often noticed as having been borrowed from the Pisan school, of angels withdrawing the curtains of the couch to look down upon the dead, was brought forward with increasing prominence by every succeeding sculptor; but, as we draw nearer to the Renaissance period, we find that the *angels* become of less importance, and the *curtains* of more. With the Pisans, the curtains are introduced as a motive for the angels; with the Renaissance sculptors, the angels are introduced merely as a motive for the curtains, which become every day more huge and elaborate. In the monument of Mocenigo, they have already expanded into a tent, with a pole in the centre of it; and in that of Foscari, for the first time, the *angels are absent altogether;* while the curtains are arranged in the form of an enormous French tent-bed, and are sustained at the flanks by two diminutive figures in Roman armour; substituted for the angels, merely that the sculptor might *show his knowledge* of classical costume. And now observe how often a fault in feeling induces also a fault in style. In the old tombs, the angels used to stand on or by the side of the sarcophagus; but their places are here to be occupied by the Virtues; and therefore, to sustain the diminutive Roman figures at the necessary height, each has a whole Corinthian pillar to himself, a pillar whose shaft is eleven feet high, and some three or four feet round: and because this was not high enough, it is put on a pedestal four feet and a half high; and has a spurred base besides of its own, a tall capital, then a huge bracket above the capital, and then another pedestal above the bracket, and on the top of all the diminutive figure who has charge of the curtains.

Under the canopy, thus arranged, is placed the sarcophagus with its recumbent figure. The statues of the Virgin and the saints have disappeared from it. In their stead, its panels are filled with half length figures of Faith, Hope, and Charity; while Temperance and Fortitude are at the Doge's feet. Justice and Prudence at his head, figures now the size of life, yet nevertheless recognizable only by their attributes; for, except that Hope raises her eyes, there is no difference in the character or expression of any of their faces,—they are nothing more than handsome Venetian women, in rather full and courtly dresses, and tolerably well thrown into postures for effect from below. Fortitude could not of course be placed in a graceful one without some sacrifice of her character, but that was of no consequence in the eyes of the sculptors of this period, so she leans back languidly, and nearly overthrows her own column; while Temperance, and Justice opposite to her, as neither the left hand of the one nor the right hand of the other could be seen from below, have been *left with one hand each.* . . .

But the most significant change in the treatment of these tombs, with respect to our immediate object, is in the form of the sarcophagus. It was above noted that, exactly in proportion to the degree of the pride of life expressed in any monument, would be also the fear of death; and therefore, as these tombs increase in splendour, in size, and beauty of workmanship, we perceive a gradual desire to *take away from the definite character of the sarcophagus.* In the earliest times, as we have seen, it was a gloomy mass of stone; gradually it became charged with religious sculpture; but never with the slightest desire to disguise its form, until towards the middle of the fifteenth century. It then becomes enriched with flower-work and hidden by the Virtues: and, finally, losing its four-square form, it is modelled on graceful types of ancient vases, made as little like a coffin as possible, and refined away in various elegances, till it becomes, at last, a mere pedestal or stage for the portrait statue. This statue, in the meantime, has been gradually coming back to life, through a curious series of transitions. The Vendramin monument* is one of the last which shows, or pretends to show, the recumbent figure laid in death. A few years later, this idea became disagreeable to polite minds; and, lo! the figures, which before had been laid at rest upon the tomb pillow, raised themselves on their elbows, and began to look round them. The soul of the sixteenth century dared not contemplate its body in death. . . .

* The Doge Andrea Vendramin died in 1478 and, after a brief, disastrous reign, was interred in an elaborate monument in the Church of SS. Giovanni e Paolo.

As of the intermediate monumental type, so also of this, the last and most gross, there are unfortunately many examples in our own country; but the most wonderful, by far, are still at Venice. I shall, however, particularise only two; the first, that of the Doge John Pesaro, in the Frari. It is to be observed that we have passed over a considerable interval of time; we are now in the latter half of the seventeenth century; the progress of corruption has in the meantime been incessant, and sculpture has here lost its taste and learning as well as its feeling. The monument is a huge accumulation of theatrical scenery in marble: four colossal negro caryatides, grinning and horrible, with faces of black marble and white eyes, sustain the first story of it; above this, two monsters, long-necked, half dog and half dragon, sustain an ornamental sarcophagus, on the top of which the full length statue of the Doge in robes of state stands forward with its arms expanded, like an actor courting applause, under a huge canopy of metal, like the roof of a bed, painted crimson and gold; on each side of him are sitting figures of genii, and unintelligible personifications gesticulating in Roman armour; below, between the negro caryatides, are two ghastly figures in bronze, half corpse, half skeleton, carrying tablets on which is written the eulogium: but in large letters, graven in gold, the following words are the first and last that strike the eye; the first two phrases, one on each side, on tablets in the lower story, the last under the portrait statue above:

Vixit annos LXX.   Devixit anno MDCLIX.
"Hic revixit anno MDCLXIX."

We have here, at last, the horrible images of death in violent contrast with the defiant monument, which pretends to bring the resurrection down to earth, "Hic revixit;" and it seems impossible for false taste and base feeling to sink lower. Yet even this monument is surpassed by one in St. John and Paul. . . .

There, towering from the pavement to the vaulting of

the church, behold a mass of marble, sixty or seventy feet in
height, of mingled yellow and white, the yellow carved into
the form of an enormous curtain, with ropes, fringes, and
tassels, sustained by cherubs; in front of which, in the now
usual stage attitudes, advance the statues of the Doge Bertuc-
cio Valier, his son the Doge Silvester Valier, and his son's
wife, Elisabeth. The statues of the Doges, though mean and
Polonius-like, are partly redeemed by the Ducal robes; but
that of the Dogaressa is a consummation of grossness, vanity,
and ugliness,—the figure of a large and wrinkled woman,
with elaborate curls in stiff projection round her face, covered from her shoulders to her feet with ruffs, furs, lace,
jewels, and embroidery. Beneath and around are scattered
Virtues, Victories, Fames, genii,—the entire company of the
monumental stage assembled, as before a drop scene, executed by various sculptors, and deserving attentive study as
exhibiting every condition of false taste and feeble conception. The Victory in the centre is peculiarly interesting; the
lion by which she is accompanied, springing on a dragon,
has been intended to look terrible, but the incapable sculptor could not conceive any form of dreadfulness, could not
even make the lion look angry. It looks only lachrymose;
and its lifted forepaws, there being no spring nor motion in
its body, give it the appearance of a dog begging. The in-
scriptions under the two principal statues are as follows:

> *"Bertucius Valier, Duke,*
> *Great in wisdom and eloquence,*
> *Greater in his Hellespontic victory,*
> *Greatest in the Prince his son,*
> *Died in the year 1658."*

> *"Elisabeth Quirina,*
> *The wife of Silvester,*
> *Distinguished by Roman virtue,*
> *By Venetian piety,*
> *And by the Ducal crown,*
> *Died 1708."*

The writers of this age were generally anxious to make the world aware that they understood the degrees of comparison, and a large number of epitaphs are principally constructed with this object . . . but the latter of these epitaphs is also interesting, from its mention, in an age now altogether given up to the pursuit of worldly honour, of that "Venetian piety" which once truly distinguished the city from all others; and of which some form and shadow, remaining still, served to point an epitaph, and to feed more cunningly and speciously the pride which could not be satiated with the sumptuousness of the sepulchre.

[Vol. III, Chap. 2]

Grotesque Renaissance

In the close of the last chapter it was noted that the phases of transition in the moral temper of the falling Venetians, during their fall, were from pride to infidelity, and from infidelity to the unscrupulous *pursuit of pleasure*. During the last years of the existence of the state, the minds both of the nobility and the people seem to have been set simply upon the attainment of the means of self-indulgence. There was not strength enough in them to be proud, nor forethought enough to be ambitious. One by one the possessions of the state were abandoned to its enemies; one by one the channels of its trade were forsaken by its own languor, or occupied and closed against it by its more energetic rivals; and the time, the resources, and the thoughts of the nation were exclusively occupied in the invention of such fantastic and costly pleasures as might best amuse their apathy, lull their remorse, or disguise their ruin.

The architecture raised at Venice during this period is among the worst and basest ever built by the hands of men, being especially distinguished by a spirit of brutal mockery and insolent jest, which, exhausting itself in deformed and monstrous sculpture, can sometimes be hardly otherwise defined than as the perpetuation in stone of the ribaldries of drunkenness. On such a period, and on such work, it is painful to dwell, and I had not originally intended to do so; but I found that the entire spirit of the Renaissance could not be comprehended unless it was followed to its consummation; and that there were many most interesting questions arising out of the study of this particular spirit of jesting, with reference to which I have called it the *Grotesque* Renaissance. For it is not this period alone which is distinguished by such a spirit. There is jest—perpetual, careless, and not unfrequently obscene—in the most noble work of the Gothic periods; and it becomes, therefore, of the greatest possible importance to examine into the nature and essence of the Grotesque itself, and to ascertain in what respect it is that the jesting of art in its highest flight differs from its jesting in its utmost degradation.

The place where we may best commence our inquiry is one renowned in the history of Venice, the space of ground before the Church of Santa Maria Formosa; a spot which, after the Rialto and St. Mark's Place, ought to possess a peculiar interest in the mind of the traveller, in consequence of its connexion with the most touching and true legend of the Brides of Venice. That legend is related at length in every Venetian history, and, finally, has been told by the poet Rogers, in a way which renders it impossible for any one to tell it after him. I have only, therefore, to remind the reader that the capture of the brides took place in the cathedral church, St. Pietro di Castello; and that this of Santa Maria Formosa is connected with the tale, only because it was yearly visited with prayers by the Venetian maidens, on the anniversary of their ancestors' deliverance. For that deliverance, their thanks were to be rendered to the Virgin; and there was no church then dedicated to the Virgin in Venice except this.

Neither of the cathedral church, nor of this dedicated to St. Mary the Beautiful, is one stone left upon another. But from that which has been raised on the site of the latter, we may receive a most important lesson, introductory to our immediate subject, if first we glance back to the traditional history of the church which has been destroyed.

No more honourable epithet than "traditional" can be attached to what is recorded concerning it, yet I should grieve to lose the legend of its first erection. The Bishop of Uderzo, driven by the Lombards from his bishopric, as he was praying beheld in a vision the Virgin Mother, who ordered him to found a church in her honour, in the place where he should see a white cloud rest. And when he went out, the white cloud went before him; and on the place where it rested he built a church, and it was called the Church of St. Mary the Beautiful, from the loveliness of the form in which she appeared in the vision. . . .

There is now but one landmark to guide the steps of the traveller to the place where the white cloud rested, and the shrine was built to St. Mary the Beautiful. Yet the spot is still worth his pilgrimage, for he may receive a lesson upon it, though a painful one. Let him first fill his mind with the fair images of the ancient festival, and then seek that landmark, the tower of the modern church, built upon the place where the daughters of Venice knelt yearly with her noblest lords; and let him look at the head that is carved on the base of the tower, still dedicated to St. Mary the Beautiful.

A head,—huge, inhuman, and monstrous,—leering in bestial degradation, too foul to be either pictured or described, or to be beheld for more than an instant: yet let it be endured for that instant; for in that head is embodied the type of the evil spirit to which Venice was abandoned in the fourth period of her decline; and it is well that we should see and feel the full horror of it on this spot, and know what pestilence it was that came and breathed upon her beauty, until it melted away like the white cloud from the ancient field of Santa Maria Formosa.

This head is one of many hundreds which disgrace the latest buildings of the city, all more or less agreeing in their

expression of sneering mockery, in most cases enhanced by
thrusting out the tongue. Most of them occur upon the
bridges, which were among the very last works undertaken
by the republic, several, for instance, upon the Bridge of
Sighs; and they are evidences of a delight in the contemplation of bestial vice, and the expression of low sarcasm,
which is, I believe, the most hopeless state into which the
human mind can fall. This spirit of idiotic mockery is, as I
have said, the most striking characteristic of the last period
of the Renaissance, which, in consequence of the character
thus imparted to its sculpture, I have called grotesque; but
it must be our immediate task, and it will be a most interesting one, to distinguish between this base grotesqueness, and
that magnificent condition of fantastic imagination, which
was above noticed as one of the chief elements of the Northern Gothic mind. . . .

First, then, it seems to me that the grotesque is, in almost
all cases, composed of two elements, one ludicrous, the other
fearful; that, as one or the other of these elements prevails,
the grotesque falls into two branches, sportive grotesque
and terrible grotesque; but that we cannot legitimately
consider it under these two aspects, because there are hardly
any examples which do not in some degree combine both
elements: there are few grotesques so utterly playful as to
be overcast with no shade of fearfulness, and few so fearful
as absolutely to exclude all ideas of jest. But although we
cannot separate the grotesque itself into two branches, we
may easily examine separately the two conditions of mind
which it seems to combine; and consider successively what
are the kinds of jest, and what the kinds of fearfulness,
which may be legitimately expressed in the various walks of
art, and how their expressions actually occur in the Gothic
and Renaissance schools.

Now all the forms of art which result from the comparatively recreative exertion of minds more or less blunted or
encumbered by other cares and toils, the art which we may

call generally art of the wayside, as opposed to that which is the business of men's lives, is, in the best sense of the word, Grotesque. And it is noble or inferior, first according to the tone of the minds which have produced it, and in proportion to their knowledge, wit, love of truth, and kindness; secondly, according to the degree of strength they have been able to give forth; but yet, however much we may find in it needing to be forgiven, always delightful so long as it is the work of good and ordinarily intelligent men. And its delightfulness ought mainly to consist *in those very imperfections* which mark it for work done in times of rest. It is not its own merit so much as the enjoyment of him who produced it, which is to be the source of the spectator's pleasure; it is to the strength of his sympathy, not to the accuracy of his criticism, that it makes appeal; and no man can indeed be a lover of what is best in the higher walks of art who has not feeling and charity enough to join in the rude sportiveness of hearts that have escaped out of prison, and to be thankful for the flowers which men have laid their burdens down to sow by the wayside. . . .

We have next to consider the expression throughout of the minds of men who indulge themselves in unnecessary play. It is evident that a large number of these men will be more refined and more highly educated than those who only play necessarily; their power of pleasure-seeking implies, in general, fortunate circumstances of life. It is evident also that their play will not be so hearty, so simple, or so joyful; and this deficiency of brightness will affect it in proportion to its unnecessary and unlawful continuance, until at last it becomes a restless and dissatisfied indulgence in excitement, or a painful delving after exhausted springs of pleasure.

The art through which this temper is expressed will, in all probability, be refined and sensual,—therefore, also assuredly feeble; and because, in the failure of the joyful energy of the mind, there will fail, also, its perceptions and its sympathies, it will be entirely deficient in expression of character and acuteness of thought, but will be peculiarly

restless, manifesting its desire for excitement in idle changes
of subject and purpose. Incapable of true imagination, it
will seek to supply its place by exaggerations, incoherences,
and monstrosities; and the form of the grotesque to which
it gives rise will be an incongruous chain of hackneyed
graces, idly thrown together,—prettinesses or sublimities,
not of its own invention, associated in forms which will be
absurd without being fantastic, and monstrous without being terrible. And because, in the continual pursuit of pleasure, men lose both cheerfulness and charity, there will be
small hilarity, but much malice, in this grotesque; yet a
weak malice, incapable of expressing its own bitterness, not
having grasp enough of truth to become forcible, and exhausting itself in impotent or disgusting caricature.

Of course, there are infinite ranks and kinds of this grotesque, according to the natural power of the minds which
originate it, and to the degree in which they have lost themselves. Its highest condition is that which first developed
itself among the enervated Romans, and which was brought
to the highest perfection of which it was capable by Raphael
in the arabesques of the Vatican. It may be generally described as an elaborate and luscious form of nonsense. Its
lower conditions are found in the common upholstery and
decorations which, over the whole of civilised Europe, have
sprung from this poisonous root; an artistical pottage, composed of nymphs, cupids, and satyrs, with shreddings of
heads and paws of meek wild beasts, and nondescript vegetables. And the lowest of all are those which have not even
graceful models to recommend them, but arise out of the
corruption of the higher schools, mingled with clownish or
bestial satire, as is the case in the later Renaissance of
Venice, which we were above examining. It is almost impossible to believe the depth to which the human mind can
be debased in following this species of grotesque. In a recent
Italian garden, the favourite ornaments frequently consist
of stucco images, representing, in dwarfish caricature, the
most disgusting types of manhood and womanhood which

can be found amidst the dissipation of the modern drawing-room; yet without either veracity or humour, and dependent, for whatever interest they possess, upon simple grossness of expression and absurdity of costume. Grossness, of one kind or another, is, indeed, an unfailing characteristic of the style; either latent, as in the refined sensuality of the more graceful arabesques, or, in the worst examples, manifested in every species of obscene conception and abominable detail. In the head, described in the opening of this chapter, at Santa Maria Formosa, the *teeth* are represented as *decayed.* . . .

The difficulty which, as I above stated, exists in distinguishing the playful from the terrible grotesque arises out of this cause: that the mind, under certain phases of excitement, *plays* with *terror,* and summons images which, if it were in another temper, would be awful, but of which, either in weariness or in irony, it refrains for the time to acknowledge the true terribleness. And the mode in which this refusal takes place distinguishes the noble from the ignoble grotesque. For the master of the noble grotesque knows the depth of all at which he seems to mock, and would feel it at another time, or feels it in a certain undercurrent of thought even while he jests with it; but the workman of the ignoble grotesque can feel and understand nothing, and mocks at all things with the laughter of the idiot and the cretin. . . .

In the true grotesque, a man of naturally strong feeling is accidentally or resolutely apathetic; in the false grotesque, a man naturally apathetic is forcing himself into temporary excitement. The horror which is expressed by the one comes upon him whether he will or not; that which is expressed by the other is sought out by him, and elaborated by his art. And therefore, also, because the fear of the one is true, and of true things, however fantastic its expression may be, there will be reality in it, and force. It is not a manufactured terribleness, whose author, when he had finished it, knew not if it would terrify any one else or not: but it is a terribleness taken from the life; a spectre which the workman indeed saw, and which, as it appalled him, will appal us also. But the other workman never felt any Divine fear; he never shuddered when he heard the cry from the burning towers of the earth,

"*Venga Medusa; sì lo farem di smalto.*"

He is stone already, and needs no gentle hand laid upon his eyes to save him.* . . .

There is, however, often another cause of difference than this. The true grotesque being the expression of the *repose* or play of a *serious* mind, there is a false grotesque opposed to it, which is the result of the *full exertion* of a *frivolous* one. . . . And herein lies the real distinction between the base grotesque of Raphael and the Renaissance, above alluded to, and the true Gothic grotesque. Those grotesques or arabesques of the Vatican, and other such work, which have become the patterns of ornamentation in modern times, are the fruit of great minds degraded to base objects. The care, skill, and science, applied to the distribution of the leaves, and the drawing of the figures, are intense, admirable, and accurate; therefore, they ought to have produced a grand and serious work, not a tissue of nonsense. If we can draw the human head perfectly, and are masters of its expression and its beauty, we have no business to cut it off, and hang it up by the hair at the end of a garland. If we can draw the human body in the perfection of its grace and movement, we have no business to take away its limbs, and terminate it with a bunch of leaves. Or rather, our doing so will imply that there is something wrong with us; that, if we can consent to use our best powers for such base and vain trifling, there must be something wanting in the powers themselves; and that, however skilful we may be, or however learned, we are wanting both in the earnestness

* *Inferno*, IX, 53. "Let Medusa come, so that we may change him into stone": thus the Furies threaten Dante, whose eyes Virgil shields from the mortal sight of Medusa.

which can apprehend a noble truth, and in the thoughtfulness which can feel a noble fear. No Divine terror will ever be found in the work of the man who wastes a colossal strength in elaborating toys; for the first lesson which that terror is sent to teach us is the value of the human soul, and the shortness of mortal time. . . .

It seems probable that nothing is so refreshing to the vulgar mind as some exercise of this [satiric] faculty, more especially on the failings of their superiors; and that, wherever the lower orders are allowed to express themselves freely, we shall find humour, more or less caustic, becoming a principal feature in their work. The classical and Renaissance manufactures of modern times having silenced the independent language of the operative, his humour and satire pass away in the word-wit which has of late become the especial study of the group of authors headed by Charles Dickens; all this power was formerly thrown into noble art, and became permanently expressed in the sculptures of the cathedral. It was never thought that there was anything discordant or improper in such a position: for the builders evidently felt very deeply a truth of which, in modern times, we are less cognizant: that folly and sin are, to a certain extent, synonymous, and that it would be well for mankind in general if all could be made to feel that wickedness is as contemptible as it is hateful. So that the vices were permitted to be represented under the most ridiculous forms, and the coarsest wit of the workman to be exhausted in conpleting the degradation of the creatures supposed to be subjected to them. . . .

Nor, indeed, is this altogether avoidable, for it is not possible to express intense wickedness without some condition of degradation. Malice, subtlety, and pride, in their extreme, cannot be written upon noble forms; and I am aware of no effort to represent the Satanic mind in the angelic form which has succeeded in painting. Milton succeeds only because he separately describes the movements of the mind, and therefore leaves himself at liberty to make the form heroic; but that form is never distinct enough to be painted. Dante, who will not leave even external forms obscure, degrades them before he can feel them to be demoniacal; so also John Bunyan: both of them, I think, having firmer faith than Milton's in their own creations, and deeper insight into the nature of sin. Milton makes his fiends too noble, and misses the foulness, inconstancy, and fury of wickedness. His Satan possesses some virtues, not the less virtues for being applied to evil purpose. Courage, resolution, patience, deliberation in counsel, this latter being eminently a wise and holy character, as opposed to the "Insania" of excessive sin: and all this, if not a shallow and false, is a smoothed and artistical, conception. On the other hand, I have always felt that there was a peculiar grandeur in the indescribable ungovernable fury of Dante's fiends, ever shortening its own powers, and disappointing its own purposes; the deaf, blind, speechless, unspeakable rage, fierce as the lightning, but erring from its mark or turning senselessly against itself, and still further debased by foulness of form and action. Something is indeed to be allowed for the rude feelings of the time, but I believe all such men as Dante are sent into the world at the time when they can do their work best; and that, it being appointed for him to give to mankind the most vigorous realisation possible both of Hell and Heaven, he was born both in the country and at the time which furnished the most stern opposition of Horror and Beauty, and permitted it to be written in the clearest terms. And, therefore, though there are passages in the *Inferno* which it would be impossible for any poet now to write, I look upon it as all the more perfect for them. For there can be no question but that one characteristic of excessive vice is indecency, a general baseness in its thoughts and acts concerning the body,* and that the full portraiture of it cannot be given without marking, and that in the

* Let the reader examine, with especial reference to this subject, the general character of the language of Iago. [Ruskin's note.]

strongest lines, this tendency to corporeal degradation; which, in the time of Dante, could be done frankly, but cannot now. And, therefore, I think the twenty-first and twenty-second books of the *Inferno* the most perfect portraitures of fiendish nature which we possess; and, at the same time, in their mingling of the extreme of horror (for it seems to me that the silent swiftness of the first demon, "con l' ali aperte e sovra i pie leggiero," cannot be surpassed in dreadfulness*) with ludicrous actions and images, they present the most perfect instances with which I am acquainted of the terrible grotesque. But the whole of the *Inferno* is full of this grotesque, as well as the *Faërie Queen;* and these two poems, together with the works of Albert Dürer, will enable the reader to study it in its noblest forms, without reference to Gothic cathedrals. . . .

From what we have seen to be its nature, we must, I think, be led to one most important conclusion: that wherever the human mind is healthy and vigorous in all its proportions, great in imagination and emotion no less than in intellect, and not overborne by an undue or hardened pre-eminence of the mere reasoning faculties, there the grotesque will exist in full energy. And, accordingly, I believe that there is no test of greatness in periods, nations, or men, more sure than the development, among them or in them, or a noble grotesque; and no test of comparative smallness or limitation, of one kind or another, more sure than the absence of grotesque invention, or incapability of understanding it. I think that the central man of all the world, as representing in perfect balance the imaginative, moral, and intellectual faculties, all at their highest, is Dante; and in him the grotesque reaches at once the most distinct and the most noble development to which it was ever brought in the human mind. The two other greatest men whom Italy has produced, Michael Angelo and Tintoret, show the same element in no less original strength, but oppressed in the one by his science, and in both by the spirit of the age in which they lived;

* xxi, 33: "With wings outspread, and feet of nimblest tread."

never, however, absent even in Michael Angelo, but stealing
forth continually in a strange and spectral way, lurking in
folds of raiment and knots of wild hair, and mountainous
confusions of crabby limb and cloudy drapery; and in
Tintoret, ruling the entire conceptions of his greatest works
to such a degree that they are an enigma or an offence, even
to this day, to all the petty disciples of a formal criticism.
Of the grotesque in our own Shakespeare I need hardly
speak, nor of its intolerableness to his French critics; nor
of that of Æschylus and Homer, as opposed to the lower
Greek writers; and so I believe it will be found, at all periods, in all minds of the first order. . . .

The development of [the grotesque in late Renaissance
Venice] took place under different laws from those which
regulate it in any other European city. For, great as we have
seen the Byzantine mind show itself to be in other directions, it was marked as that of a declining nation by the
absence of the grotesque element, and, owing to its influence, the early Venetian Gothic remained inferior to all
other schools in this particular character. Nothing can well
be more wonderful than its instant failure in any attempt
at the representation of ludicrous or fearful images, more
especially when it is compared with the magnificent grotesque of the neighbouring city of Verona, in which the
Lombard influence had full sway. Nor was it until the last
links of connexion with Constantinople had been dissolved,
that the strength of the Venetian mind could manifest itself
in this direction. But it had then a new enemy to encounter.
The Renaissance laws altogether checked its imagination in
architecture; and it could only obtain permission to express
itself by starting forth in the work of the Venetian painters,
filling them with monkeys and dwarfs, even amidst the most
serious subjects, and leading Veronese and Tintoret to the
most unexpected and wild fantasies of form and colour.
We may be deeply thankful for this peculiar reserve of
the Gothic grotesque character to the last days of Venice.

All over the rest of Europe it had been strongest in the days of imperfect art; magnificently powerful throughout the whole of the thirteenth century, tamed gradually in the fourteenth and fifteenth, and expiring in the sixteenth amidst anatomy and laws of art. But at Venice, it had not been received when it was elsewhere in triumph, and it fled to the lagoons for shelter when elsewhere it was oppressed. And it was arrayed by the Venetian painters in robes of state, and advanced by them to such honour as it had never received in its days of widest dominion; while, in return, it bestowed upon their pictures that fulness, piquancy, decision of parts, and mosaic-like intermingling of fancies, alternately brilliant and sublime, which were exactly what was most needed for the development of their unapproachable colour-power. . . .

Such, then, were the general tone and progress of the Venetian mind, up to the close of the seventeenth century. First, serious, religious, and sincere; then, though serious still, comparatively deprived of conscientiousness, and apt to decline into stern and subtle policy: in the first case, the spirit of the noble grotesque not showing itself in art at all, but only in speech and action; in the second case, developing itself in painting, through accessories and vivacities of composition, while perfect dignity was always preserved in portraiture. A third phase rapidly developed itself.

Once more, and for the last time, let me refer the reader to the important epoch of the death of the Doge Tomaso Mocenigo in 1423, long ago indicated as the commencement of the decline of the Venetian power. That commencement is marked not merely by the words of the dying Prince, but by a great and clearly legible sign. It is recorded, that on the accession of his successor, Foscari, to the throne, "SIFESTEGGIO DALLA CITTA UNO ANNO INTERO:" "The city kept festival for a whole year." Venice had in her childhood sown, in tears, the harvest she was to reap in rejoicing. She now sowed in laughter the seeds of death.

Thenceforward, year after year, the nation drank with

deeper thirst from the fountains of forbidden pleasure, and dug for springs, hitherto unknown, in the dark places of the earth. In the ingenuity of indulgence, in the varieties of vanity, Venice surpassed the cities of Christendom, as of old she had surpassed them in fortitude and devotion; and as once the powers of Europe stood before her judgment-seat, to receive the decisions of her justice, so now the youth of Europe assembled in the halls of her luxury, to learn from her the arts of delight.

It is as needless as it is painful to trace the steps of her final ruin. That ancient curse was upon her, the curse of the Cities of the Plain, "Pride, fulness of bread, and abundance of idleness." By the inner burning of her own passions, as fatal as the fiery rain of Gomorrah, she was consumed from her place among the nations; and her ashes are choking the channels of the dead, salt sea.

[Vol. III, Chap. 3]

Society

It is tempting to take 1860—the year *Modern Painters* was completed and the precise mid-point of Ruskin's life—as the dividing line on one side of which falls his career as art critic and on the other, with the publication of *Unto This Last* also in 1860, his career as a critic of society. But the change was one of emphasis, not of direction. During the 1850s Ruskin had become less concerned with the study of art than with the creation of social conditions under which the arts might flourish. "Beautiful art," he told his audiences, "can only be produced by people who have beautiful things about them, and leisure to look at them." But England had turned her cities into furnaces and her artisans into slaves of the machine. This is the theme of "Modern Manufacture and Design," and it runs throughout the lectures Ruskin gave in the industrial Midlands in the late 1850s. Published as *The Political Economy of Art* (1857) and *The Two Paths* (1859), the lectures are an expansion of "The Nature of Gothic" and a prelude to *Unto This Last*.

Victorian England was so hostile to the message of *Unto This Last* that for more than a decade after its publication the book was virtually unread. Ruskin was denounced as a monger of heresies who must be crushed, lest his wild words open a "moral floodgate . . . and drown us all." If the uproar over *Unto This Last* now seems excessive, we need only recall that Ruskin attacked every principle held sacred by the economists and industrialists of the age, and that the book appeared at a time when the life of the industrial worker was barely above the level of animal survival. Yet the reforms which Ruskin advocated in *Unto This Last* are almost item for item those effected in the past half century, and we are slowly realizing the balance of his program. It would require a revolution to undo the bloodless revolution which his book helped bring about.

Clement Attlee, who was converted to socialism after reading the works of Ruskin and his disciple William Morris, dates the birth of the Labour Party in 1906, when twenty-nine independent Labourites were returned to the House of Commons; according to a questionnaire circulated among them, the book which most profoundly influenced their thought was *Unto This Last*. By 1910 one hundred thousand copies had been sold and several unauthorized editions had been printed in America. Translations appeared in French, German, and Italian; and a then obscure disciple of Ruskin prepared an edition in Gujarati, an Indic dialect.

Gandhi entitled his translation *Sarvodaya*, or "The Welfare of All." His phrase renders perfectly the point of the book and the parable from which its title derives. Over the protests of those who had labored through the heat of the day, the master of the vineyard paid all alike the same wage, even those who were hired at the eleventh hour: "Friend, I do thee no wrong. . . . Take that thine is, and go thy way: I will give unto this last, even as unto thee." Ruskin's state is a secular image of the Lord's vineyard, in which labor is not forced to compete against itself and capital provides a living wage for those who work or are forced into idleness.

Gospel parables appear irrelevant to a treatise on economics if one holds that the subject is concerned exclusively with marketable commodities, and not at all with the human beings who make and consume them. But Ruskin insisted that the market place cannot be sealed off from the rest of life and that economics, when not simply statistics, is indissolubly linked to ethics. He perceived that the political economists were as deluded in deriving their principles from a hypothetical Economic Man, devoid of all motives save acquisitiveness, as were the aestheticians with their hypothetical Aesthetic Man, a mere disembodied perceiver of beauty. Ruskin's contribution to economics rests on his humanization of the concept of value. The whole argument of *Unto This Last* culminates in a single sentence: "There is no Wealth but Life."

Unto This Last first appeared serially in the *Cornhill Magazine,* under the editorship of Thackeray. Because of the hostility the articles aroused, Thackeray was compelled to notify Ruskin that the fourth installment would have to be the last. It was a felicitous injunction. In the final essay Ruskin said all that was essential, the remainder spilling over into a lesser sequel, *Munera Pulveris.* The result was the finest achievement of Ruskin's middle years.

Throughout the 1860s Ruskin continued to channel his energies into social criticism. But he was no longer capable of the sustained and disciplined coherence he had achieved in *The Stones of Venice* and *Unto This Last.* Nor had he yet learned to make a virtue of his vagaries, as he did in the 1870s, when he created in *Fors Clavigera* a new genre uniquely suited to his erratic gifts. The public lecture now became his characteristic form. Although *Sesame and Lilies* (1865) and *The Crown of Wild Olive* (1866) contain some of his most memorable writing, they are not properly books but collections of miscellaneous addresses on related themes.

They are above all angry lectures, full of rage at the barbarism of a professedly Christian society. Their energy arises from the same burning outrage at injustice and pretended piety that had inflamed the Prophets. And Ruskin takes the Prophets' bold license of insulting his hearers. The heart of his address "Of Kings' Treasuries" is an indictment of the illiteracy and cruelty of his seemingly literate, compassionate audience. Only a nation which despises compassion could tolerate the newspaper account he cites of a half-blind cobbler who was found starved to death in his lodgings. Ruskin condemns his audience precisely as he condemned himself for enjoying luxury in the midst of poverty. "The cruelest man living," he wrote in *Unto This Last,* "could not sit at his feast, unless he sat blindfold." Ruskin sat with eyes opened and, unable to forgive himself, could not forgive others. A letter he wrote to Charles Eliot Norton in 1863 reveals his anxious inner conflict more starkly than anything he said in public: "I am . . . tormented between the longing for rest . . . and the sense of the terrific call of human crime for resistance and of human misery for help—though it seems to me as the voice of a river of blood which can but sweep me down in the midst of its black clots, helpless."

Ruskin had come to despise the reputation he had won in his earlier books as an eloquent adjudicator of taste. Something of his contempt for this popular misconception finds its way into the savagely satiric passages of his lecture on "Traffic." He had been invited to address the citizens of Bradford on the proper style for their new stock exchange. But the invitation went out ten years too late. Ruskin had ceased to care about architectural styles when he saw his plea for the spirit of Gothic parodied by dismal churches and gingerbread pubs. And so, instead of advising his audience on the latest mode in pinnacles, he attacked their corrupted taste and, through it, the Mammonite values of the whole nation. The lecture is a brilliant distillation of all that Ruskin had learned in the two decades since he had written the opening lines of *The Seven Lamps.*

—J. D. R.

THE TWO PATHS

*Modern Manufacture and Design**

The changes in the state of this country are now so rapid, that it would be wholly absurd to endeavour to lay down laws of art education for it under its present aspect and circumstances; and therefore I must necessarily ask, how much of it do you seriously intend within the next fifty years to be coal-pit, brick-field, or quarry? For the sake of distinctness of conclusion, I will suppose your success absolute: that from shore to shore the whole of the island is to be set as thick with chimneys as the masts stand in the docks of Liverpool: that there shall be no meadows in it; no trees; no gardens; only a little corn grown upon the housetops, reaped and threshed by steam: that you do not leave even room for roads, but travel either over the roofs of your mills, on viaducts; or under their floors, in tunnels: that, the smoke having rendered the light of the sun unserviceable, you work always by the light of your own gas: that no acre of English ground shall be without its shaft and its engine; and therefore, no spot of English ground left, on which it shall be possible to stand, without a definite and calculable chance of being blown off it, at any moment, into small pieces.

Under these circumstances, (if this is to be the future of England,) no designing or any other development of beautiful art will be possible. Do not vex your minds, nor waste your money with any thought or effort in the matter. Beauti-

* Delivered at the Mechanics' Institute, Bradford, March 1, 1859.

ful art can only be produced by people who have beautiful things about them, and leisure to look at them; and unless you provide some elements of beauty for your workmen to be surrounded by, you will find that no elements of beauty can be invented by them.

I was struck forcibly by the bearing of this great fact upon our modern efforts at ornamentation in an afternoon walk, last week, in the suburbs of one of our large manufacturing towns. I was thinking of the difference in the effect upon the designer's mind, between the scene which I then came upon, and the scene which would have presented itself to the eyes of any designer of the Middle Ages, when he left his workshop. Just outside the town I came upon an old English cottage, or mansion, I hardly know which to call it, set close under the hill, and beside the river, perhaps built somewhere in the Charleses' times, with mullioned windows and a low arched porch; round which, in the little triangular garden, one can imagine the family as they used to sit in old summer times, the ripple of the river heard faintly through the sweetbriar hedge, and the sheep on the far-off wolds shining in the evening sunlight. There, uninhabited for many and many a year, it had been left in unregarded havoc of ruin; the garden-gate still swung loose to its latch; the garden, blighted utterly into a field of ashes, not even a weed taking root there; the roof torn into shapeless rents; the shutters hanging about the windows in rags of rotten wood; before its gate, the stream which had gladdened it now soaking slowly by, black as ebony and thick with curdling scum; the bank above it trodden into unctuous, sooty slime: far in front of it, between it and the old hills, the furnaces of the city foaming forth perpetual plague of sulphurous darkness; the volumes of their storm clouds coiling low over a waste of grassless fields, fenced from each other, not by hedges, but by slabs of square stone, like gravestones, riveted together with iron.

That was your scene for the designer's contemplation in his afternoon walk at Rochdale. Now fancy what was the

scene which presented itself, in his afternoon walk, to a designer of the Gothic school of Pisa—Nino Pisano, or any of
his men.

On each side of a bright river he saw rise a line of brighter
palaces, arched and pillared, and inlaid with deep red
porphyry, and with serpentine; along the quays before their
gates were riding troops of knights, noble in face and form,
dazzling in crest and shield; horse and man one labyrinth of
quaint colour and gleaming light—the purple, and silver,
and scarlet fringes flowing over the strong limbs and clashing
mail, like sea-waves over rocks at sunset. Opening on each
side from the river were gardens, courts, and cloisters; long
successions of white pillars among wreaths of vine; leaping
of fountains through buds of pomegranate and orange: and
still along the garden paths, and under and through the
crimson of the pomegranate shadows, moving slowly, groups
of the fairest women that Italy ever saw—fairest, because
purest and thoughtfullest; trained in all high knowledge, as
in all courteous art—in dance, in song, in sweet wit, in lofty
learning, in loftier courage, in loftiest love—able alike to
cheer, to enchant, or save, the souls of men. Above all this
scenery of perfect human life, rose dome and bell-tower,
burning with white alabaster and gold: beyond dome and
bell-tower the slopes of mighty hills, hoary with olive; far
in the north, above a purple sea of peaks of solemn Apennine, the clear, sharp-cloven Carrara mountains sent up
their steadfast flames of marble summit into amber sky; the
great sea itself, scorching with expanse of light, stretching
from their feet to the Gorgonian isles; and over all these,
ever present, near or far—seen through the leaves of vine,
or imaged with all its march of clouds in the Arno's stream,
or set with its depth of blue close against the golden hair
and burning cheek of lady and knight,—the untroubled
and sacred sky, which was to all men, in those days of innocent faith, indeed the unquestioned abode of spirits, as
the earth was of men; and which opened straight through
its gates of cloud and veils of dew into the awfulness of the

eternal world;—a heaven in which every cloud that passed was literally the chariot of an angel, and every ray of its Evening and Morning streamed from the throne of God.

What think you of that for a school of design?

I do not bring this contrast before you as a ground of hopelessness in our task; neither do I look for any possible renovation of the Republic of Pisa, at Bradford, in the nineteenth century; but I put it before you in order that you may be aware precisely of the kind of difficulty you have to meet, and may then consider with yourselves how far you can meet it. To men surrounded by the depressing and monotonous circumstances of English manufacturing life, depend upon it, design is simply impossible. This is the most distinct of all the experiences I have had in dealing with the modern workman. He is intelligent and ingenious in the highest degree—subtle in touch and keen in sight: but he is, generally speaking, wholly destitute of designing power. And if you want to give him the power, you must give him the materials, and put him in the circumstances for it. Design is not the offspring of idle fancy: it is the studied result of accumulative observation and delightful habit. Without observation and experience, no design— without peace and pleasurableness in occupation, no design —and all the lecturings, and teachings, and prizes, and principles of art, in the world, are of no use, so long as you don't surround your men with happy influences and beautiful things. It is impossible for them to have right ideas about colour, unless they see the lovely colours of nature unspoiled; impossible for them to supply beautiful incident and action in their ornament, unless they see beautiful incident and action in the world about them. Inform their minds, refine their habits, and you form and refine their designs; but keep them illiterate, uncomfortable, and in the midst of unbeautiful things, and whatever they do will still be spurious, vulgar, and valueless.

I repeat, that I do not ask you nor wish you to build a new Pisa for them. We don't want either the life or the decorations of the thirteenth century back again; and the circumstances with which you must surround your workmen are those simply of happy modern English life, because the designs you have now to ask for from your workmen are such as will make modern English life beautiful. All that gorgeousness of the Middle Ages, beautiful as it sounds in description, noble as in many respects it was in reality, had, nevertheless, for foundation and for end, nothing but the pride of life—the pride of the so-called superior classes; a pride which supported itself by violence and robbery, and led in the end to the destruction both of the arts themselves and the States in which they flourished.

The great lesson of history is, that all the fine arts hitherto—having been supported by the selfish power of the noblesse, and never having extended their range to the comfort or the relief of the mass of the people—the arts, I say, thus practised, and thus matured, have only accelerated the ruin of the States they adorned; and at the moment when, in any kingdom, you point to the triumphs of its greatest artists, you point also to the determined hour of the kingdom's decline. The names of great painters are like passing bells: in the name of Velasquez, you hear sounded the fall of Spain; in the name of Titian, that of Venice; in the name of Leonardo, that of Milan; in the name of Raphael, that of Rome. And there is profound justice in this; for in proportion to the nobleness of the power is the guilt of its use for purposes vain or vile; and hitherto the greater the art, the more surely has it been used, and used solely, for the decoration of pride, or the provoking of sensuality. Another course lies open to us. We may abandon the hope—or if you like the words better—we may disdain the temptation, of the pomp and grace of Italy in her youth. For us there can be no more the throne of marble—for us no more the vault of gold—but for us there is the loftier and lovelier privilege of bringing the power and charm of art within the reach of the humble and the poor; and as the magnificence of past ages failed by its narrowness and its pride, ours may prevail and continue, by its universality and its lowliness. . . .

And you must remember always that your business, as manufacturers, is to form the market, as much as to supply it. If, in short-sighted and reckless eagerness for wealth, you catch at every humour of the populace as it shapes itself into momentary demand—if, in jealous rivalry with neighbouring States, or with other producers, you try to attract attention by singularities, novelties, and gaudinesses—to make every design an advertisement, and pilfer every idea of a successful neighbour's, that you may insidiously imitate it, or pompously eclipse—no good design will ever be possible to you, or perceived by you. You may, by accident, snatch the market; or, by energy, command it; you may obtain the confidence of the public, and cause the ruin of opponent houses; or you may, with equal justice of fortune, be ruined by them. But whatever happens to you, this, at least, is certain, that the whole of your life will have been spent in corrupting public taste and encouraging public extravagance. Every preference you have won by gaudiness must have been based on the purchaser's vanity; every demand you have created by novelty has fostered in the consumer a habit of discontent; and when you retire into inactive life, you may, as a subject of consolation for your declining years, reflect that precisely according to the extent of your past operations, your life has been successful in retarding the arts, tarnishing the virtues, and confusing the manners of your country.

The Roots of Honour

Among the delusions which at different periods have possessed themselves of the minds of large masses of the human
race, perhaps the most curious—certainly the least creditable—is the modern *soi-disant* science of political economy,
based on the idea that an advantageous code of social action
may be determined irrespectively of the influence of social
affection.

Of course, as in the instances of alchemy, astrology, witchcraft, and other such popular creeds, political economy has
a plausible idea at the root of it. "The social affections,"
says the economist, "are accidental and disturbing elements
in human nature; but avarice and the desire of progress are
constant elements. Let us eliminate the inconstants, and,
considering the human being merely as a covetous machine,
examine by what laws of labour, purchase, and sale, the
greatest accumulative result in wealth is obtainable. Those
laws once determined, it will be for each individual afterwards to introduce as much of the disturbing affectionate
element as he chooses, and to determine for himself the
result on the new conditions supposed."

This would be a perfectly logical and successful method
of analysis, if the accidentals afterwards to be introduced
were of the same nature as the powers first examined. Supposing a body in motion to be influenced by constant and
inconstant forces, it is usually the simplest way of examining its course to trace it first under the persistent conditions,

and afterwards introduce the causes of variation. But the disturbing elements in the social problem are not of the same nature as the constant ones: they alter the essence of the creature under examination the moment they are added; they operate, not mathematically, but chemically, introducing conditions which render all our previous knowledge unavailable. We made learned experiments upon pure nitrogen, and have convinced ourselves that it is a very manageable gas: but, behold! the thing which we have practically to deal with is its chloride; and this, the moment we touch it on our established principles, sends us and our apparatus through the ceiling.

Observe, I neither impugn nor doubt the conclusion of the science if its terms are accepted. I am simply uninterested in them, as I should be in those of a science of gymnastics which assumed that men had no skeletons. It might be shown, on that supposition, that it would be advantageous to roll the students up into pellets, flatten them into cakes, or stretch them into cables; and that when these results were effected, the re-insertion of the skeleton would be attended with various inconveniences to their constitution. The reasoning might be admirable, the conclusions true, and the science deficient only in applicability. Modern political economy stands on a precisely similar basis. Assuming, not that the human being has no skeleton, but that it is all skeleton, it founds an ossifant theory of progress on this negation of a soul; and having shown the utmost that may be made of bones, and constructed a number of interesting geometrical figures with death's-head and humeri, successfully proves the inconvenience of the reappearance of a soul among these corpuscular structures. I do not deny the truth of this theory: I simply deny its applicability to the present phase of the world.

This inapplicability has been curiously manifested during the embarrassment caused by the late strikes of our workmen. Here occurs one of the simplest cases, in a pertinent and positive form, of the first vital problem which political economy has to deal with (the relation between employer and employed); and, at a severe crisis, when lives in multitudes and wealth in masses are at stake, the political economists are helpless—practically mute: no demonstrable solution of the difficulty can be given by them, such as may convince or calm the opposing parties. Obstinately the masters take one view of the matter; obstinately the operatives another; and no political science can set them at one.

It would be strange if it could, it being not by 'science" of any kind that men were ever intended to be set at one. Disputant after disputant vainly strives to show that the interests of the masters are, or are not, antagonistic to those of the men: none of the pleaders ever seeming to remember that it does not absolutely or always follow that the persons must be antagonistic because their interests are. If there is only a crust of bread in the house, and mother and children are starving, their interests are not the same. If the mother eats it, the children want it; if the children eat it, the mother must go hungry to her work. Yet it does not necessarily follow that there will be "antagonism" between them, that they will fight for the crust, and that the mother, being strongest, will get it, and eat it. Neither, in any other case, whatever the relations of the persons may be, can it be assumed for certain that, because their interests are diverse, they must necessarily regard each other with hostility, and use violence or cunning to obtain the advantage.

Even if this were so, and it were as just as it is convenient to consider men as actuated by no other moral influences than those which affect rats or swine, the logical conditions of the question are still indeterminable. It can never be shown generally either that the interests of master and labourer are alike, or that they are opposed; for, according to circumstances, they may be either. It is, indeed, always the interest of both that the work should be rightly done, and a just price obtained for it; but, in the division of profits, the gain of the one may or may not be the loss of the other. It is not the master's interest to pay wages so low as to leave the men sickly and depressed, nor the workman's interest to be paid high wages if the smallness of the master's profit hinders him from enlarging his business, or conducting it in a safe and liberal way. A stoker ought not to desire high pay if the company is too poor to keep the engine-wheels in repair.

And the varieties of circumstances which influence these reciprocal interests are so endless, that all endeavour to deduce rules of action from balance of expediency is in vain. And it is meant to be in vain. For no human actions ever were intended by the Maker of men to be guided by balances of expediency, but by balances of justice. He has therefore rendered all endeavours to determine expediency futile for evermore. No man ever knew, or can know, what will be the ultimate result to himself, or to others, of any given line of conduct. But every man may know, and most of us do know, what is a just and unjust act. And all of us may know also, that the consequences of justice will be ultimately the best possible, both to others and ourselves, though we can neither say what *is* best, or how it is likely to come to pass.

I have said balances of justice, meaning, in the term justice, to include affection,—such affection as one man *owes* to another. All right relations between master and operative, and all their best interests, ultimately depend on these.

We shall find the best and simplest illustration of the relations of master and operative in the position of domestic servants.

We will suppose that the master of a household desires only to get as much work out of his servants as he can, at the rate of wages he gives. He never allows them to be idle; feeds them as poorly and lodges them as ill as they will endure, and in all things pushes his requirements to the exact point beyond which he cannot go without forcing the servant to leave him. In doing this, there is no violation on his part of what is commonly called "justice." He agrees with the domestic for his whole time and service, and takes them;—the limits of hardship in treatment being fixed by the practice of other masters in his neighbourhood; that is to say, by the current rate of wages for domestic labour. If the servant can get a better place, he is free to take one, and the master can only tell what is the real market value of his labour, by requiring as much as he will give.

This is the politico-economical view of the case, according to the doctors of that science; who assert that by this procedure the greatest average of work will be obtained from the servant, and therefore the greatest benefit to the community, and through the community, by reversion, to the servant himself.

That, however, is not so. It would be so if the servant were an engine of which the motive power was steam, magnetism, gravitation, or any other agent of calculable force. But he being, on the contrary, an engine whose motive power is a Soul, the force of this very peculiar agent, as an unknown quantity, enters into all the political economist's equations, without his knowledge, and falsifies every one of their results. The largest quantity of work will not be done by this curious engine for pay, or under pressure, or by help of any kind of fuel which may be supplied by the chaldron. It will be done only when the motive force, that is to say, the will or spirit of the creature, is brought to its greatest strength by its own proper fuel: namely, by the affections. . . .

In any case, and with any person, this unselfish treatment will produce the most effective return. Observe, I am here considering the affections wholly as a motive power; not at all as things in themselves desirable or noble, or in any other way abstractedly good. I look at them simply as an anomalous force, rendering every one of the ordinary political economist's calculations nugatory; while, even if he desired to introduce this new element into his estimates, he has no power of dealing with it; for the affections only become a true motive power when they ignore every other motive and condition of political economy. Treat the servant kindly, with the idea of turning his gratitude to account, and you will get, as you deserve, no gratitude, nor any value for your kindness; but treat him kindly without any economical purpose, and all economical purposes will be answered; in this, as in all other matters, whosoever will save his life shall lose it, whoso loses it shall find it.*

The next clearest and simplest example of relation between master and operative is that which exists between the commander of a regiment and his men.

Supposing the officer only desires to apply the rules of discipline so as, with least trouble to himself, to make the regiment most effective, he will not be able, by any rules or administration of rules, on this selfish principle, to develop the full strength of his subordinates. If a man of sense and firmness, he may, as in the former instance, produce a better result than would be obtained by the irregular kindness of a weak officer; but let the sense and firmness be the same in both cases, and assuredly the officer who has the most direct personal relations with his men, the most care for their interests, and the most value for their lives, will develop

* The difference between the two modes of treatment, and between their effective material results, may be seen very accurately by a comparison of the relations of Esther and Charlie in *Bleak House* with those of Miss Brass and the Marchioness in *Master Humphrey's Clock.*

The essential value and truth of Dickens's writings have been unwisely lost sight of by many thoughtful persons, merely because he presents his truth with some colour of caricature. Allowing for his manner of telling them, the things he tells us are always true. I wish that he could think it right to limit his brilliant exaggeration to works written only for public amusement; and when he takes up a subject of high national importance, such as that which he handled in *Hard Times,* that he would use severer and more accurate analysis. The usefulness of that work (to my mind, in several respects the greatest he has written) is with many persons seriously diminished because Mr. Bounderby is a dramatic monster, instead of a characteristic example of a worldly master; and Stephen Blackpool a dramatic perfection, instead of a characteristic example of an honest workman. But let us not lose the use of Dickens's wit and insight, because he chooses to speak in a circle of stage fire. [Ruskin's note.]

their effective strength, through their affection for his own person, and trust in his character, to a degree wholly unattainable by other means. This law applies still more stringently as the numbers concerned are larger: a charge may often be successful, though the men dislike their officers; a battle has rarely been won, unless they loved their general.

Passing from these simple examples to the more complicated relations existing between a manufacturer and his workmen, we are met first by certain curious difficulties, resulting, apparently, from a harder and colder state of moral elements. It is easy to imagine an enthusiastic affection existing among soldiers for the colonel. Not so easy to imagine an enthusiastic affection among cotton-spinners for the proprietor of the mill. A body of men associated for purposes of robbery (as a Highland clan in ancient times) shall be animated by perfect affection, and every member of it be ready to lay down his life for the life of his chief. But a band of men associated for purposes of legal production and accumulation is usually animated, it appears, by no such emotions, and none of them are in any wise willing to give his life for the life of his chief. Not only are we met by this apparent anomaly, in moral matters, but by others connected with it, in administration of system. For a servant or a soldier is engaged at a definite rate of wages, for a definite period; but a workman at a rate of wages variable according to the demand for labour, and with the risk of being at any time thrown out of his situation by chances of trade. Now, as, under these contingencies, no action of the affections can take place, but only an explosive action of disaffections, two points offer themselves for consideration in the matter.

The first—How far the rate of wages may be so regulated as not to vary with the demand for labour.

The second—How far it is possible that bodies of workmen may be engaged and maintained at such fixed rate of wages (whatever the state of trade may be), without enlarging or diminishing their number, so as to give them permanent interest in the establishment with which they are connected, like that of the domestic servants in an old family, or an *esprit de corps,* like that of the soldiers in a crack regiment.

The first question is, I say, how far it may be possible to fix the rate of wages, irrespectively of the demand for labour.

Perhaps one of the most curious facts in the history of human error is the denial by the common political economist of the possibility of thus regulating wages; while, for all the important, and much of the unimportant, labour, on the earth, wages are already so regulated.

We do not sell our prime-ministership by Dutch auction; nor, on the decease of a bishop, whatever may be the general advantages of simony, do we (yet) offer his diocese to the clergyman who will take the episcopacy at the lowest contract. We (with exquisite sagacity of political economy!) do indeed sell commissions; but not openly, generalships: sick, we do not inquire for a physician who takes less than a guinea; litigious, we never think of reducing six-and-eight-pence to four-and-sixpence; caught in a shower, we do not canvass the cabmen, to find one who values his driving at less than sixpence a mile.

It is true that in all these cases there is, and in every conceivable case there must be, ultimate reference to the presumed difficulty of the work, or number of candidates for the office. If it were thought that the labour necessary to make a good physician would be gone through by a sufficient number of students with the prospect of only half-guinea fees, public consent would soon withdraw the unnecessary half-guinea. In this ultimate sense, the price of labour is indeed always regulated by the demand for it; but, so far as the practical and immediate administration of the matter is regarded, the best labour always has been, and is, as *all* labour ought to be, paid by an invariable standard.

"What!" the reader perhaps answers amazedly: "pay good and bad workmen alike?"

Certainly. The difference between one prelate's sermons

and his successor's—or between one physician's opinion and another's—is far greater, as respects the qualities of mind involved, and far more important in result to you personally, than the difference between good and bad laying of bricks (though that is greater than most people suppose). Yet you pay with equal fee, contentedly, the good and bad workmen upon your soul, and the good and bad workmen upon your body; much more may you pay, contentedly, with equal fees, the good and bad workmen upon your house.

"Nay, but I choose my physician and (?) my clergyman, thus indicating my sense of the quality of their work." By all means, also, choose your bricklayer; that is the proper reward of the good workman, to be "chosen." The natural and right system respecting all labour is, that it should be paid at a fixed rate, but the good workman employed, and the bad workman unemployed. The false, unnatural, and destructive system is when the bad workman is allowed to offer his work at half-price, and either take the place of the good, or force him by his competition to work for an inadequate sum.

This equality of wages, then, being the first object toward which we have to discover the directest available road; the second is, as above stated, that of maintaining constant numbers of workmen in employment, whatever may be the accidental demand for the article they produce.

I believe the sudden and extensive inequalities of demand, which necessarily arise in the mercantile operations of an active nation, constitute the only essential difficulty which has to be overcome in a just organization of labour. The subject opens into too many branches to admit of being investigated in a paper of this kind; but the following general facts bearing on it may be noted.

The wages which enable any workman to live are necessarily higher, if his work is liable to intermission, than if it is assured and continuous; and however severe the struggle for work may become, the general law will always hold, that men must get more daily pay if, on the average, they can only calculate on work three days a week than they would require if they were sure of work six days a week. Supposing that a man cannot live on less than a shilling a day, his seven shillings he must get, either for three days' violent work, or six days' deliberate work. The tendency of all modern mercantile operations is to throw both wages and trade into the form of a lottery, and to make the workman's pay depend on intermittent exertion, and the principal's profit on dexterously used chance.

In what partial degree, I repeat, this may be necessary in consequence of the activities of modern trade, I do not here investigate; contenting myself with the fact, that in its fatalest aspects it is assuredly unnecessary, and results merely from love of gambling on the part of the masters, and from ignorance and sensuality in the men. The masters cannot bear to let any opportunity of gain escape them, and frantically rush at every gap and breach in the walls of Fortune, raging to be rich, and affronting, with impatient covetousness, every risk of ruin, while the men prefer three days of violent labour, and three days of drunkenness, to six days of moderate work and wise rest. . . .

I have already alluded to the difference hitherto existing between regiments of men associated for purposes of violence, and for purposes of manufacture; in that the former appear capable of self-sacrifice—the latter, not; which singular fact is the real reason of the general lowness of estimate in which the profession of commerce is held, as compared with that of arms. Philosophically, it does not, at first sight, appear reasonable (many writers have endeavoured to prove it unreasonable) that a peaceable and rational person, whose trade is buying and selling, should be held in less honour than an unpeaceable and often irrational person, whose trade is slaying. Nevertheless, the consent of mankind has always, in spite of the philosophers, given precedence to the soldier.

And this is right.

For the soldier's trade, verily and essentially, is not slaying, but being slain. This, without well knowing its own meaning, the world honours it for. A bravo's trade is slaying; but the world has never respected bravos more than merchants: the reason it honours the soldier is, because he holds his life at the service of the State. Reckless he may be —fond of pleasure or of adventure—all kinds of bye-motives and mean impulses may have determined the choice of his profession, and may affect (to all appearance exclusively) his daily conduct in it; but our estimate of him is based on this ultimate fact—of which we are well assured—that put him in a fortress breach, with all the pleasures of the world behind him, and only death and his duty in front of him, he will keep his face to the front; and he knows that his choice may be put to him at any moment—and has beforehand taken his part—virtually takes such part continually— does, in reality, die daily.

Not less is the respect we pay to the lawyer and physician, founded ultimately on their self-sacrifice. Whatever the learning or acuteness of a great lawyer, our chief respect for him depends on our belief that, set in a judge's seat, he will strive to judge justly, come of it what may. Could we suppose that he would take bribes, and use his acuteness and legal knowledge to give plausibility to iniquitous decisions, no degree of intellect would win for him our respect. Nothing will win it, short of our tacit conviction, that in all important acts of his life justice is first with him; his own interest, second.

In the case of a physician, the ground of the honour we render him is clearer still. Whatever his science, we would shrink from him in horror if we found him regard his patients merely as subjects to experiment upon; much more, if we found that, receiving bribes from persons interested in their deaths, he was using his best skill to give poison in the mask of medicine.

Finally, the principle holds with utmost clearness as it respects clergymen. No goodness of disposition will excuse want of science in a physician, or of shrewdness in an advocate; but a clergyman, even though his power of intellect be small, is respected on the presumed ground of his unselfishness and serviceableness.

Now, there can be no question but that the tact, foresight, decision, and other mental powers, required for the successful management of a large mercantile concern, if not such as could be compared with those of a great lawyer, general, or divine, would at least match the general conditions of mind required in the subordinate officers of a ship, or of a regiment, or in the curate of a country parish. If, therefore, all the efficient members of the so-called liberal professions are still, somehow, in public estimate of honour, preferred before the head of a commercial firm, the reason must lie deeper than in the measurement of their several powers of mind.

And the essential reason for such preference will be found to lie in the fact that the merchant is presumed to act always selfishly. His work may be very necessary to the community; but the motive of it is understood to be wholly personal. The merchant's first object in all his dealings must be (the public believe) to get as much for himself, and leave as little to his neighbour (or customer) as possible. Enforcing this upon him, by political statute, as the necessary principle of his action; recommending it to him on all occasions, and themselves reciprocally adopting it, proclaiming vociferously, for law of the universe, that a buyer's function is to cheapen, and a seller's to cheat,—the public, nevertheless, involuntarily condemn the man of commerce for his compliance with their own statement, and stamp him for ever as belonging to an inferior grade of human personality.

This they will find, eventually, they must give up doing. They must not cease to condemn selfishness; but they will have to discover a kind of commerce which is not exclusively selfish. Or, rather, they will have to discover that there never was, or can be, any other kind of commerce; that this which they have called commerce was not commerce at all, but cozening; and that a true merchant differs as much from a merchant according to laws of modern political economy, as the hero of the *Excursion* from Autolycus. They will find that commerce is an occupation which gentlemen will every day see more need to engage in, rather than in the businesses of talking to men, or slaying them; that, in true commerce, as in true preaching, or true fighting, it is necessary to admit the idea of occasional voluntary loss;—that sixpences have to be lost, as well as lives, under a sense of duty; that the market may have its martyrdoms as well as the pulpit; and trade its heroisms as well as war.

May have—in the final issue, must have—and only has not had yet, because men of heroic temper have always been misguided in their youth into other fields; not recognizing what is in our days, perhaps, the most important of all fields; so that, while many a zealous person loses his life in trying to teach the form of a gospel, very few will lose a hundred pounds in showing the practice of one.

The fact is, that people never have had clearly explained to them the true functions of a merchant with respect to other people. I should like the reader to be very clear about this.

Five great intellectual professions, relating to daily necessities of life, have hitherto existed—three exist necessarily, in every civilized nation:

The Soldier's profession is to *defend* it.

The Pastor's to *teach* it.

The Physician's to *keep it in health*.

The Lawyer's to *enforce justice* in it.

The Merchant's to *provide* for it.

And the duty of all these men is, on due occasion, to *die* for it.

"On due occasion," namely:—

The Soldier, rather than leave his post in battle.

The Physician, rather than leave his post in plague.

The Pastor, rather than teach Falsehood.

The Lawyer, rather than countenance Injustice.

The Merchant—what is *his* "due occasion" of death?

It is the main question for the merchant, as for all of us. For, truly, the man who does not know when to die, does not know how to live.

Observe, the merchant's function (or manufacturer's, for in the broad sense in which it is here used the word must be understood to include both) is to provide for the nation. It is no more his function to get profit for himself out of that provision than it is a clergyman's function to get his stipend. This stipend is a due and necessary adjunct, but not the object of his life, if he be a true clergyman, any more than his fee (or honorarium) is the object of life to a true physician. Neither is his fee the object of life to a true merchant. All three, if true men, have a work to be done irrespective of fee—to be done even at any cost, or for quite the contrary of fee; the pastor's function being to teach, the physician's to heal, and the merchant's, as I have said, to provide. That is to say, he has to understand to their very root the qualities of the thing he deals in, and the means of obtaining or producing it; and he has to apply all his sagacity and energy to the producing or obtaining it in perfect state, and distributing it at the cheapest possible price where it is most needed.

And because the production or obtaining of any commodity involves necessarily the agency of many lives and hands, the merchant becomes in the course of his business the master and governor of large masses of men in a more direct, though less confessed way, than a military officer or pastor; so that on him falls, in great part, the responsibility for the kind of life they lead: and it becomes his duty, not only to be always considering how to produce what he sells, in the purest and cheapest forms, but how to make the various employments involved in the production, or transference of it, most beneficial to the men employed.

And as into these two functions, requiring for their right exercise the highest intelligence, as well as patience, kindness, and tact, the merchant is bound to put all his energy, so for their just discharge he is bound, as soldier or physician is bound, to give up, if need be, his life, in such way as it may be demanded of him. Two main points he has in his providing function to maintain: first, his engagements (faithfulness to engagements being the real root of all possibilities, in commerce); and, secondly, the perfectness and purity of the thing provided; so that, rather than fail in any engagement, or consent to any deterioration, adulteration, or unjust and exorbitant price of that which he provides, he is bound to meet fearlessly any form of distress, poverty, or labour, which may, through maintenance of these points, come upon him.

Again: in his office as governor of the men employed by him, the merchant or manufacturer is invested with a distinctly paternal authority and responsibility. In most cases, a youth entering a commercial establishment is withdrawn altogether from home influence; his master must become his father, else he has, for practical and constant help, no father at hand: in all cases the master's authority, together with the general tone and atmosphere of his business, and the character of the men with whom the youth is compelled in the course of it to associate, have more immediate and pressing weight than the home influence, and will usually neutralize it either for good or evil; so that the only means which the master has of doing justice to the men employed by him is to ask himself sternly whether he is dealing with such subordinate as he would with his own son, if compelled by circumstances to take such a position.

Supposing the captain of a frigate saw it right, or were by any chance obliged, to place his own son in the position of a common sailor: as he would then treat his son, he is bound always to treat every one of the men under him. So, also, supposing the master of a manufactory saw it right, or were by any chance obliged, to place his own son in the position of an ordinary workman; as he would then treat his son, he is bound always to treat every one of his men. This is the only effective, true, or practical RULE which can be given on this point of political economy.

And as the captain of a ship is bound to be the last man

to leave his ship in case of wreck, and to share his last crust with the sailors in case of famine, so the manufacturer, in any commercial crisis or distress, is bound to take the suffering of it with his men, and even to take more of it for himself than he allows his men to feel; as a father would in a famine, shipwreck, or battle, sacrifice himself for his son.

All which sounds very strange: the only real strangeness in the matter being, nevertheless, that it should so sound. For all this is true, and that not partially nor theoretically, but everlastingly and practically: all other doctrine than this respecting matters political being false in premises, absurd in deduction, and impossible in practice, consistently with any progressive state of national life; all the life which we now possess as a nation showing itself in the resolute denial and scorn, by a few strong minds and faithful hearts, of the economic principles taught to our multitudes, which principles, so far as accepted, lead straight to national destruction. Respecting the modes and forms of destruction to which they lead, and, on the other hand, respecting the farther practical working of true polity, I hope to reason farther in a following paper.

The Veins of Wealth

The answer which would be made by any ordinary political economist to the statements contained in the preceding paper, is in few words as follows:—

"It is indeed true that certain advantages of a general nature may be obtained by the development of social affections. But political economists never professed, nor profess, to take advantages of a general nature into consideration. Our science is simply the science of getting rich. So far from being a fallacious or visionary one, it is found by experience to be practically effective. Persons who follow its precepts do actually become rich, and persons who disobey them become poor. Every capitalist of Europe has acquired his fortune by following the known laws of our science, and increases his capital daily by an adherence to them. It is vain to bring forward tricks of logic, against the force of accomplished facts. Every man of business knows by experience how money is made, and how it is lost."

Pardon me. Men of business do indeed know how they themselves made their money, or how, on occasion, they lost it. Playing a long-practised game, they are familiar with the chances of its cards, and can rightly explain their losses and gains. But they neither know who keeps the bank of the gambling-house, nor what other games may be played with the same cards, nor what other losses and gains, far away among the dark streets, are essentially, though invisibly, dependent on theirs in the lighted rooms. They have learned a few, and only a few, of the laws of mercantile economy; but not one of those of political economy.

Primarily, which is very notable and curious, I observe that men of business rarely know the meaning of the word "rich." At least, if they know, they do not in their reasonings allow for the fact, that it is a relative word, implying its opposite "poor" as positively as the word "north" implies its opposite "south." Men nearly always speak and write as if riches were absolute, and it were possible, by following certain scientific precepts, for everybody to be rich. Whereas riches are a power like that of electricity, acting only through inequalities or negations of itself. The force of the guinea you have in your pocket depends wholly on the default of a guinea in your neighbour's pocket. If he did not want it, it would be of no use to you; the degree of power it possesses depends accurately upon the need or desire he has for it,—and the art of making yourself rich, in the ordinary mercantile economist's sense, is therefore equally and necessarily the art of keeping your neighbour poor.

I would not contend in this matter (and rarely in any matter) for the acceptance of terms. But I wish the reader clearly and deeply to understand the difference between the two economies, to which the terms "Political" and "Mercantile" might not unadvisedly be attached.

Political economy (the economy of a State, or of citizens) consists simply in the production, preservation, and distribution, at fittest time and place, of useful or pleasurable things. The farmer who cuts his hay at the right time; the shipwright who drives his bolts well home in sound wood; the builder who lays good bricks in well-tempered mortar; the housewife who takes care of her furniture in the parlour, and guards against all waste in her kitchen; and the singer who rightly disciplines, and never overstrains her voice, are all political economists in the true and final sense: adding continually to the riches and well-being of the nation to which they belong.

But mercantile economy, the economy of "merces" or of "pay," signifies the accumulation, in the hands of individuals, of legal or moral claim upon, or power over, the labour of others; every such claim implying precisely as much poverty or debt on one side, as it implies riches or right on the other. . . .

Now, the establishment of such inequality cannot be shown in the abstract to be either advantageous or disadvantageous to the body of the nation. The rash and absurd assumption that such inequalities are necessarily advantageous, lies at the root of most of the popular fallacies on the subject of political economy. For the eternal and inevitable law in this matter is, that the beneficialness of the inequality depends, first, on the methods by which it was accomplished; and, secondly, on the purposes to which it is applied. Inequalities of wealth, unjustly established, have assuredly injured the nation in which they exist during their establishment; and, unjustly directed, injure it yet more during their existence. But inequalities of wealth, justly established, benefit the nation in the course of their establishment; and, nobly used, aid it yet more by their existence. That is to say, among every active and well-governed people, the various strength of individuals, tested by full exertion and specially applied to various need, issues in unequal, but harmonious results, receiving reward or authority according to its class and service; while, in the inactive or ill-governed nation, the gradations of decay and the victories of treason work out also their own rugged system of subjection and success; and substitute, for the melodious inequalities of concurrent power, the iniquitous dominances and depressions of guilt and misfortune.

Thus the circulation of wealth in a nation resembles that of the blood in the natural body. There is one quickness of the current which comes of cheerful emotion or wholesome exercise; and another which comes of shame or of fever. There is a flush of the body which is full of warmth and life; and another which will pass into putrefaction.

The analogy will hold down even to minute particulars. For as diseased local determination of the blood involves depression of the general health of the system, all morbid local action of riches will be found ultimately to involve a weakening of the resources of the body politic.

The mode in which this is produced may be at once understood by examining one or two instances of the development of wealth in the simplest possible circumstances.

Suppose two sailors cast away on an uninhabited coast, and obliged to maintain themselves there by their own labour for a series of years.

If they both kept their health, and worked steadily and in amity with each other, they might build themselves a convenient house, and in time come to possess a certain quantity of cultivated land, together with various stores laid up for future use. All these things would be real riches or property; and, supposing the men both to have worked equally hard, they would each have right to equal share or use of it. Their political economy would consist merely in careful preservation and just division of these possessions. Perhaps, however, after some time one or other might be dissatisfied with the results of their common farming; and they might in consequence agree to divide the land they had brought under the spade into equal shares, so that each might thenceforward work in his own field, and live by it. Suppose that after this arrangement had been made, one of them were to fall ill, and be unable to work on his land at a critical time—say of sowing or harvest.

He would naturally ask the other to sow or reap for him.

Then his companion might say, with perfect justice, "I will do this additional work for you; but if I do it, you must promise to do as much for me at another time. I will count how many hours I spend on your ground, and you shall give me a written promise to work for the same number of hours on mine, whenever I need your help, and you are able to give it."

Suppose the disabled man's sickness to continue, and that under various circumstances, for several years, requiring the help of the other, he on each occasion gave a written pledge to work, as soon as he was able, at his companion's orders, for the same number of hours which the other had given up to him. What will the positions of the two men be when the invalid is able to resume work?

Considered as a "Polis," or state, they will be poorer than they would have been otherwise: poorer by the withdrawal of what the sick man's labour would have produced in the interval. His friend may perhaps have toiled with an energy quickened by the enlarged need, but in the end his own land and property must have suffered by the withdrawal of so much of his time and thought from them: and the united property of the two men will be certainly less than it would have been if both had remained in health and activity.

But the relations in which they stand to each other are also widely altered. The sick man has not only pledged his labour for some years, but will probably have exhausted his own share of the accumulated stores, and will be in consequence for some time dependent on the other for food, which he can only "pay" or reward him for by yet more deeply pledging his own labour.

Supposing the written promises to be held entirely valid (among civilized nations their validity is secured by legal measures), the person who had hitherto worked for both might now, if he chose, rest altogether, and pass his time in idleness, not only forcing his companion to redeem all the engagements he had already entered into, but exacting from him pledges for further labour, to an arbitrary amount, for what food he had to advance to him.

There might not, from first to last, be the least illegality (in the ordinary sense of the word) in the arrangement; but if a stranger arrived on the coast at this advanced epoch of their political economy, he would find one man commercially Rich; the other commercially Poor. He would see, perhaps, with no small surprise, one passing his days in idleness; the other labouring for both, and living sparely, in the hope of recovering his independence at some distant period.

This is, of course, an example of one only out of many ways in which inequality of possession may be established between different persons, giving rise to the Mercantile forms of Riches and Poverty. In the instance before us, one of the men might from the first have deliberately chosen to be idle, and to put his life in pawn for present ease; or he might have mismanaged his land, and been compelled to have recourse to his neighbour for food and help, pledging his future labour for it. But what I want the reader to note especially is the fact, common to a large number of typical cases of this kind, that the establishment of the mercantile wealth which consists in a claim upon labour, signifies a political diminution of the real wealth which consists in substantial possessions.

Take another example, more consistent with the ordinary course of affairs of trade. Suppose that three men, instead of two, formed the little isolated republic, and found themselves obliged to separate, in order to farm different pieces of land at some distance from each other along the coast: each estate furnishing a distinct kind of produce, and each more or less in need of the material raised on the other.

Suppose that the third man, in order to save the time of all three, undertakes simply to superintend the transference of commodities from one farm to the other; on condition of receiving some sufficiently remunerative share of every parcel of goods conveyed, or of some other parcel received in exchange for it.

If this carrier or messenger always brings to each estate, from the other, what is chiefly wanted, at the right time, the operations of the two farmers will go on prosperously, and the largest possible result in produce, or wealth, will be attained by the little community. But suppose no intercourse between the landowners is possible, except through the travelling agent; and that, after a time, this agent, watching the course of each man's agriculture, keeps back the articles with which he has been entrusted until there comes a period of extreme necessity for them, on one side or other, and then exacts in exchange for them all that the distressed farmer can spare of other kinds of produce: it is easy to see that by ingeniously watching his opportunities, he might possess himself regularly of the greater part of the superfluous produce of the two estates, and at last, in some year of severest trial or scarcity, purchase both for himself and maintain the former proprietors thenceforward as his labourers or servants.

This would be a case of commercial wealth acquired on the exactest principles of modern political economy. But more distinctly even than in the former instance, it is manifest in this that the wealth of the State, or of the three men considered as a society, is collectively less than it would have been had the merchant been content with juster profit. The operations of the two agriculturists have been cramped to the utmost; and the continual limitations of the supply of things they wanted at critical times, together with the failure of courage consequent on the prolongation of a struggle for mere existence, without any sense of permanent gain, must have seriously diminished the effective results of their labour; and the stores finally accumulated in the merchant's hands will not in any wise be of equivalent value to those which, had his dealings been honest, would have filled at once the granaries of the farmers and his own.

The whole question, therefore, respecting not only the advantage, but even the quantity, of national wealth, resolves itself finally into one of abstract justice. It is impossible to conclude, of any given mass of acquired wealth, merely by the fact of its existence, whether it signifies good or evil to the nation in the midst of which it exists. Its real value depends on the moral sign attached to it, just as sternly as that of a mathematical quantity depends on the algebraical sign attached to it. Any given accumulation of commercial wealth may be indicative, on the one hand, of faithful industries, progressive energies, and productive ingenuities: or, on the other, it may be indicative of mortal luxury, merciless tyranny, ruinous chicane. Some treasures are heavy with human tears, as an ill-stored harvest with untimely rain; and some gold is brighter in sunshine than it is in substance.

And these are not, observe, merely moral or pathetic attributes of riches, which the seeker of riches may, if he chooses, despise; they are, literally and sternly, material attributes of riches, depreciating or exalting, incalculably, the monetary signification of the sum in question. One mass of money is the outcome of action which has created,—another, of action which has annihilated,—ten times as much in the gathering of it; such and such strong hands have been paralyzed, as if they had been numbed by nightshade: so many strong men's courage broken, so many productive operations hindered; this and the other false direction given to labour, and lying image of prosperity set up, on Dura plains dug into seven-times-heated furnaces. That which seems to be wealth may in verity be only the gilded index of far-reaching ruin; a wrecker's handful of coin gleaned from the beach to which he has beguiled an argosy; a camp-follower's bundle of rags unwrapped from the breasts of goodly soldiers dead; the purchase-pieces of potter's fields, wherein shall be buried together the citizen and the stranger.

And therefore, the idea that directions can be given for the gaining of wealth, irrespectively of the consideration of its moral sources, or that any general and technical law of purchase and gain can be set down for national practice, is perhaps the most insolently futile of all that ever beguiled men through their vices. So far as I know, there is not in history record of anything so disgraceful to the human intellect as the modern idea that the commercial text, "Buy in the cheapest market and sell in the dearest," represents, or under any circumstances could represent, an available principle of national economy. Buy in the cheapest market?—yes; but what made your market cheap? Charcoal may be cheap among your roof timbers after a fire, and bricks may be cheap in your streets after an earthquake; but fire and earthquake may not therefore be national benefits. Sell in the dearest?—Yes, truly; but what made your market dear? You sold your bread well to-day: was it to a dying man who gave his last coin for it, and will never need bread more; or to a rich man who to-morrow will buy your farm over your head; or to a soldier on his way to pillage the bank in which you have put your fortune?

None of these things you can know. One thing only you can know: namely, whether this dealing of yours is a just and faithful one, which is all you need concern yourself about respecting it; sure thus to have done your own part in bringing about ultimately in the world a state of things which will not issue in pillage or in death. And thus every question concerning these things merges itself ultimately in the great question of justice. . . .

It has been shown that the chief value and virtue of money consists in its having power over human beings; that, without this power, large material possessions are useless, and to any person possessing such power, comparatively unnecessary. But power over human beings is attainable by other means than by money. As I said a few pages back, the money power is always imperfect and doubtful; there are many things which cannot be reached with it, others which cannot be retained by it. Many joys may be given to men which cannot be bought for gold, and many fidelities found in them which cannot be rewarded with it.

Trite enough,—the reader thinks. Yes: but it is not so trite,—I wish it were,—that in this moral power, quite inscrutable and immeasurable though it be, there is a monetary value just as real as that represented by more ponderous currencies. A man's hand may be full of invisible gold, and the wave of it, or the grasp, shall do more than another's with a shower of bullion. This invisible gold, also, does not necessarily diminish in spending. Political economists will do well some day to take heed of it, though they cannot take measure.

But farther. Since the essence of wealth consists in its authority over men, if the apparent or nominal wealth fail in this power, it fails in essence; in fact, ceases to be wealth at all. It does not appear lately in England, that our authority over men is absolute. The servants show some disposition to rush riotously upstairs, under an impression that their wages are not regularly paid. We should augur ill of any gentleman's property to whom this happened every other day in his drawing-room.

So, also, the power of our wealth seems limited as respects the comfort of the servants, no less than their quietude. The persons in the kitchen appear to be ill-dressed, squalid, half-starved. One cannot help imagining that the riches of the establishment must be of a very theoretical and documentary character.

Finally. Since the essence of wealth consists in power over men, will it not follow that the nobler and the more in number the persons are over whom it has power, the greater the wealth? Perhaps it may even appear, after some consideration, that the persons themselves *are* the wealth— that these pieces of gold with which we are in the habit of guiding them, are, in fact, nothing more than a kind of Byzantine harness or trappings, very glittering and beautiful in barbaric sight, wherewith we bridle the creatures; but that if these same living creatures could be guided without the fretting and jingling of the Byzants in their mouths and ears, they might themselves be more valuable than their bridles. In fact, it may be discovered that the true veins of wealth are purple—and not in Rock, but in Flesh—perhaps even that the final outcome and consummation of all wealth is in the producing as many as possible full-breathed, bright-eyed, and happy-hearted human creatures. Our modern wealth, I think, has rather a tendency the other way;—most political economists appearing to consider multitudes of human creatures not conducive to wealth, or at best conducive to it only by remaining in a dim-eyed and narrow-chested state of being.

Nevertheless, it is open, I repeat, to serious question, which I leave to the reader's pondering, whether, among national manufactures, that of Souls of a good quality may not at last turn out a quite leadingly lucrative one? Nay, in some far-away and yet undreamt-of hour, I can even imagine that England may cast all thoughts of possessive wealth back to the barbaric nations among whom they first arose; and that, while the sands of the Indus and adamant of Golconda may yet stiffen the housings of the charger, and flash from the turban of the slave, she, as a Christian mother, may at last attain to the virtues and the treasures of a Heathen one, and be able to lead forth her Sons, saying,—

"These are MY *Jewels."**

Ad Valorem

[We have seen] that just payment of labour consisted in a sum of money which would approximately obtain equiva-

---

* Said by the unadorned Cornelia of her sons, the Gracchi.

lent labour at a future time: we have now to examine the means of obtaining such equivalence. Which question involves the definition of Value, Wealth, Price, and Produce.

None of these terms are yet defined so as to be understood by the public. But the last, Produce, which one might have thought the clearest of all, is, in use, the most ambiguous; and the examination of the kind of ambiguity attendant on its present employment will best open the way to our work.

In his chapter on Capital, Mr. J. S. Mill instances, as a capitalist, a hardware manufacturer, who, having intended to spend a certain portion of the proceeds of his business in buying plate and jewels, changes his mind, and "pays it as wages to additional workpeople." The effect is stated by Mr. Mill to be, that "more food is appropriated to the consumption of productive labourers."

Now I do not ask, though, had I written this paragraph, it would surely have been asked of me, What is to become of the silversmiths? If they are truly unproductive persons, we will acquiesce in their extinction. And though in another part of the same passage, the hardware merchant is supposed also to dispense with a number of servants, whose "food is thus set free for productive purposes," I do not inquire what will be the effect, painful or otherwise, upon the servants, of this emancipation of their food. But I very seriously inquire why ironware is produce, and silverware is not? That the merchant consumes the one, and sells the other, certainly does not constitute the difference, unless it can be shown (which, indeed, I perceive it to be becoming daily more and more the aim of tradesmen to show) that commodities are made to be sold, and not to be consumed. The merchant is an agent of conveyance to the consumer in one case, and is himself the consumer in the other: but the labourers are in either case equally productive, since they have produced goods to the same value, if the hardware and the plate are both goods.

And what distinction separates them? It is indeed possible that in the "comparative estimate of the moralist," with which Mr. Mill says political economy has nothing to do (III. i. 2), a steel fork might appear a more substantial production than a silver one: we may grant also that knives, no less than forks, are good produce; and scythes and ploughshares serviceable articles. But, how of bayonets? Supposing the hardware merchant to effect large sales of *these*, by help of the "setting free" of the food of his servants and his silversmith,—is he still employing productive labourers, or, in Mr. Mill's words, labourers who increase "the stock of permanent means of enjoyment" (I. iii. 4)? Or if, instead of bayonets, he supply bombs, will not the absolute and final "enjoyment" of even these energetically productive articles (each of which costs ten pounds) be dependent on a proper choice of time and place for their *enfantement;* choice, that is to say, depending on those philosophical considerations with which political economy has nothing to do?

I should have regretted the need of pointing out inconsistency in any portion of Mr. Mill's work, had not the value of his work proceeded from its inconsistencies. He deserves honour among economists by inadvertently disclaiming the principles which he states, and tacitly introducing the moral considerations with which he declares his science has no connection. Many of his chapters are, therefore, true and valuable; and the only conclusions of his which I have to dispute are those which follow from his premises.

Thus, the idea which lies at the root of the passage we have just been examining, namely, that labour applied to produce luxuries will not support so many persons as labour applied to produce useful articles, is entirely true; but the instance given fails—and in four directions of failure at once—because Mr. Mill has not defined the real meaning of usefulness. The definition which he has given—"capacity to satisfy a desire, or serve a purpose" (III. i. 2)—applies equally to the iron and silver; while the true definition—

which he has not given, but which nevertheless underlies the false verbal definition in his mind, and comes out once or twice by accident (as in the words "any support to life or strength" in I. iii. 5)—applies to some articles of iron, but not to others, and to some articles of silver, but not to others. It applies to ploughs, but not to bayonets; and to forks, but not to filigree.

The eliciting of the true definitions will give us the reply to our first question, "What is value?" respecting which, however, we must first hear the popular statements.

"The word 'value,' when used without adjunct, always means, in political economy, value in exchange" (Mill, III. i. 2). So that, if two ships cannot exchange their rudders, their rudders are, in politico-economic language, of no value to either.

But "the subject of political economy is wealth."—(Preliminary remarks, page 1.)

And wealth "consists of all useful and agreeable objects which possess exchangeable value."—(Preliminary remarks, page 10.)

It appears, then, according to Mr. Mill, that usefulness and agreeableness underlie the exchange value, and must be ascertained to exist in the thing, before we can esteem it an object of wealth.

Now, the economical usefulness of a thing depends not merely on its own nature, but on the number of people who can and will use it. A horse is useless, and therefore unsaleable, if no one can ride,—a sword, if no one can strike, and meat, if no one can eat. Thus every material utility depends on its relative human capacity.

Similarly: The agreeableness of a thing depends not merely on its own likeableness, but on the number of people who can be got to like it. The relative agreeableness, and therefore saleableness, of "a pot of the smallest ale," and of "Adonis painted by a running brook," depends virtually on the opinion of Demos, in the shape of Christopher Sly.

That is to say, the agreeableness of a thing depends on its relatively human disposition.* Therefore, political economy, being a science of wealth, must be a science respecting human capacities and dispositions. But moral considerations have nothing to do with political economy (III. i. 2). Therefore, moral considerations have nothing to do with human capacities and dispositions. I do not wholly like the look of this conclusion. . . .

Much store has been set for centuries upon the use of our English classical education. It were to be wished that our well-educated merchants recalled to mind always this much of their Latin schooling,—that the nominative of *valorem* (a word already sufficiently familiar to them) is *valor;* a word which, therefore, ought to be familiar to them. *Valor,* from *valere,* to be well or *strong* (ὑγιαίνω);— strong, *in* life (if a man), or valiant; strong, *for* life (if a thing), or valuable. To be "valuable," therefore, is to "avail towards life." A truly valuable or availing thing is that which leads to life with its whole strength. In proportion as it does not lead to life, or as its strength is broken, it is less valuable; in proportion as it leads away from life, it is unvaluable or malignant.

The value of a thing, therefore, is independent of opinion, and of quantity. Think what you will of it, gain how much you may of it, the value of the thing itself is neither greater nor less. For ever it avails, or avails not; no estimate can raise, no disdain repress, the power which it holds from the Maker of things and of men.

* These statements sound crude in their brevity; but will be found of the utmost importance when they are developed. Thus, in the above instance, economists have never perceived that disposition to buy is a wholly *moral* element in demand: that is to say, when you give a man half a crown, it depends on his disposition whether he is rich or poor with it—whether he will buy disease, ruin, and hatred, or buy health, advancement, and domestic love. And thus the agreeableness or exchange value of every offered commodity depends on production, not merely of the commodity, but of buyers of it; therefore on the education of buyers, and on all the moral elements by which their disposition to buy this, or that, is formed. [Ruskin's note.]

The real science of political economy, which has yet to be distinguished from the bastard science, as medicine from witchcraft, and astronomy from astrology, is that which teaches nations to desire and labour for the things that lead to life: and which teaches them to scorn and destroy the things that lead to destruction. And if, in a state of infancy, they supposed indifferent things, such as excrescences of shell-fish, and pieces of blue and red stone, to be valuable, and spent large measures of the labour which ought to be employed for the extension and ennobling of life, in diving or digging for them, and cutting them into various shapes,— or if, in the same state of infancy, they imagine precious and beneficent things, such as air, light, and cleanliness, to be valueless,—or if, finally, they imagine the conditions of their own existence, by which alone they can truly possess or use anything, such, for instance, as peace, trust, and love, to be prudently exchangeable, when the markets offer, for gold, iron, or excrescences of shells—the great and only science of Political Economy teaches them, in all these cases, what is vanity, and what substance; and how the service of Death, the Lord of Waste, and of eternal emptiness, differs from the service of Wisdom, the Lady of Saving, and of eternal fulness; she who has said, "I will cause those that love me to inherit Substance; and I will Fill their treasures."*

The "Lady of Saving," in a profounder sense than that of the savings bank, though that is a good one: Madonna della Salute,—Lady of Health,—which, though commonly spoken of as if separate from wealth, is indeed a part of wealth. This word, "wealth," it will be remembered, is the next we have to define.

"To be wealthy," says Mr. Mill, "is to have a large stock of useful articles."

I accept this definition. Only let us perfectly understand it. My opponents often lament my not giving them enough logic: I fear I must at present use a little more than they

* Proverbs 8:21.

will like: but this business of Political Economy is no light one, and we must allow no loose terms in it.

We have, therefore, to ascertain in the above definition, first, what is the meaning of "having," or the nature of Possession. Then what is the meaning of "useful," or the nature of Utility.

And first of possession. At the crossing of the transepts of Milan Cathedral has lain, for three hundred years, the embalmed body of St. Carlo Borromeo. It holds a golden crosier, and has a cross of emeralds on its breast. Admitting the crosier and emeralds to be useful articles, is the body to be considered as "having" them? Do they, in the politico-economical sense of property, belong to it? If not, and if we may, therefore, conclude generally that a dead body cannot possess property, what degree and period of animation in the body will render possession possible?

As thus: lately in a wreck of a Californian ship, one of the passengers fastened a belt about him with two hundred pounds of gold in it, with which he was found afterwards at the bottom. Now, as he was sinking—had he the gold? or had the gold him?

And if, instead of sinking him in the sea by its weight, the gold had struck him on the forehead, and thereby caused incurable disease—suppose palsy or insanity,—would the gold in that case have been more a "possession" than in the first? Without pressing the inquiry up through instances of gradually increasing vital power over the gold (which I will, however, give, if they are asked for), I presume the reader will see that possession, or "having," is not an absolute, but a gradated, power; and consists not only in the quantity or nature of the thing possessed, but also (and in a greater degree) in its suitableness to the person possessing it and in his vital power to use it.

And our definition of Wealth, expanded, becomes: "The possession of useful articles, *which we can use.*" This is a very serious change. For wealth, instead of depending merely on a "have," is thus seen to depend on a "can." Gladiator's death, on a "habet"; but soldier's victory, and State's salvation, on a "quo plurimum posset." (Liv. VII. 6.) And what we reasoned of only as accumulation of material, is seen to demand also accumulation of capacity.*

So much for our verb. Next for our adjective. What is the meaning of "useful"?

The inquiry is closely connected with the last. For what is capable of use in the hands of some persons, is capable, in the hands of others, of the opposite of use, called commonly "from-use," or "ab-use." And it depends on the person, much more than on the article, whether its usefulness or ab-usefulness will be the quality developed in it. Thus, wine, which the Greeks, in their Bacchus, made rightly the type of all passion, and which, when used, "cheereth god and man" (that is to say, strengthens both the divine life, or reasoning power, and the earthy, or carnal power, of man); yet, when abused, becomes "Dion[y]sos," hurtful especially to the divine part of man, or reason. And again, the body itself, being equally liable to use and to abuse, and, when rightly disciplined, serviceable to the State, both for war and labour,—but when not disciplined, or abused, valueless to the State, and capable only of continuing the private or single existence of the individual (and that but

* In *Munera Pulveris*, Chapter I, Ruskin further elucidates this point:
"'Value' signifies the strength, or 'availing' of anything towards the sustaining of life, and is always twofold; that is to say, primarily, INTRINSIC, and secondarily, EFFECTUAL . . .
"Intrinsic value is the absolute power of anything to support life. . . . It does not in the least affect the intrinsic value of the wheat, the air, or the flowers, that men refuse or despise them. Used or not, their own power is in them, and that particular power is in nothing else.
"But in order that this value of theirs may become effectual, a certain state is necessary in the recipient of it. The digesting, breathing, and perceiving functions must be perfect in the human creature before the food, air, or flowers can become of their full values to it. *The production of effectual value, therefore, always involves two needs: first, the production of a thing essentially useful; then the production of the capacity to use it.* Where the intrinsic value and acceptant capacity come together there is Effectual value, or wealth; where there is either no intrinsic value, or no acceptant capacity, there is no effectual value; that is to say, no wealth."

feebly)—the Greeks called such a body an "idiotic" or "private" body, from their word signifying a person employed in no way directly useful to the State; whence finally, our "idiot," meaning a person entirely occupied with his own concerns.

Hence, it follows that if a thing is to be useful, it must be not only of an availing nature, but in availing hands. Or, in accurate terms, usefulness is value in the hands of the valiant; so that this science of wealth being, as we have just seen, when regarded as the science of Accumulation, accumulative of capacity as well as of material,—when regarded as the Science of Distribution, is distribution not absolute, but discriminate; not of every thing to every man, but of the right thing to the right man. A difficult science, dependent on more than arithmetic.

Wealth, therefore, is "THE POSSESSION OF THE VALUABLE BY THE VALIANT"; and in considering it as a power existing in a nation, the two elements, the value of the thing, and the valour of its possessor, must be estimated together. Whence it appears that many of the persons commonly considered wealthy, are in reality no more wealthy than the locks of their own strong boxes are, they being inherently and eternally incapable of wealth; and operating for the nation, in an economical point of view, either as pools of dead water, and eddies in a stream (which, so long as the stream flows, are useless, or serve only to drown people, but may become of importance in a state of stagnation should the stream dry); or else, as dams in a river, of which the ultimate service depends not on the dam, but the miller; or else, as mere accidental stays and impediments, acting not as wealth, but (for we ought to have a correspondent term) as "illth," causing various devastation and trouble around them in all directions; or lastly, act not at all, but are merely animated conditions of delay, (no use being possible of anything they have until they are dead,) in which last condition they are nevertheless often useful *as* delays, and "impedimenta," if a nation is apt to move too fast.

This being so, the difficulty of the true science of Political Economy lies not merely in the need of developing manly character to deal with material value, but in the fact, that while the manly character and material value only form wealth by their conjunction, they have nevertheless a mutually destructive operation on each other. For the manly character is apt to ignore, or even cast away, the material value:—whence that of Pope:—

> *"Sure, of qualities demanding praise,*
> *More go to ruin fortunes, than to raise."*

And on the other hand, the material value is apt to undermine the manly character; so that it must be our work, in the issue, to examine what evidence there is of the effect of wealth on the minds of its possessors; also, what kind of person it is who usually sets himself to obtain wealth, and succeeds in doing so; and whether the world owes more gratitude to rich or to poor men, either for their moral influence upon it, or for chief goods, discoveries, and practical advancements. I may, however, anticipate future conclusions, so far as to state that in a community regulated only by laws of demand and supply, but protected from open violence, the persons who become rich are, generally speaking, industrious, resolute, proud, covetous, prompt, methodical, sensible, unimaginative, insensitive, and ignorant. The persons who remain poor are the entirely foolish, the entirely wise, the idle, the reckless, the humble, the thoughtful, the dull, the imaginative, the sensitive, the well-informed, the improvident, the irregularly and impulsively wicked, the clumsy knave, the open thief, and the entirely merciful, just, and godly person.

Thus far, then, of wealth. Next, we have to ascertain the nature of PRICE; that is to say, of exchange value, and its expression by currencies.

Note first, of exchange, there can be no *profit* in it. It is only in labour there can be profit—that is to say, a "making in advance," or "making in favour of" (from proficio). In exchange, there is only advantage, *i.e.*, a bringing of vantage or power to the exchanging persons. Thus, one man, by sowing and reaping, turns one measure of corn into two measures. That is Profit. Another, by digging and forging, turns one spade into two spades. That is Profit. But the man who has two measures of corn wants sometimes to dig; and the man who has two spades wants sometimes to eat:— They exchange the gained grain for the gained tool; and both are the better for the exchange; but though there is much advantage in the transaction, there is no profit. Nothing is constructed or produced. Only that which had been before constructed is given to the person by whom it can be used. If labour is necessary to effect the exchange, that labour is in reality involved in the production, and, like all other labour, bears profit. Whatever number of men are concerned in the manufacture, or in the conveyance, have share in the profit; but neither the manufacture nor the conveyance are the exchange, and in the exchange itself there is no profit. . . .

The Science of Exchange, or, as I hear it has been proposed to call it, of "Catallactics," considered as one of gain, is, therefore, simply nugatory; but considered as one of acquisition, it is a very curious science, differing in its data and basis from every other science known. Thus:—if I can exchange a needle with a savage for a diamond, my power of doing so depends either on the savage's ignorance of social arrangements in Europe, or on his want of power to take advantage of them, by selling the diamond to any one else for more needles. If, farther, I make the bargain as completely advantageous to myself as possible, by giving to the savage a needle with no eye in it (reaching, thus a sufficiently satisfactory type of the perfect operation of catallactic science), the advantage to me in the entire transaction depends wholly upon the ignorance, powerlessness, or heedlessness of the person dealt with. Do away with these, and catallactic advantage becomes impossible. So far, therefore, as the science of exchange relates to the advantage of one of the exchanging persons only, it is founded on the ignorance or incapacity of the opposite person. Where these vanish, it also vanishes. It is therefore a science founded on nescience, and an art founded on artlessness. But all other sciences and arts, except this, have for their object the doing away with their opposite nescience and artlessness. *This* science, alone of sciences, must, by all available means, promulgate and prolong its opposite nescience; otherwise the science itself is impossible. It is, therefore, peculiarly and alone the science of darkness; probably a bastard science —not by any means a *divina scientia,* but one begotten of another father, that father who, advising his children to turn stones into bread, is himself employed in turning bread into stones, and who, if you ask a fish of him (fish not being producible on his estate), can but give you a serpent.

The general law, then, respecting just or economical exchange, is simply this:—There must be advantage on both sides (or if only advantage on one, at least no disadvantage on the other) to the persons exchanging; and just payment for his time, intelligence, and labour, to any intermediate person effecting the transaction (commonly called a merchant); and whatever advantage there is on either side, and whatever pay is given to the intermediate person, should be thoroughly known to all concerned. All attempt at concealment implies some practice of the opposite, or undivine science, founded on nescience. Whence another saying of the Jew merchant's*—"As a nail between the stone joints, so doth sin stick fast between buying and selling." . . .

The last word which we have to define is "Production."

I have hitherto spoken of all labour as profitable; because it is impossible to consider under one head the quality or value of labour, and its aim. But labour of the best quality may be various in aim. It may be either constructive ("gathering," from con and struo), as agriculture; nugatory, as jewel-cutting; or destructive ("scattering," from de and

---

* Solomon, whose "sayings on commerce" Ruskin had quoted in the third chapter of *Unto This Last.*

struo), as war. It is not, however, always easy to prove labour, apparently nugatory, to be actually so; generally, the formula holds good: "he that gathereth not, scattereth"; thus, the jeweller's art is probably very harmful in its ministering to a clumsy and inelegant pride. So that, finally, I believe nearly all labour may be shortly divided into positive and negative labour: positive, that which produces life; negative, that which produces death; the most directly negative labour being murder, and the most directly positive, the bearing and rearing of children. . . .

Labour being thus various in its result, the prosperity of any nation is in exact proportion to the quantity of labour which it spends in obtaining and employing means of life. Observe,—I say, obtaining and employing; that is to say, not merely wisely producing, but wisely distributing and consuming. Economists usually speak as if there were no good in consumption absolute. So far from this being so, consumption absolute is the end, crown, and perfection of production; and wise consumption is a far more difficult art than wise production. Twenty people can gain money for one who can use it; and the vital question, for individual and for nation, is, never "how much do they make?" but "to what purpose do they spend?"

The reader may, perhaps, have been surprised at the slight reference I have hitherto made to "capital," and its functions. It is here the place to define them.

Capital signifies "head, or source, or root material"—it is material by which some derivative or secondary good is produced. It is only capital proper (caput vivum, not caput mortuum) when it is thus producing something different from itself. It is a root, which does not enter into vital function till it produces something else than a root: namely, fruit. That fruit will in time again produce roots; and so all living capital issues in reproduction of capital; but capital which produces nothing but capital is only root producing root; bulb issuing in bulb, never in tulip; seed issuing in seed, never in bread. The Political Economy of Europe has hitherto devoted itself wholly to the multiplication, or (less even) the aggregation, of bulbs. It never saw, nor conceived, such a thing as a tulip. Nay, boiled bulbs they might have been—glass bulbs—Prince Rupert's drops,* consummated in powder (well, if it were glass-powder and not gunpowder), for any end or meaning the economists had in defining the laws of aggregation. We will try and get a clearer notion of them.

The best and simplest general type of capital is a well-made ploughshare. Now, if that ploughshare did nothing but beget other ploughshares, in a polypous manner,—however the great cluster of polypous plough might glitter in the sun, it would have lost its function of capital. It becomes true capital only by another kind of splendour,—when it is seen "splendescere sulco," to grow bright in the furrow; rather with diminution of its substance, than addition, by the noble friction. And the true home question, to every capitalist and to every nation, is not, "how many ploughs have you?" but, "where are your furrows?" not—"how quickly will this capital reproduce itself?"—but, "what will it do during reproduction?" What substance will it furnish, good for life? what work construct, protective of life? if none, its own reproduction is useless—if worse than none,— (for capital may destroy life as well as support it), its own reproduction is worse than useless; it is merely an advance from Tisiphone, on mortgage—not a profit by any means. . . .

This being the real nature of capital, it follows that there are two kinds of true production, always going on in an active State: one of seed, and one of food; or production for the Ground, and for the Mouth; both of which are by covetous persons thought to be production only for the granary; whereas the function of the granary is but intermediate and conservative, fulfilled in distribution; else it ends in nothing but mildew, and nourishment of rats and

* Molten drops of glass, elongated and solidified by falling into water. If the tapered end is broken, the whole disintegrates into dust.

worms. And since production for the Ground is only useful with future hope of harvest, all *essential* production is for the Mouth; and is finally measured by the mouth; hence, as I said above, consumption is the crown of production; and the wealth of a nation is only to be estimated by what it consumes.

The want of any clear sight of this fact is the capital error, issuing in rich interest and revenue of error among the political economists. Their minds are continually set on money-gain, not on mouth-gain; and they fall into every sort of net and snare, dazzled by the coin-glitter as birds by the fowler's glass; or rather (for there is not much else like birds in them) they are like children trying to jump on the heads of their own shadows; the money-gain being only the shadow of the true gain, which is humanity.

The final object of political economy, therefore, is to get good method of consumption, and great quantity of consumption: in other words, to use everything, and to use it nobly; whether it be substance, service, or service perfecting substance. The most curious error in Mr. Mill's entire work, (provided for him originally by Ricardo,) is his endeavour to distinguish between direct and indirect service, and consequent assertion that a demand for commodities is not demand for labour (I. v. 9, *et seq.*). He distinguishes between labourers employed to lay out pleasure grounds, and to manufacture velvet; declaring that it makes material difference to the labouring classes in which of these two ways a capitalist spends his money; because the employment of the gardeners is a demand for labour, but the purchase of velvet is not. Error colossal, as well as strange. It will, indeed, make a difference to the labourer whether we bid him swing his scythe in the spring winds, or drive the loom in pestilential air; but, so far as his pocket is concerned, it makes to him absolutely no difference whether we order him to make green velvet, with seed and a scythe, or red velvet, with silk and scissors. Neither does it anywise concern him whether, when the velvet is made, we consume it by walking on it, or wearing it, so long as our consumption of it is wholly selfish. But if our consumption is to be in anywise unselfish, not only our mode of consuming the articles we require interests him, but also the *kind* of article we require with a view to consumption. As thus (returning for a moment to Mr. Mill's great hardware theory): it matters, so far as the labourer's immediate profit is concerned, not an iron filing whether I employ him in growing a peach, or forging a bombshell; but my probable mode of consumption of those articles matters seriously. Admit that it is to be in both cases "unselfish," and the difference, to him, is final, whether when his child is ill, I walk into his cottage and give it the peach, or drop the shell down his chimney, and blow his roof off.

The worst of it, for the peasant, is, that the capitalist's consumption of the peach is apt to be selfish, and of the shell, distributive; but, in all cases, this is the broad and general fact, that on due catallactic commercial principles, *somebody's* roof must go off in fulfilment of the bomb's destiny. You may grow for your neighbour, at your liking, grapes or grape-shot; he will also, catallactically, grow grapes or grape-shot for you, and you will each reap what you have sown.

It is, therefore, the manner and issue of consumption which are the real tests of production. Production does not consist in things laboriously made, but in things serviceably consumable; and the question for the nation is not how much labour it employs, but how much life it produces. For as consumption is the end and aim of production, so life is the end and aim of consumption.

I left this question to the reader's thought two months ago, choosing rather that he should work it out for himself than have it sharply stated to him. But now, the ground being sufficiently broken (and the details into which the several questions, here opened, must lead us, being too complex for discussion in the pages of a periodical, so that I must pursue them elsewhere), I desire, in closing the series of introductory papers, to leave this one great fact clearly stated. THERE IS NO WEALTH BUT LIFE. Life, including all its powers of love, of joy, and of admiration. That country is the richest which nourishes the greatest number of noble and happy human beings; that man is richest who, having perfected the functions of his own life to the utmost, has also the widest helpful influence, both personal, and by means of his possessions, over the lives of others.

A strange political economy; the only one, nevertheless, that ever was or can be: all political economy founded on self-interest being but the fulfilment of that which once brought schism into the Policy of angels, and ruin into the Economy of Heaven.

"The greatest number of human beings noble and happy." But is the nobleness consistent with the number? Yes, not only consistent with it, but essential to it. The maximum of life can only be reached by the maximum of virtue. In this respect the law of human population differs wholly from that of animal life. The multiplication of animals is checked only by want of food, and by the hostility of races; the population of the gnat is restrained by the hunger of the swallow, and that of the swallow by the scarcity of gnats. Man, considered as an animal, is indeed limited by the same laws: hunger, or plague, or war, are the necessary and only restraints upon his increase,—effectual restraints hitherto,—his principal study having been how most swiftly to destroy himself, or ravage his dwelling-places, and his highest skill directed to give range to the famine, seed to the plague, and sway to the sword. But, considered as other than an animal, his increase is not limited by these laws. It is limited only by the limits of his courage and his love. Both of these *have* their bounds; and ought to have; his race has its bounds also; but these have not yet been reached, nor will be reached for ages.

In all the ranges of human thought I know none so melancholy as the speculations of political economists on the population question. It is proposed to better the condition of the labourer by giving him higher wages. "Nay," says the economist,—"if you raise his wages, he will either people down to the same point of misery at which you found him, or drink your wages away." He will. I know it. Who gave him this will? Suppose it were your own son of whom you spoke, declaring to me that you dared not take him into your firm, nor even give him his just labourer's wages, because if you did he would die of drunkenness, and leave half a score of children to the parish. "Who gave your son these dispositions?"—I should enquire. Has he them by inheritance or by education? By one or other they *must* come; and as in him, so also in the poor. Either these poor are of a race essentially different from ours, and unredeemable (which, however often implied, I have heard none yet openly say), or else by such care as we have ourselves received, we may make them continent and sober as ourselves—wise and dispassionate as we are— models arduous of imitation. "But," it is answered, "they cannot receive education." Why not? That is precisely the point at issue. Charitable persons suppose the worst fault of the rich is to refuse the people meat; and the people cry for their meat, kept back by fraud, to the Lord of Multitudes. Alas! it is not meat of which the refusal is cruelest, or to which the claim is validest. The life is more than the meat. The rich not only refuse food to the poor; they refuse wisdom; they refuse virtue; they refuse salvation. Ye sheep without shepherd, it is not the pasture that has been shut from you, but the Presence. . . .

If, on due and honest thought over these things, it seems that the kind of existence to which men are now summoned by every plea of pity and claim of right, may, for some time at least, not be a luxurious one;—consider whether, even supposing it guiltless, luxury would be desired by any of us, if we saw clearly at our sides the suffering which accompanies it in the world. Luxury is indeed possible in the future—innocent and exquisite; luxury for all, and by the help of all; but luxury at present can only be enjoyed by the ignorant; the cruelest man living could not sit at his feast, unless he sat blindfold. Raise the veil boldly; face the light; and if, as yet, the light of the eye can only be through tears, and the light of the body through sackcloth, go thou forth weeping, bearing precious seed, until the time come, and the kingdom, when Christ's gift of bread, and bequest of peace, shall be "Unto this last as unto thee"; and when, for earth's severed multitudes of the wicked and the weary, there shall be holier reconciliation than that of the narrow home, and calm economy, where the Wicked cease—not from trouble, but from troubling—and the Weary are at rest.

THE CROWN OF WILD OLIVE

*Traffic**

My good Yorkshire friends, you asked me down here among your hills that I might talk to you about this Exchange you are going to build: but, earnestly and seriously asking you to pardon me, I am going to do nothing of the kind. I cannot talk, or at least can say very little, about this same Exchange. I must talk of quite other things, though not willingly;—I could not deserve your pardon, if, when you invited me to speak on one subject, I *wilfully* spoke on another. But I cannot speak, to purpose, of anything about which I do not care; and most simply and sorrowfully I have to tell you, in the outset, that I do *not* care about this Exchange of yours.

If, however, when you sent me your invitation, I had answered, "I won't come, I don't care about the Exchange of Bradford," you would have been justly offended with me, not knowing the reasons of so blunt a carelessness. So I have come down, hoping that you will patiently let me tell you why, on this and many other such occasions, I now remain silent, when formerly I should have caught at the opportunity of speaking to a gracious audience.

In a word, then, I do not care about this Exchange—because *you* don't; and because you know perfectly well I cannot make you. Look at the essential conditions of the case, which you, as business men, know perfectly well, though perhaps you think I forget them. You are going to

* Delivered in the Town Hall, Bradford, April 21, 1864.

spend £30,000, which to you, collectively, is nothing; the buying a new coat is, as to the cost of it, a much more important matter of consideration to me, than building a new Exchange is to you. But you think you may as well have the right thing for your money. You know there are a great many odd styles of architecture about; you don't want to do anything ridiculous; you hear of me, among others, as a respectable architectural man-milliner; and you send for me, that I may tell you the leading fashion; and what is, in our shops, for the moment, the newest and sweetest thing in pinnacles.

Now, pardon me for telling you frankly, you cannot have good architecture merely by asking people's advice on occasion. All good architecture is the expression of national life and character; and it is produced by a prevalent and eager national taste, or desire for beauty. And I want you to think a little of the deep significance of this word "taste"; for no statement of mine has been more earnestly or oftener controverted than that good taste is essentially a moral quality. "No," say many of my antagonists, "taste is one thing, morality is another. Tell us what is pretty: we shall be glad to know that; but we need no sermons—even were you able to preach them, which may be doubted."

Permit me, therefore, to fortify this old dogma of mine somewhat. Taste is not only a part and an index of morality; —it is the ONLY morality. The first, and last, and closest trial question to any living creature is, "What do you like?" Tell me what you like, and I'll tell you what you are. Go out into the street, and ask the first man or woman you meet, what their "taste" is; and if they answer candidly, you know them, body and soul. "You, my friend in the rags, with the unsteady gait, what do *you* like?" "A pipe, and a quartern of gin." I know you. "You, good woman, with the quick step and tidy bonnet, what do you like?" "A swept hearth, and a clean tea-table; and my husband opposite me, and a baby at my breast." Good, I know you also. "You, little girl with the golden hair and the soft eyes, what do you like?"

"My canary, and a run among the wood hyacinths." "You, little boy with the dirty hands, and the low forehead, what do you like?" "A shy at the sparrows, and a game at pitch farthing." Good; we know them all now. What more need we ask?

"Nay," perhaps you answer; "we need rather to ask what these people and children do, than what they like. If they *do* right, it is no matter that they like what is wrong; and if they *do* wrong, it is no matter that they like what is right. Doing is the great thing; and it does not matter that the man likes drinking, so that he does not drink; nor that the little girl likes to be kind to her canary, if she will not learn her lessons; nor that the little boy likes throwing stones at the sparrows, if he goes to the Sunday school." Indeed, for a short time, and in a provisional sense, this is true. For if, resolutely, people do what is right, in time to come they like doing it. But they only are in a right moral state when they *have* come to like doing it; and as long as they don't like it, they are still in a vicious state. The man is not in health of body who is always thinking of the bottle in the cupboard, though he bravely bears his thirst; but the man who heartily enjoys water in the morning, and wine in the evening, each in its proper quantity and time. And the entire object of true education is to make people not merely *do* the right things, but *enjoy* the right things:— not merely industrious, but to love industry—not merely learned, but to love knowledge—not merely pure, but to love purity—not merely just, but to hunger and thirst after justice.

But you may answer or think, "Is the liking for outside ornaments,—for pictures, or statues, or furniture, or architecture, a moral quality?" Yes, most surely, if a rightly set liking. Taste for *any* pictures or statues is not a moral quality, but taste for good ones is. Only here again we have to define the word "good." I don't mean by "good," clever—or learned—or difficult in the doing. Take a picture by Teniers, of sots quarrelling over their dice; it is an entirely clever picture; so clever that nothing in its kind has ever been done equal to it; but it is also an entirely base and evil picture. It is an expression of delight in the prolonged contemplation of a vile thing, and delight in that is an "unmannered," or "immoral" quality. It is "bad taste" in the profoundest sense—it is the taste of the devils. On the other hand, a picture of Titian's, or a Greek statue, or a Greek coin, or a Turner landscape, expresses delight in the perpetual contemplation of a good and perfect thing. That is an entirely moral quality—it is the taste of the angels. And all delight in fine art, and all love of it, resolve themselves into simple love of that which deserves love. That deserving is the quality which we call "loveliness"—(we ought to have an opposite word, hateliness, to be said of the things which deserve to be hated); and it is not an indifferent nor optional thing whether we love this or that; but it is just the vital function of all our being. What we *like* determines what we *are,* and is the sign of what we are; and to teach taste is inevitably to form character.

As I was thinking over this, in walking up Fleet Street the other day, my eye caught the title of a book standing open in a bookseller's window. It was—"On the necessity of the diffusion of taste among all classes." "Ah," I thought to myself, "my classifying friend, when you have diffused your taste, where will your classes be? The man who likes what you like, belongs to the same class with you, I think. Inevitably so. You may put him to other work if you choose; but, by the condition you have brought him into, he will dislike the work as much as you would yourself. You get hold of a scavenger or a costermonger, who enjoyed the Newgate Calendar for literature, and 'Pop goes the Weasel' for music. You think you can make him like Dante and Beethoven? I wish you joy of your lessons; but if you do, you have made a gentleman of him:—he won't like to go back to his costermongering."

And so completely and unexceptionally is this so, that, if I had time to-night, I could show you that a nation can-

not be affected by any vice, or weakness, without expressing
it, legibly, and for ever, either in bad art, or by want of art;
and that there is no national virtue, small or great, which is
not manifestly expressed in all the art which circumstances
enable the people possessing that virtue to produce. Take,
for instance, your great English virtue of enduring and
patient courage. You have at present in England only one
art of any consequence—that is, iron-working. You know
thoroughly well how to cast and hammer iron. Now, do
you think, in those masses of lava which you build volcanic
cones to melt, and which you forge at the mouths of the
Infernos you have created; do you think, on those iron
plates, your courage and endurance are not written for ever,
—not merely with an iron pen, but on iron parchment? And
take also your great English vice—European vice—vice of
all the world—vice of all other worlds that roll or shine in
heaven, bearing with them yet the atmosphere of hell—
the vice of jealousy, which brings competition into your
commerce, treachery into your councils, and dishonour into
your wars—that vice which has rendered for you, and for
your next neighbouring nation, the daily occupations of
existence no longer possible, but with the mail upon your
breasts and the sword loose in its sheath; so that at last, you
have realised for all the multitudes of the two great peoples
who lead the so-called civilization of the earth,—you have
realised for them all, I say, in person and in policy, what
was once true only of the rough Border riders of your
Cheviot hills—

> "*They carved at the meal*
> *With gloves of steel,*

And they drank the red wine through the helmet barr'd;"*—
do you think that this national shame and dastardliness of
heart are not written as legibly on every rivet of your iron
armour as the strength of the right hands that forged it?

Friends, I know not whether this thing be the more

* *Lay of the Last Minstrel*, I, 31 ff.

ludicrous or the more melancholy. It is quite unspeakably both. Suppose, instead of being now sent for by you, I had been sent for by some private gentleman, living in a suburban house, with his garden separated only by a fruit wall from his next door neighbour's; and he had called me to consult with him on the furnishing of his drawing-room. I begin looking about me, and find the walls rather bare; I think such and such a paper might be desirable—perhaps a little fresco here and there on the ceiling—a damask curtain or so at the windows. "Ah," says my employer, "damask curtains, indeed! That's all very fine, but you know I can't afford that kind of thing just now!" "Yet the world credits you with a splendid income!" "Ah, yes," says my friend, "but do you know, at present I am obliged to spend it nearly all in steel-traps?" "Steel-traps! for whom?" "Why, for that fellow on the other side the wall, you know: we're very good friends, capital friends; but we are obliged to keep our traps set on both sides of the wall; we could not possibly keep on friendly terms without them, and our spring guns. The worst of it is, we are both clever fellows enough; and there's never a day passes that we don't find out a new trap, or a new gun-barrel, or something; we spend about fifteen millions a year each in our traps, take it altogether; and I don't see how we're to do with less." A highly comic state of life for two private gentlemen! but for two nations, it seems to me, not wholly comic. Bedlam would be comic, perhaps, if there were only one madman in it; and your Christmas pantomime is comic, when there is only one clown in it; but when the whole world turns clown, and paints itself red with its own heart's blood instead of vermilion, it is something else than comic, I think.

Mind, I know a great deal of this is play, and willingly allow for that. You don't know what to do with yourselves for a sensation: fox-hunting and cricketing will not carry you through the whole of this unendurably long mortal life: you liked pop-guns when you were schoolboys, and

rifles and Armstrongs are only the same things better made:
but then the worst of it is, that what was play to you when
boys, was not play to the sparrows; and what is play to
you now, is not play to the small birds of State neither;
and for the black eagles, you are somewhat shy of taking
shots at them, if I mistake not.*

I must get back to the matter in hand, however. Believe
me, without farther instance, I could show you, in all time,
that every nation's vice, or virtue, was written in its art:
the soldiership of early Greece; the sensuality of late Italy;
the visionary religion of Tuscany; the splendid human
energy of Venice. I have no time to do this to-night (I
have done it elsewhere before now); but I proceed to apply
the principle to ourselves in a more searching manner.

I notice that among all the new buildings which cover
your once wild hills, churches and schools are mixed in due,
that is to say, in large proportion, with your mills and mansions; and I notice also that the churches and schools are
almost always Gothic, and the mansions and mills are never
Gothic. May I ask the meaning of this? for, remember, it is
peculiarly a modern phenomenon. When Gothic was invented, houses were Gothic as well as churches; and when
the Italian style superseded the Gothic, churches were
Italian as well as houses. If there is a Gothic spire to the
cathedral of Antwerp, there is a Gothic belfry to the Hôtel
de Ville at Brussels; if Inigo Jones builds an Italian White-
hall, Sir Christopher Wren builds an Italian St. Paul's.
But now you live under one school of architecture, and
worship under another. What do you mean by doing this?
Am I to understand that you are thinking of changing your
architecture back to Gothic; and that you treat your
churches experimentally, because it does not matter what
mistakes you make in a church? Or am I to understand that
you consider Gothic a pre-eminently sacred and beautiful
mode of building, which you think, like the fine frankin-

* An allusion to England's reluctance to aid the Danes in their struggle against Prussia and Austria.

cense, should be mixed for the tabernacle only, and re-served for your religious services? For if this be the feeling, though it may seem at first as if it were graceful and rev-erent, at the root of the matter, it signifies neither more nor less than that you have separated your religion from your life.

For consider what a wide significance this fact has: and remember that it is not you only, but all the people of England, who are behaving thus, just now.

You have all got into the habit of calling the church "the house of God." I have seen, over the doors of many churches, the legend actually carved, *"This* is the house of God and this is the gate of heaven." Now, note where that legend comes from, and of what place it was first spoken. A boy leaves his father's house to go on a long journey on foot, to visit his uncle: he has to cross a wild hill-desert; just as if one of your own boys had to cross the wolds to visit an uncle at Carlisle. The second or third day your boy finds himself somewhere between Hawes and Brough, in the midst of the moors, at sunset. It is stony ground, and boggy; he cannot go one foot farther that night. Down he lies, to sleep, on Wharnside, where best he may, gathering a few of the stones together to put under his head;—so wild the place is, he cannot get anything but stones. And there, lying under the broad night, he has a dream; and he sees a ladder set up on the earth, and the top of it reaches to heaven, and the angels of God are seen ascending and descending upon it. And when he wakes out of his sleep, he says, "How dreadful is this place; surely this is none other than the house of God, and this is the gate of heaven." This PLACE, observe; not this church; not this city; not this stone, even, which he puts up for a memorial—the piece of flint on which his head has lain. But this *place;* this windy slope of Wharnside; this moorland hollow, torrent-bitten, snow-blighted; this *any* place where God lets down the ladder. And how are you to know where that will be? or how are you to determine where it may be, but by being ready for it always? Do you

know where the lightning is to fall next? You *do* know
that, partly; you can guide the lightning; but you cannot
guide the going forth of the Spirit, which is as that lightning when it shines from the east to the west.

But the perpetual and insolent warping of that strong
verse to serve a merely ecclesiastical purpose, is only one
of the thousand instances in which we sink back into gross
Judaism. We call our churches "temples." Now, you know
perfectly well they are *not* temples. They have never had,
never can have, anything whatever to do with temples. They
are "synagogues"—"gathering places"—where you gather
yourselves together as an assembly; and by not calling them
so, you again miss the force of another mighty text—"Thou,
when thou prayest, shalt not be as the hypocrites are; for
they love to pray standing in the *churches*" [we should
translate it], "that they may be seen of men. But thou, when
thou prayest, enter into thy closet, and when thou hast shut
thy door, pray to thy Father,"—which is, not in chancel nor
in aisle, but "in secret."

Now, you feel, as I say this to you—I know you feel—
as if I were trying to take away the honour of your churches.
Not so; I am trying to prove to you the honour of your
houses and your hills; not that the Church is not sacred—
but that the whole Earth is. I would have you feel what
careless, what constant, what infectious sin there is in all
modes of thought, whereby, in calling your churches only
"holy," you call your hearths and homes "profane"; and
have separated yourselves from the heathen by casting all
your household gods to the ground, instead of recognizing,
in the places of their many and feeble Lares, the presence
of your One and Mighty Lord and Lar.

"But what has all this to do with our Exchange?" you ask
me, impatiently. My dear friends, it has just everything to do
with it; on these inner and great questions depend all the
outer and little ones; and if you have asked me down here
to speak to you, because you had before been interested in
anything I have written, you must know that all I have yet

said about architecture was to show this. The book I called *The Seven Lamps* was to show that certain right states of temper and moral feeling were the magic powers by which all good architecture, without exception, had been produced. *The Stones of Venice* had, from beginning to end, no other aim than to show that the Gothic architecture of Venice had arisen out of, and indicated in all its features, a state of pure national faith, and of domestic virtue; and that its Renaissance architecture had arisen out of, and in all its features indicated, a state of concealed national infidelity, and of domestic corruption. And now, you ask me what style is best to build in, and how can I answer, knowing the meaning of the two styles, but by another question —do you mean to build as Christians or as infidels? And still more—do you mean to build as honest Christians or as honest Infidels? as thoroughly and confessedly either one or the other? You don't like to be asked such rude questions. I cannot help it; they are of much more importance than this Exchange business; and if they can be at once answered, the Exchange business settles itself in a moment. But before I press them farther, I must ask leave to explain one point clearly.

In all my past work, my endeavour has been to show that good architecture is essentially religious—the production of a faithful and virtuous, not of an infidel and corrupted people. But in the course of doing this, I have had also to show that good architecture is not *ecclesiastical*. People are so apt to look upon religion as the business of the clergy, not their own, that the moment they hear of anything depending on "religion," they think it must also have depended on the priesthood; and I have had to take what place was to be occupied between these two errors, and fight both, often with seeming contradiction. Good architecture is the work of good and believing men; therefore, you say, at least some people say, "Good architecture must essentially have been the work of the clergy, not of the laity." No—a thousand times no; good architecture has always been the work of the commonalty, *not* of the clergy.

"What," you say, "those glorious cathedrals—the pride of Europe—did their builders not form Gothic architecture?" No; they corrupted Gothic architecture. Gothic was formed in the baron's castle, and the burgher's street. It was formed by the thoughts, and hands, and powers of labouring citizens and warrior kings. By the monk it was used as an instrument for the aid of his superstition: when that superstition became a beautiful madness, and the best hearts of Europe vainly dreamed and pined in the cloister, and vainly raged and perished in the crusade,—through that fury of perverted faith and wasted war, the Gothic rose also to its loveliest, most fantastic, and, finally, most foolish dreams; and in those dreams was lost.

I hope, now, that there is no risk of your misunderstanding me when I come to the gist of what I want to say to-night;—when I repeat, that every great national architecture has been the result and exponent of a great national religion. You can't have bits of it here, bits there—you must have it everywhere or nowhere. It is not the monopoly of a clerical company—it is not the exponent of a theological dogma—it is not the hieroglyphic writing of an initiated priesthood; it is the manly language of a people inspired by resolute and common purpose, and rendering resolute and common fidelity to the legible laws of an undoubted God.

Now there have as yet been three distinct schools of European architecture. I say, European, because Asiatic and African architectures belong so entirely to other races and climates, that there is no question of them here; only, in passing, I will simply assure you that whatever is good or great in Egypt, and Syria, and India, is just good or great for the same reasons as the buildings on our side of the Bosphorus. We Europeans, then, have had three great religions: the Greek, which was the worship of the God of Wisdom and Power; the Mediæval, which was the worship of the God of Judgment and Consolation; the Renaissance, which was the worship of the God of Pride and Beauty: these three we have had—they are past,—and now, at last, we English have got a fourth religion, and a God of our own, about which I want to ask you. But I must explain these three old ones first.

I repeat, first, the Greeks essentially worshipped the God of Wisdom; so that whatever contended against their religion,—to the Jews a stumbling-block,—was, to the Greeks —*Foolishness.*

The first Greek idea of deity was that expressed in the word, of which we keep the remnant in our words *"Di-*urnal" and *"Di*-vine"—the god of *Day,* Jupiter the revealer. Athena is his daughter, but especially daughter of the Intellect, springing armed from the head. We are only with the help of recent investigation beginning to penetrate the depth of meaning couched under the Athenaic symbols: but I may note rapidly, that her ægis, the mantle with the serpent fringes, in which she often, in the best statues, is represented as folding up her left hand, for better guard; and the Gorgon, on her shield, are both representative mainly of the chilling horror and sadness (turning men to stone, as it were,) of the outmost and superficial spheres of knowledge—that knowledge which separates, in bitterness, hardness, and sorrow, the heart of the full-grown man from the heart of the child. For out of imperfect knowledge spring terror, dissension, danger, and disdain; but from perfect knowledge, given by the full-revealed Athena, strength and peace, in sign of which she is crowned with the olive spray, and bears the resistless spear.

This then, was the Greek conception of purest Deity; and every habit of life, and every form of his art developed themselves from the seeking this bright, serene, resistless wisdom; and setting himself, as a man, to do things evermore rightly and strongly; not with any ardent affection or ultimate hope; but with a resolute and continent energy of will, as knowing that for failure there was no consolation, and for sin there was no remission. And the Greek architecture rose unerring, bright, clearly defined, and self-contained.

Next followed in Europe the great Christian faith, which was essentially the religion of Comfort. Its great doctrine is the remission of sins; for which cause, it happens, too often, in certain phases of Christianity, that sin and sickness themselves are partly glorified, as if, the more you had to be healed of, the more divine was the healing. The practical result of this doctrine, in art, is a continual contemplation of sin and disease, and of imaginary states of purification from them; thus we have an architecture conceived in a mingled sentiment of melancholy and aspiration, partly severe, partly luxuriant, which will bend itself to every one of our needs, and every one of our fancies, and be strong or weak with us, as we are strong or weak ourselves. It is, of all architecture, the basest, when base people build it— of all, the noblest, when built by the noble.

And now note that both these religions—Greek and Mediæval—perished by falsehood in their own main purpose. The Greek religion of Wisdom perished in a false philosophy—"Oppositions of science, falsely so called." The Mediæval religion of Consolation perished in false comfort; in remission of sins given lyingly. It was the selling of absolution that ended the Mediæval faith; and I can tell you more, it is the selling of absolution which, to the end of time, will mark false Christianity. Pure Christianity gives her remission of sins only by *ending* them; but false Christianity gets her remission of sins by *compounding for* them. And there are many ways of compounding for them. We English have beautiful little quiet ways of buying absolution, whether in low Church or high, far more cunning than any of Tetzel's trading.*

Then, thirdly, there followed the religion of Pleasure, in which all Europe gave itself to luxury, ending in death. First, *bals masqués* in every saloon, and then guillotines in every square. And all these three worships issue in vast temple building. Your Greek worshipped Wisdom, and built

* Johann Tetzel, whose sale of papal indulgences aroused Luther's wrath and led ultimately to the Reformation.

you the Parthenon—the Virgin's temple. The Mediæval
worshipped Consolation, and built you Virgin temples also
—but to our Lady of Salvation. Then the Revivalist worshipped beauty, of a sort, and built you Versailles and the
Vatican. Now, lastly, will you tell me what *we* worship,
and what *we* build?

You know we are speaking always of the real, active,
continual, national worship; that by which men act, while
they live; not that which they talk of, when they die. Now,
we have, indeed, a nominal religion, to which we pay tithes
of property and sevenths of time; but we have also a practical and earnest religion, to which we devote nine-tenths
of our property, and six-sevenths of our time. And we dispute a great deal about the nominal religion: but we are all
unanimous about this practical one; of which I think you
will admit that the ruling goddess may be best generally
described as the "Goddess of Getting-on," or "Britannia of
the Market." The Athenians had an "Athena Agoraia," or
Athena of the Market; but she was a subordinate type of
their goddess, while our Britannia Agoraia is the principal
type of ours. And all your great architectural works are, of
course, built to her. It is long since you built a great cathedral; and how you would laugh at me if I proposed building a cathedral on the top of one of these hills of yours, to
make it an Acropolis! But your railroad mounds, vaster
than the walls of Babylon; your railroad stations, vaster
than the temple of Ephesus, and innumerable; your chimneys, how much more mighty and costly than cathedral
spires! your harbour-piers; your warehouses; your exchanges!—all these are built to your great Goddess of "Getting-on"; and she has formed, and will continue to form,
your architecture, as long as you worship her; and it is
quite vain to ask me to tell you how to build to *her;* you
know far better than I.

There might, indeed, on some theories, be a conceivably
good architecture for Exchanges—that is to say, if there
were any heroism in the fact or deed of exchange, which
might be typically carved on the outside of your building.

For, you know, all beautiful architecture must be adorned with sculpture or painting; and for sculpture or painting, you must have a subject. And hitherto it has been a received opinion among the nations of the world that the only right subjects for either, were *heroisms* of some sort. Even on his pots and his flagons, the Greek put a Hercules slaying lions, or an Apollo slaying serpents, or Bacchus slaying melancholy giants, and earthborn despondencies. On his temples, the Greek put contests of great warriors in founding states, or of gods with evil spirits. On his houses and temples alike, the Christian put carvings of angels conquering devils; or of hero-martyrs exchanging this world for another: subject inappropriate, I think, to our direction of exchange here. And the Master of Christians not only left His followers without any orders as to the sculpture of affairs of exchange on the outside of buildings, but gave some strong evidence of His dislike of affairs of exchange within them. And yet there might surely be a heroism in such affairs; and all commerce become a kind of selling of doves, not impious. The wonder has always been great to me, that heroism has never been supposed to be in anywise consistent with the practice of supplying people with food, or clothes; but rather with that of quartering one's self upon them for food, and stripping them of their clothes. Spoiling of armour is an heroic deed in all ages; but the selling of clothes, old, or new, has never taken any colour of magnanimity. Yet one does not see why feeding the hungry and clothing the naked should ever become base businesses, even when engaged in on a large scale. If one could contrive to attach the notion of conquest to them anyhow! so that, supposing there were anywhere an obstinate race, who refused to be comforted, one might take some pride in giving them compulsory comfort! and, as it were, *"occupying* a country" with one's gifts, instead of one's armies? If one could only consider it as much a victory to get a barren field sown, as to get an eared field stripped; and contend who should build villages, instead of who should "carry" them! Are not all forms of heroism conceivable in doing these serviceable deeds? You doubt who is strongest? It might be ascertained by push of spade, as well as push of sword. Who is wisest? There are witty things to be thought of in planning other business than campaigns. Who is bravest? There are always the elements to fight with, stronger than men; and nearly as merciless.

The only absolutely and unapproachably heroic element in the soldier's work seems to be—that he is paid little for it—and regularly: while you traffickers, and exchangers, and others occupied in presumably benevolent business, like to be paid much for it—and by chance. I never can make out how it is that a *knight*-errant does not expect to be paid for his trouble, but a *pedlar*-errant always does;—that people are willing to take hard knocks for nothing, but never to sell ribands cheap; that they are ready to go on fervent crusades, to recover the tomb of a buried God, but never on any travels to fulfil the orders of a living one;—that they will go anywhere barefoot to preach their faith, but must be well bribed to practise it, and are perfectly ready to give the Gospel gratis, but never the loaves and fishes.

If you chose to take the matter up on any such soldierly principle; to do your commerce, and your feeding of nations, for fixed salaries; and to be as particular about giving people the best food, and the best cloth, as soldiers are about giving them the best gunpowder, I could carve something for you on your exchange worth looking at. But I can only at present suggest decorating its frieze with pendant purses; and making its pillars broad at the base, for the sticking of bills. And in the innermost chambers of it there might be a statue of Britannia of the Market, who may have, perhaps advisably, a partridge for her crest, typical at once of her courage in fighting for noble ideas, and of her interest in game; and round its neck, the inscription in golden letters, "Perdix fovit quæ non peperit."* Then, for

* Jerem. xvii. 11, (best in Septuagint and Vulgate). "As the partridge, fostering what she brought not forth, so he that getteth riches, not by right, shall leave them in the midst of his days, and at his end shall be a fool." [Ruskin's note.]

her spear, she might have a weaver's beam; and on her shield, instead of St. George's Cross, the Milanese boar, semi-fleeced, with the town of Gennesaret proper, in the field; and the legend, "In the best market," and her corslet, of leather, folded over her heart in the shape of a purse, with thirty slits in it, for a piece of money to go in at, on each day of the month. And I doubt not but that people would come to see your exchange, and its goddess, with applause.

Nevertheless, I want to point out to you certain strange characters in this goddess of yours. She differs from the great Greek and Mediæval deities essentially in two things —first, as to the continuance of her presumed power; secondly, as to the extent of it.

1st, as to the Continuance.

The Greek Goddess of Wisdom gave continual increase of wisdom, as the Christian Spirit of Comfort (or Comforter) continual increase of comfort. There was no question, with these, of any limit or cessation of function. But with your Agora Goddess, that is just the most important question. Getting on—but where to? Gathering together—but how much? Do you mean to gather always—never to spend? If so, I wish you joy of your goddess, for I am just as well off as you, without the trouble of worshipping her at all. But if you do not spend, somebody else will—somebody else must. And it is because of this (among many other such errors) that I have fearlessly declared your so-called science of Political Economy to be no science; because, namely, it has omitted the study of exactly the most important branch of the business—the study of *spending*. For spend you must, and as much as you make, ultimately. You gather corn:— will you bury England under a heap of grain; or will you, when you have gathered, finally eat? You gather gold:—will you make your house-roofs of it, or pave your streets with it? That is still one way of spending it. But if you keep it, that you may get more, I'll give you more; I'll give you all the gold you want—all you can imagine—if you can tell me what you'll do with it. You shall have thousands of gold pieces;—thousands of thousands—millions—mountains, of gold: where will you keep them? Will you put an Olympus of silver upon a golden Pelion—make Ossa like a wart? Do you think the rain and dew would then come down to you, in the streams from such mountains, more blessedly than they will down the mountains which God has made for you, of moss and whinstone? But it is not gold that you want to gather! What is it? greenbacks? No; not those neither. What is it then—is it ciphers after a capital I? Cannot you practise writing ciphers, and write as many as you want! Write ciphers for an hour every morning, in a big book, and say every evening, I am worth all those noughts more than I was yesterday. Won't that do? Well, what in the name of Plutus is it you want? Not gold, not greenbacks, not ciphers after a capital I? You will have to answer, after all, "No; we want, somehow or other, money's *worth.*" Well, what is that? Let your Goddess of Getting-on discover it, and let her learn to stay therein.

But there is yet another question to be asked respecting this Goddess of Getting-on. The first was of the continuance of her power; the second is of its extent.

Pallas and the Madonna were supposed to be all the world's Pallas, and all the world's Madonna. They could teach all men, and they could comfort all men. But, look strictly into the nature of the power of your Goddess of Getting-on; and you will find she is the Goddess—not of everybody's getting on—but only of somebody's getting on. This is a vital, or rather deathful, distinction. Examine it in your own ideal of the state of national life which this Goddess is to evoke and maintain. I asked you what it was, when I was last here;—you have never told me. Now, shall I try to tell you?

Your ideal of human life then is, I think, that it should be passed in a pleasant undulating world, with iron and coal everywhere underneath it. On each pleasant bank of this world is to be a beautiful mansion, with two wings; and stables, and coach-houses; a moderately-sized park; a large garden and hot-houses; and pleasant carriage drives through the shrubberies. In this mansion are to live the favoured votaries of the Goddess; the English gentleman, with his gracious wife, and his beautiful family; he always able to have the boudoir and the jewels for the wife, and the beautiful ball dresses for the daughters, and hunters for the sons, and a shooting in the Highlands for himself. At the bottom of the bank, is to be the mill; not less than a quarter of a mile long, with one steam engine at each end, and two in the middle, and a chimney three hundred feet high. In this mill are to be in constant employment from eight hundred to a thousand workers, who never drink, never strike, always go to church on Sunday, and always express themselves in respectful language.

Is not that, broadly, and in the main features, the kind of thing you propose to yourselves? It is very pretty indeed, seen from above; not at all so pretty, seen from below. For, observe, while to one family this deity is indeed the Goddess of Getting-on, to a thousand families she is the Goddess of *not* Getting-on. "Nay," you say, "they have all their chance." Yes, so has every one in a lottery, but there must always be the same number of blanks. "Ah! but in a lottery it is not skill and intelligence which take the lead, but blind chance." What then! do you think the old practice, that "they should take who have the power, and they should keep who can," is less iniquitous, when the power has become power of brains instead of fist? and that, though we may not take advantage of a child's or a woman's weakness, we may of a man's foolishness? "Nay, but finally, work must be done, and someone must be at the top, someone at the bottom." Granted, my friends. Work must always be, and captains of work must always be; and if you in the least remember the tone of any of my writings, you must know that they are thought unfit for this age, because they are always insisting on need of government, and speaking with scorn of liberty. But I beg you to observe that there is a wide difference between being captains or governors of work, and taking the profits of it. It does not follow, because you are general of an army, that you are to take all the treasure, or land, it wins (if it fight for treasure or land); neither, because you are king of a nation, that you are to consume all the profits of the nation's work. Real kings, on the contrary, are known invariably by their doing quite the reverse of this—by their taking the least possible quantity of the nation's work for themselves. There is no test of real kinghood so infallible as that. Does the crowned creature live simply, bravely, unostentatiously? probably he *is* a King. Does he cover his body with jewels, and his table with delicates? in all probability he is *not* a King. It is possible he may be, as Solomon was; but that is when the nation shares his splendour with him. Solomon made gold, not only to be in his own palace as stones, but to be in Jerusalem as stones. But, even so, for the most part, these splendid kinghoods expire in ruin, and only the true kinghoods live, which are of royal labourers governing loyal labourers; who, both leading rough lives, establish the true dynasties. Conclusively you will find that because you are king of a nation, it does not follow that you are to gather for yourself all the wealth of that nation; neither, because you are king of a small part of the nation, and lord over the means of its maintenance—over field, or mill, or mine,—are you to take all the produce of that piece of the foundation of national existence for yourself.

You will tell me I need not preach against these things, for I cannot mend them. No, good friends, I cannot; but you can, and you will; or something else can and will. Even good things have no abiding power—and shall these evil things persist in victorious evil? All history shows, on the contrary, that to be the exact thing they never can do. Change *must* come; but it is ours to determine whether change of growth, or change of death. Shall the Parthenon be in ruins on its rock, and Bolton priory in its meadow, but these mills of yours be the consummation of the buildings of the earth, and their wheels be as the wheels of eternity? Think you that "men may come, and men may go," but—mills—go on forever? Not so; out of these, better or worse shall come; and it is for you to choose which.

I know that none of this wrong is done with deliberate purpose. I know, on the contrary, that you wish your workmen well; that you do much for them, and that you desire to do more for them, if you saw your way to such benevolence safely. I know that even all this wrong and misery are brought about by a warped sense of duty, each of you striving to do his best; but, unhappily, not knowing for whom this best should be done. And all our hearts have been betrayed by the plausible impiety of the modern economist, telling us that, "To do the best for ourselves, is finally to do the best for others." Friends, our great Master said not so; and most absolutely we shall find this world is not made so. Indeed, to do the best for others, is finally to do the best for ourselves; but it will not do to have our eyes fixed on that issue. The Pagans had got beyond that. Hear what a Pagan says of this matter; hear what were, perhaps, the last written words of Plato,—if not the last actually written (for this we cannot know), yet assuredly in fact and power his parting words—in which, endeavouring to give full crowning and harmonious close to all his thoughts, and to speak the sum of them by the imagined sentence of the Great Spirit, his strength and his heart fail him, and the words cease, broken off for ever.

They are at the close of the dialogue called *Critias,* in which he describes, partly from real tradition, partly in ideal dream, the early state of Athens; and the genesis, and order, and religion, of the fabled isle of Atlantis; in which genesis he conceives the same first perfection and final degeneracy of man, which in our own Scriptural tradition is expressed by saying that the Sons of God inter-married with the daughters of men, for he supposes the earliest race to have been indeed the children of God; and to have corrupted themselves, until "their spot was not the spot of his children." And this, he says, was the end; that indeed "through many generations, so long as the God's nature in them yet was full, they were submissive to the sacred laws, and carried themselves lovingly to all that had kindred with them in divineness; for their uttermost spirit was faithful and true, and in every wise great; so that, in *all meekness of wisdom, they dealt with each other,* and took all the chances of life; and despising all things except virtue, they cared little what happened day by day, and *bore lightly the burden* of gold and of possessions; for they saw that, if *only their common love and virtue increased, all these things would be increased together with them;* but to set their esteem and ardent pursuit upon material possession would be to lose that first, and their virtue and affection together with it. And by such reasoning, and what of the divine nature remained in them, they gained all this greatness of which we have already told; but when the God's part of them faded and became extinct, being mixed again and again, and effaced by the prevalent mortality; and the human nature at last exceeded, they then became unable to endure the courses of fortune; and fell into shapelessness of life, and baseness in the sight of him who could see, having lost everything that was fairest of their honour; while to the blind hearts which could not discern the true life, tending to happiness, it seemed that they were then chiefly noble and happy, being filled with all iniquity of inordinate possession and power. Whereupon, the God of Gods, whose Kinghood is in laws, beholding a once just nation thus cast into misery, and desiring to lay such punishment upon them as might make them repent into restraining, gathered together all the gods into his dwelling place, which from heaven's centre overlooks whatever has part in creation; and having assembled them, he said"——

The rest is silence.* Last words of the chief wisdom of the heathen, spoken of this idol of riches; this idol of yours; this golden image, high by measureless cubits, set up where your green fields of England are furnace-burnt into the

* The last words of Hamlet.

likeness of the plain of Dura: this idol, forbidden to us, first of all idols, by our own Master and faith; forbidden to us also by every human lip that has ever, in any age or people, been accounted of as able to speak according to the purposes of God. Continue to make that forbidden deity your principal one, and soon no more art, no more science, no more pleasure will be possible. Catastrophe will come; or, worse than catastrophe, slow mouldering and withering into Hades. But if you can fix some conception of a true human state of life to be striven for—life, good for all men, as for yourselves; if you can determine some honest and simple order of existence; following those trodden ways of wisdom, which are pleasantness, and seeking her quiet and withdrawn paths, which are peace;—then, and so sanctifying wealth into "commonwealth," all your art, your literature, your daily labours, your domestic affection, and citizen's duty, will join and increase into one magnificent harmony. You will know then how to build, well enough; you will build with stone well, but with flesh better; temples not made with hands, but riveted of hearts; and that kind of marble, crimson-veined, is indeed eternal.

SESAME AND LILIES

Of Kings' Treasuries*

"You shall each have a cake of sesame,—and ten pound."
LUCIAN: The Fisherman

My first duty this evening is to ask your pardon for the ambiguity of title under which the subject of lecture has been announced: for indeed I am not going to talk of kings, known as regnant, nor of treasuries, understood to contain wealth; but of quite another order of royalty, and another material of riches, than those usually acknowledged. I had even intended to ask your attention for a little while on trust, and (as sometimes one contrives, in taking a friend to see a favourite piece of scenery) to hide what I wanted most to show, with such imperfect cunning as I might, until we unexpectedly reached the best point of view by winding paths. But—and as also I have heard it said, by men practised in public address, that hearers are never so much fatigued as by the endeavour to follow a speaker who gives them no clue to his purpose,—I will take the slight mask off at once, and tell you plainly that I want to speak to you about the treasures hidden in books; and about the way we find them, and the way we lose them. A grave subject, you will say; and a wide one! Yes; so wide that I shall make no effort to touch the compass of it. I will try only to bring before you a few simple thoughts about reading, which press themselves upon me every day more deeply, as I watch

* Delivered in the Town Hall, Rusholme, December 6, 1864.

the course of the public mind with respect to our daily enlarging means of education; and the answeringly wider spreading on the levels, of the irrigation of literature. . . .

First of all, I tell you earnestly and authoritatively (I *know* I am right in this), you must get into the habit of looking intensely at words, and assuring yourself of their meaning, syllable by syllable—nay, letter by letter. For though it is only by reason of the opposition of letters in the function of signs, to sounds in the function of signs, that the study of books is called "literature," and that a man versed in it is called, by the consent of nations, a man of letters instead of a man of books, or of words, you may yet connect with that accidental nomenclature this real fact:—that you might read all the books in the British Museum (if you could live long enough), and remain an utterly "illiterate," uneducated person; but that if you read ten pages of a good book, letter by letter,—that is to say, with real accuracy,—you are for evermore in some measure an educated person. The entire difference between education and non-education (as regards the merely intellectual part of it), consists in this accuracy. . . . A few words well chosen, and distinguished, will do work that a thousand cannot, when every one is acting, equivocally, in the function of another. Yes; and words, if they are not watched, will do deadly work sometimes. There are masked words droning and skulking about us in Europe just now,—(there never were so many, owing to the spread of a shallow, blotching, blundering, infectious "information," or rather deformation, everywhere, and to the teaching of catechisms and phrases at school instead of human meanings)—there are masked words abroad, I say, which nobody understands, but which everybody uses, and most people will also fight for, live for, or even die for, fancying they mean this or that, or the other, of things dear to them: for such words wear chameleon cloaks—"ground-lion" cloaks, of the colour of the ground of any man's fancy: on that ground they lie in wait, and rend them with a spring from it. There never were creatures of prey so mischievous, never diplomatists so cunning, never poisoners so deadly, as these masked words; they are the unjust stewards of all men's ideas: whatever fancy or favourite instinct a man most cherishes, he gives to his favourite masked word to take care of for him; the word at last comes to have an infinite power over him,— you cannot get at him but by its ministry. . . .

And now, merely for example's sake, I will with your permission, read a few lines of a true book with you, carefully; and see what will come out of them. I will take a book perfectly known to you all. No English words are more familiar to us, yet few perhaps have been read with less sincerity. I will take these few following lines of *Lycidas*:—

> "*Last came, and last did go,*
> *The pilot of the Galilean lake.*
> *Two massy keys he bore of metals twain,*
> *(The golden opes, the iron shuts amain,)*
> *He shook his mitred locks, and stern bespake,*
> *'How well could I have spared for thee, young swain,*
> *Enow of such as for their bellies' sake*
> *Creep, and intrude, and climb into the fold!*
> *Of other care they little reckoning make,*
> *Than how to scramble at the shearers' feast,*
> *And shove away the worthy bidden guest;*
> *Blind mouths! that scarce themselves know how to hold*
> *A sheep-hook, or have learn'd aught else, the least*
> *That to the faithful herdman's art belongs!*
> *What recks it them? What need they? They are sped;*
> *And when they list, their lean and flashy songs*
> *Grate on their scrannel pipes of wretched straw;*
> *The hungry sheep look up, and are not fed,*
> *But, swoln with wind, and the rank mist they draw,*
> *Rot inwardly, and foul contagion spread;*
> *Besides what the grim wolf with privy paw*
> *Daily devours apace, and nothing said.*' "

Let us think over this passage, and examine its words. First, is it not singular to find Milton assigning to St.

Peter, not only his full episcopal function, but the very types of it which Protestants usually refuse most passionately? His "mitred" locks! Milton was no Bishop-lover; how comes St. Peter to be "mitred"? "Two massy keys he bore." Is this, then, the power of the keys claimed by the Bishops of Rome? and is it acknowledged here by Milton only in a poetical licence, for the sake of its picturesqueness, that he may get the gleam of the golden keys to help his effect?

Do not think it. Great men do not play stage tricks with the doctrines of life and death: only little men do that. Milton means what he says; and means it with his might too—is going to put the whole strength of his spirit presently into the saying of it. For though not a lover of false bishops, he *was* a lover of true ones; and the Lake-pilot is here, in his thoughts, the type and head of true episcopal power. For Milton reads that text, "I will give unto thee the keys of the kingdom of heaven," quite honestly. Puritan though he be, he would not blot it out of the book because there have been bad bishops; nay, in order to understand *him*, we must understand that verse first; it will not do to eye it askance, or whisper it under our breath, as if it were a weapon of an adverse sect. It is a solemn, universal assertion, deeply to be kept in mind by all sects. But perhaps we shall be better able to reason on it if we go on a little farther, and come back to it. For clearly this marked insistence on the power of the true episcopate is to make us feel more weightily what is to be charged against the false claimants of episcopate; or generally, against false claimants of power and rank in the body of the clergy; they who, "for their bellies' sake, creep, and intrude, and climb into the fold."

Never think Milton uses those three words to fill up his verse, as a loose writer would. He needs all the three;—especially those three, and no more than those—"creep," and "intrude," and "climb"; no other words would or could serve the turn, and no more could be added. For they exhaustively comprehend the three classes, correspondent to the three characters, of men who dishonestly seek ecclesi-

astical power. First, those who *"creep"* into the fold; who do
not care for office, nor name, but for secret influence, and do
all things occultly and cunningly, consenting to any servility
of office or conduct, so only that they may intimately discern, and unawares direct, the minds of men. Then those
who "intrude" (thrust, that is) themselves into the fold,
who by natural insolence of heart, and stout eloquence of
tongue, and fearlessly perseverant self-assertion, obtain hearing and authority with the common crowd. Lastly, those
who "climb," who, by labour and learning, both stout and
sound, but selfishly exerted in the cause of their own ambition, gain high dignities and authorities, and become
"lords over the heritage," though not "ensamples to the
flock."

Now go on:—

> *"Of other care they little reckoning make,*
> *Than how to scramble at the shearers' feast,*
> *Blind mouths—"*

I pause again, for this is a strange expression; a broken
metaphor, one might think, careless and unscholarly.

Not so: its very audacity and pithiness are intended to
make us look close at the phrase and remember it. Those
two monosyllables express the precisely accurate contraries
of right character, in the two great offices of the Church—
those of bishop and pastor.

A "Bishop" means "a person who sees."

A "Pastor" means "a person who feeds."

The most unbishoply character a man can have is therefore to be Blind.

The most unpastoral is, instead of feeding, to want to
be fed,—to be a Mouth.

Take the two reverses together, and you have "blind
mouths." We may advisably follow out this idea a little.
Nearly all the evils in the Church have arisen from bishops
desiring *power* more than *light*. They want authority, not
outlook. Whereas their real office is not to rule; though

it may be vigorously to exhort and rebuke: it is the king's
office to rule; the bishop's office is to *oversee* the flock; to
number it, sheep by sheep; to be ready always to give full
account of it. Now it is clear he cannot give account of the
souls, if he has not so much as numbered the bodies, of his
flock. The first thing, therefore, that a bishop has to do is
at least to put himself in a position in which, at any moment, he can obtain the history, from childhood, of every
living soul in his diocese, and of its present state. Down in
that back street, Bill and Nancy, knocking each other's
teeth out!—Does the bishop know all about it? Has he his
eye upon them? Has he *had* his eye upon them? Can he
circumstantially explain to us how Bill got into the habit
of beating Nancy about the head? If he cannot, he is no
bishop, though he had a mitre as high as Salisbury steeple;
he is no bishop,—he has sought to be at the helm instead of
the masthead; he has no sight of things. "Nay," you say,
"it is not his duty to look after Bill in the back street."
What! the fat sheep that have full fleeces—you think it is
only those he should look after while (go back to your
Milton) "the hungry sheep look up, and are not fed, besides
what the grim wolf, with privy paw" (bishops knowing
nothing about it), "daily devours apace, and nothing said"?

"But that's not our idea of a bishop." Perhaps not; but
it was St. Paul's; and it was Milton's. They may be right,
or we may be; but we must not think we are reading either
one or the other by putting our meaning into their words.

I go on.

"But swoln with wind, and the rank mist they draw."

This is to meet the vulgar answer that "if the poor are
not looked after in their bodies, they are in their souls;
they have spiritual food."

And Milton says, "They have no such thing as spiritual
food; they are only swollen with wind." At first you may
think that is a coarse type, and an obscure one. But again,
it is a quite literally accurate one. Take up your Latin and

Greek dictionaries, and find out the meaning of "Spirit."
It is only a contraction of the Latin word "breath," and
an indistinct translation of the Greek word for "wind."
The same word is used in writing, "The wind bloweth
where it listeth"; and in writing, "So is every one that is
born of the Spirit"; born of the *breath*, that is; for it means
the breath of God, in soul and body. We have the true sense
of it in our words "inspiration" and "expire." Now, there
are two kinds of breath with which the flock may be filled,
—God's breath, and man's. The breath of God is health,
and life, and peace to them, as the air of heaven is to the
flocks on the hills; but man's breath—the word which *he*
calls spiritual—is disease and contagion to them, as the fog
of the fen. They rot inwardly with it; they are puffed up by
it, as a dead body by the vapours of its own decomposition.
This is literally true of all false religious teaching; the first
and last, and fatalest sign of it, is that "puffing up." Your
converted children, who teach their parents; your converted
convicts, who teach honest men; your converted dunces,
who, having lived in cretinous stupefaction half their lives,
suddenly awaking to the fact of there being a God, fancy
themselves therefore His peculiar people and messengers;
your sectarians of every species, small and great, Catholic or
Protestant, of high church or low, in so far as they think
themselves exclusively in the right and others wrong; and,
pre-eminently, in every sect, those who hold that men can
be saved by thinking rightly instead of doing rightly, by
word instead of act, and wish instead of work;—these are
the true fog children—clouds, these, without water; bodies,
these, of putrescent vapour and skin, without blood or flesh:
blown bagpipes for the fiends to pipe with—corrupt, and
corrupting,—"Swollen with wind, and the rank mist they
draw."

Lastly, let us return to the lines respecting the power of
the keys, for now we can understand them. Note the difference between Milton and Dante in their interpretation of
this power: for once, the latter is weaker in thought; he

supposes *both* the keys to be of the gate of heaven; one is of gold, the other of silver: they are given by St. Peter to the sentinel angel; and it is not easy to determine the meaning either of the substances of the three steps of the gate, or of the two keys. But Milton makes one, of gold, the key of heaven; the other, of iron, the key of the prison in which the wicked teachers are to be bound who "have taken away the key of knowledge, yet entered not in themselves."

We have seen that the duties of bishop and pastor are to see, and feed; and of all who do so it is said, "He that watereth, shall be watered also himself." But the reverse is truth also. He that watereth not, shall be *withered* himself; and he that seeth not, shall himself be shut out of sight— shut into the perpetual prison-house. And that prison opens here, as well as hereafter: he who is to be bound in heaven must first be bound on earth. That command to the strong angels, of which the rock-apostle is the image, "Take him, and bind him hand and foot, and cast him out," issues, in its measure, against the teacher, for every help withheld, and for every truth refused, and for every falsehood enforced; so that he is more strictly fettered the more he fetters, and farther outcast as he more and more misleads, till at last the bars of the iron cage close upon him, and as "the golden opes, the iron shuts amain."

We have got something out of the lines, I think, and much more is yet to be found in them; but we have done enough by way of example of the kind of word-by-word examination of your author which is rightly called "reading"; watching every accent and expression, and putting ourselves always in the author's place, annihilating our own personality, and seeking to enter into his, so as to be able assuredly to say, "Thus Milton thought," not "Thus *I* thought, in mis-reading Milton." . . .

Having then faithfully listened to the great teachers, that you may enter into their Thoughts, you have yet this higher advance to make;—you have to enter into their Hearts. As you go to them first for clear sight, so you must stay with them, that you may share at last their just and mighty Passion. Passion, or "sensation." I am not afraid of the word; still less of the thing. You have heard many outcries against sensation lately; but, I can tell you, it is not less sensation we want, but more. The ennobling difference between one man and another,—between one animal and another,—is precisely in this, that one feels more than another. If we were sponges, perhaps sensation might not be easily got for us; if we were earthworms, liable at every instant to be cut in two by the spade, perhaps too much sensation might not be good for us. But being human creatures, it *is* good for us; nay, we are only human in so far as we are sensitive, and our honour is precisely in proportion to our passion.

You know I said of that great and pure society of the Dead, that it would allow "no vain or vulgar person to enter there." What do you think I meant by a "vulgar" person? What do you yourselves mean by "vulgarity"? You will find it a fruitful subject of thought; but, briefly, the essence of all vulgarity lies in want of sensation. Simple and innocent vulgarity is merely an untrained and undeveloped bluntness of body and mind; but in true inbred vulgarity, there is a dreadful callousness, which, in extremity, becomes capable of every sort of bestial habit and crime, without fear, without pleasure, without horror, and without pity. It is in the blunt hand and the dead heart, in the diseased habit, in the hardened conscience, that men become vulgar; they are for ever vulgar, precisely in proportion as they are incapable of sympathy,—of quick understanding,—of all that, in deep insistence on the common, but most accurate term, may be called the "tact" or "touch-faculty," of body and soul: that tact which the Mimosa has in trees, which the pure woman has above all creatures; fineness and fulness of sensation, beyond reason;—the guide and sanctifier of reason itself. Reason can but determine what is true: —it is the God-given passion of humanity which alone can recognise what God has made good.

We come then to that great concourse of the Dead, not merely to know from them what is True, but chiefly to feel with them what is just. Now, to feel with them, we must be like them; and none of us can become that without pains. As the true knowledge is disciplined and tested knowledge,—not the first thought that comes, so the true passion is disciplined and tested passion,—not the first passion that comes. The first that come are the vain, the false, the treacherous; if you yield to them they will lead you wildly and far, in vain pursuit. . . . So the anxiety is ignoble, with which you linger over the course and catastrophe of an idle tale; but do you think the anxiety is less, or greater, with which you watch, or *ought* to watch, the dealings of fate and destiny with the life of an agonized nation? Alas! it is the narrowness, selfishness, minuteness, of your sensation that you have to deplore in England at this day;—sensation which spends itself in bouquets and speeches: in revellings and junketings; in sham fights and gay puppet shows, while you can look on and see noble nations murdered, man by man, without an effort or a tear.* . . .

No nation can last, which has made a mob of itself, however generous at heart. It must discipline its passions, and direct them, or they will discipline *it,* one day, with scorpion whips. Above all, a nation cannot last as a money-making mob: it cannot with impunity,—it cannot with existence,—go on despising literature, despising science, despising art, despising nature, despising compassion, and concentrating its soul on Pence. Do you think these are harsh or wild words? Have patience with me but a little longer. I will prove their truth to you, clause by clause.

(I.) I say first we have despised literature. What do we, as a nation, care about books? How much do you think we spend altogether on our libraries, public or private, as compared with what we spend on our horses? If a man spends lavishly on his library, you call him mad—a bibliomaniac.

* An allusion to Russia's brutal suppression of the Polish insurrection in 1864, a few months before Ruskin delivered this lecture.

But you never call any one a horsemaniac, though men ruin
themselves every day by their horses, and you do not hear
of people ruining themselves by their books. Or, to go
lower still, how much do you think the contents of the
book-shelves of the United Kingdom, public and private,
would fetch, as compared with the contents of its wine-
cellars? What position would its expenditure on literature
take, as compared with its expenditure on luxurious eating?
We talk of food for the mind, as of food for the body: now
a good book contains such food inexhaustibly; it is a provision for life, and for the best part of us; yet how long
most people would look at the best book before they would
give the price of a large turbot for it? . . . The very cheapness of literature is making even wise people forget that if
a book is worth reading, it is worth buying. No book is
worth anything which is not worth *much;* nor is it serviceable, until it has been read, and re-read, and loved, and
loved again; and marked, so that you can refer to the passages you want in it, as a soldier can seize the weapon he
needs in an armoury, or a housewife bring the spice she
needs from her store. Bread of flour is good; but there is
bread, sweet as honey, if we would eat it, in a good book;
and the family must be poor indeed, which, once in their
lives, cannot, for such multipliable barley-loaves, pay their
baker's bill. We call ourselves a rich nation, and we are
filthy and foolish enough to thumb each other's books out
of circulating libraries!

(II.) I say we have despised science. "What!" you exclaim,
"are we not foremost in all discovery, and is not the whole
world giddy by reason, or unreason, of our inventions?"
Yes; but do you suppose that is national work? That work
is all done *in spite of* the nation; by private people's zeal
and money. We are glad enough, indeed, to make our profit
of science; we snap up anything in the way of a scientific
bone that has meat on it, eagerly enough; but if the scientific man comes for a bone or a crust to *us,* that is another
story. What have we publicly done for science? We are

obliged to know what o'clock it is, for the safety of our ships, and therefore we pay for an observatory; and we allow ourselves, in the person of our Parliament, to be annually tormented into doing something, in a slovenly way, for the British Museum; sullenly apprehending that to be a place for keeping stuffed birds in, to amuse our children. . . .

(III.) I say you have despised Art! "What!" you again answer, "have we not Art exhibitions, miles long? and do we not pay thousands of pounds for single pictures? and have we not Art schools and institutions, more than ever nation had before?" Yes, truly, but all that is for the sake of the shop. You would fain sell canvas as well as coals, and crockery as well as iron; you would take every other nation's bread out of its mouth if you could; not being able to do that, your ideal of life is to stand in the thoroughfares of the world, like Ludgate apprentices, screaming to every passer-by, "What d'ye lack?" You know nothing of your own faculties or circumstances; you fancy that, among your damp, flat, fat fields of clay, you have as quick art-fancy as the Frenchman among his bronzed vines, or the Italian under his volcanic cliffs;—that Art may be learned, as bookkeeping is, and when learned, will give you more books to keep. You care for pictures, absolutely, no more than you do for the bills pasted on your dead walls. There is always room on the walls for the bills to be read,—never for the pictures to be seen. You do not know what pictures you have (by repute) in the country, nor whether they are false or true, nor whether they are taken care of or not; in foreign countries, you calmly see the noblest existing pictures in the world rotting in abandoned wreck—(in Venice you saw the Austrian guns deliberately pointed at the palaces containing them*), and if you heard that all the fine pictures in Europe were made into sand-bags to-morrow

* During the bombardment and occupation of Venice, Ruskin wrote that "hardly a single palace escaped without three or four balls through its roof: three came into the Scuola di San Rocco, tearing their way through the pictures of Tintoret, of which the ragged fragments were still hanging from the ceiling in 1851."

on the Austrian forts, it would not trouble you so much as the chance of a brace or two of game less in your own bags, in a day's shooting. That is your national love of Art.

(IV.) You have despised Nature; that is to say, all the deep and sacred sensations of natural scenery. The French revolutionists made stables of the cathedrals of France; you have made race-courses of the cathedrals of the earth. Your *one* conception of pleasure is to drive in railroad carriages round their aisles, and eat off their altars. You have put a railroad-bridge over the falls of Schaffhausen. You have tunnelled the cliffs of Lucerne by Tell's chapel; you have destroyed the Clarens shore of the Lake of Geneva; there is not a quiet valley in England that you have not filled with bellowing fire; there is not a particle left of English land which you have not trampled coal ashes into—nor any foreign city in which the spread of your presence is not marked among its fair old streets and happy gardens by a consuming white leprosy of new hotels and perfumers' shops: the Alps themselves, which your own poets used to love so reverently, you look upon as soaped poles in a bear-garden, which you set yourselves to climb and slide down again, with "shrieks of delight." When you are past shrieking, having no human articulate voice to say you are glad with, you fill the quietude of their valleys with gunpowder blasts, and rush home, red with cutaneous eruption of conceit, and voluble with convulsive hiccough of self-satisfaction. I think nearly the two sorrowfullest spectacles I have ever seen in humanity, taking the deep inner significance of them, are the English mobs in the valley of Chamouni, amusing themselves with firing rusty howitzers; and the Swiss vintagers of Zurich expressing their Christian thanks for the gift of the vine, by assembling in knots in the "towers of the vineyards," and slowly loading and firing horse-pistols from morning till evening. It is pitiful, to have dim conceptions of duty; more pitiful, it seems to me, to have conceptions like these, of mirth.

Lastly. You despise compassion. There is no need of

words of mine for proof of this. I will merely print one of
the newspaper paragraphs which I am in the habit of cutting out and throwing into my store-drawer; here is one
from a *Daily Telegraph* of an early date this year (1867*);
(date which, though by me carelessly left unmarked, is easily
discoverable; for on the back of the slip there is the an-
nouncement that "yesterday the seventh of the special services of this year was performed by the Bishop of Ripon in
St. Paul's";) it relates only one of such facts as happen now
daily; this by chance having taken a form in which it came
before the coroner. I will print the paragraph in red. Be
sure, the facts themselves are written in that colour, in a
book which we shall all of us, literate or illiterate, have to
read our page of, some day.

*An inquiry was held on Friday by Mr. Richards, deputy
coroner, at the White Horse Tavern, Christ Church, Spitalfields, respecting the death of Michael Collins, aged 58 years.
Mary Collins, a miserable-looking woman, said that she
lived with the deceased and his son in a room at 2, Cobb's
Court, Christ Church. Deceased was a "translator" of boots.
Witness went out and bought old boots; deceased and his
son made them into good ones, and then witness sold them
for what she could get at the shops, which was very little
indeed. Deceased and his son used to work night and day
to try and get a little bread and tea, and pay for the room
(2s. a week), so as to keep the home together. On Friday-
night-week deceased got up from his bench and began to
shiver. He threw down the boots, saying, "Somebody else
must finish them when I am gone for I can do no more."
There was no fire, and he said, "I would be better if I was
warm." Witness therefore took two pairs of translated boots
to sell at the shop, but she could only get 14d. for the two
pairs, for the people at the shop said, "We must have our
profit." Witness got 14 lb. of coal, and a little tea and bread.*

* An error for the *Morning Post* of February 13, 1865. Apparently
Ruskin added the quotation after giving the lecture in its original
form in December, 1864.

Her son sat up the whole night to make the "translations," to get money, but deceased died on Saturday morning. The family never had enough to eat.—Coroner: "It seems to me deplorable that you did not go into the workhouse." Witness: "We wanted the comforts of our little home." A juror asked what the comforts were, for he only saw a little straw in the corner of the room, the windows of which were broken. The witness began to cry, and said that they had a quilt and other little things. The deceased said he never would go into the workhouse. In summer, when the season was good, they sometimes made as much as 10s. profit in the week. They then always saved towards the next week, which was generally a bad one. In winter they made not half so much. For three years they had been getting from bad to worse.—Cornelius Collins said that he had assisted his father since 1847. They used to work so far into the night that both nearly lost their eyesight. Witness now had a film over his eyes. Five years ago deceased applied to the parish for aid. The relieving officer gave him a 4 lb. loaf, and told him if he came again he should "get the stones." That disgusted deceased, and he would have nothing to do with them since. They got worse and worse until last Friday week, when they had not even a halfpenny to buy a candle. Deceased then lay down on the straw, and said he could not live till morning.—A juror: "You are dying of starvation yourself, and you ought to go into the house until the summer."—Witness: "If we went in we should die. When we come out in the summer we should be like people dropped from the sky. No one would know us, and we would not have even a room. I could work now if I had food, for my sight would get better." Dr. G. P. Walker said deceased died from syncope, from exhaustion from want of food. The deceased had had no bedclothes. For four months he had had nothing but bread to eat. There was not a particle of fat in the body. There was no disease, but, if there had been medical attendance, he might have survived the syncope or fainting. The Coroner having remarked

*upon the painful nature of the case, the jury returned the
following verdict: "That deceased died from exhaustion
from want of food and the common necessaries of life; also
through want of medical aid."*

"Why would witness not go into the workhouse?" you
ask. Well, the poor seem to have a prejudice against the
workhouse which the rich have not; for of course everyone
who takes a pension from Government goes into the workhouse on a grand scale: only the workhouses for the rich do
not involve the idea of work, and should be called play-
houses. But the poor like to die independently, it appears;
perhaps if we made the play-houses for them pretty and
pleasant enough, or gave them their pensions at home, and
allowed them a little introductory peculation with the
public money, their minds might be reconciled to the conditions. Meantime, here are the facts: we make our relief
either so insulting to them, or so painful, that they rather
die than take it at our hands; or, for third alternative, we
leave them so untaught and foolish that they starve like
brute creatures, wild and dumb, not knowing what to do,
or what to ask. I say, you despise compassion; if you did
not, such a newspaper paragraph would be as impossible in
a Christian country as a deliberate assassination permitted
in its public streets. "Christian," did I say? Alas! if we were
but wholesomely *un*-Christian, it would be impossible: it is
our imaginary Christianity that helps us to commit these
crimes, for we revel and luxuriate in our faith, for the lewd
sensation of it; dressing *it* up, like everything else, in fiction.
The dramatic Christianity of the organ and aisle, of dawn-
service and twilight-revival—the Christianity, which we do
not fear to mix the mockery of, pictorially, with our play
about the devil, in our Satanellas,—Roberts,—Fausts;*
chanting hymns through traceried windows for background
effect, and artistically modulating the "Dio" through varia-

* Balfe's *Satanella: or the Power of Love*, an opera produced in London in 1858; Meyerbeer's *Robert le Diable*; and, of course, Gounod's
Faust.

tion on variation of mimicked prayer: (while we distribute tracts, next day, for the benefit of uncultivated swearers, upon what we suppose to be the signification of the Third Commandment;—) this gas-lighted, and gas-inspired Christianity, we are triumphant in, and draw back the hem of our robes from the touch of the heretics who dispute it. But to do a piece of common Christian righteousness in a plain English word or deed; to make Christian law any rule of life, and found one National act or hope thereon,—we know too well what our faith comes to for that! You might sooner get lightning out of incense smoke than true action or passion out of your modern English religion. You had better get rid of the smoke, and the organ pipes, both: leave them, and the Gothic windows, and the painted glass, to the property man; give up your carburetted hydrogen ghost in one healthy expiration, and look after Lazarus at the doorstep. For there is a true Church wherever one hand meets another helpfully, and that is the only holy or Mother Church which ever was, or ever shall be.

All these pleasures then, and all these virtues, I repeat, you nationally despise. . . . Our National wish and purpose are only to be amused; our National religion is the performance of church ceremonies, and preaching of soporific truths (or untruths) to keep the mob quietly at work, while we amuse ourselves; and the necessity for this amusement is fastening on us, as a feverous disease of parched throat and wandering eyes—senseless, dissolute, merciless. How literally that word *Dis*-Ease, the Negation and impossibility of Ease, expresses the entire moral state of our English Industry and its Amusements!

When men are rightly occupied, their amusement grows out of their work, as the colour-petals out of a fruitful flower;—when they are faithfully helpful and compassionate, all their emotions become steady, deep, perpetual, and vivifying to the soul as the natural pulse to the body. But now, having no true business, we pour our whole masculine energy into the false business of money-making; and having no true emotion, we must have false emotions dressed up for us to play with, not innocently, as children with dolls, but guiltily and darkly, as the idolatrous Jews with their pictures on cavern walls, which men had to dig to detect. The justice we do not execute, we mimic in the novel and on the stage; for the beauty we destroy in nature, we substitute the metamorphosis of the pantomime, and (the human nature of us imperatively requiring awe and sorrow of *some* kind) for the noble grief we should have borne with our fellows, and the pure tears we should have wept with them, we gloat over the pathos of the police court, and gather the night-dew of the grave.

It is difficult to estimate the true significance of these things; the facts are frightful enough;—the measure of national fault involved in them is perhaps not as great as it would at first seem. We permit, or cause, thousands of deaths daily, but we mean no harm; we set fire to houses, and ravage peasants' fields, yet we should be sorry to find we had injured anybody. We are still kind at heart; still capable of virtue, but only as children are. Chalmers,* at the end of his long life, having had much power with the public, being plagued in some serious matter by a reference to "public opinion," uttered the impatient exclamation, "The public is just a great baby!" And the reason that I have allowed all these graver subjects of thought to mix themselves up with an inquiry into methods of reading, is that, the more I see of our national faults or miseries, the more they resolve themselves into conditions of childish illiterateness and want of education in the most ordinary habits of thought. It is, I repeat, not vice, not selfishness, not dullness of brain, which we have to lament; but an unreachable schoolboy's recklessness, only differing from the true schoolboy's in its incapacity of being helped, because it acknowledges no master.

There is a curious type of us given in one of the lovely, neglected works of the last of our great painters. It is a

* Thomas Chalmers (1780–1847), Scottish theologian and preacher.

drawing of Kirkby Lonsdale churchyard, and of its brook, and valley, and hills, and folded morning sky beyond. And unmindful alike of these, and of the dead who have left these for other valleys and for other skies, a group of school-boys have piled their little books upon a grave, to strike them off with stones. So, also, we play with the words of the dead that would teach us, and strike them far from us with our bitter, reckless will; little thinking that those leaves which the wind scatters had been piled, not only upon a gravestone, but upon the seal of an enchanted vault—nay, the gate of a great city of sleeping kings, who would awake for us and walk with us, if we knew but how to call them by their names. How often, even if we lift the marble entrance gate, do we but wander among those old kings in their repose, and finger the robes they lie in, and stir the crowns on their foreheads; and still they are silent to us, and seem but a dusty imagery, because we know not the incantation of the heart that would wake them;—which, if they once heard, they would start up to meet us in their power of long ago, narrowly to look upon us, and consider us; and, as the fallen kings of Hades meet the newly fallen, saying, "Art thou also become weak as we—art thou also become one of us?"* so would these kings, with their un-dimmed, unshaken diadems, meet us, saying, "Art thou also become pure and mighty of heart as we—art thou also be-come one of us?"

---

* Isaiah 14:10.

Solitude

In Jacob's deathbed prophecy to his son Reuben—"Unstable as water, thou shalt not excel"—Ruskin saw a judgment upon his own work. His reader, too, cannot fail to note the growing instability of temper which marks Ruskin's writing after the publication of *Unto This Last* in 1860. The agonies and obsessions of his personal life increasingly obtrude into his books, at once robbing them of coherence and enriching them with a strangely moving poignance.

The most important of these intrusions was Ruskin's love for Rose La Touche, whom he met in 1858. She was then a brilliant child thirty years his junior. As his fondness for Rose developed into an overmastering passion, she became more and more withdrawn, until her extreme sensitivity first lapsed into morbid religious fervor, then into insanity and early death. When she was eighteen, she responded to Ruskin's urgent, abject entreaties of marriage by sending him Biblical texts and bidding him renounce his "heathenism" and "sins against God." Ruskin's frequent invectives against evangelical piety in his writings of the 1860s (see the penultimate paragraph of "The Mystery of Life and Its Arts") are veiled pleas that Rose understand his unorthodox religious position and abandon the sick excesses of her own.

Ruskin had always been drawn to the innocence and sexually unchallenging beauty of girlhood. As Rose grew into maturity, more and more alienated from Ruskin and

from reality, she became fixed in his mind as the untroubled child who had once gathered flowers in his garden
at Herne Hill, the ageless little girl whom we meet in the
closing pages of *Præterita*. She also appears in Letter 20
("Benediction") of *Fors Clavigera,* in the guise of the young
St. Ursula. The sleeping saint in Carpaccio's *Dream of St.
Ursula* lies in deathlike stillness, her slender body covered
with a sheet which rises and falls "in a narrow unbroken
wave, like the shape of the coverlid of the last sleep, when
the turf scarcely rises." Ruskin's recurrent descriptions of
the painting form a part of his larger obsession with Rose.
He was learning to create out of the wreck of his personal
life the central but hidden subject of his books.

During the fertile but febrile years preceding his mental
collapse in 1878, Ruskin wrote about political economy and
the motion of snakes, botany and Florentine engraving,
Greek myths and criminal law, the stratification of the Alps
and the education of little girls. Physically as well as in-
tellectually he spent these years in transit, shifting from
subject to subject as rapidly as he hastened from place to
place, seeking an anchorage he could not find and fleeing
a chaos he was powerless to avoid.

The resilience of Ruskin's mind, however, was as remarkable as its hectic imbalance. Although his social criticism in *Time and Tide* (1867) is continually warped by
anxious autobiographical digressions, only a year later he
wrote the most exquisitely controlled of all his lectures,
"The Mystery of Life and Its Arts." Stylistically, this elegy
to his abandoned hopes is a tour de force. Ruskin introduces into modern English the rich resonances of Donne
and Browne, the majestic sonorities of the King James
Bible. The haunting solemnity of his cadences has the effect
of implicating the cosmos itself in his grief. A verse from
the Bible serves as his leitmotiv: "What is your life? It is
even as a vapour that appeareth for a little time, and then
vanisheth away." In *Modern Painters* Ruskin had written
of the cloud as a luminous veil lightly interposed between

the face of nature and the face of God. Here the fleeting
yet impenetrable cloud symbolizes his own darkened spirit,
his sense of the thick, unfathomable mystery of life, the
evanescence of its arts, the futility of its labors. The lecture
is a beautifully sane, beautifully structured statement of
despair.

Ruskin closed his work of the 1860s with *The Queen of
the Air,* a re-creation of the Greek sense of the gods and
their ruling presence throughout nature. The subtitle—"A
Study of the Greek Myths of Cloud and Storm"—is mis-
leading, for the book is less a study of certain myths than a
hymn to Athena, an incantation of astonishing yet elusive
power. Ruskin employs a prose not of statement but of
prayer, which at its best achieves the condition of music
and should be so read, precisely as one reads Eliot's *Four
Quartets.* Of course a study of myths ought not to attempt
the effects of music or poetry, but Ruskin does not so much
trace their origins or meanings as reanimate, through a
miracle of style, the god-haunted groves of Greece in which
the myths were born.

But *The Queen of the Air* cannot be wholly trusted or
understood. In the chaotic final chapter Ruskin seems to
have entered a "world of unreason and illusion, and [to
wander] there without a compass and a guide—or any light
save the fitful flashes of his beautiful genius." Such was the
impression Henry James formed on meeting Ruskin in
1869. James accurately gauged the extent of Ruskin's "unreason" but underestimated his vitality, his almost infinite
resourcefulness in shaping great art out of great illness. In
the next twenty years Ruskin was to create two perfect
expressions of his genius, *Fors Clavigera* and *Præterita,* the
one a chronicle of his torment and the other, composed in
lucid intervals between attacks of madness, the richest in
peace of all that he wrote.

Weary and obviously ill, Ruskin went to Italy immediately after completing *The Queen of the Air.* While at
Lugano he learned of his appointment to the newly en-

dowed Slade Professorship of Fine Art. He returned to England, where his new duties at Oxford imposed a direction on the dangerous wanderings of his thought. The early Slade lectures are orderly, temperate, almost courtly in their grace of statement. But the lectures are works of consolidation rather than of discovery. The aim of the professorship as Ruskin conceived it was to convince his students, many of whom were born to privilege and destined to positions of patronage and power, that the beauty which is truly to be a joy forever must be a joy for all.

Ruskin's most enduring achievement in the 1870s was not his lectures on art but a collection of letters to the workmen of Great Britain which he began "as a byework to quiet my conscience, that I might be happy in . . . my own proper life of Art-teaching, at Oxford and elsewhere." The letters comprising *Fors Clavigera* were published monthly from 1871 until Ruskin's breakdown in 1878; thereafter publication was intermittent, the series ending with the Christmas letter of 1884. The dates are revealing, for they confirm the fact that *Fors* was written in part as a guilty reaction to Ruskin's work as Professor of Fine Art. Within a year of his inaugural lecture, he published the first issue of *Fors;* the last appeared on the eve of his final resignation from Oxford. Only then did he feel free to indulge in the pleasing labor of *Præterita.*

Fors is first and most simply an anatomy of the folly, ugliness, and brutality of the age. Its 600,000 words record Ruskin's lonely pilgrimage through Europe and his cry of *nausée* at the horror of the earthly city. *Fors* is also the diary of a nobly gifted mind, disturbed but not deceived by its sickness. There are letters which, in the magnitude of their isolation, open out on a terrifying night of the soul. As Cardinal Manning phrased it, reading them is like listening to the beating of one's heart in a nightmare.

The image is perfect, for it conveys not only the peculiar loneliness of *Fors* but its frightening immediacy. Ruskin is closer to his reader in *Fors,* yet more alienated from the world he describes, than in any other of his books. As his hold on reality became more tenuous, his style became more intimate, until on the pages of *Fors* one seems to touch the lineaments of thought itself without the intervening medium of words.

Certain letters lead nowhere, but capture with a fixed intensity some isolated moment of feeling. *Fors* was written as much to arrest these moments, to transmit them whole from Ruskin's to the reader's mind, as to propound a scheme of social reform. Early in the letters Ruskin abandoned his customary salutation—"My friends"—and ceased to sign his name at their close. His anonymity was the sign of his own estrangement; yet he could no more cease writing the letters than refrain from noting in his diary the blank or hostile faces which passed him in the streets. *Fors* was his final link with a communicable world before "the solitude at last became too great to be endured."

Ruskin's dread of that fearful solitude is the subject of the great Christmas letter of 1874. The tone ranges from the quiet irony which Ruskin directs against himself at its opening to a raging denunciation of the cannibalistic world, "mad for money and lust, tearing each other to pieces, and starving each other to death." The relief Ruskin derived from violent language he also found in the wild inconsequence of wit. He affected the very madness he feared, assuming an antic disposition in order to say in jest what no man could say in earnest and still be thought sane. "If I took off the Harlequin's mask for a moment," he wrote, "you would say I was simply mad." Ruskin's stratagem is Hamlet's stratagem, born of the same fear and cloaking the same inner bafflement. Indeed, the mind which animates *Fors* is as swift and subtle as Hamlet's, yet as tempestuous as Lear's and as wayward as the Fool's.

One mark of Ruskin's folly throughout *Fors* is his reckless and absolute candor. Remarkably personal, the letters express the idiosyncrasies and convictions of a man who is simply and guilelessly the center of his universe. Yet they are wholly devoid of posturing or illusion. Perhaps because we habitually associate the objective with the impersonal, we cannot comprehend a mind which is at once so passionately disinterested, yet so passionately itself.

Using *Fors* as his forum, Ruskin hoped to transform the industrial wasteland of England into a fruitful garden open to all. For this purpose he gave much of his time and fortune to found the Guild of St. George, the affairs of which form a recurrent theme loosely connecting the letters. He succeeded in recruiting some fifty "Companions of St. George," many of whom lived on the Guild's lands and subscribed to its principles of "dressing the earth and keeping it, feeding human lips, clothing human bodies, kindling human souls." Although the Guild still survives as a corporate body, it achieved far less than Ruskin had desired and is dwarfed in significance by the letters which brought it into being.

In the 1880s Ruskin progressively withdrew from his role as Master of the Guild. Despite recurrent periods of insanity, he continued to write on a widening number of subjects. In 1880–81 he published *Fiction, Fair and Foul,* a series of essays on contemporary literature. The first essay is one of his most brilliant excursions into literary criticism. He defines a new genre, the novel of the city, the morbid violence of which he traces to a kind of death-wish engendered by the tedium, depersonalization, and anxious rootlessness of modern urban culture.

In 1884 Ruskin gave his last Slade lecture and published the final issue of *Fors*. He had brought the ragged ends of his career as art and social critic to a close and was free to write his autobiography. The shift in tone from the tempestuousness of *Fors* to the placidity of *Præterita* is astonishing. There are no outbursts of rage, no traces of his obsession with the ominous storm cloud which mar almost all that he wrote during his professorship. The key to this change is *The Storm-Cloud of the Nineteenth Century,* which served as a catharsis enabling him to return in

Præterita to the clear skies and crystal streams of his childhood.

In part the lecture on *The Storm-Cloud* (1884) represents a "pathetic fallacy," a confusion of Ruskin's altered response to nature with an imagined decline in nature herself. He describes the storm cloud as vile and diabolic, seemingly "made of dead men's souls" and accompanied by a plague wind whose "sound is a hiss instead of a wail." The lurid skies of *The Storm-Cloud* are the obverse of the luminous heavens of *Modern Painters,* opposing faces of a single power to which Ruskin, throughout his life, was incapable of indifference. After 1870, however, he came to believe that the elements were locked in a cosmic combat of good and evil. As "the black Devil cloud" gained mastery, he felt that nature had betrayed him and that man, in a kind of vicious collusion, had polluted the earth and air. This is the burden of the apocalyptic close of *The Storm-Cloud,* with its alarming prophecy of "blanched Sun,—blighted grass,—blinded man" and of an earth made desolate and uninhabitable.

The evocativeness of Ruskin's prose in *The Storm-Cloud* has obscured the accuracy of his observations. He had indeed observed a new kind of cloud which looked "as if it were made of poisonous smoke" and which, if not sent by Satan, was sufficiently lethal on one occasion to raise the weekly death rate in London by 40 percent. The cloud originated not in the heavens but in the chimneys of industrialized England. The height of Ruskin's weather obsession also coincided, in England at least, with a period of abnormally high rainfall, extreme cold, and diminished sunshine. The data he cites in *The Storm-Cloud* were based on fanatically precise but morbidly heightened responses to atmospheric conditions. Indeed, if one were to plot a graph of his mental state, the curve would almost exactly parallel the weather of the moment. The same hyperesthesia which painfully magnified Ruskin's responses to light and sound now turned the skies of England into "a raging enemy."

Ruskin was not alone in portraying a decline in nature from benevolence to evil. *Modern Painters* and *The Storm-Cloud* recapitulate, at both ends of his career, one of the crucial realizations of his century: that the benign Nature of Wordsworth was in fact red in tooth and claw. With that discovery, the pastoral landscapes of the Romantic poets gave way to the sinister, blighted terrain of Tennyson's "The Holy Grail," of Browning's "Childe Roland," and of their prose counterparts, Hardy's blasted heaths and Ruskin's *Storm-Cloud.*

—J. D. R.

SESAME AND LILIES

The Mystery of Life and Its Arts*

When I accepted the privilege of addressing you today, I
was not aware of a restriction with respect to the topics of
discussion which may be brought before this Society†—a
restriction which, though entirely wise and right under the
circumstances contemplated in its introduction, would necessarily have disabled me, thinking as I think, from pre-
paring any lecture for you on the subject of art in a form
which might be permanently useful. Pardon me, therefore,
in so far as I must transgress such limitation; for indeed my
infringement will be of the letter—not of the spirit—of your
commands. In whatever I may say touching the religion
which has been the foundation of art, or the policy which
has contributed to its power, if I offend one, I shall offend
all; for I shall take no note of any separations in creeds, or
antagonisms in parties: neither do I fear that ultimately I
shall offend any, by proving—or at least stating as capable
of positive proof—the connection of all that is best in the
crafts and arts of man, with the simplicity of his faith, and
the sincerity of his patriotism.

But I speak to you under another disadvantage, by which
I am checked in frankness of utterance, not here only, but
everywhere: namely, that I am never fully aware how far
my audiences are disposed to give me credit for real knowl-

* Delivered in the Exhibition Palace, Dublin, May 13, 1868.
† That no reference should be made to religious questions. [Ruskin's
note.]

edge of my subject, or how far they grant me attention only because I have been sometimes thought an ingenious or pleasant essayist upon it. For I have had what, in many respects, I boldly call the misfortune, to set my words sometimes prettily together; not without a foolish vanity in the poor knack that I had of doing so: until I was heavily punished for this pride, by finding that many people thought of the words only, and cared nothing for their meaning. Happily, therefore, the power of using such pleasant language—if indeed it ever were mine—is passing away from me; and whatever I am now able to say at all, I find myself forced to say with great plainness. For my thoughts have changed also, as my words have; and whereas in earlier life, what little influence I obtained was due perhaps chiefly to the enthusiasm with which I was able to dwell on the beauty of the physical clouds, and of their colours in the sky; so all the influence I now desire to retain must be due to the earnestness with which I am endeavouring to trace the form and beauty of another kind of cloud than those; the bright cloud of which it is written—"What is your life? It is even as a vapour that appeareth for a little time, and then vanisheth away."*

I suppose few people reach the middle or latter period of their age, without having, at some moment of change or disappointment, felt the truth of those bitter words; and been startled by the fading of the sunshine from the cloud of their life into the sudden agony of the knowledge that the fabric of it was as fragile as a dream, and the endurance of it as transient as the dew. But it is not always that, even at such times of melancholy surprise, we can enter into any true perception that this human life shares in the nature of it, not only the evanescence, but the mystery of the cloud; that its avenues are wreathed in darkness, and its forms and courses no less fantastic, than spectral and obscure; so that not only in the vanity which we cannot grasp, but in the

* James 4:14.

shadow which we cannot pierce, it is true of this cloudy life of ours, that "man walketh in a vain shadow, and disquieteth himself in vain."

And least of all, whatever may have been the eagerness of our passions, or the height of our pride, are we able to understand in its depth the third and most solemn character in which our life is like those clouds of heaven; that to it belongs not only their transience, not only their mystery, but also their power; that in the cloud of the human soul there is a fire stronger than the lightning, and a grace more precious than the rain; and that though of the good and evil it shall one day be said alike, that the place that knew them knows them no more, there is an infinite separation between those whose brief presence had there been a blessing, like the mist of Eden that went up from the earth to water the garden, and those whose place knew them only as a drifting and changeful shade, of whom the heavenly sentence is, that they are "wells without water; clouds that are carried with a tempest, to whom the mist of darkness is reserved for ever."

To those among us, however, who have lived long enough to form some just estimate of the rate of the changes which are, hour by hour in accelerating catastrophe, manifesting themselves in the laws, the arts, and the creeds of men, it seems to me, that now at least, if never at any former time, the thoughts of the true nature of our life, and of its powers and responsibilities, should present themselves with absolute sadness and sternness. And although I know that this feeling is much deepened in my own mind by disappointment, which, by chance, has attended the greater number of my cherished purposes, I do not for that reason distrust the feeling itself, though I am on my guard against an exaggerated degree of it: nay, I rather believe that in periods of new effort and violent change, disappointment is a wholesome medicine; and that in the secret of it, as in the twilight so beloved by Titian, we may see the colours of things with deeper truth than in the most dazzling sunshine. And because these truths about the works of men, which I want to bring to-day before you, are most of them sad ones, though at the same time helpful; and because also I believe that your kind Irish hearts will answer more gladly to the truthful expression of a personal feeling, than to the exposition of an abstract principle, I will permit myself so much unreserved speaking of my own causes of regret, as may enable you to make just allowance for what, according to your sympathies, you will call either the bitterness, or the insight, of a mind which has surrendered its best hopes, and been foiled in its favourite aims.

I spent the ten strongest years of my life, (from twenty to thirty,) in endeavouring to show the excellence of the work of the man whom I believed, and rightly believed, to be the greatest painter of the schools of England since Reynolds. I had then perfect faith in the power of every great truth of beauty to prevail ultimately, and take its right place in usefulness and honour; and I strove to bring the painter's work into this due place, while the painter was yet alive. But he knew, better than I, the uselessness of talking about what people could not see for themselves. He always discouraged me scornfully, even when he thanked me—and he died before even the superficial effect of my work was visible. I went on, however, thinking I could at least be of use to the public, if not to him, in proving his power. My books got talked about a little. The prices of modern pictures, generally, rose, and I was beginning to take some pleasure in a sense of gradual victory, when, fortunately or unfortunately, an opportunity of perfect trial undeceived me at once, and for ever. The Trustees of the National Gallery commissioned me to arrange the Turner drawings there, and permitted me to prepare three hundred examples of his studies from nature, for exhibition at Kensington. At Kensington they were, and are, placed for exhibition; but they are not exhibited, for the room in which they hang is always empty.

Well—this showed me at once, that those ten years of my

life had been, in their chief purpose, lost. For that, I did not so much care; I had, at least, learned my own business thoroughly, and should be able, as I fondly supposed, after such a lesson, now to use my knowledge, with better effect. But what I did care for was the—to me frightful—discovery, that the most splendid genius in the arts might be permitted by Providence to labour and perish uselessly; that in the very fineness of it there might be something rendering it invisible to ordinary eyes; but that, with this strange excellence, faults might be mingled which would be as deadly as its virtues were vain; that the glory of it was perishable, as well as invisible, and the gift and grace of it might be to us as snow in summer and as rain in harvest.

That was the first mystery of life to me. But, while my best energy was given to the study of painting, I had put collateral effort, more prudent if less enthusiastic, into that of architecture; and in this I could not complain of meeting with no sympathy. Among several personal reasons which caused me to desire that I might give this, my closing lecture on the subject of art here, in Ireland, one of the chief was, that in reading it, I should stand near the beautiful building,—the engineer's school of your college,—which was the first realization I had the joy to see, of the principles I had, until then, been endeavouring to teach! but which, alas, is now, to me, no more than the richly canopied monument of one of the most earnest souls that ever gave itself to the arts, and one of my truest and most loving friends, Benjamin Woodward. Nor was it here in Ireland only that I received the help of Irish sympathy and genius. When to another friend, Sir Thomas Deane, with Mr. Woodward, was entrusted the building of the museum at Oxford, the best details of the work were executed by sculptors who had been born and trained here; and the first window of the façade of the building, in which was inaugurated the study of natural science in England, in true fellowship with literature, was carved from my design by an Irish sculptor.

You may perhaps think that no man ought to speak of

disappointment, to whom, even in one branch of labour, so much success was granted. Had Mr. Woodward now been beside me, I had not so spoken; but his gentle and passionate spirit was cut off from the fulfilment of its purposes, and the work we did together is now become vain. It may not be so in future; but the architecture we endeavoured to introduce is inconsistent alike with the reckless luxury, the deforming mechanism, and the squalid misery of modern cities; among the formative fashions of the day, aided, especially in England, by ecclesiastical sentiment, it indeed obtained notoriety; and sometimes behind an engine furnace, or a railroad bank, you may detect the pathetic discord of its momentary grace, and, with toil, decipher its floral carvings choked with soot. I felt answerable to the schools I loved, only for their injury. I perceived that this new portion of my strength had also been spent in vain; and from amidst streets of iron, and palaces of crystal, shrank back at last to the carving of the mountain and colour of the flower.

And still I could tell of failure, and failure repeated, as years went on; but I have trespassed enough on your patience to show you, in part, the causes of my discouragement. Now let me more deliberately tell you its results. You know there is a tendency in the minds of many men, when they are heavily disappointed in the main purposes of their life, to feel, and perhaps in warning, perhaps in mockery, to declare, that life itself is a vanity. Because it has disappointed them, they think its nature is of disappointment always, or at best, of pleasure that can be grasped by imagination only; that the cloud of it has no strength nor fire within; but is a painted cloud only, to be delighted in, yet despised. You know how beautifully Pope has expressed this particular phase of thought:—

> "Meanwhile opinion gilds, with varying rays,
> These painted clouds that beautify our days;
> Each want of happiness by hope supplied,
> And each vacuity of sense, by pride.

Hope builds as fast as Knowledge can destroy;
In Folly's cup, still laughs the bubble joy.
One pleasure past, another still we gain,
*And not a vanity is given in vain."**

But the effect of failure upon my own mind has been just the reverse of this. The more that my life disappointed me, the more solemn and wonderful it became to me. It seemed, contrarily to Pope's saying, that the vanity of it *was* indeed given in vain; but that there was something behind the veil of it, which was not vanity. It became to me not a painted cloud, but a terrible and impenetrable one: not a mirage, which vanished as I drew near, but a pillar of darkness, to which I was forbidden to draw near. For I saw that both my own failure, and such success in petty things as in its poor triumph seemed to me worse than failure, came from the want of sufficiently earnest effort to understand the whole law and meaning of existence, and to bring it to noble and due end; as, on the other hand, I saw more and more clearly that all enduring success in the arts, or in any other occupation, had come from the ruling of lower purposes, not by a conviction of their nothingness, but by a solemn faith in the advancing power of human nature, or in the promise, however dimly apprehended, that the mortal part of it would one day be swallowed up in immortality; and that, indeed, the arts themselves never had reached any vital strength or honour, but in the effort to proclaim this immortality, and in the service either of great and just religion, or of some unselfish patriotism, and law of such national life as must be the foundation of religion.

Nothing that I have ever said is more true or necessary—nothing has been more misunderstood or misapplied—than my strong assertion that the arts can never be right themselves, unless their motive is right. It is misunderstood this way: weak painters, who have never learned their business, and cannot lay a true line, continually come to me, crying

* *Essay on Man*, II, 283–90.

out—"Look at this picture of mine; it *must* be good, I had such a lovely motive. I have put my whole heart into it, and taken years to think over its treatment." Well, the only answer for these people is—if one had the cruelty to make it —"Sir, you cannot think over *any*thing in any number of years,—you haven't the head to do it; and though you had fine motives, strong enough to make you burn yourself in a slow fire, if only first you could paint a picture, you can't paint one, nor half an inch of one; you haven't the hand to do it."

But, far more decisively we have to say to the men who *do* know their business, or may know it if they choose— "Sir, you have this gift, and a mighty one; see that you serve your nation faithfully with it. It is a greater trust than ships and armies: you might cast *them* away, if you were their captain, with less treason to your people than in casting your own glorious power away, and serving the devil with it instead of men. Ships and armies you may replace if they are lost, but a great intellect, once abused, is a curse to the earth for ever."

This, then, I meant by saying that the arts must have noble motive. This also I said respecting them, that they never had prospered, nor could prosper, but when they had such true purpose, and were devoted to the proclamation of divine truth or law. And yet I saw also that they had always failed in this proclamation—that poetry, and sculpture, and painting, though only great when they strove to teach us something about the gods, never had taught us anything trustworthy about the gods, but had always betrayed their trust in the crisis of it, and, with their powers at the full reach, became ministers to pride and to lust. And I felt also, with increasing amazement, the unconquerable apathy in ourselves and hearers, no less than in these the teachers; and that while the wisdom and rightness of every act and art of life could only be consistent with a right understanding of the ends of life, we were all plunged as in a languid dream— our hearts fat, and our eyes heavy, and our ears closed, lest the inspiration of hand or voice should reach us—lest we should see with our eyes, and understand with our hearts, and be healed.

This intense apathy in all of us is the first great mystery of life; it stands in the way of every perception, every virtue. There is no making ourselves feel enough astonishment at it. That the occupations or pastimes of life should have no motive, is understandable; but—That life itself should have no motive—that we neither care to find out what it may lead to, nor to guard against its being forever taken away from us—here is a mystery indeed. For just suppose I were able to call at this moment to anyone in this audience by name, and to tell him positively that I knew a large estate had been lately left to him on some curious conditions; but that though I knew it was large, I did not know how large, nor even where it was—whether in the East Indies or the West, or in England, or at the Antipodes. I only knew it was a vast estate, and that there was a chance of his losing it altogether if he did not soon find out on what terms it had been left to him. Suppose I were able to say this positively to any single man in this audience, and he knew that I did not speak without warrant, do you think that he would rest content with that vague knowledge, if it were anywise possible to obtain more? Would he not give every energy to find some trace of the facts, and never rest till he had ascertained where this place was, and what it was like? And suppose he were a young man, and all he could discover by his best endeavor was that the estate was never to be his at all, unless he persevered, during certain years of probation, in an orderly and industrious life; but that, according to the rightness of his conduct, the portion of the estate assigned to him would be greater or less, so that it literally depended on his behavior from day to day whether he got ten thousand a year, or thirty thousand a year, or nothing whatever —would you not think it strange if the youth never troubled himself to satisfy the conditions in any way, nor ever to know what was required of him, but lived exactly as he chose, and never inquired whether his chances of the estate were increasing or passing away? Well, you know that this is actually and literally so with the greater number of the educated persons now living in Christian countries. Nearly every man and woman in any company such as this, outwardly professes to believe—and a large number unquestionably think they believe—much more than this; not only that a quite unlimited estate is in prospect for them if they please the Holder of it, but that the infinite contrary of such a possession—an estate of perpetual misery—is in store for them if they displease this great Land-Holder, this great Heaven-Holder. And yet there is not one in a thousand of these human souls that cares to think, for ten minutes of the day, where this estate is or how beautiful it is, or what kind of life they are to lead in it, or what kind of life they must lead to obtain it.

You fancy that you care to know this: so little do you care that, probably, at this moment many of you are displeased with me for talking of the matter! You came to hear about the Art of this world, not about the Life of the next, and you are provoked with me for talking of what you can hear any Sunday in church. But do not be afraid. I will tell you something before you go about pictures, and carvings, and pottery, and what else you would like better to hear of than the other world. Nay, perhaps you say, "We want you to talk of pictures and pottery, because we are sure that you know something of them, and you know nothing of the other world." Well—I don't. That is quite true. But the very strangeness and mystery of which I urge you to take notice, is in this—that I do not;—nor you either. Can you answer a single bold question unflinchingly about that other world?—Are you sure there is a heaven? Sure there is a hell? Sure that men are dropping before your faces through the pavements of these streets into eternal fire, or sure that they are not? Sure that at your own death you are going to be delivered from all sorrow, to be endowed with all virtue, to be gifted with all felicity, and raised into perpetual companionship with a King, compared to whom the kings of the earth are as grasshoppers, and the nations as the dust of His feet? Are you sure of this? or, if not sure, do any of us so much as care to make it sure? and, if not, how can anything that we do be right—how can anything we think be wise? what honour can there be in the arts that amuse us, or what profit in the possessions that please?

Is not this a mystery of life?

But farther, you may, perhaps, think it a beneficent ordinance for the generality of men that they do not, with earnestness or anxiety, dwell on such questions of the future because the business of the day could not be done if this kind of thought were taken by all of us for the morrow. Be it so: but at least we might anticipate that the greatest and wisest of us, who were evidently the appointed teachers of the rest, would set themselves apart to seek out whatever could be surely known of the future destinies of their race; and to teach this in no rhetorical or ambiguous manner, but in the plainest and most severely earnest words.

Now, the highest representatives of men who have thus endeavoured, during the Christian era, to search out these deep things, and relate them, are Dante and Milton. There are none who for earnestness of thought, for mastery of word, can be classed with these. I am not at present, mind you, speaking of persons set apart in any priestly or pastoral office, to deliver creeds to us, or doctrines; but of men who try to discover and set forth, as far as by human intellect is possible, the facts of the other world. Divines may perhaps teach us how to arrive there, but only these two poets have in any powerful manner striven to discover, or in any definite words professed to tell, what we shall see and become there; or how those upper and nether worlds are, and have been, inhabited.

And what have they told us? Milton's account of the most important event in his whole system of the universe, the fall of the angels, is evidently unbelievable to himself; and the more so, that it is wholly founded on, and in a great part spoiled and degraded from, Hesiod's account of the decisive war of the younger gods with the Titans. The rest of his poem is a picturesque drama, in which every artifice of invention is visibly and consciously employed; not a single fact being, for an instant, conceived as tenable by any living faith. Dante's conception is far more intense, and, by himself, for the time, not to be escaped from; it is indeed a vision, but a vision only, and that one of the wildest that ever entranced a soul—a dream in which every grotesque type or phantasy of heathen tradition is renewed, and adorned; and the destinies of the Christian Church, under their most sacred symbols, become literally subordinate to the praise, and are only to be understood by the aid, of one dear Florentine maiden.

I tell you truly that, as I strive more with this strange lethargy and trance in myself, and awake to the meaning and power of life, it seems daily more amazing to me that men such as these should dare to play with the most precious truths, (or the most deadly untruths,) by which the whole human race listening to them could be informed, or deceived;—all the world their audiences for ever, with pleased ear, and passionate heart;—and yet, to this submissive infinitude of souls, and evermore succeeding and succeeding multitude, hungry for bread of life, they do but play upon sweetly modulated pipes; with pompous nomenclature adorn the councils of hell; touch a troubadour's guitar to the courses of the suns; and fill the openings of eternity, before which prophets have veiled their faces, and which angels desire to look into, with idle puppets of their scholastic imagination, and melancholy lights of frantic faith in their lost mortal love.

Is not this a mystery of life?

But more. We have to remember that these two great teachers were both of them warped in their temper, and thwarted in their search for truth. They were men of intellectual war, unable, through darkness of controversy, or stress of personal grief, to discern where their own ambition modified their utterances of the moral law; or their own agony mingled with their anger at its violation. But greater men than these have been—innocent-hearted—too great for contest. Men, like Homer and Shakespeare, of so un-recognized personality, that it disappears in future ages, and becomes ghostly, like the tradition of a lost heathen god. Men, therefore, to whose unoffended, uncondemning sight, the whole of human nature reveals itself in a pathetic weakness, with which they will not strive; or in mournful and transitory strength, which they dare not praise. And all Pagan and Christian Civilization thus becomes subject to them. It does not matter how little, or how much, any of us have read, either of Homer or Shakespeare; everything round us, in substance, or in thought, has been moulded by them. All Greek gentlemen were educated under Homer. All Roman gentlemen, by Greek literature. All Italian, and French, and English gentlemen, by Roman literature, and by its principles. Of the scope of Shakespeare, I will say only, that the intellectual measure of every man since born, in the domains of creative thought, may be assigned to him, according to the degree in which he has been taught by Shakespeare. Well, what do these two men, centres of mortal intelligence, deliver to us of conviction respecting what it most behoves that intelligence to grasp? What is their hope —their crown of rejoicing? what manner of exhortation have they for us, or of rebuke? what lies next their own hearts, and dictates their undying words? Have they any peace to promise to our unrest—any redemption to our misery?

Take Homer first, and think if there is any sadder image of human fate than the great Homeric story. The main features in the character of Achilles are its intense desire of justice, and its tenderness of affection. And in that bitter song of the *Iliad*, this man, though aided continually by the wisest of the gods, and burning with the desire of justice in his heart, becomes yet, through ill-governed passion, the most unjust of men: and, full of the deepest tenderness in his heart, becomes yet, through ill-governed passion, the most cruel of men. Intense alike in love and in friendship, he loses, first his mistress, and then his friend; for the sake of the one, he surrenders to death the armies of his own land; for the sake of the other, he surrenders all. Will a man lay down his life for his friend? Yea—even for his *dead* friend, this Achilles, though goddess-born, and goddess-taught, gives up his kingdom, his country, and his life—casts alike the innocent and guilty, with himself, into one gulf of slaughter, and dies at last by the hand of the basest of his adversaries.

Is not this a mystery of life?

But what, then, is the message to us of our own poet, and searcher of hearts, after fifteen hundred years of Christian faith have been numbered over the graves of men? Are his words more cheerful than the Heathen's—is his hope more near—his trust more sure—his reading of fate more happy? Ah, no! He differs from the Heathen poet chiefly in this—that he recognizes, for deliverance, no gods nigh at hand; and that, by petty chance—by momentary folly—by broken message—by fool's tyranny—or traitor's snare, the strongest and most righteous are brought to their ruin, and perish without word of hope. He indeed, as part of his rendering of character, ascribes the power and modesty of habitual devotion to the gentle and the just. The death-bed of Katharine is bright with visions of angels; and the great soldier-king, standing by his few dead, acknowledges the presence of the Hand that can save alike by many or by few. But observe that from those who with deepest spirit, meditate, and with deepest passion, mourn, there are no such words as these; nor in their hearts are any such consolations. Instead of the perpetual sense of the helpful presence of the Deity, which, through all heathen tradition, is the source of heroic strength, in battle, in exile, and in the valley of the shadow of death, we find only in the great Christian poet, the consciousness of a moral law, through which "the gods are just, and of our pleasant vices make

instruments to scourge us"; and of the resolved arbitration
of the destinies, that conclude into precision of doom what
we feebly and blindly began; and force us, when our indiscretion serves us, and our deepest plots do pall, to the confession, that "there's a divinity that shapes our ends, rough
hew them how we will."*

Is not this a mystery of life?

Be it so, then. About this human life that is to be, or that
is, the wise religious men tell us nothing that we can trust;
and the wise contemplative men, nothing that can give us
peace. But there is yet a third class, to whom we may turn—
the wise practical men. We have sat at the feet of the poets
who sang of heaven, and they have told us their dreams.
We have listened to the poets who sang of earth, and they
have chanted to us dirges and words of despair. But there
is one class of men more:—men, not capable of vision, nor
sensitive to sorrow, but firm of purpose—practised in business; learned in all that can be, (by handling,) known. Men,
whose hearts and hopes are wholly in this present world,
from whom, therefore, we may surely learn, at least, how,
at present, conveniently to live in it. What will *they* say to
us, or show us by example? These kings—these councillors—
these statesmen and builders of kingdoms—these capitalists
and men of business, who weigh the earth, and the dust of
it, in a balance. They know the world, surely; and what is
the mystery of life to us, is none to them. They can surely
show us how to live, while we live, and to gather out of the
present world what is best.

I think I can best tell you their answer, by telling you a
dream I had once. For though I am no poet, I have dreams
sometimes:—I dreamed I was at a child's May-day party, in
which every means of entertainment had been provided for
them by a wise and kind host. It was in a stately house, with
beautiful gardens attached to it; and the children had been
set free in the rooms and gardens, with no care whatever
but how to pass their afternoon rejoicingly. They did not,

* *King Lear,* V, iii, 170–171; *Hamlet,* V, ii, 10–11.

indeed, know much about what was to happen next day; and some of them, I thought, were a little frightened, because there was a chance of their being sent to a new school where there were examinations; but they kept the thoughts of that out of their heads as well as they could, and resolved to enjoy themselves. The house, I said, was in a beautiful garden, and in the garden were all kinds of flowers; sweet, grassy banks for rest; and smooth lawns for play; and pleasant streams and woods; and rocky places for climbing. And the children were happy for a little while, but presently they separated themselves into parties; and then each party declared it would have a piece of the garden for its own, and that none of the others should have anything to do with that piece. Next, they quarrelled violently which pieces they would have; and at last the boys took up the thing, as boys should do, "practically," and fought in the flower-beds till there was hardly a flower left standing; then they trampled down each other's bits of the garden out of spite; and the girls cried till they could cry no more; and so they all lay down at last breathless in the ruin, and waited for the time when they were to be taken home in the evening.*

Meanwhile, the children in the house had been making themselves happy also in their manner. For them, there had been provided every kind of indoor pleasure: there was music for them to dance to; and the library was open, with all manner of amusing books; and there was a museum full of the most curious shells, and animals, and birds; and there was a workshop, with lathes and carpenter's tools, for the ingenious boys; and there were pretty fantastic dresses, for the girls to dress in; and there were microscopes, and kaleidoscopes; and whatever toys a child could fancy; and a table, in the dining-room, loaded with everything nice to eat.

* I have sometimes been asked what this means. I intended it to set forth the wisdom of men in war contending for kingdoms, and what follows to set forth their wisdom in peace, contending for wealth. [Ruskin's note.]

But, in the midst of all this, it struck two or three of the more "practical" children, that they would like some of the brass-headed nails that studded the chairs; and so they set to work to pull them out. Presently, the others, who were reading, or looking at shells, took a fancy to do the like; and, in a little while, all the children, nearly, were spraining their fingers, in pulling out brass-headed nails. With all that they could pull out, they were not satisfied; and then, everybody wanted some of somebody else's. And at last, the really practical and sensible ones declared, that nothing was of any real consequence, that afternoon, except to get plenty of brass-headed nails; and that the books, and the cakes, and the microscopes were of no use at all in themselves, but only, if they could be exchanged for nail-heads. And at last they began to fight for nail-heads, as the others fought for the bits of garden. Only here and there, a despised one shrank away into a corner, and tried to get a little quiet with a book, in the midst of the noise; but all the practical ones thought of nothing else but counting nail-heads all the afternoon—even though they knew they would not be allowed to carry so much as one brass knob away with them. But no—it was—"who has most nails? I have a hundred, and you have fifty; or, I have a thousand, and you have two. I must have as many as you before I leave the house, or I cannot possibly go home in peace." At last, they made so much noise that I awoke, and thought to myself, "What a false dream that is, of *children!*" The child is the father of the man; and wiser. Children never do such foolish things. Only men do.

But there is yet one last class of persons to be interrogated. The wise religious men we have asked in vain; the wise contemplative men, in vain; the wise worldly men, in vain. But there is another group yet. In the midst of this vanity of empty religion—of tragic contemplation—of wrathful and wretched ambition, and dispute for dust, there is yet one great group of persons, by whom all these disputers live —the persons who have determined, or have had it by a beneficent Providence determined for them, that they will do something useful; that whatever may be prepared for them hereafter, or happen to them here, they will, at least, deserve the food that God gives them by winning it honourably: and that, however fallen from the purity, or far from the peace, of Eden, they will carry out the duty of human dominion, though they have lost its felicity; and dress and keep the wilderness, though they no more can dress or keep the garden.

These,—hewers of wood, and drawers of water,—these, bent under burdens, or torn of scourges—these, that dig and weave—that plant and build; workers in wood, and in marble, and in iron—by whom all food, clothing, habitation, furniture, and means of delight are produced, for themselves, and for all men besides; men, whose deeds are good, though their words may be few; men, whose lives are serviceable, be they never so short, and worthy of honour, be they never so humble;—from these, surely, at least, we may receive some clear message of teaching; and pierce, for an instant, into the mystery of life, and of its arts.

Yes; from these, at last, we do receive a lesson. But I grieve to say, or rather—for that is the deeper truth of the matter—I rejoice to say—this message of theirs can only be received by joining them—not by thinking about them.

You sent for me to talk to you of art; and I have obeyed you in coming. But the main thing I have to tell you is,—that art must not be talked about. The fact that there is talk about it at all, signifies that it is ill done, or cannot be done. No true painter ever speaks, or ever has spoken, much of his art. The greatest speak nothing. Even Reynolds is no exception, for he wrote of all that he could not himself do, and was utterly silent respecting all that he himself did.

The moment a man can really do his work he becomes speechless about it. All words become idle to him—all theories.

Does a bird need to theorize about building its nest, or boast of it when built? All good work is essentially done that way—without hesitation, without difficulty, without boasting; and in the doers of the best, there is an inner and involuntary power which approximates literally to the instinct of an animal—nay, I am certain that in the most perfect human artists, reason does *not* supersede instinct, but is added to an instinct as much more divine than that of the lower animals as the human body is more beautiful than theirs; that a great singer sings not with less instinct than the nightingale, but with more—only more various, applicable, and governable; that a great architect does not build with less instinct than the beaver or the bee, but with more—with an innate cunning of proportion that embraces all beauty, and a divine ingenuity of skill that improvises all construction. But be that as it may—be the instinct less or more than that of inferior animals—like or unlike theirs, still the human art is dependent on that first, and then upon an amount of practice, of science,—and of imagination disciplined by thought, which the true possessor of it knows to be incommunicable, and the true critic of it, inexplicable, except through long process of laborious years. That journey of life's conquest, in which hills over hills, and Alps on Alps arose, and sank,—do you think you can make another trace it painlessly, by talking? Why, you cannot even carry us up an Alp, by talking. You can guide us up it, step by step, no otherwise—even so, best silently. You girls, who have been among the hills, know how the bad guide chatters and gesticulates, and it is "Put your foot here"; and "Mind how you balance yourself there"; but the good guide walks on quietly, without a word, only with his eyes on you when need is, and his arm like an iron bar, if need be.

In that slow way, also, art can be taught—if you have faith in your guide, and will let his arm be to you as an iron bar when need is. But in what teacher of art have you such faith? Certainly not in me; for, as I told you at first, I know well enough it is only because you think I can talk, not because you think I know my business, that you let me speak to you at all. If I were to tell you anything that seemed to you strange you would not believe it, and yet it would only be in telling you strange things that I could be of use to you. I could be of great use to you—infinite use—with brief saying, if you would believe it; but you would not, just because the thing that would be of real use would displease you. You are all wild, for instance, with admiration of Gustave Doré. Well, suppose I were to tell you, in the strongest terms I could use, that Gustave Doré's art was bad—bad, not in weakness,—not in failure,—but bad with dreadful power—the power of the Furies and the Harpies mingled, enraging, and polluting; that so long as you looked at it, no perception of pure or beautiful art was possible for you. Suppose I were to tell you that! What would be the use? Would you look at Gustave Doré less? Rather, more, I fancy. On the other hand, I could soon put you into good humour with me, if I chose. I know well enough what you like, and how to praise it to your better liking. I could talk to you about moonlight, and twilight, and spring flowers, and autumn leaves, and the Madonnas of Raphael—how motherly! and the Sibyls of Michael Angelo—how majestic! and the Saints of Angelico—how pious! and the Cherubs of Correggio—how delicious! Old as I am, I could play you a tune on the harp yet, that you would dance to. But neither you nor I should be a bit the better or wiser; or, if we were, our increased wisdom could be of no practical effect. For, indeed, the arts, as regards teachableness, differ from the sciences also in this, that their power is founded not merely on facts which can be communicated, but on dispositions which require to be created. Art is neither to be achieved by effort of thinking, nor explained by accuracy of speaking. It is the instinctive and necessary result of power, which can only be developed through the mind of successive generations, and which finally burst into life under social conditions as slow of growth as the faculties they regulate. Whole æras of mighty history are summed, and the passions of dead myriads are concentrated, in the existence of a noble art; and if that noble art were among us, we should feel it and rejoice; not caring in the least to hear lectures on it; and since it is not among us, be assured we have to go back to the root of it, or, at least, to the place where the stock of it is yet alive, and the branches began to die.

And now, may I have your pardon for pointing out, partly with reference to matters which are at this time of greater moment than the arts—that if we undertook such recession to the vital germ of national arts that have decayed, we should find a more singular arrest of their power in Ireland than in any other European country? For in the eighth century Ireland possessed a school of art in her manuscripts and sculpture, which, in many of its qualities—apparently in all essential qualities of decorative invention—was quite without rival; seeming as if it might have advanced to the highest triumphs in architecture and in painting. But there was one fatal flaw in its nature, by which it was stayed, and stayed with a conspicuousness of pause to which there is no parallel: so that, long ago, in tracing the progress of European schools from infancy to strength, I chose for the students of Kensington, in a lecture since published, two characteristic examples of early art, of equal skill; but in the one case, skill which was progressive—in the other, skill which was at pause. In the one case, it was work receptive of correction—hungry for correction; and in the other, work which inherently rejected correction. I chose for them a corrigible Eve, and an incorrigible Angel, and I grieve to say that the incorrigible Angel was also an Irish Angel!*

And the fatal difference lay wholly in this. In both pieces of art there was an equal falling short of the needs of fact; but the Lombardic Eve knew she was in the wrong, and the Irish Angel thought himself all right. The eager Lombardic sculptor, though firmly insisting on his childish idea, yet

* Ruskin here alludes to *two* incorrigible Irish Angels, one in an eighth-century Irish psalter, and the other, Rose La Touche, whom he had vainly hoped would be present in his Dublin audience. The corrigible Eve is sculpted on the pulpit of S. Ambrogio in Milan.

showed in the irregular broken touches of the features, and the imperfect struggle for softer lines in the form, a perception of beauty and law that he could not render; there was the strain of effort, under conscious imperfection, in every line. But the Irish missal-painter had drawn his angel with no sense of failure, in happy complacency, and put red dots into the palm of each hand, and rounded the eyes into perfect circles, and, I regret to say, left the mouth out altogether, with perfect satisfaction to himself.

May I without offence ask you to consider whether this mode of arrest in ancient Irish art may not be indicative of points of character which even yet, in some measure, arrest your national power? I have seen much of Irish character, and have watched it closely, for I have also much loved it. And I think the form of failure to which it is most liable is this,—that being generous-hearted, and wholly intending always to do right, it does not attend to the external laws of right, but thinks it must necessarily do right because it means to do so, and therefore does wrong without finding it out; and then, when the consequences of its wrong come upon it, or upon others connected with it, it cannot conceive that the wrong is in anywise of its causing or of its doing, but flies into wrath, and a strange agony of desire for justice, as feeling itself wholly innocent, which leads it farther astray, until there is nothing that it is not capable of doing with a good conscience.

But mind, I do not mean to say that, in past or present relations between Ireland and England, you have been wrong, and we right. Far from that, I believe that in all great questions of principle, and in all details of administration of law, you have been usually right, and we wrong; sometimes in misunderstanding you, sometimes in resolute iniquity to you. Nevertheless, in all disputes between states, though the stronger is nearly always mainly in the wrong, the weaker is often so in a minor degree; and I think we sometimes admit the possibility of our being in error, and you never do.

And now, returning to the broader question, what these arts and labours of life have to teach us of its mystery, this is the first of their lessons—that the more beautiful the art, the more it is essentially the work of people who *feel themselves wrong;*—who are striving for the fulfilment of a law, and the grasp of a loveliness, which they have not yet attained, which they feel even farther and farther from attaining the more they strive for it. And yet, in still deeper sense, it is the work of people who know also that they are right. The very sense of inevitable error from their purpose marks the perfectness of that purpose, and the continued sense of failure arises from the continued opening of the eyes more clearly to all the sacredest laws of truth.

This is one lesson. The second is a very plain, and greatly precious one: namely—that whenever the arts and labours of life are fulfilled in this spirit of striving against misrule, and doing whatever we have to do, honourably and perfectly, they invariably bring happiness, as much as seems possible to the nature of man. In all other paths by which that happiness is pursued there is disappointment, or destruction: for ambition and for passion there is no rest—no fruition; the fairest pleasures of youth perish in a darkness greater than their past light: and the loftiest and purest love too often does but inflame the cloud of life with endless fire of pain. But, ascending from lowest to highest, through every scale of human industry, that industry worthily followed, gives peace. Ask the labourer in the field, at the forge, or in the mine; ask the patient, delicate-fingered artisan, or the strong-armed, fiery-hearted worker in bronze, and in marble, and with the colours of light; and none of these, who are true workmen, will ever tell you, that they have found the law of heaven an unkind one—that in the sweat of their face they should eat bread, till they return to the ground; nor that they ever found it an unrewarded obedience, if, indeed, it was rendered faithfully to the command—"Whatsoever thy hand findeth to do—do it with thy might."

These are the two great and constant lessons which our labourers teach us of the mystery of life. But there is another, and a sadder one, which they cannot teach us, which we must read on their tombstones.

"Do it with thy might." There have been myriads upon myriads of human creatures who have obeyed this law—who have put every breath and nerve of their being into its toil—who have devoted every hour, and exhausted every faculty—who have bequeathed their unaccomplished thoughts at death—who, being dead, have yet spoken, by majesty of memory, and strength of example. And, at last, what has all this "Might" of humanity accomplished, in six thousand years of labour and sorrow? What has it *done?* Take the three chief occupations and arts of men, one by one, and count their achievements. Begin with the first—the lord of them all—Agriculture. Six thousand years have passed since we were set to till the ground, from which we were taken. How much of it is tilled? How much of that which is, wisely or well? In the very centre and chief garden of Europe—where the two forms of parent Christianity have had their fortresses—where the noble Catholics of the Forest Cantons, and the noble Protestants of the Vaudois valleys, have maintained, for dateless ages, their faiths and liberties—there the unchecked Alpine rivers yet run wild in devastation; and the marshes, which a few hundred men could redeem with a year's labour, still blast their helpless inhabitants into fevered idiotism. That is so, in the centre of Europe! While, on the near coast of Africa, once the Garden of the Hesperides, an Arab woman, but a few sunsets since, ate her child, for famine. And, with all the treasures of the East at our feet, we, in our own dominion, could not find a few grains of rice, for a people that asked of us no more; but stood by, and saw five hundred thousand of them perish of hunger.*

Then, after agriculture, the art of kings, take the next head of human arts—Weaving; the art of queens, honoured

* During the famine in the province of Orissa, in India.

of all noble Heathen women, in the person of their virgin goddess—honoured of all Hebrew women, by the word of their wisest king—"She layeth her hands to the spindle, and her hands hold the distaff; she stretcheth out her hand to the poor. She is not afraid of the snow for her household, for all her household are clothed with scarlet. She maketh herself covering of tapestry; her clothing is silk and purple. She maketh fine linen, and selleth it, and delivereth girdles to the merchant.* What have we done in all these thousands of years with this bright art of Greek maid and Christian matron? Six thousand years of weaving, and have we learned to weave? Might not every naked wall have been purple with tapestry, and every feeble breast fenced with sweet colours from the cold? What have we done? Our fingers are too few, it seems, to twist together some poor covering for our bodies. We set our streams to work for us, and choke the air with fire, to turn our spinning-wheels— and,—*are we yet clothed?* Are not the streets of the capitals of Europe foul with sale of cast clouts and rotten rags? Is not the beauty of your sweet children left in wretchedness of disgrace, while, with better honour, nature clothes the brood of the bird in its nest, and the suckling of the wolf in her den? And does not every winter's snow robe what you have not robed, and shroud what you have not shrouded; and every winter's wind bear up to heaven its wasted souls, to witness against you hereafter, by the voice of their Christ, —"I was naked, and ye clothed me not"?

Lastly—take the Art of Building—the strongest—proudest—most orderly—most enduring of the arts of man; that of which the produce is in the surest manner accumulative, and need not perish, or be replaced; but if once well done, will stand more strongly than the unbalanced rocks—more prevalently than the crumbling hills. The art which is associated with all civic pride and sacred principle; with which men record their power—satisfy their enthusiasm— make sure their defence—define and make dear their habi-

* Proverbs 31:19–22,24.

tation. And in six thousand years of building, what have we done? Of the greater part of all that skill and strength, *no* vestige is left, but fallen stones, that encumber the fields and impede the streams. But, from this waste of disorder, and of time, and of rage, what *is* left to us? Constructive and progressive creatures that we are, with ruling brains, and forming hands, capable of fellowship, and thirsting for fame, can we not contend, in comfort, with the insects of the forest, or, in achievement, with the worm of the sea? The white surf rages in vain against the ramparts built by poor atoms of scarcely nascent life; but only ridges of formless ruin mark the places where once dwelt our noblest multitudes. The ant and the moth have cells for each of their young, but our little ones lie in festering heaps, in homes that consume them like graves; and night by night, from the corners of our streets, rises up the cry of the homeless—"I was a stranger, and ye took me not in."

Must it be always thus? Is our life for ever to be without profit—without possession? Shall the strength of its generations be as barren as death; or cast away their labour, as the wild fig-tree casts her untimely figs? Is it all a dream then—the desire of the eyes and the pride of life—or, if it be, might we not live in nobler dream than this? The poets and prophets, the wise men, and the scribes, though they have told us nothing about a life to come, have told us much about the life that is now. They have had—they also,—their dreams, and we have laughed at them. They have dreamed of mercy, and of justice; they have dreamed of peace and good-will; they have dreamed of labour undisappointed, and of rest undisturbed; they have dreamed of fulness in harvest, and overflowing in store; they have dreamed of wisdom in council, and of providence in law; of gladness of parents, and strength of children, and glory of grey hairs. And at these visions of theirs we have mocked, and held them for idle and vain, unreal and unaccomplishable. What have we accomplished with our realities? Is this what has come of our worldly wisdom, tried against their folly? this, our mightiest possible, against their impotent ideal? or, have we only wandered among the spectra of a baser felicity, and chased phantoms of the tombs, instead of visions of the Almighty; and walked after the imaginations of our evil hearts, instead of after the counsels of Eternity, until our lives—not in the likeness of the cloud of heaven, but of the smoke of hell—have become "as a vapour, that appeareth for a little time, and then vanisheth away"?

Does it vanish then? Are you sure of that?—sure, that the nothingness of the grave will be a rest from this troubled nothingness; and that the coiling shadow, which disquiets itself in vain, cannot change into the smoke of the torment that ascends for ever? Will any answer that they *are* sure of it, and that there is no fear, nor hope, nor desire, nor labour, whither they go? Be it so: will you not, then, make as sure of the Life that now is, as you are of the Death that is to come? Your hearts are wholly in this world—will you not give them to it wisely, as well as perfectly? And see, first of all, that you *have* hearts, and sound hearts, too, to give. Because you have no heaven to look for, is that any reason that you should remain ignorant of this wonderful and infinite earth, which is firmly and instantly given you in possession? Although your days are numbered, and the following darkness sure, is it necessary that you should share the degradation of the brute, because you are condemned to its mortality; or live the life of the moth, and of the worm, because you are to companion them in the dust? Not so; we may have but a few thousands of days to spend, perhaps hundreds only—perhaps tens; nay, the longest of our time and best, looked back on, will be but as a moment, as the twinkling of an eye; still we are men, not insects; we are living spirits, not passing clouds. "He maketh the winds His messengers; the momentary fire, His minister;" and shall we do less than *these?* Let us do the work of men while we bear the form of them; and, as we snatch our narrow portion of time out of Eternity, snatch also our narrow inheritance of passion out of Immortality—even though our lives *be* as a vapour, that appeareth for a little time, and then vanisheth away.

But there are some of you who believe not this—who think this cloud of life has no such close—that it is to float, revealed and illumined, upon the floor of heaven, in the day when He cometh with clouds, and every eye shall see Him. Some day, you believe, within these five, or ten, or twenty years, for every one of us the judgment will be set, and the books opened. If that be true, far more than that must be true. Is there but one day of judgment? Why, for us every day is a day of judgment—every day is a Dies Iræ, and writes its irrevocable verdict in the flame of its West. Think you that judgment waits till the doors of the grave are opened? It waits at the doors of your houses—it waits at the corners of your streets; we are in the midst of judgment—the insects that we crush are our judges—the moments we fret away are our judges—the elements that feed us, judge, as they minister—and the pleasures that deceive us, judge, as they indulge. Let us, for our lives, do the work of Men while we bear the form of them, if indeed those lives are *Not* as a vapour, and do *Not* vanish away.

"The work of men"—and what is that? Well, we may any of us know very quickly, on the condition of being wholly ready to do it. But many of us are for the most part thinking, not of what we are to do, but of what we are to get; and the best of us are sunk into the sin of Ananias, and it is a mortal one—we want to keep back part of the price; and we continually talk of taking up our cross, as if the only harm in a cross was the *weight* of it—as if it was only a thing to be carried, instead of to be—crucified upon. "They that are His have crucified the flesh, with the affections and lusts." Does that mean, think you, that in time of national distress, of religious trial, of crisis for every interest and hope of humanity—none of us will cease jesting, none cease idling, none put themselves to any wholesome work, none take so much as a tag of lace off their footmen's coats, to save the world? Or does it rather mean, that they are ready to leave houses, lands, and kindreds—yes, and life, if need be? Life!—some of us are ready enough to throw

that away, joyless as we have made it. But "*station* in Life"
—how many of us are ready to quit *that?* Is it not always
the great objection, where there is question of finding something useful to do—"We cannot leave our stations in Life"?

Those of us who really cannot—that is to say, who can
only maintain themselves by continuing in some business
or salaried office, have already something to do; and all that
they have to see to is, that they do it honestly and with all
their might. But with most people who use that apology,
"remaining in the station of life to which Providence has
called them" means keeping all the carriages, and all the
footmen and large houses they can possibly pay for; and,
once for all, I say that if ever Providence *did* put them
into stations of that sort—which is not at all a matter of
certainty—Providence is just now very distinctly calling
them out again. Levi's station in life was the receipt of
custom; and Peter's, the shore of Galilee; and Paul's, the
antechambers of the High Priest,—which "station in life"
each had to leave, with brief notice.

And, whatever our station in life may be, at this crisis,
those of us who mean to fulfil our duty ought first to live
on as little as we can; and, secondly, to do all the wholesome work for it we can, and to spend all we can spare in
doing all the sure good we can.

And sure good is, first in feeding people, then in dressing
people, then in lodging people, and lastly in rightly pleasing people, with arts, or sciences, or any other subject of
thought.

I say first in feeding; and, once for all, do not let yourselves be deceived by any of the common talk of "indiscriminate charity." The order to us is not to feed the deserving hungry, nor the industrious hungry, nor the amiable
and well-intentioned hungry, but simply to feed the hungry.
It is quite true, infallibly true, that if any man will not
work, neither should he eat—think of that, and every time
you sit down to your dinner, ladies and gentlemen, say
solemnly, before you ask a blessing, "How much work have

I done to-day for my dinner?" But the proper way to enforce that order on those below you, as well as on yourselves, is not to leave vagabonds and honest people to starve together, but very distinctly to discern and seize your vagabond; and shut your vagabond up out of honest people's way, and very sternly then see that, until he has worked, he does *not* eat. But the first thing is to be sure you have the food to give; and, therefore, to enforce the organization of vast activities in agriculture and in commerce, for the production of the wholesomest food, and proper storing and distribution of it, so that no famine shall any more be possible among civilized beings. There is plenty of work in this business alone, and at once, for any number of people who like to engage in it.

Secondly, dressing people—that is to say, urging every one within reach of your influence to be always neat and clean, and giving them means of being so. In so far as they absolutely refuse, you must give up the effort with respect to them, only taking care that no children within your sphere of influence shall any more be brought up with such habits; and that every person who is willing to dress with propriety shall have encouragement to do so. And the first absolutely necessary step towards this is the gradual adoption of a consistent dress for different ranks of persons, so that their rank shall be known by their dress; and the restriction of the changes of fashion within certain limits. All which appears for the present quite impossible; but it is only so far even difficult as it is difficult to conquer our vanity, frivolity, and desire to appear what we are not. And it is not, nor ever shall be, creed of mine, that these mean and shallow vices are unconquerable by Christian women.

And then, thirdly, lodging people, which you may think should have been put first, but I put it third, because we must feed and clothe people where we find them, and lodge them afterwards. And providing lodgment for them means a great deal of vigorous legislature, and cutting down of vested interests that stand in the way, and after that, or before that, so far as we can get it, thorough sanitary and remedial action in the houses that we have; and then the building of more, strongly, beautifully, and in groups of limited extent, kept in proportion to their streams, and walled round, so that there may be no festering and wretched suburb anywhere, but clean and busy street within, and the open country without, with a belt of beautiful garden and orchard round the walls, so that from any part of the city perfectly fresh air and grass, and sight of far horizon, might be reachable in a few minutes' walk. This the final aim; but in immediate action every minor and possible good to be instantly done, when, and as, we can; roofs mended that have holes in them—fences patched that have gaps in them—walls buttressed that totter—and floors propped that shake; cleanliness and order enforced with our own hands and eyes, till we are breathless, every day. And all the fine arts will healthily follow. I myself have washed a flight of stone stairs all down, with bucket and broom, in a Savoy inn, where they hadn't washed their stairs since they first went up them; and I never made a better sketch than that afternoon.

These, then, are the three first needs of civilized life; and the law for every Christian man and woman is, that they shall be in direct service toward one of these three needs, as far as is consistent with their own special occupation, and if they have no special business, then wholly in one of these services. And out of such exertion in plain duty all other good will come; for in this direct contention with material evil, you will find out the real nature of all evil; you will discern by the various kinds of resistance, what is really the fault and main antagonism to good; also you will find the most unexpected helps and profound lessons given, and truths will come thus down to us which the speculation of all our lives would never have raised us up to. You will find nearly every educational problem solved, as soon as you truly want to do something; everybody will become of use in their own fittest way, and will learn what is best for them to know in that use. Competitive examination will then, and not till then, be wholesome, because it will be daily, and calm, and in practice; and on these familiar arts, and minute, but certain and serviceable knowledges, will be surely edified and sustained the greater arts and splendid theoretical sciences.

But much more than this. On such holy and simple practice will be founded, indeed, at last, an infallible religion. The greatest of all the mysteries of life, and the most terrible, is the corruption of even the sincerest religion, which is not daily founded on rational, effective, humble, and helpful action. Helpful action, observe! for there is just one law, which, obeyed, keeps all religions pure—forgotten, makes them all false. Whenever in any religious faith, dark or bright, we allow our minds to dwell upon the points in which we differ from other people, we are wrong, and in the devil's power. That is the essence of the Pharisee's thanksgiving—"Lord, I thank Thee that I am not as other men are." At every moment of our lives we should be trying to find out, not in what we differ from other people, but in what we agree with them; and the moment we find we can agree as to anything that should be done, kind or good, (and who but fools couldn't?) then do it; push at it together: you can't quarrel in a side-by-side push; but the moment that even the best men stop pushing, and begin talking, they mistake their pugnacity for piety, and it's all over. I will not speak of the crimes which in past times have been committed in the name of Christ, nor of the follies which are at this hour held to be consistent with obedience to Him; but I *will* speak of the morbid corruption and waste of vital power in religious sentiment, by which the pure strength of that which should be the guiding soul of every nation, the splendour of its youthful manhood, and spotless light of its maidenhood, is averted or cast away. You may see continually girls who have never been taught to do a single useful thing thoroughly; who cannot sew, who cannot cook, who cannot cast an account, nor prepare a medicine, whose whole life has been passed either in play or in pride; you will find girls like these, when they are earnest-hearted, cast all their innate passion of religious spirit, which was meant by God to support them through the irksomeness of daily toil, into grievous and vain meditation over the meaning of the great Book, of which no syllable was ever yet to be understood but through a deed; all the instinctive wisdom and mercy of their womanhood made vain, and the glory of their pure consciences warped into fruitless agony concerning questions which the laws of common serviceable life would have either solved for them in an instant, or kept out of their way. Give such a girl any true work that will make her active in the dawn, and weary at night, with the consciousness that her fellow-creatures have indeed been the better for her day, and the powerless sorrow of her enthusiasm will transform itself into a majesty of radiant and beneficent peace.

So with our youths. We once taught them to make Latin verses, and called them educated; now we teach them to leap and to row, to hit a ball with a bat, and call them educated. Can they plough, can they sow, can they plant at the right time, or build with a steady hand? Is it the effort of their lives to be chaste, knightly, faithful, holy in thought, lovely in word and deed? Indeed it is, with some, nay, with many, and the strength of England is in them, and the hope; but we have to turn their courage from the toil of war to the toil of mercy; and their intellect from dispute of words to discernment of things; and their knighthood from the errantry of adventure to the state and fidelity of a kingly power. And then, indeed, shall abide, for them and for us, an incorruptible felicity, and an infallible religion; shall abide for us Faith, no more to be assailed by temptation, no more to be defended by wrath and by fear;—shall abide with us Hope, no more to be quenched by the years that overwhelm, or made ashamed by the shadows that betray:—shall abide for us, and with us, the greatest of these; the abiding will, the abiding name of our Father. For the greatest of these is Charity.

THE QUEEN OF THE AIR

Athena Keramitis*

Whatever the origin of species may be, or however those species, once formed, may be influenced by external accident, the groups into which birth or accident reduce them have distinct relation to the spirit of man. It is perfectly possible, and ultimately conceivable, that the crocodile and the lamb may have descended from the same ancestral atom of protoplasm; and that the physical laws of the operation of calcareous slime and of meadow grass, on that protoplasm, may in time have developed the opposite natures and aspects of the living frames; but the practically important fact for us is the existence of a power which creates that calcareous earth itself;—which creates that, separately, and quartz, separately, and gold, separately, and charcoal, separately; and then so directs the relations of these elements that the gold may destroy the souls of men by being yellow; and the charcoal destroy their souls by being hard and bright; and the quartz represent to them an ideal purity; and the calcareous earth, soft, may beget crocodiles, and dry and hard, sheep; and that the aspects and qualities of these two products, crocodiles and lambs, may be, the one repellent to the spirit of man, the other attractive to it, in a quite inevitable way, representing to him states of moral evil and good, and becoming myths to him of destruction or

* "Athena in the Earth," a study of the "relations of Athena to the vital force in material organism."

redemption, and, in the most literal sense, "Words" of God. . . .

Now we have two orders of animals to take some note of in connection with Athena, and one vast order of plants, which will illustrate this matter very sufficiently for us.

The two orders of animals are the serpent and the bird; the serpent, in which the breath, or spirit, is less than in any other creature, and the earth-power greatest:—the bird, in which the breath, or spirit, is more full than in any other creature, and the earth-power least.

We will take the bird first. It is little more than a drift of the air brought into form by plumes; the air is in all its quills, it breathes through its whole frame and flesh, and glows with air in its flying, like a blown flame: it rests upon the air, subdues it, surpasses it, outraces it;—*is* the air, conscious of itself, conquering itself, ruling itself.

Also, into the throat of the bird is given the voice of the air. All that in the wind itself is weak, wild, useless in sweetness, is knit together in its song. As we may imagine the wild form of the cloud closed into the perfect form of the bird's wings, so the wild voice of the cloud into its ordered and commanded voice; unwearied, rippling through the clear heaven in its gladness, interpreting all intense passion through the soft spring nights, bursting into acclaim and rapture of choir at daybreak, or lisping and twittering among the boughs and hedges through heat of day, like little winds that only make the cowslip bells shake, and ruffle the petals of the wild rose.

Also, upon the plumes of the bird are put the colours of the air: on these the gold of the cloud, that cannot be gathered by any covetousness; the rubies of the clouds, that are not the price of Athena, but *are* Athena; the vermilion of the cloud-bar, and the flame of the cloud-crest, and the snow of the cloud, and its shadow, and the melted blue of the deep wells of the sky—all these, seized by the creating spirit, and woven by Athena herself into films and threads of plume; with wave on wave following and fading along breast, and throat, and opened wings, infinite as the dividing of the foam and the sifting of the sea-sand:—even the white down of the cloud seeming to flutter up between the stronger plumes, seen, but too soft for touch.

And so the Spirit of the Air is put into, and upon, this created form; and it becomes, through twenty centuries, the symbol of Divine help, descending, as the Fire, to speak, but as the Dove, to bless.

Next, in the serpent we approach the source of a group of myths, world-wide, founded on great and common human instincts, respecting which I must note one or two points which bear intimately on all our subject. For it seems to me that the scholars who are at present occupied in interpretation of human myths have most of them forgotten that there are any such things as natural myths; and that the dark sayings of men may be both difficult to read, and not always worth reading; but the dark sayings of nature will probably become clearer for the looking into, and will very certainly be worth reading. And, indeed, all guidance to the right sense of the human and variable myths will probably depend on our first getting at the sense of the natural and invariable ones. The dead hieroglyph may have meant this or that—the living hieroglyph means always the same; but remember, it is just as much a hieroglyph as the other; nay, more,—a "sacred or reserved sculpture," a thing with an inner language. The serpent crest of the king's crown, or of the god's, on the pillars of Egypt, is a mystery; but the serpent itself, gliding past the pillar's foot, is it less a mystery? Is there, indeed, no tongue, except the mute forked flash from its lips, in that running brook of horror on the ground?

Why that horror? We all feel it, yet how imaginative it is, how disproportioned to the real strength of the creature! There is more poison in an ill-kept drain,—in a pool of dish-washings at a cottage door,—than in the deadliest asp of Nile. Every back-yard which you look down into from the railway, as it carries you out by Vauxhall or Deptford,

holds its coiled serpent: all the walls of those ghastly suburbs are enclosures of tank temples for serpent worship;
yet you feel no horror in looking down into them, as you
would if you saw the livid scales and lifted head. There is
more venom, mortal, inevitable, in a single word sometimes,
or in the gliding entrance of a wordless thought, than ever
"vanti Libia con sua rena."* But that horror is of the myth,
not of the creature. There are myriads lower than this, and
more loathsome, in the scale of being; the links between
dead matter and animation drift everywhere unseen. But
it is the strength of the base element that is so dreadful in
the serpent; it is the very omnipotence of the earth. That
rivulet of smooth silver—how does it flow, think you? It
literally rows on the earth, with every scale for an oar; it
bites the dust with the ridges of its body. Watch it, when it
moves slowly:—A wave, but without wind! a current, but
with no fall! all the body moving at the same instant, yet
some of it to one side, some to another, or some forward,
and the rest of the coil backwards; but all with the same
calm will and equal way—no contraction, no extension;
one soundless, causeless march of sequent rings, and spectral procession of spotted dust, with dissolution in its fangs,
dislocation in its coils. Startle it;—the winding stream will
become a twisted arrow;—the wave of poisoned life will
lash through the grass like a cast lance. It scarcely breathes
with its one lung (the other shrivelled and abortive); it is
passive to the sun and shade, and is cold or hot like a
stone; yet, "it can outclimb the monkey, outswim the fish,
outleap the jerboa, outwrestle the athlete, and crush the
tiger." It is a divine hieroglyph of the demoniac power of
the earth,—of the entire earthly nature. As the bird is the
clothed power of the air, so this is the clothed power of the
dust; as the bird the symbol of the spirit of life, so this of
the grasp and sting of death.

* In the *Inferno*, XXIV, 82–89, Dante describes a throng of serpents
so hideous that they "let Libya no longer boast of [the power of] her
sands" to engender monstrosities and plagues.

Hence the continual change in the interpretation put upon it in various religions. As the worm of corruption, it is the mightiest of all adversaries of the gods—the special adversary of their light and creative power—Python against Apollo. As the power of the earth against the air, the giants are serpent-bodied in the Gigantomachia; but as the power of the earth upon the seed—consuming it into new life ("that which thou sowest is not quickened except it die")— serpents sustain the chariot of the spirit of agriculture.

Yet, on the other hand, there is a power in the earth to take away corruption, and to purify, (hence the very fact of burial, and many uses of earth, only lately known); and in this sense, the serpent is a healing spirit,—the representative of Æsculapius, and of Hygieia; and is a sacred earth-type in the temple of the Dew;—being there especially a symbol of the native earth of Athens; so that its departure from the temple was a sign to the Athenians that they were to leave their homes. And then, lastly, as there is a strength and healing in the earth, no less than the strength of air, so there is conceived to be a wisdom of earth no less than a wisdom of the spirit; and when its deadly power is killed, its guiding power becomes true; so that the Python serpent is killed at Delphi, where yet the oracle is from the breath of the earth.

You must remember, however, that in this, as in every other instance, I take the myth at its central time. This is only the meaning of the serpent to the Greek mind which could conceive an Athena. Its first meaning to the nascent eyes of men, and its continued influence over degraded races, are subjects of the most fearful mystery. Mr. Fergusson has just collected the principal evidence bearing on the matter in a work of very great value,* and if you read his opening chapters, they will put you in possession of the circumstances needing chiefly to be considered. I cannot touch upon any of them here, except only to point out that, though the doctrine of the so-called "corruption of human

* James Fergusson, *Tree and Serpent Worship; or, Illustrations of Mythology and Art in India,* 1868.

nature," asserting that there is nothing but evil in humanity, is just as blasphemous and false as a doctrine of the
corruption of physical nature would be, asserting there was
nothing but evil in the earth,—there is yet the clearest evidence of a disease, plague, or cretinous imperfection of
development, hitherto allowed to prevail against the greater
part of the races of men; and this in monstrous ways, more
full of mystery than the serpent-being itself. I have gathered
for you to-night only instances of what is beautiful in Greek
religion; but even in its best time there were deep corruptions in other phases of it, and degraded forms of many
of its deities, all originating in a misunderstood worship of
the principle of life; while in the religions of lower races,
little else than these corrupted forms of devotion can be
found;—all having a strange and dreadful consistency with
each other, and infecting Christianity, even at its strongest
periods, with fatal terror of doctrine, and ghastliness of sym-
bolic conception, passing through fear into frenzied grotesque, and thence into sensuality.

In the Psalter of S. Louis itself, half of its letters are
twisted snakes; there is scarcely a wreathed ornament, employed in Christian dress, or architecture, which cannot be
traced back to the serpent's coil; and there is rarely a piece
of monkish decorated writing in the world, that is not
tainted with some ill-meant vileness of grotesque—nay, the
very leaves of the twisted ivy-pattern of the fourteenth century can be followed back to wreaths for the foreheads of
bacchanalian gods. And truly, it seems to me, as I gather in
my mind the evidences of insane religion, degraded art,
merciless war, sullen toil, detestable pleasure, and vain or
vile hope, in which the nations of the world have lived since
first they could bear record of themselves—it seems to me,
I say, as if the race itself were still half-serpent, not extricated yet from its clay; a lacertine breed of bitterness—the
glory of it emaciate with cruel hunger, and blotted with
venomous stain: and the track of it, on the leaf a glittering
slime, and in the sand a useless furrow.

FORS CLAVIGERA*

The White-Thorn Blossom

"For lo, the winter is past,
The rain is over and gone,
The flowers appear on the earth,
The time of the singing of birds is come,

Arise, O my fair one, my dove,
And come."†

DENMARK HILL, 1st May, 1871.

My Friends,—It has been asked of me, very justly, why I
have hitherto written to you of things you were little likely
to care for, in words which it was difficult for you to understand.

---

* The source of this most allusive of Ruskin's titles was Horace's
image of "implacable Fate, the Nail-bearer" (*Odes* i. 35). The first
word of the title means Chance or Accident, but Ruskin used it
interchangeably in the three senses of Force, Fortitude, and Fortune.
Clavigera means Club-bearer (*clava* plus *gero*, to bear), Key-bearer
(*clavis*), and Nail-bearer (*clavus*). Force with the club represents the
wise and strong man armed; Fortitude with the key represents Patience, the portress at the gate of Art; Fortune with the nail represents the fixed power of Necessity. With the third meaning of Fors,
Ruskin also associated the Three Fates of the Greeks which control
the thread of our destiny. Each of these meaning shades into all the
others, until the title comes finally to represent the Fate which wove
the tragic pattern of Ruskin's life and the Chance which led him to
mirror that pattern with such an anarchy of digression throughout
the book.
† Song of Solomon 2:11–13.

I have no fear but that you will one day understand all my poor words,—the saddest of them, perhaps, too well. But I have great fear that you may never come to understand these written above, which are part of a king's love-song, in one sweet May, of many long since gone.

I fear that for you the wild winter's rain may never pass, —the flowers never appear on the earth;—that for you no bird may ever sing;—for you no perfect Love arise, and fulfil your life in peace.

"And why not for us, as for others?" will you answer me so, and take my fear for you as an insult?

Nay, it is no insult;—nor am I happier than you. For me, the birds do not sing, nor ever will. But they would, for you, if you cared to have it so. When I told you that you would never understand that love-song, I meant only that you would not desire to understand it.

Are you again indignant with me? Do you think, though you should labour, and grieve, and be trodden down in dishonour all your days, at least you can keep that one joy of Love, and that one honour of Home? Had you, in-deed, kept that, you had kept all. But no men yet, in the history of the race, have lost it so piteously. In many a coun-try, and many an age, women have been compelled to la-bour for their husbands' wealth, or bread; but never until now were they so homeless as to say, like the poor Samari-tan, "I have no husband." Women of every country and people have sustained without complaint the labour of fellowship: for the women of the latter days in England it has been reserved to claim the privilege of isolation.

This, then, is the end of your universal education and civilization, and contempt of the ignorance of the Middle Ages, and of their chivalry. Not only do you declare your-selves too indolent to labour for daughters and wives, and too poor to support them; but you have made the neglected and distracted creatures hold it for an honour to be inde-pendent of you, and shriek for some hold of the mattock for themselves. Believe it or not, as you may, there has not been so low a level of thought reached by any race, since they grew to be male and female out of star-fish, or chick-weed, or whatever else they have been made from, by nat-ural selection,—according to modern science.

That modern science also, Economic and of other kinds, has reached its climax at last. For it seems to be the ap-pointed function of the nineteenth century to exhibit in all things the elect pattern of perfect Folly, for a warning to the farthest future. Thus the statement of principle which I quoted to you in my last letter, from the circular of the Emigration Society, that it is over-production which is the cause of distress, is accurately the most foolish thing, not only hitherto ever said by men, but which it is possible for men ever to say, respecting their own business. It is a kind of opposite pole (or negative acme of mortal stupidity) to Newton's discovery of gravitation as an acme of mortal wisdom:—as no wise being on earth will ever be able to make such another wise discovery, so no foolish being on earth will ever be capable of saying such another foolish thing, through all the ages.

And the same crisis has been exactly reached by our nat-ural science and by our art. It has several times chanced to me, since I began these papers, to have the exact thing shown or brought to me that I wanted for illustration, just in time—and it happened that on the very day on which I published my last letter, I had to go to the Kensington Museum; and there I saw the most perfectly and roundly ill-done thing which, as yet, in my whole life I ever saw produced by art. It had a tablet in front of it, bearing this inscription:—

"Statue in black and white marble, a Newfoundland Dog standing on a Serpent, which rests on a marble cushion, the pedestal ornamented with pietra dura fruits in relief.— English. Present Century. No. I."

It was so very right for me, the Kensington people having been good enough to number it "I.," the thing itself being almost incredible in its one-ness; and, indeed, such a punctual accent over the iota of Miscreation,—so absolutely and exquisitely miscreant, that I am not myself capable of conceiving a Number two, or three, or any rivalship or association with it whatsoever. The extremity of its unvirtue consisted, observe, mainly in the quantity of instruction which was abused in it. It showed that the persons who produced it had seen everything, and practised everything; and misunderstood everything they saw, and misapplied everything they did. They had seen Roman work, and Florentine work, and Byzantine work, and Gothic work; and misunderstanding of everything had passed through them as the mud does through earthworms, and here at last was their worm-cast of a Production.

But the second chance that came to me that day, was more significant still. From the Kensington Museum I went to an afternoon tea, at a house where I was sure to meet some nice people. And among the first I met was an old friend who had been hearing some lectures on botany at the Kensington Museum, and been delighted by them. She is the kind of person who gets good out of everything, and she was quite right in being delighted; besides that, as I found by her account of them, the lectures were really interesting, and pleasantly given. She had expected botany to be dull, and had not found it so, and "had learned so much." On hearing this, I proceeded naturally to inquire what; for my idea of her was that before she went to the lectures at all, she had known more botany than she was likely to learn by them. So she told me that she had learned first of all that "there were seven sorts of leaves." Now I have always a great suspicion of the number Seven; because when I wrote the *Seven Lamps of Architecture,* it required all the ingenuity I was master of to prevent them from becoming Eight, or even Nine, on my hands. So I thought to myself that it would be very charming if there were only seven sorts of leaves; but that, perhaps, if one looked the woods and forests of the world carefully through, it was just possible that one might discover as many as eight sorts; and then where would my friend's new knowledge of Botany be?

So I said, "That was very pretty; but what more?" Then my friend told me that she had no idea, before, that petals were leaves. On which, I thought to myself that it would not have been any great harm to her if she had remained under her old impression that petals were petals. But I said, "That was very pretty, too; and what more?" So then my friend told me that the lecturer said, "the object of his lectures would be entirely accomplished if he could convince his hearers that there was no such thing as a flower." Now, in that sentence you have the most perfect and admirable summary given you of the general temper and purposes of modern science. It gives lectures on Botany, of which the object is to show that there is no such thing as a flower; on Humanity, to show that there is no such thing as a Man; and on Theology, to show there is no such thing as a God. No such thing as a Man, but only a Mechanism; no such thing as a God, but only a series of forces. The two faiths are essentially one: if you feel yourself to be only a machine, constructed to be a Regulator of minor machinery, you will put your statue of such science on your Holborn Viaduct, and necessarily recognize only major machinery as regulating *you*.

I must explain the real meaning to you, however, of that saying of the Botanical lecturer, for it has a wide bearing. Some fifty years ago the poet Goethe discovered that all the parts of plants had a kind of common nature, and would change into each other. Now this was a true discovery, and a notable one; and you will find that, in fact, all plants are composed of essentially two parts—the leaf and root—one loving the light, the other darkness; one liking to be clean, the other to be dirty; one liking to grow for the most part up, the other for the most part down; and each having faculties and purposes of its own. But the pure one which loves the light has, above all things, the purpose of being married to another leaf, and having child-leaves, and children's children of leaves, to make the earth fair for ever. And when the leaves marry, they put on wedding-robes, and are more glorious than Solomon in all his glory, and they have feasts of honey, and we call them "Flowers."

In a certain sense, therefore, you see the lecturer was quite right. There are no such things as Flowers—there are only —gladdened Leaves. Nay, farther than this, there may be a dignity in the less happy, but unwithering leaf, which is, in some sort, better than the brief lily of its bloom;— which the great poets always knew,—well;—Chaucer, before Goethe; and the writer of the first Psalm, before Chaucer. The Botanical lecturer was, in a deeper sense than he knew, right.

But in the deepest sense of all, the Botanical lecturer was, to the extremity of wrongness, wrong; for leaf, and root, and fruit, exist, all of them, only—that there may be flowers. He disregarded the life and passion of the creature, which were its essence. Had he looked for these, he would have recognized that in the thought of Nature herself, there is, in a plant, nothing else but its flowers.

Now in exactly the sense that modern Science declares there is no such thing as a Flower, it has declared there is no such thing as a Man, but only a transitional form of Ascidians and apes. It may, or may not be true—it is not of the smallest consequence whether it be or not. The real fact is, that, rightly seen with human eyes, there is nothing else but man; that all animals and beings beside him are only made that they may change into him; that the world truly exists only in the presence of Man, acts only in the passion of Man. The essence of light is in his eyes,—the centre of Force in his soul,—the pertinence of action in his deeds.

And all true science—which my Savoyard guide rightly scorned me when he thought I had not,—all true science is "savoir vivre."* But all your modern science is the contrary of that. It is "savoir mourir."

* In the previous issue of *Fors* Ruskin had written of Joseph Couttet, his Alpine guide, who used to remark, in quiet exasperation at the young Ruskin's gloom, "Le pauvre enfant, il ne sait pas vivre!"

And of its very discoveries, such as they are, it cannot make use.

That telegraphic signalling was a discovery; and conceivably, some day, may be a useful one. And there was some excuse for your being a little proud when, about last sixth of April (Cœur-de-Lion's death-day, and Albert Dürer's), you knotted a copper wire all the way to Bombay, and flashed a message along it, and back.

But what was the message, and what the answer? Is India the better for what you said to her? Are you the better for what she replied?

If not, you have only wasted an all-round-the-world's length of copper wire,—which is, indeed, about the sum of your doing. If you had had, perchance, two words of common-sense to say, though you had taken wearisome time and trouble to send them;—though you had written them slowly in gold, and sealed them with a hundred seals, and sent a squadron of ships of the line to carry the scroll, and the squadron had fought its way round the Cape of Good Hope, through a year of storms, with loss of all its ships but one,—the two words of common-sense would have been worth the carriage, and more. But you have not anything like so much as that to say, either to India, or to any other place.

You think it a great triumph to make the sun draw brown landscapes for you. That was also a discovery, and some day may be useful. But the sun had drawn landscapes before for you, not in brown, but in green, and blue, and all imaginable colours, here in England. Not one of you ever looked at them then; not one of you cares for the loss of them now, when you have shut the sun out with smoke, so that he can draw nothing more, except brown blots through a hole in a box. There was a rocky valley between Buxton and Bakewell, once upon a time, divine as the Vale of Tempe; you might have seen the Gods there morning and evening—Apollo and all the sweet Muses of the light—walking in fair procession on the lawns of it, and to and fro among the pinnacles of its crags. You cared neither for

Gods nor grass, but for cash (which you did not know the way to get); you thought you could get it by what the *Times* calls "Railroad Enterprise." You Enterprised a Railroad through the valley—you blasted its rocks away, heaped thousands of tons of shale into its lovely stream. The valley is gone, and the Gods with it; and now, every fool in Buxton can be at Bakewell in half-an-hour, and every fool in Bakewell at Buxton; which you think a lucrative process of exchange—you Fools Everywhere.

To talk at a distance, when you have nothing to say, though you were ever so near; to go fast from this place to that, with nothing to do either at one or the other: these are powers certainly. Much more, power of increased Production, if you, indeed, had got it, would be something to boast of. But are you so entirely sure that you *have* got it— that the mortal disease of plenty, and afflictive affluence of good things, are all you have to dread? . . .

There are three Material things, not only useful, but essential to Life. No one "knows how to live" till he has got them.

These are, Pure Air, Water, and Earth.

There are three Immaterial things, not only useful, but essential to Life. No one knows how to live till he has got them.

These are, Admiration, Hope, and Love.*

Admiration—the power of discerning and taking delight in what is beautiful in visible Form, and lovely in human Character; and, necessarily, striving to produce what is beautiful in form, and to become what is lovely in character.

Hope—the recognition, by true Foresight, of better things to be reached hereafter, whether by ourselves or others; necessarily issuing in the straightforward and undisappointable effort to advance, according to our proper power, the gaining of them.

Love, both of family and neighbour, faithful, and satisfied.

* Cf. Wordsworth, *The Excursion*, IV, 763: "We live by Admiration, Hope, and Love."

These are the six chiefly useful things to be got by Political Economy, when it *has* become a science. I will briefly tell you what modern Political Economy—the great "savoir mourir"—is doing with them.

The first three, I said, are Pure Air, Water, and Earth.

Heaven gives you the main elements of these. You can destroy them at your pleasure, or increase, almost without limit, the available quantities of them.

You can vitiate the air by your manner of life, and of death, to any extent. You might easily vitiate it so as to bring such a pestilence on the globe as would end all of you. You, or your fellows, German and French, are at present busy in vitiating it to the best of your power in every direction; chiefly at this moment with corpses, and animal and vegetable ruin in war: changing men, horses, and garden-stuff into noxious gas. But everywhere, and all day long, you are vitiating it with foul chemical exhalations; and the horrible nests, which you call towns, are little more than laboratories for the distillation into heaven of venomous smokes and smells, mixed with effluvia from decaying animal matter, and infectious miasmata from purulent disease.

On the other hand, your power of purifying the air, by dealing properly and swiftly with all substances in corruption; by absolutely forbidding noxious manufactures; and by planting in all soils the trees which cleanse and invigorate earth and atmosphere,—is literally infinite. You might make every breath of air you draw, food.

Secondly, your power over the rain and river-waters of the earth is infinite. You can bring rain where you will, by planting wisely and tending carefully;—drought where you will, by ravage of woods and neglect of the soil. You might have the rivers of England as pure as the crystal of the rock; beautiful in falls, in lakes, in living pools; so full of fish that you might take them out with your hands instead of nets. Or you may do always as you have done now, turn every river of England into a common sewer, so that you cannot so much as baptize an English baby but with filth, unless you hold its face out in the rain; and even *that* falls dirty.

Then for the third, Earth,—meant to be nourishing for you, and blossoming. You have learned, about it, that there is no such thing as a flower; and as far as your scientific hands and scientific brains, inventive of explosive and deathful, instead of blossoming and life-giving, Dust, can contrive, you have turned the Mother-Earth, Demeter, into the Avenger-Earth, Tisiphone—with the voice of your brother's blood crying out of it, in one wild harmony round all its murderous sphere.

This is what you have done for the three Material Useful Things.

Then for the Three Immaterial Useful Things. For Admiration, you have learnt contempt and conceit. There is no lovely thing ever yet done by man that you care for, or can understand; but you are persuaded you are able to do much finer things yourselves. You gather, and exhibit together, as if equally instructive, what is infinitely bad, with what is infinitely good. You do not know which is which; you instinctively prefer the Bad, and do more of it. You instinctively hate the Good, and destroy it.*

Then, secondly, for Hope. You have not so much spirit of it in you as to begin any plan which will not pay until ten years; nor so much intelligence of it in you (either politicians or workmen) as to be able to form one clear idea of what you would like your country to become.

---

* Last night (I am writing this on the 18th of April) I got a letter from Venice, bringing me the, I believe, too well-grounded, report that the Venetians have requested permission from the government of Italy to pull down their Ducal Palace, and "rebuild" it. Put up a horrible model of it, in its place, that is to say, for which their architects may charge a commission. Meantime, all their canals are choked with human dung, which they are too poor to cart away, but throw out at their windows.

And all the great thirteenth-century cathedrals in France have been destroyed, within my own memory, only that architects might charge commission for putting up false models of them in their place. [Ruskin's note.]

Then, thirdly, for Love. You were ordered by the Founder of your religion to love your neighbour as yourselves.

You have founded an entire Science of Political Economy, on what you have stated to be the constant instinct of man —the desire to defraud his neighbour.

And you have driven your women mad, so that they ask no more for Love, nor for fellowship with you; but stand against you, and ask for "justice."

Are there any of you who are tired of all this? Any of you, Landlords or Tenants? Employers or Workmen?

Are there any landlords,—any masters,—who would like better to be served by men than by iron devils?

Any tenants, any workmen, who can be true to their leaders and to each other? who can vow to work and to live faithfully, for the sake of the joy of their homes?

Will any such give the tenth of what they have, and of what they earn,—not to emigrate with, but to stay in England with; and do what is in their hands and hearts to make her a happy England?

I am not rich (as people now estimate riches), and great part of what I have is already engaged in maintaining art-workmen, or for other objects more or less of public utility. The tenth of whatever is left to me, estimated as accurately as I can (you shall see the accounts), I will make over to you in perpetuity, with the best security that English law can give, on Christmas Day of this year, with engagement to add the tithe of whatever I earn afterwards. Who else will help, with little or much? the object of such fund being, to begin, and gradually—no matter how slowly—to increase, the buying and securing of land in England, which shall not be built upon, but cultivated by Englishmen, with their own hands, and such help of force as they can find in wind and wave.

I do not care with how many, or how few, this thing is begun, nor on what inconsiderable scale,—if it be but in two or three poor men's gardens. So much, at least, I can buy, myself, and give them. If no help come, I have done

and said what I could, and there will be an end. If any help
come to me, it is to be on the following conditions:—We
will try to take some small piece of English ground, beautiful, peaceful, and fruitful. We will have no steam-engines
upon it, and no railroads; we will have no untended or un-
thought-of creatures on it; none wretched, but the sick;
none idle but the dead. We will have no liberty upon it;
but instant obedience to known law, and appointed persons: no equality upon it; but recognition of every better-
ness that we can find, and reprobation of every worseness.
When we want to go anywhere, we will go there quietly and
safely, not at forty miles an hour in the risk of our lives;
when we want to carry anything anywhere, we will carry it
either on the backs of beasts, or on our own, or in carts,
or boats; we will have plenty of flowers and vegetables in
our gardens, plenty of corn and grass in our fields,—and
few bricks. We will have some music and poetry; the children shall learn to dance to it and sing it;—perhaps some
of the old people, in time, may also. We will have some art,
moreover; we will at least try if, like the Greeks, we can't
make some pots. The Greeks used to paint pictures of gods
on their pots; we, probably, cannot do as much, but we
may put some pictures of insects on them, and reptiles;—
butterflies, and frogs, if nothing better. There was an excellent old potter in France who used to put frogs and vipers
into his dishes, to the admiration of mankind; we can surely
put something nicer than that. Little by little, some higher
art and imagination may manifest themselves among us;
and feeble rays of science may dawn for us. Botany, though
too dull to dispute the existence of flowers; and history,
though too simple to question the nativity of men;—nay—
even perhaps an uncalculating and uncovetous wisdom, as
of rude Magi, presenting, at such nativity, gifts of gold and
frankincense.

Faithfully yours,
JOHN RUSKIN
[Letter 5]

Charitas

DENMARK HILL, 1st *July*, 1871.

My Friends,—It seldom chances, my work lying chiefly among stones, clouds, and flowers, that I am brought into any freedom of intercourse with my fellow-creatures; but since the fighting in Paris* I have dined out several times, and spoken to the persons who sat next me, and to others when I went upstairs; and done the best I could to find out what people thought about the fighting, or thought they ought to think about it, or thought they ought to say. I had, of course, no hope of finding any one thinking what they ought to do. But I have not yet, a little to my surprise, met with any one who either appeared to be sadder, or professed himself wiser for anything that has happened.

It is true that I am neither sadder nor wiser, because of it, myself. But then I was so sad before, that nothing could make me sadder; and getting wiser has always been to me a very slow process (sometimes even quite stopping for whole days together), so that if two or three new ideas fall in my way at once, it only puzzles me; and the fighting in Paris has given me more than two or three.

The newest of all these new ones, and, in fact, quite a glistering and freshly minted idea to me, is the Parisian notion of Communism, as far as I understand it (which I don't profess to do altogether, yet, or I should be wiser than I was, with a vengeance).

For, indeed, I am myself a Communist of the old school —reddest also of the red; and was on the very point of saying so at the end of my last letter; only the telegram about the Louvre's being on fire stopped me, because I thought the Communists of the new school, as I could not

* On May 25, 1871, troops of the national government occupied Paris and, after several days of bloody fighting, subdued the radical forces of the Paris Commune.

at all understand them, might not quite understand me. For we Communists of the old school think that our property belongs to everybody, and everybody's property to us; so of course I thought the Louvre belonged to me as much as to the Parisians, and expected they would have sent word over to me, being an Art Professor, to ask whether I wanted it burnt down. But no message or intimation to that effect ever reached me. . . .

Will you be at the pains, now, however, to learn rightly, and once for all, what Communism is? First, it means that everybody must work in common, and do common or simple work for his dinner; and that if any man will not do it, he must not have his dinner. . . . The second [law] respects property, and it is that the public, or common, wealth, shall be more and statelier in all its substance than private or singular wealth; that is to say (to come to my own special business for a moment) that there shall be only cheap and few pictures, if any, in the insides of houses, where nobody but the owner can see them; but costly pictures, and many, on the outsides of houses, where the people can see them: also that the Hôtel-de-Ville, or Hotel of the whole Town, for the transaction of its common business, shall be a magnificent building, much rejoiced in by the people, and with its tower seen far away through the clear air; but that the hotels for private business or pleasure, cafés, taverns, and the like, shall be low, few, plain, and in back streets. . . . And, finally and chiefly, it is an absolute law of old Communism that the fortunes of private persons should be small, and of little account in the State; but the common treasure of the whole nation should be of superb and precious things in redundant quantity, as pictures, statues, precious books; gold and silver vessels, preserved from ancient times; gold and silver bullion laid up for use, in case of any chance need of buying anything suddenly from foreign nations; noble horses, cattle, and sheep, on the public lands; and vast spaces of land for culture, exercise, and garden, round the cities, full of flowers, which, being everybody's property, nobody could gather; and of birds which, being everybody's property, nobody could shoot. And, in a word, that instead of a common poverty, or national debt, which every poor person in the nation is taxed annually to fulfil his part of, there should be a common wealth, or national reverse of debt, consisting of pleasant things, which every poor person in the nation should be summoned to receive his dole of, annually; and of pretty things, which every person capable of admiration, foreigners as well as natives, should unfeignedly admire, in an æsthetic, and not a covetous manner. . . .

You see, also, that we dark-red Communists, since we exist only in giving, must, on the contrary, hate with a perfect hatred all manner of thieving: even to Cœur-de-Lion's tar-and-feather extreme;* and of all thieving, we dislike thieving on trust most (so that, if we ever get to be strong enough to do what we want, and chance to catch hold of any failed bankers, their necks will not be worth half-an-hour's purchase). So also, as we think virtue diminishes in the honour and force of it in proportion to income, we think vice increases in the force and shame of it, and is worse in kings and rich people than in poor; and worse on a large scale than on a narrow one; and worse when deliberate than hasty. So that we can understand one man's coveting a piece of vineyard-ground for a garden of herbs, and stoning the master of it (both of them being Jews);—and yet the dogs ate queen's flesh for that, and licked king's blood!† but for two nations—both Christian—to covet their neighbours' vineyards, all down beside the River of their border, and slay until the River itself runs red! The little pool of Samaria!—shall all the snows of the Alps, or the salt pool of the Great Sea, wash their armour, for these?

* In a previous letter Ruskin had cited King Richard's decree that the heads of thieves be shaven, covered with molten pitch, and feathered.
† For the stoning to death of Naboth, and the Lord's vengeance upon King Ahab and Jezebel for his murder, see I Kings 21–22 and II Kings 9.

I promised . . . that I would tell you the main meaning and bearing of the war, and its results to this day:—now that you know what Communism is, I can tell you these briefly, and, what is more to the purpose, how to bear yourself in the midst of them.

The first reason for all wars, and for the necessity of national defences, is that the majority of persons, high and low, in all European nations, are Thieves, and, in their hearts, greedy of their neighbours' goods, land, and fame.

But besides being Thieves, they are also fools, and have never yet been able to understand that if Cornish men want pippins cheap, they must not ravage Devonshire—that the prosperity of their neighbours is, in the end, their own also; and the poverty of their neighbours, by the communism of God, becomes also in the end their own. "Invidia," jealousy of your neighbour's good, has been, since dust was first made flesh, the curse of man; and "Charitas," the desire to do your neighbour grace, the one source of all human glory, power, and material Blessing. . . .

Occult Theft,—Theft which hides itself even from itself, and is legal, respectable, and cowardly,—corrupts the body and soul of man, to the last fibre of them. And the guilty Thieves of Europe, the real sources of all deadly war in it, are the Capitalists—that is to say, people who live by percentages on the labour of others; instead of by fair wages for their own. The *Real* war in Europe, of which this fighting in Paris is the Inauguration, is between these and the workman, such as these have made him. They have kept him poor, ignorant, and sinful, that they might, without his knowledge, gather for themselves the produce of his toil. At last, a dim insight into the fact of this dawns on him; and such as they have made him he meets them, and *will* meet. . . .

Ever faithfully yours,

JOHN RUSKIN
[Letter 7]

Val di Nievole

PISA, 29*th April*, 1872.

My Friends,—You would pity me, if you knew how seldom I see a newspaper, just now; but I chanced on one yesterday, and found that all the world was astir about the marriage of the Marquis of B., and that the Pope had sent him, on that occasion, a telegraphic blessing of superfine quality.

I wonder what the Marquis of B. has done to deserve to be blessed to that special extent, and whether a little mild beatitude, sent here to Pisa, might not have been better spent. For, indeed, before getting hold of the papers, I had been greatly troubled, while drawing the east end of the Duomo, by three fellows who were leaning against the Leaning Tower, and expectorating loudly and copiously, at intervals of half a minute each, over the white marble base of it, which they evidently conceived to have been constructed only to be spit upon. They were all in rags, and obviously proposed to remain in rags all their days, and pass what leisure of life they could obtain, in spitting. There was a boy with them, in rags also, and not less expectorant, but having some remains of human activity in him still (being not more than twelve years old); and he was even a little interested in my brushes and colours, but rewarded himself, after the effort of some attention to these, by revolving slowly round the iron railing in front of me like a pensive squirrel. This operation at last disturbed me so much, that I asked him if there were no other railings in Pisa he could turn upside down over, but these. "Sono cascato, Signor—" "I tumbled over them, please, Sir," said he, apologetically, with infinite satisfaction in his black eyes.

Now it seemed to me that these three moist-throated men and the squirrelline boy stood much more in need of a paternal blessing than the Marquis of B.—a blessing, of course, with as much of the bloom off it as would make it consistent with the position in which Providence had placed them; but enough, in its moderate way, to bring the good out of them instead of the evil. For there was all manner of good in them, deep and pure—yet for ever to be dormant; and all manner of evil, shallow and superficial, yet for ever to be active and practical, as matters stood that day, under the Leaning Tower.

Lucca, 7th May.—Eight days gone, and I've been working hard, and looking my carefullest; and seem to have done nothing, nor begun to see these places, though I've known them thirty years, and though Mr. Murray's Guide says one may see Lucca, and its Ducal Palace and Piazza, the Cathedral, the Baptistery, nine churches, and the Roman amphitheatre, and take a drive round the ramparts, in the time between the stopping of one train and the starting of the next.

I wonder how much time Mr. Murray would allow for the view I had to-day, from the tower of the Cathedral, up the valley called of "Niévole,"—now one tufted softness of fresh springing leaves, far as the eye can reach. You know something of the produce of the hills that bound it, and perhaps of its own: at least, one used to see "Fine Lucca Oil" often enough in the grocers' windows (petroleum has, I suppose, now taken its place), and the staple of Spitalfields was, I believe, first woven with Lucca thread.

The actual manner of production of these good things is thus:—The Val di Niévole is some five miles wide by thirty long, and is simply one field of corn or rich grass land, undivided by hedges; the corn two feet high, and more, to-day. Quite Lord Derby's style of agriculture, you think? No; not quite. Undivided by hedges, the fields are yet meshed across and across by an intricate network of posts and chains. The posts are maple-trees, and the chains, garlands of vine. The meshes of this net each enclose two or three acres of the cornland, with a row of mulberry-trees up the middle of it, for silk. There are poppies, and bright ones too, about the banks and roadsides; but the corn of Val di Niévole is too proud to grow with poppies, and is set with wild gladiolus instead, deep violet. Here and there a mound of crag rises out of the fields, crested with stone-pine, and studded all over with the large stars of the white rock-cistus. Quiet streams, filled with close crowds of the golden waterflag, wind beside meadows painted with purple orchis. On each side of the great plain is a wilderness of hills, veiled at their feet with a grey cloud of olive woods; above, sweet with glades of chestnut; peaks of more distant blue, still, to-day, embroidered with snow, are rather to be thought of as vast precious stones than mountains, for all the state of the world's palaces has been hewn out of their marble.

I was looking over all this from under the rim of a large bell, beautifully embossed, with a St. Sebastian upon it, and some lovely thin-edged laurel leaves, and an inscription saying that the people should be filled with the fat of the land, if they listened to the voice of the Lord. The bell-founder of course meant, by the voice of the Lord, the sound of his own bell; and all over the plain, one could see towers rising above the vines voiced in the same manner. Also much trumpeting and fiddling goes on below, to help the bells, on holy days; and, assuredly, here is fat enough of land to be filled with, if listening to these scrapings and tinklings were indeed the way to be filled.

The laurel leaves on the bell were so finely hammered that I felt bound to have a ladder set against the lip of it, that I might examine them more closely; and the sacristan and bell-ringer were so interested in this proceeding that they got up, themselves, on the cross-beams, and sat like two jackdaws, looking on, one on each side; for which expression of sympathy I was deeply grateful, and offered the bell-ringer, on the spot, two bank-notes for tenpence each. But they were so rotten with age, and so brittle and black with tobacco, that, having unadvisedly folded them up small in my purse, the patches on their backs had run their corners through them, and they came out tattered like so much tinder. The bell-ringer looked at them hopelessly, and gave me them back. I promised him some better patched ones, and folded the remnants of tinder up carefully, to be kept at Coniston* (where we have still a tenpenceworth or so of copper,—though no olive oil)—for specimens of the currency of the new Kingdom of Italy.

Such are the monuments of financial art, attained by a nation which has lived in the fattest of lands for at least three thousand years, and for the last twelve hundred of them has had at least some measure of Christian benediction, with help from bell, book, candle, and, recently, even from gas. . . .

Rome, 12th May.—I am writing at the window of a new inn, whence I have a view of a large green gas-lamp, and of a pond, in rustic rock-work, with four large black ducks in it; also of the top of the Pantheon; sundry ruined walls; tiled roofs innumerable; and a palace about a quarter of a mile long, and the height, as near as I can guess, of Folkestone cliffs under the New Parade; all which I see to advantage over a balustrade veneered with an inch of marble over four inches of cheap stone, carried by balusters of cast iron, painted and sanded, but with the rust coming through, —this being the proper modern recipe in Italy for balustrades which may meet the increasing demand of travellers for splendour of abode. (By the way, I see I can get a pretty little long vignette view of the roof of the Pantheon, and some neighbouring churches, through a chink between the veneering and the freestone.)

Standing in this balcony, I am within three hundred yards of the greater Church of St. Mary, from which Castruccio Castracani walked to St. Peter's on 17th January, 1328, carrying the sword of the German Empire, with which he was appointed to gird its Emperor, on his taking possession of Rome, by Castruccio's help, in spite of the Pope. The Lord of the Val di Niévole wore a dress of superb damask silk, doubtless the best that the worms of Lucca mulberry-trees could spin; and across his breast an embroidered scroll, inscribed, "He is what God made him,"

* Ruskin's home at Brantwood, on the shore of Coniston Lake.

and across his shoulders, behind, another scroll, inscribed, "And he shall be what God will make."

On the 3rd of August, that same year, he recovered Pistoja from the Florentines, and rode home to his own Lucca in triumph, being then the greatest war-captain in Europe, and Lord of Pisa, Pistoja, Lucca, half the coast of Genoa, and three hundred fortified castles in the Apennines; on the 3rd of September he lay dead in Lucca, of fever. "Crushed before the moth;" as the silkworms also, who were boiled before even they became so much as moths, to make his embroidered coat for him. And, humanly speaking, because he had worked too hard in the trenches of Pistoja, in the dog-days, with his armour on, and with his own hands on the mattock, like the good knight he was.

Nevertheless, his sword was no gift for the King of Italy, if the Lucchese had thought better of it. For those three hundred castles of his were all Robber-castles, and he, in fact, only the chief captain of the three hundred thieves who lived in them. In the beginning of his career these "towers of the Lunigiana belonged to gentlemen who had made brigandage in the mountains, or piracy on the sea, the sole occupation of their youth. Castruccio united them round him, and called to his little court all the exiles and adventurers who were wandering from town to town, in search of war or pleasures."

And, indeed, to Professors of Art, the Apennine between Lucca and Pistoja is singularly delightful to this day, because of the ruins of these robber-castles on every mound, and of the pretty monasteries and arcades of cloister beside them. But how little we usually estimate the real relation of these picturesque objects! The homes of Baron and Clerk, side by side, established on the hills. Underneath, in the plain, the peasant driving his oxen. The Baron lives by robbing the peasant, and the Clerk by blessing the Baron. . . .

Now then, for Mr. Fawcett:—

At the 146th page of the edition of his *Manual* [*of Politi-*

cal Economy], you will find it stated that the interest of money consists of three distinct parts:

1. Reward for abstinence.
2. Compensation for the risk of loss.
3. Wages for the labour of superintendence.

I will reverse this order in examining the statements; for the only real question is as to the first, and we had better at once clear the other two away from it.

(3.) Wages for the labour of superintendence.

By giving the capitalist *wages* at all, we put him at once into the class of labourers, which in my November letter I showed you is partly right; but, *by Mr. Fawcett's definition,* and in the broad results of business, he is *not* a labourer. So far as he is one, of course, like any other, he is to be paid for his work. There is no question but that the partner who superintends any business should be paid for superintendence; but the question before us is only respecting *payment for doing nothing*. I have, for instance, at this moment £15,000 of Bank Stock, and receive £1200 odd, a year, from the Bank, but I have never received the slightest intimation from the directors that they wished for my assistance in the superintendence of that establishment;— (more shame for them). But even in cases where the partners are active, it does not follow that the one who has most money in the business is either fittest to superintend it, or likely to do so; it is indeed probable that a man who has made money already will know how to make more; and it is necessary to attach some importance to property as the sign of sense: but your business is to choose and pay your superintendent for his sense, and not for his money. Which is exactly what Mr. Carlyle has been telling you for some time; and both he and all his disciples entirely approve of interest, if you are indeed prepared to define that term as payment for the exercise of common-sense spent in the service of the person who pays for it. I reserve yet awhile, however, what is to be said, as hinted in my first letter, about the sale of ideas.

(2.) Compensation for risk.

Does Mr. Fawcett mean by "compensation for risk," protection from it, or reward for running it? Every business involves a certain quantity of risk, which is properly covered by every prudent merchant, but he does not expect to make a profit out of his risks, nor calculate on a percentage on his insurance. If he prefer not to insure, does Professor Fawcett mean that his customers ought to compensate him for his anxiety; and that while the definition of the first part of interest is extra payment for prudence, the definition of the second part of interest is extra payment for *im*prudence? Or, does Professor Fawcett mean, what is indeed often the fact, that interest for money represents such reward for risk as people may get across the green cloth at Homburg or Monaco? Because so far as what used to be business is, in modern political economy, gambling, Professor Fawcett will please to observe that what one gamester gains another loses. You cannot get anything out of Nature, or from God, by gambling;—only out of your neighbour: and to the quantity of interest of money thus gained, you are mathematically to oppose a precisely equal *dis*interest of somebody else's money.

These second and third reasons for interest then, assigned by Professor Fawcett, have evidently nothing whatever to do with the question. What I want to know is, why the Bank of England is paying me £1200 a year. It certainly does not pay me for superintendence. And so far from receiving my dividend as compensation for risk, I put my money into the bank because I thought it exactly the safest place to put it in. But nobody can be more anxious than I to find it proper that I should have £1200 a year. Finding two of Mr. Fawcett's reasons fail me utterly, I cling with tenacity to the third, and hope the best from it.

The third, or first,—and now too sorrowfully the last— of the Professor's reasons, is this, that my £1200 are given me as "the reward of abstinence." It strikes me, upon this, that if I had not my £15,000 of Bank Stock I should be a good deal more abstinent than I am, and that nobody would then talk of rewarding me for it. It might be possible to find even cases of very prolonged and painful abstinence, for which no reward has yet been adjudged by less abstinent England. Abstinence may, indeed, have its reward, nevertheless; but not by increase of what we abstain from, unless there be a law of growth for it, unconnected with our abstinence. "You cannot have your cake and eat it." Of course not; and if you don't eat it, you have your cake; but not a cake and a half! Imagine the complex trial of schoolboy minds, if the law of nature about cakes were, that if you ate none of your cake to-day, you would have ever so much bigger a cake to-morrow!—which is Mr. Fawcett's notion of the law of nature about money; and, alas, many a man's beside,—it being no law of nature whatever, but absolutely contrary to all her laws, and not to be enacted by the whole force of united mankind.

Not a cake and a quarter to-morrow, dunce, however abstinent you are—only the cake you have,—if the mice don't get at it in the night.

Interest, then, is not, it appears, payment for labour; it is not reward for risk; it is not reward for abstinence.

What is it?

One of two things it is;—taxation, or usury. Of which in my next letter. Meantime believe me

Faithfully yours,

J. RUSKIN

[Letter 18]

Benediction

VENICE, *3rd July,* 1872.

My Friends,—You probably thought I had lost my temper, and written inconsiderately, when I called the whistling of the Lido steamer "accursed."

I never wrote more considerately; using the longer and weaker word "accursed" instead of the simple and proper one, "cursed," to take away, as far as I could, the appearance of unseemly haste; and using the expression itself on set purpose, not merely as the fittest for the occasion, but because I have more to tell you respecting the general benediction engraved on the bell of Lucca, and the particular benediction bestowed on the Marquis of B.; several things more, indeed, of importance for you to know, about blessing and cursing.

Some of you may perhaps remember the saying of St. James about the tongue: "Therewith bless we God, and therewith curse we men; out of the same mouth proceedeth blessing and cursing. My brethren, these things ought not so to be."

It is not clear whether St. James means that there should be no cursing at all (which I suppose he does), or merely that the blessing and cursing should not be uttered by the same lips. But his meaning, whatever it was, did not, in the issue, matter; for the Church of Christendom has always ignored this text altogether, and appointed the same persons in authority to deliver, on all needful occasions, benediction or malediction, as either might appear to them due; while our own most learned sect, wielding State power, has not only appointed a formal service of malediction in Lent, but commanded the Psalms of David, in which the blessing and cursing are inlaid as closely as the black and white in a mosaic floor, to be solemnly sung through once a month.

I do not wish, however, to-day to speak to you of the practice of the churches; but of your own, which, observe, is in one respect singularly different. All the churches, of late years, paying less and less attention to the discipline of their people, have felt an increasing compunction in cursing them when they did wrong; while also, the wrong doing, through such neglect of discipline, becoming every day more complex, ecclesiastical authorities perceived that, if delivered with impartiality, the cursing must be so general, and the blessing so defined, as to give their services an entirely unpopular character.

Now, there is a little screw steamer just passing, with no deck, an omnibus cabin, a flag at both ends, and a single passenger; she is not twelve yards long, yet the beating of her screw has been so loud across the lagoon for the last five minutes, that I thought it must be a large new steamer coming in from the sea, and left my work to go and look.

Before I had finished writing that last sentence, the cry of a boy selling something black out of a basket on the quay became so sharply distinguished above the voices of the always debating gondoliers, that I must needs stop again, and go down to the quay to see what he had got to sell. They were half-rotten figs, shaken down, untimely, by the midsummer storms: his cry of "Fighiaie" scarcely ceased, being delivered, as I observed, just as clearly between his legs, when he was stooping to find an eatable portion of the black mess to serve a customer with, as when he was standing up. His face brought the tears into my eyes, so open, and sweet, and capable it was; and so sad. I gave him three very small halfpence, but took no figs, to his surprise: he little thought how cheap the sight of him and his basket was to me, at the money; nor what this fruit "that could not be eaten, it was so evil," sold cheap before the palace of the Dukes of Venice, meant, to any one who could read signs, either in earth, or her heaven and sea.*

Well, the blessing, as I said, not being now often legitimately applicable to particular people by Christian priests, they gradually fell into the habit of giving it of pure grace and courtesy to their congregations; or more especially to poor persons, instead of money, or to rich ones, in exchange for it,—or generally to any one to whom they wished to be polite: while, on the contrary, the cursing, having now become widely applicable, and even necessary, was left to be understood, but not expressed; and at last, to all practical purpose, abandoned altogether (the rather that it had become very disputable whether it ever did any one the least mischief); so that, at this time being, the Pope, in his charmingest manner, blesses the bridecake of the Marquis of B.,

* See Jeremiah 24:8 and Revelation 6:13.

making, as it were, an ornamental confectionery figure of himself on the top of it; but has not, in anywise, courage to curse the King of Italy, although that penniless monarch has confiscated the revenues of every time-honoured religious institution in Italy. . . .

4th July.

First, it is necessary that you should understand accurately the difference between swearing and cursing, vulgarly so often confounded. They are entirely different things: the first is invoking the witness of a Spirit to an assertion you wish to make; the second is invoking the assistance of a Spirit, in a mischief you wish to inflict. When ill-educated and ill-tempered people clamorously confuse the two invocations, they are not, in reality, either cursing or swearing; but merely vomiting empty words indecently. True swearing and cursing must always be distinct and solemn; here is an old Latin oath, for instance, which, though borrowed from a stronger Greek one, and much diluted, is still grand:—

*"I take to witness the Earth, and the stars, and the sea; the two lights of heaven; the falling and rising of the year; the dark power of the gods of sorrow; the sacredness of unbending Death; and may the Father of all things hear me, who sanctifies covenants with his lightning. For I lay my hand on the altar, and by the fires thereon, and the gods to whom they burn, I swear that no future day shall break this peace for Italy, nor violate the covenant she has made."**

That is old swearing: but the lengthy forms of it appearing partly burdensome to the celerity, and partly superstitious to the wisdom, of modern minds, have been abridged, —in England, for the most part, into the extremely simple "By God"; in France into "Sacred name of God" (often the first word of the sentence only pronounced), and in Italy into "Christ" or "Bacchus"; the superiority of the former Deity being indicated by omitting the preposition before

* The oath of Latinus in *The Aeneid*, XII, 197–202.

the name. The oaths are "Christ,"—never "by Christ"; and "by Bacchus,"—never "Bacchus."

Observe also that swearing is only by extremely ignorant persons supposed to be an infringement of the Third Commandment. It is disobedience to the teaching of Christ; but the Third Commandment has nothing to do with the matter. People do not take the name of God in vain when they swear; they use it, on the contrary, very earnestly and energetically to attest what they wish to say. But when the Monster Concert at Boston* begins, on the English day, with the hymn, "The will of God be done," while the audience know perfectly well that there is not one in a thousand of them who is trying to do it, or who would have it done if he could help it, unless it was his own will too,—*that* is taking the name of God in vain, with a vengeance.

Cursing, on the other hand, is invoking the aid of a Spirit to a harm you wish to see accomplished, but which is too great for your own immediate power: and to-day I wish to point out to you what intensity of faith in the existence and activity of a spiritual world is evinced by the curse which is characteristic of the English tongue.

For, observe, habitual as it has become, there is still so much life and sincerity in the expression, that we all feel our passion partly appeased in its use; and the more serious the occasion, the more practical and effective the cursing becomes. In Mr. Kinglake's *History of the Crimean War,* you will find the —th Regiment at Alma is stated to have been materially assisted in maintaining position quite vital to the battle by the steady imprecation delivered at it by its colonel for half-an-hour on end. No quantity of benediction would have answered the purpose; the colonel might have said, "Bless you, my children," in the tenderest tones, as often as he pleased,—yet not have helped his men to keep their ground.

I want you therefore, first, to consider how it happens

---

* A musical festival and International Peace Jubilee held at Boston in June 1872.

that cursing seems at present the most effectual means for encouraging human work; and whether it may not be conceivable that the work itself is of a kind which any form of effectual blessing would hinder instead of help. Then, secondly, I want you to consider what faith in a spiritual world is involved in the terms of the curse we usually employ. It has two principal forms: one complete and unqualified, "God damn your soul," implying that the soul is there, and that we cannot be satisfied with less than its destruction; the other, qualified, and on the bodily members only, "God damn your eyes and limbs." It is this last form I wish especially to examine.

For how do you suppose that either eye, or ear, or limb, *can* be damned? What is the spiritual mischief you invoke? Not merely the blinding of the eye, nor palsy of the limb; but the condemnation or judgment of them. And remember that though you are for the most part unconscious of the spiritual meaning of what you say, the instinctive satisfaction you have in saying it is as much a real movement of the spirit within you, as the beating of your heart is a real movement of the body, though you are unconscious of that also, till you put your hand on it. Put your hand also, so to speak, upon the source of the satisfaction with which you use this curse; and ascertain the law of it.

Now this you may best do by considering what it is which will make the eyes and the limbs blessed. For the precise contrary of that must be their damnation. What do you think was the meaning of that saying of Christ's, "Blessed are the eyes which see the things that ye see"? For to be made evermore incapable of seeing such things, must be the condemnation of the eyes. It is not merely the capacity of seeing sunshine, which is their blessing; but of seeing certain things under the sunshine; nay, perhaps, even without sunshine, the eye itself becoming a Sun. Therefore, on the other hand, the curse upon the eyes will not be mere blindness to the daylight, but blindness to particular things under the daylight; so that, when directed towards these, the eye itself becomes as the Night.

Again, with regard to the limbs, or general powers of the body. Do you suppose that when it is promised that "the lame man shall leap as an hart, and the tongue of the dumb sing"—(Steam-whistle interrupts me from the *Capo d'Istria*, which is lying in front of my window with her black nose pointed at the red nose of another steamer at the next pier. There are nine large ones at this instant,—half-past six, morning, 4th July,—lying between the Church of the Redeemer and the Canal of the Arsenal; one of them an iron-clad, five smoking fiercely, and the biggest,—English and half a quarter of a mile long,—blowing steam from all manner of pipes in her sides, and with such a roar through her funnel—whistle number two from *Capo d'Istria*—that I could not make any one hear me speak in this room without an effort),—do you suppose, I say, that such a form of benediction is just the same as saying that the lame man shall leap as a lion, and the tongue of the dumb mourn? Not so, but a special manner of action of the members is meant in both cases: (whistle number three from *Capo d'Istria;* I am writing on, steadily, so that you will be able to form an accurate idea, from this page, of the intervals of time in modern music. The roaring from the English boat goes on all the while, for bass to the *Capo d'Istria's* treble, and a tenth steamer comes in sight round the Armenian Monastery)—a particular kind of activity is meant, I repeat, in both cases. The lame man is to leap, (whistle fourth from *Capo d'Istria*, this time at high pressure, going through my head like a knife) as an innocent and joyful creature leaps, and the lips of the dumb to move melodiously: they are to be blest, so; may not be unblest even in silence; but are the absolute contrary of blest, in evil utterance. (Fifth whistle, a double one, from *Capo d'Istria,* and it is seven o'clock, nearly; and here's my coffee, and I must stop writing. Sixth whistle—the *Capo d'Istria* is off, with her crew of morning bathers. Seventh,—from I don't know which of the boats outside—and I count no more.)

5th July.

Yesterday, in these broken sentences, I tried to make you understand that for all human creatures there are necessarily three separate states: life positive, under blessing,—life negative, under curse,—and death, neutral between these; and, henceforward, take due note of the quite true assumption you make in your ordinary malediction, that the state of condemnation may begin in this world, and separately affect every living member of the body.

You assume the fact of these two opposite states, then; but you have no idea whatever of the meaning of your words, nor of the nature of the blessedness or condemnation you admit. I will try to make your conception clearer.

In the year 1869, just before leaving Venice, I had been carefully looking at a picture by Victor Carpaccio, representing the dream of a young princess. Carpaccio has taken much pains to explain to us, as far as he can, the kind of life she leads, by completely painting her little bedroom in the light of dawn, so that you can see everything in it. It is lighted by two doubly-arched windows, the arches being painted crimson round their edges, and the capitals of the shafts that bear them, gilded. They are filled at the top with small round panes of glass; but beneath, are open to the blue morning sky, with a low lattice across them: and in the one at the back of the room are set two beautiful white Greek cases with a plant in each; one having rich dark and pointed green leaves, the other crimson flowers, but not of any species known to me, each at the end of a branch like a spray of heath.

These flower-pots stand on a shelf which runs all round the room, and beneath the window, at about the height of the elbow, and serves to put things on anywhere: beneath it, down to the floor, the walls are covered with green cloth; but above, are bare and white. The second window is nearly opposite the bed, and in front of it is the princess's reading-table, some two feet and a half square, covered by a red cloth with a white border and dainty fringe; and beside it her seat, not at all like a reading-chair in Oxford, but a very small three-legged stool like a music-stool, covered with crimson cloth. On the table are a book set up at a slope fittest for reading, and an hour-glass. Under the shelf, near the table, so as to be easily reached by the outstretched arm, is a press full of books. The door of this has been left open, and the books, I am grieved to say, are rather in disorder, having been pulled about before the princess went to bed, and one left standing on its side.

Opposite this window, on the white wall, is a small shrine or picture (I can't see which, for it is in sharp retiring perspective) with a lamp before it, and a silver vessel hung from the lamp, looking like one for holding incense.

The bed is a broad four-poster, the posts being beautifully wrought golden or gilded rods, variously wreathed and branched, carrying a canopy of warm red. The princess's shield is at the head of it, and the feet are raised entirely above the floor of the room, on a dais which projects at the lower end so as to form a seat, on which the child has laid her crown. Her little blue slippers lie at the side of the bed,—her white dog beside them. The coverlid is scarlet, the white sheet folded half-way back over it; the young girl lies straight, bending neither at waist nor knee, the sheet rising and falling over her in a narrow unbroken wave, like the shape of the coverlid of the last sleep, when the turf scarcely rises. She is some seventeen or eighteen years old, her head is turned towards us on the pillow, the cheek resting on her hand, as if she were thinking, yet utterly calm in sleep, and almost colourless. Her hair is tied with a narrow riband, and divided into two wreaths, which encircle her head like a double crown. The white nightgown hides the arm raised on the pillow, down to the wrist.

At the door of the room an angel enters (the little dog,

though lying awake, vigilant, takes no notice). He is a very small angel, his head just rises a little above the shelf round the room, and would only reach as high as the princess's chin, if she were standing up. He has soft grey wings, lustre-less; and his dress, of subdued blue, has violet sleeves, open above the elbow, and showing white sleeves below. He comes in without haste, his body, like a mortal one, casting shadow from the light through the door behind, his face perfectly quiet; a palm-branch in his right hand—a scroll in his left.

So dreams the princess, with blessed eyes, that need no earthly dawn. It is very pretty of Carpaccio to make her dream out the angel's dress so particularly, and notice the slashed sleeves; and to dream so little an angel—very nearly a doll angel,—bringing her the branch of palm, and mes-sage. But the lovely characteristic of all is the evident delight of her continual life. Royal power over herself, and happi-ness in her flowers, her books, her sleeping, and waking, her prayers, her dreams, her earth, her heaven.

After I had spent my morning over this picture, I had to go to Verona by the afternoon train. In the carriage with me were two American girls with their father and mother, people of the class which has lately made so much money, suddenly, and does not know what to do with it: and these two girls, of about fifteen and eighteen, had evi-dently been indulged in everything (since they had had the means) which western civilization could imagine. And here they were, specimens of the utmost which the money and invention of the nineteenth century could produce in maid-enhood,—children of its most progressive race,—enjoying the full advantages of political liberty, of enlightened philo-sophical education, of cheap pilfered literature, and of lux-ury at any cost. Whatever money, machinery, or freedom of thought could do for these two children, had been done. No superstition had deceived, no restraint degraded them: —types, they could not but be, of maidenly wisdom and felicity, as conceived by the forwardest intellects of our time.

And they were travelling through a district which, if any

of the world, should touch the hearts and delight the eyes
of young girls. Between Venice and Verona! Portia's villa
perhaps in sight upon the Brenta, Juliet's tomb to be visited
in the evening,—blue against the southern sky, the hills of
Petrarch's home. Exquisite midsummer sunshine, with low
rays, glanced through the vine-leaves; all the Alps were
clear, from the Lake of Garda to Cadore, and to farthest
Tyrol. What a princess's chamber, this, if these are princesses, and what dreams might they not dream, therein!

But the two American girls were neither princesses, nor
seers, nor dreamers. By infinite self-indulgence, they had
reduced themselves simply to two pieces of white putty that
could feel pain. The flies and the dust stuck to them as to
clay, and they perceived, between Venice and Verona, nothing but the flies and the dust. They pulled down the blinds
the moment they entered the carriage, and then sprawled,
and writhed, and tossed among the cushions of it, in vain
contest, during the whole fifty miles, with every miserable
sensation of bodily affliction that could make time intolera-
ble. They were dressed in thin white frocks, coming vaguely
open at the backs as they stretched or wriggled; they had
French novels, lemons, and lumps of sugar, to beguile their
state with; the novels hanging together by the ends of string
that had once stitched them, or adhering at the corners in
densely bruised dog's-ears, out of which the girls, wetting
their fingers, occasionally extricated a gluey leaf. From time
to time they cut a lemon open, ground a lump of sugar
backwards and forwards over it till every fibre was in a
treacly pulp; then sucked the pulp, and gnawed the white
skin into leathery strings for the sake of its bitter. Only one
sentence was exchanged, in the fifty miles, on the subject
of things outside the carriage (the Alps being once visible
from a station where they had drawn up the blinds).

"Don't those snow-caps make you cool?"

"No—I wish they did."

And so they went their way, with sealed eyes and tormented limbs, their numbered miles of pain.

There are the two states for you, in clearest opposition;

Blessed, and Accursed. The happy industry, and eyes full of sacred imagination of things that are not (such sweet cosa è la fede), and the tortured indolence, and infidel eyes, blind even to the things that are.

"How do I know the princess is industrious?"

Partly by the trim state of her room,—by the hour-glass on the table,—by the evident use of all the books she has (well bound, every one of them, in stoutest leather or velvet, and with no dog's-ear), but more distinctly from another picture of her, not asleep. In that one, a prince of England has sent to ask her in marriage: and her father, little liking to part with her, sends for her to his room to ask her what she would do. He sits, moody and sorrowful; she, standing before him in a plain housewifely dress, talks quietly, going on with her needlework all the time.

A work-woman, friends, she, no less than a princess; and princess most in being so. In like manner, in a picture by a Florentine, whose mind I would fain have you know somewhat, as well as Carpaccio's—Sandro Botticelli—the girl who is to be the wife of Moses, when he first sees her at the desert-well, has fruit in her left hand, but a distaff in her right.

"To do good work, whether you live or die," it is the entrance to all Princedoms; and if not done, the day will come, and that infallibly, when you must labour for evil instead of good.

It was some comfort to me, that second of May last, at Pisa, to watch the workman's ashamed face, as he struck the old marble cross to pieces. Stolidly and languidly he dealt the blows,—down-looking,—so far as in anywise sensitive, ashamed,—and well he might be.

It was a wonderful thing to see done. This Pisan chapel, first built in 1230, then called the Oracle, or Oratory,— "Oraculum, vel Oratorium"—of the Blessed Mary of the New Bridge, afterwards called the Sea-bridge (Ponte-a-Mare), was a shrine like that of ours on the Bridge of Wakefield; a boatman's praying-place: you may still see, or might, ten years since, have seen, the use of such a thing at the mouth of Boulogne Harbour, when the mackerel boats went out in a fleet at early dawn. There used to be a little shrine at the end of the longest pier; and as the *Bonne Espérance,* or *Grâce-de-Dieu* or *Vierge Marie,* or *Notre Dame des Dunes,* or *Reine des Anges,* rose on the first surge of the open sea, their crews bared their heads, and prayed for a few seconds. So also the Pisan oarsmen looked back to their shrine, many-pinnacled, standing out from the quay above the river, as they dropped down Arno under their sea-bridge, bound for the Isles of Greece. Later, in the fifteenth century, "there was laid up in it a little branch of the Crown of Thorns of the Redeemer, which a merchant had brought home, enclosed in a little urn of Beyond-sea" (ultra-marine), and its name was changed to "St. Mary's of the Thorn."

In the year 1840 I first drew it, then as perfect as when it was built. Six hundred and ten years had only given the marble of it a tempered glow, or touched its sculpture here and there with softer shade. I daguerreotyped the eastern end of it some years later (photography being then unknown), and copied the daguerreotype, that people might not be plagued in looking, by the lustre. The frontispiece to this letter is engraved from the drawing, and will show you what the building was like.

But the last quarter of a century has brought changes, and made the Italians wiser. British Protestant missionaries explained to them that they had only got a piece of black-berry stem in their ultramarine box. German philosophical missionaries explained to them that the Crown of Thorns itself was only a graceful metaphor. French republican missionaries explained to them that chapels were inconsistent with liberty on the quay; and their own Engineering missionaries of civilization explained to them that steam-power was independent of the Madonna. And now in 1872, rowing by steam, digging by steam, driving by steam, here, behold, are a troublesome pair of human arms out of employ. So the Engineering misisonaries fit them with hammer and chisel, and set them to break up the Spina Chapel.

A costly kind of stone-breaking, this, for Italian parishes to set paupers on! Are there not rocks enough of Apennine, think you, they could break down instead? For truly, the God of their Fathers, and of their land, would rather see them mar His own work, than His children's.

Believe me, faithfully yours,

JOHN RUSKIN

[Letter 20]

The Squirrel Cage: English Servitude

ROME, 6th June, 1874.

The poor Campagna herdsman, whose seeking for St. Paul's statue the Professor of Fine Art in the University of Oxford so disgracefully failed to assist him in,* had been kneeling nearer the line of procession of the Corpus Domini than I; —in fact, quite among the rose-leaves which had been strewed for a carpet round the aisles of the Basilica. I grieve to say that I was shy of the rose-bestrewn path, myself; for the crowd waiting at the side of it had mixed up the rose-leaves with spittle so richly as to make quite a pink pomatum of them. And, indeed, the living temples of the Holy Ghost which in any manner bestir themselves here among the temples,—whether of Roman gods or Christian saints, —have merely and simply the two great operations upon them of filling their innermost adyta with dung, and making their pavements slippery with spittle; the Pope's new tobacco manufactory under the Palatine,—an infinitely more important object now, in all views of Rome from the west, than either the Palatine or the Capital,—greatly aid-

---

* An allusion to the previous Letter, in which Ruskin, in answer to the peasant's question, had guided him to the presumed site of St. Paul's grave, rather than to the saint's statue.

ing and encouraging this especial form of lustration: while
the still more ancient documents of Egyptian religion—the
obelisks of the Piazza del Popolo, and of the portico of
St. Peter's—are entirely eclipsed by the obelisks of our
English religion, lately elevated, in full view from the Pin-
cian and the Montorio, with smoke coming out of the top
of them. And farther, the entire eastern district of Rome,
between the two Basilicas of the Lateran and St. Lorenzo,
is now one mass of volcanic ruin;—a desert of dust and
ashes, the lust of wealth exploding there, out of a crater
deeper than Etna's, and raging, as far as it can reach, in one
frantic desolation of whatever is lovely, or holy, or memorable, in the central city of the world.

For there is one fixed idea in the mind of every European
progressive politician, at this time; namely, that by a certain
application of Financial Art, and by the erection of a certain
quantity of new buildings on a colossal scale, it will be possible for society hereafter to pass its entire life in eating,
smoking, harlotry, and talk; without doing anything whatever with its hands or feet of a laborious character. . . .

And now examine the facts about England in this broad
light.

She has a vast quantity of ground still food-producing,
in corn, grass, cattle, or game. With that territory she educates her squire, or typical gentleman, and his tenantry,
to whom, together, she owes all her power in the world.
With another large portion of territory,—now continually
on the increase,—she educates a mercenary population,
ready to produce any quantity of bad articles to anybody's
order; population which every hour that passes over them
makes acceleratingly avaricious, immoral, and insane. In
the increase of that kind of territory and its people, her
ruin is just as certain as if she were deliberately exchanging
her corn-growing land, and her heaven above it, for a soil
of arsenic, and rain of nitric acid.

"Have the Arkwrights and Stephensons, then, done nothing but harm?" Nothing; but the root of all the mischief is

not in Arkwrights or Stephensons; nor in rogues or mechanics. The real root of it is the crime of the squire himself. And the method of that crime is thus. A certain quantity of the food produced by the country is paid annually
by it into the squire's hand, in the form of rent, privately,
and taxes, publicly. If he uses this food to support a food-
producing population, he increases daily the strength of the
country and his own; but if he uses it to support an idle
population, or one producing merely trinkets in iron, or
gold, or other rubbish, he steadily weakens the country, and
debases himself.

Now the action of the squire for the last fifty years has
been, broadly, to take the food from the ground of his
estate, and carry it to London, where he feeds with it a vast
number of builders, upholsterers (one of them charged me
five pounds for a footstool the other day), carriage and
harness makers, dress-makers, grooms, footmen, bad musi-
cians, bad painters, gamblers, and harlots, and in supply of
the wants of these main classes, a vast number of shopkeepers of minor useless articles. The muscles and the time
of this enormous population being wholly unproductive
—(for of course time spent in the mere process of sale is
unproductive, and much more that of the footman and
groom, while that of the vulgar upholsterer, jeweller, fid-
dler, and painter, etc., etc., is not only unproductive, but
mischievous),—the entire mass of this London population
do nothing whatever either to feed or clothe themselves; and
their vile life preventing them from all rational entertainment, they are compelled to seek some pastime in a vile
literature, the demand for which again occupies another
enormous class, who do nothing to feed or dress themselves;
finally, the vain disputes of this vicious population give employment to the vast industry of the lawyers and their clerks,
who similarly do nothing to feed or dress themselves.

Now the peasants might still be able to supply this enormous town population with food (in the form of the squire's
rent), but it cannot, without machinery, supply the flimsy

dresses, toys, metal work, and other rubbish, belonging to their accursed life. Hence over the whole country the sky is blackened and the air made pestilent, to supply London and other such towns with their iron railings, vulgar up-holstery, jewels, toys, liveries, lace, and other means of dissipation and dishonour of life. Gradually the country peo-ple cannot even supply food to the voracity of the vicious centre; and it is necessary to import food from other coun-tries, giving in exchange any kind of commodity we can attract their itching desires for, and produce by machinery. The tendency of the entire national energy is therefore to approximate more and more to the state of a squirrel in a cage, or a turnspit in a wheel, fed by foreign masters with nuts and dog's meat. And indeed, when we rightly conceive the relation of London to the country, the sight of it be-comes more fantastic and wonderful than any dream. Hyde Park, in the season, is the great rotatory form of the vast squirrel-cage; round and round it go the idle company, in their reversed streams, urging themselves to their neces-sary exercise. They cannot with safety even eat their nuts, without so much "revolution" as shall, in Venetian lan-guage, "comply with the demands of hygiene." Then they retire into their boxes, with due quantity of straw; the Bel-gravian and Piccadillian streets outside the railings being, when one sees clearly, nothing but the squirrel's box at the side of his wires. And then think of all the rest of the metropolis as the creation and ordinance of these squirrels, that they may squeak and whirl to their satisfaction, and yet be fed. Measure the space of its entirely miserable life. Begin with that diagonal which I struck from Regent Circus to Drury Lane; examine it, house by house; then go up from Drury Lane to St. Giles' Church, look into Church Lane there, and explore your Seven Dials and Warwick Street; and remember this is the very centre of the mother city,— precisely between its Parks, its great Library and Museum, its principal Theatres, and its Bank. Then conceive the East-end; and the melancholy Islington and Pentonville districts; then the ghastly spaces of southern suburb—Vauxhall, Lambeth, the Borough, Wapping, and Bermondsey. All this is the nidification of those Park Squirrels. This is the thing they have produced round themselves; this their work in the world. When they rest from their squirrellian revolutions, and die in the Lord, and their works do follow them, *these* are what will follow them. Lugubrious march of the Waterloo Road, and the Borough, and St. Giles's; the shadows of all the Seven Dials having fetched their last compass. New Jerusalem, prepared as a bride, of course, opening her gates to them;—but, pertinaciously attendant, Old Jewry outside. "Their works do follow them."

For these streets are indeed what they have built; their inhabitants the people they have chosen to educate. They took the bread and milk and meat from the people of their fields; they gave it to feed, and retain here in their service, this fermenting mass of unhappy human beings,—news-mongers, novel-mongers, picture-mongers, poison-drink-mongers, lust and death-mongers; the whole smoking mass of it one vast dead-marine storeshop,—accumulation of wreck of the Dead Sea, with every activity in it, a form of putrefaction. . . .   [Letter 44]

The Advent Collect

The accounts of the state of St. George's Fund, given without any inconvenience in crowding type, on the last leaf of this number of *Fors,* will, I hope, be as satisfactory to my subscribers as they are to me. In these days of financial operation, the subscribers to *any*thing may surely be content when they find that all their talents have been laid up in the softest of napkins; and even farther, that, though they are getting no interest themselves, that lichenous growth of vegetable gold, or mould, is duly developing itself on their capital.

The amount of subscriptions received, during the four

years of my mendicancy, might have disappointed me, if, in my own mind, I had made any appointments on the subject, or had benevolence pungent enough to make me fret at the delay in the commencement of the national felicity which I propose to bestow. On the contrary, I am only too happy to continue amusing myself in my study, with stones and pictures; and find, as I grow old, that I remain resigned to the consciousness of any quantity of surrounding vice, distress and disease, provided only the sun shine in at my window over Corpus Garden, and there are no whistles from the luggage trains passing the Waterworks.

I understand this state of even temper to be what most people call "rational"; and, indeed, it has been the result of very steady effort on my own part to keep myself, if it might be, out of Hanwell, or that other Hospital which makes the name of Christ's native village dreadful in the ear of London. For, having long observed that the most perilous beginning of trustworthy qualification for either of those establishments consisted in an exaggerated sense of self-importance; and being daily compelled, of late, to value my own person and opinions at a higher and higher rate, in proportion to my extending experience of the rarity of any similar creatures or ideas among mankind, it seemed to me expedient to correct this increasing conviction of my superior wisdom, by companionship with pictures I could not copy, and stones I could not understand:—while, that this wholesome seclusion may remain only self-imposed, I think it not a little fortunate for me that the few relations I have left are generally rather fond of me;—don't know clearly which is the next of kin,—and perceive that the administration of my inconsiderable effects would be rather troublesome than profitable to them. Not in the least, therefore, wondering at the shyness of my readers to trust me with money of theirs, I have made, during these four years past, some few experiments with money of my own,—in hopes of being able to give such account of them as might justify a more extended confidence. I am bound to state that the results, for the present, are not altogether encouraging. On my own little piece of mountain ground at Coniston I grow a large quantity of wood-hyacinths and heather, without any expense worth mentioning; but my only industrious agricultural operations have been the getting three-pounds-ten worth of hay, off a field for which I pay six pounds rent; and the surrounding with a costly wall six feet high, to keep out rabbits, a kitchen garden, which, being terraced and trim, my neighbours say is pretty; and which will probably, every third year, when the weather is not wet, supply me with a dish of strawberries.

At Carshalton, in Surrey, I have indeed had the satisfaction of cleaning out one of the springs of the Wandel, and making it pleasantly habitable by trout; but find that the fountain, instead of taking care of itself when once pure, as I expected it to do, requires continual looking after, like a child getting into a mess; and involves me besides in continual debate with the surveyors of the parish, who insist on letting all the road-washings run into it. For the present, however, I persevere, at Carshalton, against the wilfulness of the spring and the carelessness of the parish; and hope to conquer both: but I have been obliged entirely to abandon a notion I had of exhibiting ideally clean street pavement in the centre of London,—in the pleasant environs of Church Lane, St. Giles's. There I had every help and encouragement from the authorities; and hoped, with the staff of two men and a young rogue of a crossing-sweeper, added to the regular force of the parish, to keep a quarter of a mile square of the narrow streets without leaving so much as a bit of orange-peel on the footway, or an eggshell in the gutters. I failed, partly because I chose too difficult a district to begin with (the contributions of transitional mud being constant, and the inhabitants passive), but chiefly because I could no more be on the spot myself, to give spirit to the men, when I left Denmark Hill for Coniston.

I next set up a tea-shop at 29, Paddington Street W. (an

establishment which my *Fors* readers may as well know of),
to supply the poor in that neighbourhood with pure tea, in
packets as small as they chose to buy, without making a
profit on the subdivision,—larger orders being of course
equally acceptable from anybody who cares to promote
honest dealing. The result of this experiment has been my
ascertaining that the poor only like to buy their tea where
it is brilliantly lighted and eloquently ticketed; and as I
resolutely refuse to compete with my neighbouring tradesmen either in gas or rhetoric, the patient subdivision of my
parcels by the two old servants of my mother's, who manage
the business for me, hitherto passes little recognized as an
advantage by my uncalculating public. Also, steady increase
in the consumption of spirits throughout the neighbourhood faster and faster slackens the demand for tea; but I
believe none of these circumstances have checked my trade
so much as my own procrastination in painting my sign.
Owing to that total want of imagination and invention
which makes me so impartial and so accurate a writer on
subjects of political economy, I could not for months determine whether the said sign should be of a Chinese character, black upon gold; or of a Japanese, blue upon white;
or of pleasant English, rose colour on green; and still less
how far legible scale of letters could be compatible, on a
board only a foot broad, with lengthy enough elucidation
of the peculiar offices of "Mr. Ruskin's tea-shop." Meanwhile the business languishes, and the rent and taxes absorb
the profits, and something more, after the salary of my good
servants has been paid.

In all these cases, however, I can see that I am defeated
only because I have too many things on hand: and that
neither rabbits at Coniston, road-surveyors at Croydon, or
mud in St. Giles's would get the better of me, if I could give
exclusive attention to any one business: meantime, I learn
the difficulties which are to be met, and shall make the fewer
mistakes when I venture on any work with other people's
money.

I may as well, together with these confessions, print a piece written for the end of a *Fors* letter at Assisi, a month or two back, but for which I had then no room, referring to the increase of commercial, religious, and egotistic insanity, in modern society, and delicacy of the distinction implied by that long wall at Hanwell, between the persons inside it, and out.

"Does it never occur to me" (thus the letter went on) "that I may be mad myself?"

Well, I am so alone now in my thoughts and ways that if I am not mad, I should soon become so, from mere solitude, but for my *work*. But it must be manual work. Whenever I suceed in a drawing, I am happy, in spite of all that surrounds me of sorrow. It is a strange feeling;— not gratified vanity: I can have any quantity of praise I like from some sorts of people; but that does me no vital good (though dispraise does me mortal harm); whereas to succeed to my own satisfaction in a manual piece of work, is life,—to me, as to all men; and it is only the peace which comes necessarily from manual labour which in all time has kept the honest country people patient in their task of maintaining the rascals who live in towns. But we are in hard times, now, for all men's wits; for men who know the truth are like to go mad from isolation; and the fools are all going mad in "Schwärmerei,"*—only that is much the pleasanter way. Mr. Lecky, for instance, quoted in last *Fors;* how pleasant for him to think he is ever so much wiser than Aristotle; and that, as a body, the men of his generation are the wisest that ever were born—giants of intellect, according to Lord Macaulay, compared to the pigmies of Bacon's time, and the minor pigmies of Christ's time, and the minutest of all, the microscopic pigmies of Solomon's time, and, finally, the vermicular and infusorial pigmies—twenty-three millions to the cube inch—of Mr. Darwin's time, whatever that may be! How pleasant for

* Ruskin uses the word in Carlyle's sense of fanatical enthusiasms blindly shared by the masses.

Mr. Lecky to live in these days of the Anakim,—"his spear, to equal which, the tallest pine,"* etc., etc., which no man Stratford-born could have lifted, much less shaken!

But for us of the old race—few of us now left,—children who reverence our fathers, and are ashamed of ourselves; comfortless enough in that shame, and yearning for one word or glance from the graves of old, yet knowing ourselves to be of the same blood, and recognizing in our hearts the same passions, with the ancient masters of humanity;—we, who feel as men, and not as carnivorous worms; we, who are every day recognizing some inaccessible height of thought and power, and are miserable in our shortcomings,—the few of us now standing here and there, alone, in the midst of this yelping, carnivorous crowd, mad for money and lust, tearing each other to pieces, and starving each other to death, and leaving heaps of their dung and ponds of their spittle on every palace floor and altar stone,—it is impossible for us, except in the labour of our hands, not to go mad.

And the danger is tenfold greater for a man in my own position, concerned with the arts which develop the more subtle brain sensations; and, through them, tormented all day long. Mr. Leslie Stephen rightly says how much better it is to have a thick skin and a good digestion. Yes, assuredly; but what is the use of knowing that, if one hasn't? In one of my saddest moods, only a week or two ago, because I had failed twice over in drawing the lifted hand of Giotto's "Poverty"; utterly beaten and comfortless, at Assisi, I got some wholesome peace and refreshment by mere sympathy with a Bewickian little pig in the roundest and conceitedest burst of pig-blossom. His servant,—a grave old woman, with much sorrow and toil in the wrinkles of *her* skin, while his was only dimpled in its divine thickness,—was leading him, with magnanimous length of rope, down a grassy path behind the convent; stopping, of course, where he chose. Stray stalks and leaves of eatable things,

* *Paradise Lost*, I, 292 ff.

in various stages of ambrosial rottenness, lay here and there; the convent walls made more savoury by their fumigation, as Mr. Leslie Stephen says the Alpine pines are by his cigar. And the little joyful darling of Demeter shook his curly tail, and munched; and grunted the goodnaturedest of grunts, and snuffled the approvingest of snuffles, and was a balm and beatification to behold; and I would fain have changed places with him for a little while, or with Mr. Leslie Stephen for a little while,—at luncheon, suppose, —anywhere but among the Alps. But it can't be.

HÔTEL MEURICE, PARIS,
20th October, 1874.

I interrupt myself, for an instant or two, to take notice of two little things that happen to me here—arriving to breakfast by night train from Geneva.

Expecting to be cold, I had ordered fire, and sat down by it to read my letters as soon as I arrived, not noticing that the little parlour was getting much too hot. Presently, in comes the chambermaid, to put the bedroom in order, which one enters through the parlour. Perceiving that I am mismanaging myself, in the way of fresh air, as she passes through, "Il fait bien chaud, monsieur, ici," says she, reprovingly, and with entire self-possession. Now that is French servant-character of the right old school. She knows her own position perfectly, and means to stay in it, and wear her little white radiant frill of a cap all her days. She knows my position also; and has not the least fear of my thinking her impertinent because she tells me what it is right that I should know. Presently afterwards, an evidently German-importation of waiter brings me up my breakfast, which has been longer in appearing than it would have been in old times. It looks all right at first,—the napkin, china, and solid silver sugar basin, all of the old régime. Bread, butter,—yes, of the best, still. Coffee, milk, —all right too. But, at last here is a bit of the new régime. There are no sugar-tongs; and the sugar is of beetroot, and in methodically similar cakes, which I must break with my finger and thumb if I want a small piece, and put back what I don't want, for my neighbour, to-morrow.

"Civilization," this, you observe, according to Professor Liebig and Mr. John Stuart Mill. Not according to old French manners, however.

Now, my readers are continually complaining that I don't go on telling them my plan of life, under the rule of St. George's Company.

I *have* told it them, again and again, in broad terms; agricultural life, with as much refinement as I can enforce in it. But it is impossible to describe what I mean by "refinement," except in details which can only be suggested by practical need; and which cannot at all be set down at once.

Here, however, to-day, is one instance. At the best hotel in what has been supposed the most luxurious city of modern Europe,—because people are now always in a hurry to catch the train, they haven't time to use the sugar-tongs, or look for a little piece among differently sized lumps, and therefore they use their fingers; have bad sugar instead of good, and waste the ground that would grow blessed cherry trees, currant bushes, or wheat, in growing a miserable root as a substitute for the sugar-cane, which God has appointed to grow where cherries and wheat won't, and to give juice which will freeze into sweet snow as pure as hoar-frost.

Now, on the poorest farm of the St. George's Company, the servants shall have white and brown sugar of the best —or none. If we are too poor to buy sugar, we will drink our tea without; and have suet-dumpling instead of pudding. But among the earliest school lessons, and home lessons, decent behaviour at table will be primarily essential; and of such decency, one little exact point will be—the neat, patient, and scrupulous use of sugar-tongs instead of fingers. If we are too poor to have silver basins, we will have delf ones; if not silver tongs, we will have wooden ones; and the boys of the house shall be challenged to cut, and fit together, the prettiest and handiest machines of the sort they can contrive. In six months you would find more real art fancy brought out in the wooden handles and claws, than there is now in all the plate in London.

Now, there's the cuckoo-clock striking seven, just as I sit down to correct the press of this sheet, in my nursery at Herne Hill; and though I don't remember, as the murderer does in Mr. Crummles' play, having heard a cuckoo-clock strike seven—in my infancy, I do remember in my favourite *Frank,** much talk of the housekeeper's cuckoo-clock, and of the boy's ingenuity in mending it. Yet to this hour of seven in the morning, ninth December of my fifty-fifth year, I haven't the least notion how any such clock says "Cuckoo," nor a clear one even of the making of the commonest barking toy of a child's Noah's ark. I don't know how a barrel-organ produces music by being ground; nor what real function the pea has in a whistle. Physical science—all this —of a kind which would have been boundlessly interesting to me, as to all boys of mellifluous disposition, if only I had been taught it with due immediate practice, and enforcement of true manufacture, or, in pleasant Saxon, "handiwork." But there shall not be on St. George's estate a single thing in the house which the boys don't know how to make, nor a single dish on the table which the girls will not know how to cook.

By the way, I have been greatly surprised by receiving some letters of puzzled inquiry as to the meaning of my recipe, given last year, for Yorkshire Pie. Do not my readers yet at all understand that the whole gist of this book is to make people build their own houses, provide and cook their own dinners, and enjoy both? Something else besides, perhaps; but at least, and at first, those. St. Michael's mass, and Christ's mass, may eventually be associated in your minds with other things than goose and pudding; but *Fors*

* *Nicholas Nickleby,* Ch. XXIV, and Miss Maria Edgeworth's edifying nursery tale, which the young Ruskin was allowed to read when not memorizing Genesis.

demands at first no more chivalry nor Christianity from you
than that you build your houses bravely, and earn your
dinners honestly, and enjoy them both, and be content with
them both. The contentment is the main matter; you may
enjoy to any extent, but if you are discontented, your life
will be poisoned. The little pig was so comforting to me
because he was wholly content to be a little pig; and Mr.
Leslie Stephen is in a certain degree exemplary and comforting to me, because he is wholly content to be Mr. Leslie
Stephen; while I am miserable because I am always wanting
to be something else than I am. I want to be Turner; I want
to be Gainsborough; I want to be Samuel Prout; I want to
be Doge of Venice; I want to be Pope; I want to be Lord
of the Sun and Moon. The other day, when I read that
story in the papers about the dog-fight,* I wanted to be
able to fight a bulldog.

Truly, that was the only effect of the story upon me,
though I heard everybody else screaming out "how horrible
it was!" What's horrible in it? Of course it is in bad taste,
and the sign of a declining era of national honour—as all
brutal gladiatorial exhibitions are; and the stakes and rings
of the tethered combat meant precisely, for England, what
the stakes and rings of the Theater of Taormina,—where
I saw the holes left for them among the turf, blue with
Sicilian lilies, in this last April,—meant, for Greece, and
Rome. There might be something loathsome, or something
ominous, in such a story, to the old Greeks of the school of
Heracles; who used to fight with the Nemean lion, or with
Cerberus, when it was needful only, and not for money; and
whom their Argus remembered through all Trojan exile.
There might be something loathsome in it, or ominous, to
an Englishman of the school of Shakespeare or Scott; who
would fight with men only, and loved his hound. But for
you—you carnivorous cheats—what, in dog's or devil's

* I don't know how far it turned out to be true,—a fight between a
dwarf and a bulldog (both chained to stakes, as in Roman days),
described at length in some journals. [Ruskin's note.]

name, is there horrible in it for *you*? Do you suppose it isn't
more manly and virtuous to fight a bulldog, than to poison
a child, or cheat a fellow who trusts you, or leave a girl to
go wild in the streets? And don't you live, and profess to
live—and even insolently proclaim that there's no other
way of living than—by poisoning and cheating? And isn't
every woman of fashion's dress, in Europe, now set the pattern of to her by its prostitutes?

What's horrible in it? I ask you, the third time. I hate,
myself, seeing a bulldog ill-treated; for they are the gentlest
and faithfullest of living creatures if you use them well. And
the best dog I ever had was a bull-terrier, whose object in
life was to please me, and nothing else; though, if he found
he *could* please me by holding on with his teeth to an inch-
thick stick, and being swung round in the air as fast as I
could turn, that was his own idea of entirely felicitous existence. I don't like, therefore, hearing of a bulldog's being ill-
treated; but I can tell you a little thing that chanced to me
at Coniston the other day, more horrible, in the deep
elements of it, than all the dog, bulldog, or bull-fights, or
baitings, of England, Spain, and California. A fine boy, the
son of an amiable English clergyman, had come on the
coach-box round the Water-head to see me, and was telling
me of the delightful drive he had had. "Oh," he said, in the
triumph of his enthusiasm, "and just at the corner of the
wood, there was *such* a big squirrel! and the coachman
threw a stone at it, and nearly hit it!"

"Thoughtlessness — only thoughtlessness" — say you —
proud father? Well, perhaps not much worse than that.
But how *could* it be much worse? Thoughtlessness is precisely the chief public calamity of our day; and when it
comes to the pitch, in a clergyman's child, of not thinking
that a stone hurts what it hits of living things, and not
caring for the daintiest, dextrousest, innocentest living thing
in the northern forests of God's earth, except as a brown
excresence to be knocked off their branches,—nay, good
pastor of Christ's lambs, believe me, your boy had better

have been employed in thoughtfully and resolutely stoning
St. Stephen—if any St. Stephen is to be found in these
days, when men not only can't see heaven opened, but
don't so much as care to see it shut.

For they, at least, meant neither to give pain nor death
without cause,—that unanimous company who stopped
their ears,—they, and the consenting bystander who afterwards was sorry for his mistake. . . .   [Letter 48]

The Catholic Prayer

"*Deus, a quo sancta desideria, recta consilia, et justa sunt
opera, da servis tuis illam quam mundus dare non potest
pacem, ut et corda nostra mandatis tuis, et, hostium sublata
formidine, tempora, sint tuâ protectione tranquilla.*"

"*God, from whom are all holy desires, right counsels, and
just works, give to Thy servants that peace which the world
cannot, that both our hearts, in Thy commandments, and
our times, the fear of enemies being taken away, may be
calm under Thy guard.*"

The adulteration of this great Catholic prayer in our English church-service (as needless as it was senseless, since the
pure form of it contains nothing but absolutely Christian
prayer, and is as fit for the most stammering Protestant lips
as for Dante's), destroyed all the definite meaning of it, and
left merely the vague expression of desire for peace, on
quite unregarded terms. For of the millions of people who
utter the prayer at least weekly, there is not one in a thousand who is ever taught, or can for themselves find out,
either what a holy desire means, or a right counsel means, or
a just work means,—or what the world is, or what the peace
is which it cannot give. And half-an-hour after they have
insulted God by praying to Him in this deadest of all dead
languages, not understanded of the people, they leave the
church, themselves pacified in their perennial determina-

tion to put no check on their natural covetousness; to act on their own opinions, be they right or wrong; to do whatever they can make money by, be it just or unjust; and to thrust themselves, with the utmost of their soul and strength, to the highest, by them attainable, pinnacle of the most bedrummed and betrumpeted booth in the Fair of the World.

The prayer, in its pure text, is essentially, indeed, a monastic one; but it is written for the great Monastery of the Servants of God, whom the world hates. It cannot be uttered with honesty but by these; nor can it ever be answered but with the peace bequeathed to these, "not as the world giveth."

Of which peace, the nature is not to be without war, but undisturbed in the midst of war; and not without enemies, but without fear of them. It is a peace without pain, because desiring only what is holy; without anxiety, because it thinks only what is right; without disappointment, because a just work is always successful; without sorrow, because "great peace have they which love Thy Law, and nothing shall offend them"; and without terror, because the God of all battles is its Guard.

So far as any living souls in the England of this day can use, understandingly, the words of this collect, they are already, consciously or not, companions of all good labourers in the vineyard of God. For those who use it reverently, yet have never set themselves to find out what the commandments of God are, nor how lovable they are, nor how far, instead of those commandments, the laws of the world are the only code they care for, nor how far they still think their own thoughts and speak their own words, it is assuredly time to search out these things. And I believe that, after having searched them out, no sincerely good and religious person would find, whatever his own particular form of belief might be, anything which he could reasonably refuse, or which he ought in anywise to fear to profess before all men, in the following statement of creed and resolution, which must be written with their own hand, and signed, with the solemnity of a vow, by every person received into the St. George's Company.

I. I trust in the Living God, Father Almighty, Maker of heaven and earth, and of all things and creatures visible and invisible.

I trust in the kindness of His law, and the goodness of His work.

And I will strive to love Him, and keep His law, and see His work, while I live.

II. I trust in the nobleness of human nature, in the majesty of its faculties, the fulness of its mercy, and the joy of its love.

And I will strive to love my neighbour as myself, and, even when I cannot, will act as if I did.

III. I will labour, with such strength and opportunity as God gives me, for my own daily bread; and all that my hand finds to do, I will do with my might.

IV. I will not deceive, or cause to be deceived, any human being for my gain or pleasure; nor hurt, or cause to be hurt, any human being for my gain or pleasure; nor rob, or cause to be robbed, any human being for my gain or pleasure.

V. I will not kill nor hurt any living creature needlessly, nor destroy any beautiful thing, but will strive to save and comfort all gentle life, and guard and perfect all natural beauty, upon the earth.

VI. I will strive to raise my own body and soul daily into higher powers of duty and happiness; not in rivalship or contention with others, but for the help, delight, and honour of others, and for the joy and peace of my own life.

VII. I will obey all the laws of my country faithfully; and the orders of its monarch, and of all persons appointed to be in authority under its monarch, so far as such laws or commands are consistent with what I suppose to be the law of God; and when they are not, or seem in anywise to need change, I will oppose them loyally and deliberately, not with malicious, concealed, or disorderly violence.

VIII. And with the same faithfulness, and under the limits of the same obedience, which I render to the laws of my country, and the commands of its rulers, I will obey the laws of the Society called of St. George, into which I am this day received; and the orders of its masters, and of all persons appointed to be in authority under its masters, so long as I remain a Companion, called of St. George. . . .

The object of the Society, it has been stated again and again, is to buy land in England; and thereon to train into the healthiest and most refined life possible, as many Englishmen, Englishwomen, and English children, as the land we possess can maintain in comfort; to establish, for them and their descendants, a national store of continually augmenting wealth; and to organize the government of the persons, and administration of the properties, under laws which shall be just to all, and secure in their inviolable foundation on the Law of God. . . .

While, therefore, I am perfectly content, for a beginning, with our acre of rocky land given us by Mrs. Talbot, and am so little impatient for any increase that I have been quietly drawing ragged-robbin leaves in Malham Cove, instead of going to see another twenty acres promised in Worcestershire,—I am yet thinking out my system on a scale which shall be fit for wide European work. Of course the single Master of the Company cannot manage all its concerns as it extends. He must have, for his help, men holding the same relation to him which the Marshals of an army do its General;—bearing, that is to say, his own authority where he is not present; and I believe no better name than "Marshal" can be found for these. Beneath whom, there will again be the landlords, resident each in his own district; under these, the land agents, tenantry, tradesmen, and hired labourers, some of whom will be Companions, others Retainers, and others free tenants: and outside all this there will be of course an irregular cavalry, so to speak, of more or less helpful friends, who, without sharing in the work, will be glad to further it more or less, as they would any other benevolent institution. . . .

And what am I, myself then, infirm and old, who take, or claim, leadership even of these lords? God forbid that I should claim it; it is thrust and compelled on me—utterly against my will, utterly to my distress, utterly, in many things, to my shame. But I have found no other man in England, none in Europe, ready to receive it,—or even desiring to make himself capable of receiving it. Such as I am, to my own amazement, I stand — so far as I can discern—alone in conviction, in hope, and in resolution, in the wilderness of this modern world. Bred in luxury, which I perceive to have been unjust to others, and destructive to myself; vacillating, foolish, and miserably failing in all my own conduct in life—and blown about hopelessly by storms of passion—I, a man clothed in soft raiment,—I, a reed shaken with the wind, have yet this Message to all men again entrusted to me: "Behold, the axe is laid to the root of the trees. Whatsoever tree therefore bringeth not forth good fruit, shall be hewn down and cast into the fire." . . .   [Letter 58]

The Fatherland

VENICE, *9th November,* 1876, 7 *morning.*
I have set my writing-table close to the pillars of the great window of the Ca' Ferro, which I drew, in 1841, carefully, with those of the next palace, Ca' Contarini Fasan. Samuel Prout was so pleased with the sketch that he borrowed it,

and made the upright drawing from it of the palace with the rich balconies, which now represents his work very widely as a chromo-lithotint.

Between the shafts of the pillars, the morning sky is seen pure and pale, relieving the grey dome of the church of the Salute; but beside that vault, and like it, vast thunder-clouds heap themselves above the horizon, catching the light of dawn upon them where they rise, far westward, over the dark roof of the ruined Badia;—but all so massive, that half-an-hour ago, in the dawn, I scarcely knew the Salute dome and towers from theirs; while the sea-gulls, rising and falling hither and thither in clusters above the green water beyond my balcony, tell me that the south wind is wild on Adria.

"Dux inquieti turbidus Adriæ."—The Sea has her Lord, and the sea-birds are prescient of the storm; but my own England, ruler of the waves in her own proud thoughts, can she rule the tumult of her people or, pilotless, even so much as discern the thunderclouds heaped over her Galilean lake of life?

Here is a little grey cockle-shell, lying beside me, which I gathered, the other evening, out of the dust of the Island of St. Helena; and a brightly-spotted snail-shell, from the thistly sands of Lido; and I want to set myself to draw these, and describe them, in peace.

"Yes," all my friends say, "that is my business; why can't I mind it, and be happy?"

Well, good friends, I would fain please you, and myself with you; and live here in my Venetian palace, luxurious; scrutinant of dome, cloud, and cockle-shell. I could even sell my books for not inconsiderable sums of money if I chose to bribe the reviewers, pay half of all I got to the booksellers, stick bills on the lamp-posts, and say nothing but what would please the Bishop of Peterborough.*

I could say a great deal that would please him, and yet

---

* Whom the press had reported as advocating "strict neutrality" in matters of political economy.

be very good and useful; I should like much again to be
on terms with my old publisher, and hear him telling me
nice stories over our walnuts, this Christmas, after dividing
his year's spoil with me in Christmas charity. And little
enough mind have I for any work, in this seventy-seventh
year that's coming of our glorious century, wider than I
could find in the compass of my cockle-shell.

But alas! my prudent friends, little enough of all that
I have a mind to may be permitted me. For this green tide
that eddies by my threshold is full of floating corpses, and
I must leave my dinner to bury them, since I cannot save;
and put my cockle-shell in cap, and take my staff in hand,
to seek an unencumbered shore. This green sea-tide!—yes,
and if you knew it, your black and sulphurous tides also—
Yarrow, and Teviot, and Clyde, and the stream, for ever
now drumly and dark as it rolls on its way, at the ford of
Melrose.

Yes, and the fair lakes and running waters in your English park pleasure-grounds,—nay, also the great and wide
sea, that gnaws your cliffs,—yes, and Death, and Hell also,
more cruel than cliff or sea; and a more neutral episcopal
person than even my Lord of Peterborough stands, level-
barred balance in hand,—waiting (how long?) till the Sea
shall give up the dead which are in it, and Death, and Hell,
give up the dead which are in them. . . .   [Letter 72]

Star Law

VENICE, *Purification of the Virgin,* 1877.
It is eleven years to-day since the 2nd of February became
a great festival to me:* now, like all the days of all the
years, a shadow; deeper, this, in beautiful shade. The sun
has risen cloudless, and I have been looking at the light of it
on the edges of St. Ursula's flower, which is happy with
me, and has four buds bursting, and one newly open flower,

* The day on which Ruskin proposed marriage to Rose La Touche.

which the first sunbeams filled with crimson light down under every film of petal; whose jagged edges of paler rose broke over and over each other, tossed here and there into crested flakes of petal foam, as if the Adriatic breakers had all been changed into crimson leaves at the feet of Venice-Aphrodite. And my dear old Chamouni guide, Joseph Couttet, is dead; he who said of me "le pauvre enfant,—il ne sait pas vivre" and (another time) he would give me nine sous a day, to keep cows, as that was all I was worth, for aught he could see. Captain of Mont Blanc, in his time,— eleven times up it, before Alpine clubs began; like to have been left in a crevasse of the Grand Plateau, where three of his mates were left, indeed; he, fourth of the line, under Dr. Hamel, just brought out of the avalanche-snow breathing. Many a merry walk he took me in his onward years— fifty-five or so, thirty years ago. Clear in heart and mind to the last, if you let him talk; wandering a little if you wanted him to listen;—I've known younger people with somewhat of that weakness. And so, he took to his bed, and—ten days ago, as I hear, said, one evening, to his daughter Judith, "Bon soir, je pars pour l'autre monde," and so went. . . . And we are here with guides of the newest, mostly blind, and proud of finding their way always with a stick. If they trusted in their dogs, one would love them a little for their dogs' sakes. But they only vivisect their dogs.

If I don't tell you my tale of the Venetian doggie* at once, it's all over with it. How so much love and life can be got into a little tangle of floss silk, St. Theodore knows; not I; and its master is one of the best servants in this world, to one of the best masters. It was to be drowned, soon after its eyes had opened to the light of sea and sky,—a poor worthless wet flake of floss silk it had like to have been, presently. Toni pitied it, pulled it out of the water, bought

---

* The pet of Ruskin's friend, Rawdon Brown, whose gondolier, Antonio, figures in the story here told. Earlier in the letter, Ruskin had alluded to the dog and also recounted the legend of St. Theodore's slaying of a dragon.

it for certain sous, brought it home under his arm. What it learned out of his heart in that half-hour, again, St. Theodore knows;—but the mute spiritual creature has been his own, verily, from that day, and only lives for him. Toni, being a pious Toni as well as a pitiful, went this last autumn, in his holiday, to see the Pope; but did not think of taking the doggie with him (who, St. Theodore would surely have said, ought to have seen the Pope too). Whereupon, the little silken mystery wholly refused to eat. No coaxing, no tempting, no nursing, would cheer the desolate-minded thing from that sincere fast. It would drink a little, and was warmed and medicined as best might be. Toni came back from Rome in time to save it; but it was not its gay self again for many and many a day after; the terror of such loss, as yet again possible, weighing on the reviving mind (stomach, supposably, much out of order also). It greatly dislikes getting itself wet; for, indeed, the tangle of its mortal body takes half a day to dry; some terror and thrill of uncomprehended death, perhaps, remaining on it, also,—who knows? but once, after this terrible Roman grief, running along the quay cheerfully beside rowing Toni, it saw him turn the gondola's head six feet aside, as if going away. The dog dashed into the water like a mad thing. "See, now, if aught but death part thee and me."

Indistinguishable, doubtless, in its bones from a small wolf: according to Mr. Waterhouse Hawkins: but much distinguishable, by St. Theodore's theology, telling of God, down, thus far at least, in nature. Emmanuel,—with us; in Raphael, in Tobias, in all loving and lowly things; "the young man's dog went with them.". . .

I have told you the wealth of the world consists, for one great article, in its useful animals.

How to get the most you can of those, and the most serviceable?

"Rob the squires' stables, to begin with?"

No, good friends,—no. Their stables have been to them

as the first wards of Hell, locked on them in this life, for these three hundred years. But you must not open them that way, even for their own sakes.

"Poach the squires' game?"

No, good friends,—no. Down among the wild en'mies, the dust of many a true English keeper forbids you that form of theft, for ever.

"Poison the squires' hounds, and keep a blood bull terrier?"

Worse and worse—merry men, all.

No—here's the beginning. Box your own lad's ears the first time you see him shy a stone at a sparrow; and heartily, too; but put up, you and mother—(and thank God for the blessed persecution),—with every conceivable form of vermin the boy likes to bring into the house,—and go hungry yourselves rather than not feed his rat or his rabbit.

Then, secondly,—you want to be a gentleman yourself, I suppose?

Well, you can't be, as I have told you before, nor I neither; and there's an end, neither of us being born in the caste: but you may get some pieces of gentlemen's education, which will lead the way to your son's being a better man than you.

And of all essential things in a gentleman's bodily and moral training, this is really the beginning—that he should have close companionship with the horse, the dog, and the eagle. Of all birthrights and bookrights—this is his first. He needn't be a Christian,—there have been millions of Pagan gentlemen; he needn't be kind—there have been millions of cruel gentlemen; he needn't be honest,—there have been millions of crafty gentlemen. He needn't know how to read, or to write his own name. But he *must* have horse, dog, and eagle for friends. If then he has also Man for his friend, he is a noble gentleman; and if God for his Friend, a king. And if, being honest, being kind, and having God and Man for his friends, he *then* gets these three brutal friends, besides his angelic ones, he is perfect in earth, as for heaven. For, to be his friends, these must be brought up with him, and he with them. Falcon on fist, hound at foot, and horse part of himself—Eques, Ritter, Cavalier, Chevalier.

Yes;—horse and dog you understand the good of; but what's the good of the falcon, think you?

To be friends with the falcon must mean that you love to see it soar; that is to say, you love fresh air and the fields. Farther, when the Law of God is understood, you will like better to see the eagle free than the jessed hawk. And to preserve your eagles' nests, is to be a great nation. It means keeping everything that is noble; mountains and floods, and forests, and the glory and honour of them, and all the birds that haunt them. If the eagle takes more than his share, you may shoot him,—(but with the knight's arrow, not the blackguard's gun)—and not till then.

Meantime, for you are of course by no means on the direct way to the accomplishment of all this, your way to such wealth, so far as in your present power, is this: first, acknowledgment of the mystery of divine life, kindly and dreadful, throughout creation; then the taking up your own part as the Lord of this life; to protect, assist, or extinguish, as it is commanded you. Understand that a mad dog is to be slain; though with pity—infinitude of pity,—(and much more, a mad *man,* of an injurious kind; for a mad dog only bites flesh; but a mad man, spirit: get your rogue, the supremely maddest of men, with supreme pity always, but inexorably, hanged). But to all good and sane men and beasts, be true brother; and as it is best, perhaps, to begin with all things in the lowest place, begin with true brotherhood to the beast: in pure simplicity of practical help, I should like a squad of you to stand always harnessed, at the bottom of any hills you know of in Sheffield,—where the horses strain;—ready there at given hours; carts ordered not to pass at any others: at the low level, hook yourselves on before the horses; pull them up too, if need be; and dismiss them at the top with a pat and a mouthful of hay. Here's a beginning of chivalry, and gentlemanly life for you, my masters. . . . [Letter 75]

Our Battle Is Immortal

VENICE, *Sunday 4th March,* 1877.

You cannot but have noticed—any of you who read attentively,—that *Fors* has become much more distinctly Christian in its tone, during the last two years; and those of you who know with any care my former works, must feel a yet more vivid contrast between the spirit in which the preface to the *Crown of Wild Olive* was written, and that in which I am now collating for you the Mother Laws of the Trades of Venice.

This is partly because I am every day compelled, with increasing amazement, and renewed energy, to contradict the idiotic teaching of Atheism which is multiplied in your ears; but it depends far more essentially on two vital causes: the first, that since *Fors* began, "such things have befallen me" personally, which have taught me much, but of which I need not at present speak; the second, that in the work I did at Assisi in 1874, I discovered a fallacy which had underlain all my art teaching (and the teaching of Art, as I understand it, is the teaching of all things) since the year 1858. Of which I must be so far tedious to you as to give some brief account. For it is continually said of me, and I observe has been publicly repeated lately by one of my very good friends, that I have "changed my opinions" about painting and architecture. And this, like all the worst of falsehoods, has one little kernel of distorted truth in the heart of it, which it is practically necessary, now, that you, my Sheffield essayists of St. George's service,* should clearly know.

All my first books, to the end of the *Stones of Venice,* were written in the simple belief I had been taught as a child; and especially the second volume of *Modern Painters*

* That is, the workingmen-members of St. George's Guild in Sheffield, where Ruskin founded a museum centered on works donated from his own collections of minerals, manuscripts, and paintings.

was an outcry of enthusiastic praise of religious painting, in which you will find me placing Fra Angelico (see the closing paragraph of the book) above all other painters.

But during my work at Venice, I discovered the gigantic power of Tintoret, and found that there was a quite different spirit in that from the spirit of Angelico; and, analysing Venetian work carefully, I found,—and told fearlessly, in spite of my love for the masters,—that there was "no religion whatever in any work of Titian's; and that Tintoret only occasionally forgot himself into religion."—I repeat now, and reaffirm, this statement; but must ask the reader to add to it, what I partly indeed said in other places at the time, that only when Tintoret forgets himself, does he truly find himself.

Now you see that among the four pieces of art I have given you for standards to study, only one is said to be "perfect,"—Titian's. And ever since the *Stones of Venice* was written, Titian was given in all my art teaching as a standard of perfection. Conceive the weight of this problem, then, on my inner mind—how the most perfect work I knew, in my special business, could be done "wholly without religion"!

I set myself to work out that problem thoroughly in 1858, and arrived at the conclusion—which is an entirely sound one, and which did indeed alter, from that time forward, the tone and method of my teaching,—that human work must be done honourably and thoroughly, because we are now Men;—whether we ever expect to be angels, or ever were slugs, being practically no matter. We *are* now Human creatures, and must, at our peril, do Human—that is to say, affectionate, honest, and earnest work.

Farther, I found, and have always since taught, and do teach, and shall teach, I doubt not, till I die, that in resolving to do our work well, is the only sound foundation of any religion whatsoever: and that by that resolution only, and what we have done, and not by our belief, Christ will judge us, as He has plainly told us He will (though nobody believes Him) in the Resurrection.

But, beyond this, in the year 1858, I came to another conclusion, which was a false one.

My work on the Venetians in that year not only convinced me of their consummate power, but showed me that there was a great *worldly* harmony running through all they did—opposing itself to the fanaticism of the Papacy; and in this worldly harmony of human and artistic power, my own special idol, Turner, stood side by side with Tintoret; so also Velasquez, Sir Joshua, and Gainsborough, stood with Titian and Veronese; and those seven men— quite demonstrably and indisputably giants in the domain of Art, of whom in the words of Velasquez himself, "Tizian z'e quel che porta la Bandiera,"*—stood, as heads of a great Worldly Army, worshippers of Worldly visible Truth, *against* (as it seemed then to me), and assuredly distinct from, another sacred army, bearing the Rule of the Catholic Church in the strictest obedience, and headed by Cimabue, Giotto, and Angelico; worshippers not of a worldly and visible Truth, but of a visionary one, which they asserted to be higher; yet under the (as they asserted—supernatural) teaching of the Spirit of this Truth, doing less perfect work than their unassisted opposites!

All this is entirely so; fact tremendous in its unity, and difficult enough as it stands to me even now; but as it stood to me then, wholly insoluble, for I was still in the bonds of my old Evangelical faith; and, in 1858, it was with me, Protestantism or nothing: the crisis of the whole turn of my thoughts being one Sunday morning, at Turin, when, from before Paul Veronese's Queen of Sheba, and under quite overwhelmed sense of his God-given power, I went away to a Waldensian chapel, where a little squeaking idiot was preaching to an audience of seventeen old women and three louts, that they were the only children of God in Turin; and that all the people in Turin outside the chapel, and all the people in the world out of sight of Monte Viso, would be damned. I came out of the chapel, in sum of twenty

* "Titian it is who bears the banner."

years of thought, a conclusively *un*-converted man—converted by this little Piedmontest gentleman, so powerful in his organ-grinding, inside-out, as it were. "Here is an end to my 'Mother-Law' of Protestantism anyhow!—and now—what is there left?" You will find what was left, as, in much darkness and sorrow of heart I gathered it, variously taught in my books, written between 1858 and 1874. It is all sound and good, as far as it goes: whereas all that went before was so mixed with Protestant egotism and insolence, that, as you have probably heard, I won't republish, in their first form, any of those former books.

Thus then it went with me till 1874, when I had lived sixteen full years with "the religion of Humanity," for rough and strong and sure foundation of everything; but on that, building Greek and Arabian superstructure, taught me at Venice, full of sacred colour and melancholy shade. Which is the under meaning of my answer to the Capuchin (*Fors*, Aug. 1875, § 2), that I was "more a Turk than a Christian." The Capuchin insisted, as you see, nevertheless that I might have a bit of St. Francis's cloak: which accepting thankfully, I went on to Assisi, and there, by the kindness of my good friend Padre Tini, and others, I was allowed (and believe I am the first painter who *ever was* allowed) to have scaffolding erected above the high altar, and therefore above the body of St. Francis which lies in the lower chapel beneath it; and thence to draw what I could of the great fresco of Giotto, "The marriage of Poverty and Francis."

And while making this drawing, I discovered the fallacy under which I had been tormented for sixteen years,—the fallacy that Religious artists were weaker than Irreligious. I found that all Giotto's "weaknesses" (so called) were merely absences of material science. He did not know, and could not, in his day, so much of perspective as Titian,— so much of the laws of light and shade, or so much of technical composition. But I found he was in the make of him, and contents, a very much stronger and greater man than Titian; that the things I had fancied easy in his work, because they were so unpretending and simple, were nevertheless entirely inimitable; that the Religion in him, instead of weakening, had solemnized and developed every faculty of his heart and hand; and finally that his work, in all the innocence of it, was yet a human achievement and possession, quite above everything that Titian had ever done!

"But what is all this about Titian and Angelico to you," are you thinking? "We belong to cotton mills—iron mills: —what is Titian to *us!*—and to all men. Heirs only of simial life, what Angelico?"

Patience—yet for a little while. They shall both be at least something to you before St. George's Museum is six months older.

Meantime, don't be afraid that I am going to become a Roman Catholic, or that I am one, in disguise. I can no more become a *Roman*-Catholic, than again an Evangelical-Protestant. I am a "Catholic" of those Catholics, to whom the Catholic Epistle of St. James is addressed—"the Twelve Tribes which are scattered abroad"—the literally or spiritually wandering Israel of all the Earth. The St. George's creed includes Turks, Jews, infidels, and heretics; and I am myself much of a Turk, more of a Jew; alas, most of all,— an infidel; but not an atom of a heretic: Catholic, I, of the Catholics; holding only for sure God's order to His scattered Israel,—"He hath shown thee, oh man, what is good; and what doth the Lord thy God require of thee, but to do justice, and to love mercy, and to walk humbly with thy God?" . . .   [Letter 76]

The Convents of St. Quentin

BRANTWOOD, *8th February,* 1880.

It is now close on two years since I was struck by the illness which brought these Letters to an end, as a periodical series; nor did I think, on first recovery, that I should ever be able to conclude them otherwise than by a few comments in arranging their topical index.

But my strength is now enough restored to permit me to add one or two more direct pieces of teaching to the broken statements of principle which it has become difficult to gather out of the mixed substance of the book. These will be written at such leisure as I may find, and form an eighth volume, which with a thin ninth, containing indices, I shall be thankful if I can issue in this tenth year from the beginning of the work.

To-day, being my sixty-first birthday, I would ask leave to say a few words to the friends who care for me, and the readers who are anxious about me, touching the above-named illness itself. For a physician's estimate of it, indeed, I can only refer them to my physicians. But there were some conditions of it which I knew better than they could: namely, first, the precise and sharp distinction between the state of morbid inflammation of brain which gave rise to false visions (whether in sleep, or trance, or waking, in broad daylight, with perfect knowledge of the real things in the room, while yet I saw others that were not there), and the not morbid, however dangerous, states of more or less excited temper, and too much quickened thought, which gradually led up to the illness, accelerating in action during the eight or ten days preceding the actual giving way of the brain (as may be enough seen in the fragmentary writing of the first edition of my notes on the Turner exhibition); and yet, up to the transitional moment of first hallucination, entirely healthy, and in the full sense of the word "sane"; just as the natural inflammation about a heal-ing wound in flesh is sane, up to the transitional edge where it may pass at a crisis into morbific, or even mortified sub-stance. And this more or less inflamed, yet still perfectly healthy, condition of mental power, may be traced by any watchful reader, in *Fors,* nearly from its beginning,—that manner of mental ignition or irritation being for the time a great additional force, enabling me to discern more clearly, and say more vividly, what for long years it had been in my heart to say.

Now I observed that in talking of the illness, whether during its access or decline, none of the doctors ever thought of thus distinguishing what was definitely diseased in the brain action, from what was simply curative—had there been time enough—of the wounded nature in me. And in the second place, not perceiving, or at least not admitting, this difference; nor, for the most part, apprehending (except the one who really carried me through, and who never lost hope—Dr. Parsons of Hawkshead) that there *were* any mental wounds to be healed, they made, and still make, my friends more anxious about me than there is occasion for: which anxiety I partly regret, as it pains them; but much more if it makes them more doubtful than they used to be (which, for some, is saying a good deal) of the "truth and soberness" of *Fors* itself. Throughout every syllable of which, hitherto written, the reader will find one consistent purpose, and perfectly conceived system, far more deeply founded than any bruited about under their founders' names; including in its balance one vast department of human skill,—the arts,—which the vulgar economists are wholly incapable of weighing; and a yet more vast realm of human enjoyment—the spiritual affections,—which materialistic thinkers are alike incapable of imagining: a system not mine, nor Kant's, nor Comte's;—but that which Heaven has taught every true man's heart, and proved by every true man's work, from the beginning of time to this day.

I use the word "Heaven" here in an absolutely literal sense, meaning the blue sky, and the light and air of it. Men who live in that light,—"in pure sunshine, not under mixed-up shade,"*—and whose actions are open as the air, always arrive at certain conditions of moral and practical loyalty, which are wholly independent of religious opinion. These, it has been the first business of *Fors* to declare. Whether there be one God or three,—no God, or ten

* Plato, Phædrus, 239 C.

thousand,—children should have enough to eat, and their skins should be washed clean. It is not *I* who say that. Every mother's heart under the sun says that, if she has one.

Again, whether there be saints in Heaven or not, as long as its stars shine on the sea, and the thunnies swim there— every fisherman who drags a net ashore is bound to say to as many human creatures as he can, "Come and dine." And the fishmongers who destroy their fish by cartloads that they may make the poor pay dear for what is left, ought to be flogged round Billingsgate, and out of it. It is not *I* who say that. Every man's heart on sea and shore says that—if he isn't at heart a rascal. Whatever is dictated in *Fors* is dictated thus by common sense, common equity, common humanity, and common sunshine—not by me.

But farther. I have just now used the word "Heaven" in a nobler sense also: meaning, Heaven and our Father therein.

And beyond the power of its sunshine, which all men may know, *Fors* has declared also the power of its Fatherhood,— which only some men know, and others do not,—and, except by rough teaching, may not. For the wise of all the earth have said in their hearts always, "God is, and there is none beside Him;" and the fools of all the earth have said in their hearts always, "I am, and there is none beside me."

Therefore, beyond the assertion of what is visibly salutary, *Fors* contains also the assertion of what is invisibly salutary, or salvation-bringing, in Heaven, to all men who will receive such health: and beyond this an invitation— passing gradually into an imperious call—to all men who trust in God, that they purge their conscience from dead works, and join together in work separated from the fool's; pure, undefiled, and worthy of Him they trust in.

But in the third place. Besides these definitions, first, of what is useful to all the world, and then of what is useful to the wiser part of it, *Fors* contains much trivial and desultory talk by the way. Scattered up and down in it,—perhaps by the Devil's sowing tares among the wheat,

—there is much casual expression of my own personal feelings and faith, together with bits of autobiography, which were allowed place, not without some notion of their being useful, but yet imprudently, and even incontinently, because I could not at the moment hold my tongue about what vexed or interested me, or returned soothingly to my memory.

Now these personal fragments must be carefully sifted from the rest of the book, by readers who wish to understand it, and taken within their own limits,—no whit farther. For instance, when I say that "St. Ursula sent me a flower with her love," it means that I myself am in the habit of thinking of the Greek Persephone, the Latin Proserpina, and the Gothic St. Ursula, as of the same living spirit; and so far regulating my conduct by that idea as to dedicate my book on Botany to Proserpina; and to think, when I want to write anything pretty about flowers, how St. Ursula would like it said. And when on the Christmas morning in question, a friend staying in Venice brought me a pot of pinks, "with St. Ursula's love," the said pot of pinks did afterwards greatly help me in my work;—and reprove me afterwards, in its own way, for the failure of it.

All this effort, or play, of personal imagination is utterly distinct from the teaching of *Fors,* though I thought at the time its confession innocent, without in any wise advising my readers to expect messages from pretty saints, or reprobation from pots of pinks: only being urgent with them to ascertain clearly in their own minds what they *do* expect comfort or reproof from. Here, for instance (Sheffield, 12th February), I am lodging at an honest and hospitable grocer's, who has lent me his own bedroom, of which the principal ornament is a card printed in black and gold, sacred to the memory of his infant son, who died aged fourteen months, and whose tomb is represented under the figure of a broken Corinthian column, with two graceful-winged ladies putting garlands on it. He is comforted by this conception, and, in that degree, believes and feels with me:

the merely palpable fact is probably, that his child's body is lying between two tall chimneys which are covering it gradually with cinders. I am quite as clearly aware of that fact as the most scientific of my friends; and can probably see more in the bricks of the said chimneys than they. But if they can see nothing in Heaven above the chimney tops, nor conceive of anything in spirit greater than themselves, it is not because they have more knowledge than I, but because they have less sense.

Less *common*-sense,—observe: less practical insight into the things which are of instant and constant need to man.

I must yet allow myself a few more words of autobiography touching this point. The doctors said that I went mad, this time two years ago, from overwork. I had not been then working more than usual, and what was usual with me had become easy. But I went mad because nothing came of my work. People would have understood my falling crazy if they had heard that the manuscripts on which I had spent seven years of my old life had all been used to light the fire with, like Carlyle's first volume of the *French Revolution*. But they could not understand that I should be the least annoyed, far less fall ill in a frantic manner, because, after I had got them published, nobody believed a word of them. Yet the first calamity would only have been misfortune,—the second (the enduring calamity under which I toil) is humiliation,—resisted necessarily by a dangerous and lonely pride.

I spoke just now of the "wounds" of which that fire in the flesh came; and if any one ask me faithfully, what the wounds were, I can faithfully give the answer of Zechariah's silenced messenger, "Those with which I was wounded in the house of my friends." All alike, in whom I had most trusted for help, failed me in this main work: some mocked at it, some pitied, some rebuked,—all stopped their ears at the cry: and the solitude at last became too great to be endured. . . .   [Letter 88]

FICTION, FAIR AND FOUL

Essay I

On the first mild—or, at least, the first bright—day of March, in this year, I walked through what was once a country lane, between the hostelry of the Half-moon at the bottom of Herne Hill, and the secluded College of Dulwich.

In my young days, Croxted Lane was a green bye-road traversable for some distance by carts; but rarely so traversed, and, for the most part, little else than a narrow strip of untilled field, separated by blackberry hedges from the better-cared-for meadows on each side of it: growing more weeds, therefore, than they, and perhaps in spring a primrose or two—white archangel—daisies plenty, and purple thistles in autumn. A slender rivulet, boasting little of its brightness, for there are no springs at Dulwich, yet fed purely enough by the rain and morning dew, here trickled —there loitered—through the long grass beneath the hedges, and expanded itself, where it might, into moderately clear and deep pools, in which, under their veils of duck-weed, a fresh-water shell or two, sundry curious little skipping shrimps, any quantity of tadpoles in their time, and even sometimes a tittlebat, offered themselves to my boyhood's pleased, and not inaccurate, observation. There, my mother and I used to gather the first buds of the hawthorn; and there, in after years, I used to walk in the summer shadows, as in a place wilder and sweeter than our garden, to think over any passage I wanted to make better than usual in *Modern Painters.*

So, as aforesaid, on the first kindly day of this year, being thoughtful more than usual of those old times, I went to look again at the place.

Often, both in those days, and since, I have put myself hard to it, vainly, to find words wherewith to tell of beautiful things; but beauty has been in the world since the world was made, and human language can make a shift, somehow, to give account of it, whereas the peculiar forces of devastation induced by modern city life have only entered the world lately; and no existing terms of language known to me are enough to describe the forms of filth, and modes of ruin, that varied themselves along the course of Croxted Lane. The fields on each side of it are now mostly dug up for building, or cut through into gaunt corners and nooks of blind ground by the wild crossings and concurrencies of three railroads. Half a dozen handfuls of new cottages, with Doric doors, are dropped about here and there among the gashed ground: the lane itself, now entirely grassless, is a deep-rutted, heavy-hillocked cart-road, diverging gatelessly into various brickfields or pieces of waste; and bordered on each side by heaps of—Hades only knows what!—mixed dust of every unclean thing that can crumble in draught, and mildew of every unclean thing that can rot or rust in damp: ashes and rags, beer-bottles and old shoes, battered pans, smashed crockery, shreds of nameless clothes, door-sweepings, floor-sweepings, kitchen garbage, back-garden sewage, old iron, rotten timber jagged with out-torn nails, cigar-ends, pipe-bowls, cinders, bones, and ordure, indescribable; and, variously kneaded into, sticking to, or fluttering foully here and there over all these, remnants, broadcast, of every manner of newspaper, advertisement or big-lettered bill, festering and flaunting out their last publicity in the pits of stinking dust and mortal slime. . . .

It became matter of curious meditation to me what must here become of children resembling my poor little dreamy quondam self in temper, and thus brought up at the same distance from London, and in the same or better circumstances of worldly fortune; but with only Croxted Lane in its present condition for their country walk. . . . For its sense or fancy, what food, or stimulus, can it find, in that foul causeway of its youthful pilgrimage? What would have happened to myself, so directed, I cannot clearly imagine. Possibly, I might have got interested in the old iron and wood-shavings; and become an engineer or a carpenter: but for the children of to-day, accustomed, from the instant they are out of their cradles, to the sight of this infinite nastiness, prevailing as a fixed condition of the universe, over the face of nature, and accompanying all the operations of industrious man, what is to be the scholastic issue? unless, indeed, the thrill of scientific vanity in the primary analysis of some unheard-of process of corruption—or the reward of microscopic research in the sight of worms with more legs, and acari of more curious generation than ever vivified the more simply smelling plasma of antiquity.

One result of such elementary education is, however, already certain; namely, that the pleasure which we may conceive taken by the children of the coming time, in the analysis of physical corruption, guides, into fields more dangerous and desolate, the expatiation of an imaginative literature: and that the reactions of moral disease upon itself, and the conditions of languidly monstrous character developed in an atmosphere of low vitality, have become the most valued material of modern fiction, and the most eagerly discussed texts of modern philosophy.

The many concurrent reasons for this mischief may, I believe, be massed under a few general heads.

(I.) There is first the hot fermentation and unwholesome secrecy of the population crowded into large cities, each mote in the misery lighter, as an individual soul, than a dead leaf, but becoming oppressive and infectious each to his neighbour, in the smoking mass of decay. The resulting modes of mental ruin and distress are continually new; and in a certain sense, worth study in their monstrosity: they have accordingly developed a corresponding science of fiction, concerned mainly with the description of such forms of disease, like the botany of leaf-lichens.

In De Balzac's story of *Father Goriot,* a grocer makes a large fortune, of which he spends on himself as much as may keep him alive; and on his two daughters, all that can promote their pleasures or their pride. He marries them to men of rank, supplies their secret expenses, and provides for his favourite a separate and clandestine establishment with her lover. On his deathbed, he sends for this favourite daughter, who wishes to come, and hesitates for a quarter of an hour between doing so, and going to a ball at which it has been for the last month her chief ambition to be seen. She finally goes to the ball.

The story is, of course, one of which the violent contrasts and spectral catastrophe could only take place, or be conceived, in a large city. A village grocer cannot make a large fortune, cannot marry his daughters to titled squires, and cannot die without having his children brought to him, if in the neighbourhood, by fear of village gossip, if for no better cause.

(II.) But a much more profound feeling that this mere curiosity of science in morbid phenomena is concerned in the production of the carefullest forms of modern fiction. The disgrace and grief resulting from the mere trampling pressure and electric friction of town life, become to the sufferers peculiarly mysterious in their undeservedness, and frightful in their inevitableness. The power of all surroundings over them for evil; the incapacity of their own minds to refuse the pollution, and of their own wills to oppose the weight, of the staggering mass that chokes and crushes them into perdition, brings every law of healthy existence into question with them, and every alleged method of help and hope into doubt. Indignation, without any calming faith in justice, and self-contempt, without any curative self-reproach, dull the intelligence, and degrade the conscience, into sullen incredulity of all sunshine outside the dunghill, or breeze beyond the wafting of its impurity; and at last a philosophy develops itself, partly satiric, partly consolatory, concerned only with the regenerative vigour of manure, and the necessary obscurities of fimetic Providence;

showing how everybody's fault is somebody else's, how in-
fection has no law, digestion no will, and profitable dirt no
dishonour.

And thus an elaborate and ingenious scholasticism, in
what may be called the Divinity of Decomposition, has
established itself in connection with the more recent forms
of romance, giving them at once a complacent tone of
clerical dignity, and an agreeable dash of heretical impu-
dence; while the inculcated doctrine has the double advantage of needing no laborious scholarship for its foundation,
and no painful self-denial for its practice.

(III.) The monotony of life in the central streets of any
great modern city, but especially in those of London, where
every emotion intended to be derived by men from the
sight of nature, or the sense of art, is forbidden for ever,
leaves the craving of the heart for a sincere, yet changeful,
interest, to be fed from one source only. Under natural
conditions the degree of mental excitement necessary to
bodily health is provided by the course of the seasons, and
the various skill and fortune of agriculture. . . . The divine
laws of seed-time which cannot be recalled, harvest which
cannot be hastened, and winter in which no man can work,
compel the impatiences and coveting of his heart into
labour too submissive to be anxious, and rest too sweet to
be wanton. What thought can enough comprehend the
contrast between such life, and that in streets where summer and winter are only alternations of heat and cold;
where snow never fell white, nor sunshine clear; where the
ground is only a pavement, and the sky no more than the
glass roof of an arcade; where the utmost power of a storm
is to choke the gutters, and the finest magic of spring, to
change mud into dust: where—chief and most fatal difference in state—there is no interest of occupation for any of
the inhabitants but the routine of counter or desk within
doors, and the effort to pass each other without collision
outside; so that from morning to evening the only possible
variation of the monotony of the hours, and lightening of
the penalty of existence, must be some kind of mischief,

limited, unless by more than ordinary godsend of fatality, to the fall of a horse, or the slitting of a pocket?

I said that under these laws of inanition, the craving of the human heart for some kind of excitement could be supplied from *one* source only. It might have been thought by any other than a sternly tentative philosopher, that the denial of their natural food to human feelings would have provoked a reactionary desire for it; and that the dreariness of the street would have been gilded by dreams of pastoral felicity. Experience has shown the fact to be otherwise; the thoroughly trained Londoner can enjoy no other excitement than to which he has been accustomed, but asks for *that* in continually more ardent or more virulent concentration; and the ultimate power of fiction to entertain him is by varying to his fancy the modes, and defining for his dulness the horrors, of Death. In the single novel of *Bleak House* there are nine deaths (or left for death's, in the drop scene) carefully wrought out or led up to, either by way of pleasing surprise, as the baby's at the brickmaker's, or finished in their threatenings and sufferings, with as much enjoyment as can be contrived in the anticipation, and as much pathology as can be concentrated in the description. Under the following varieties of method:—

One by assassination	*Mr. Tulkinghorn.*
One by starvation, with phthisis . .	*Joe.*
One by chagrin	*Richard.*
One by spontaneous combustion .	*Mr. Krook.*
One by sorrow	*Lady Dedlock's lover.*
One by remorse	*Lady Dedlock.*
One by insanity	*Miss Flite.*
One by paralysis	*Sir Leicester.*

Besides the baby, by fever, and a lively young Frenchwoman left to be hanged.

And all this, observe, not in a tragic, adventurous, or military story, but merely as the further enlivenment of a narrative intended to be amusing; and as a properly representative average of the statistics of civilian mortality in the centre of London.

Observe further, and chiefly. It is not the mere number of deaths (which, if we count the odd troopers in the last scene, is exceeded in *Old Mortality,* and reached, within one or two, both in *Waverley* and *Guy Mannering)* that marks the peculiar tone of the modern novel. It is the fact that all these deaths, but one, are of inoffensive, or at least in the world's estimate, respectable persons; and that they are all grotesquely either violent or miserable, purporting thus to illustrate the modern theology that the appointed destiny of a large average of our population is to die like rats in a drain, either by trap or poison. Not, indeed, that a lawyer in full practice can be usually supposed as fault-less in the eye of Heaven as a dove or a woodcock; but it is not, in former divinities, thought the will of Providence that he should be dropped by a shot from a client behind his fire-screen, and retrieved in the morning by his house-maid under the chandelier. Neither is Lady Dedlock less reprehensible in her conduct than many women of fashion have been and will be: but it would not therefore have been thought poetically just, in old-fashioned morality, that she should be found by her daughter lying dead, with her face in the mud of a St. Giles's churchyard.

In the work of the great masters death is always either heroic, deserved, or quiet and natural (unless their purpose be totally and deeply tragic, when collateral meaner death is permitted, like that of Polonius or Roderigo). In *Old Mortality,* four of the deaths, Bothwell's, Ensign Grahame's, Macbriar's, and Evandale's, are magnificently heroic; Bur-ley's and Olifant's long deserved, and swift; the troopers', met in the discharge of their military duty; and the old miser's, as gentle as the passing of a cloud. . . .

Nor is it ever to be forgotten, in the comparison of Scott's with inferior work, that his own splendid powers were, even in early life, tainted, and in his latter years destroyed, by modern conditions of commercial excitement, then first, but rapidly, developing themselves. There are parts even in his best novels coloured to meet tastes which he despised; and many pages written in his later ones to lengthen his article for the indiscriminate market.

But there was one weakness of which his healthy mind remained incapable to the last. In modern stories prepared for more refined or fastidious audiences than those of Dickens, the funereal excitement is obtained, for the most part, not by the infliction of violent or disgusting death; but in the suspense, the pathos, and the more or less by all felt, and recognized, mortal phenomena of the sick-room. The temptation, to weak writers, of this order of subject is especially great, because the study of it from the living— or dying—model is so easy, and to many has been the most impressive part of their own personal experience; while, if the description be given even with mediocre accuracy, a very large section of readers will admire its truth, and cherish its melancholy. Few authors of second or third rate genius can either record or invent a probable conversation in ordinary life; but few, on the other hand, are so destitute of observant faculty as to be unable to chronicle the broken syllables and languid movements of an invalid. The easily rendered, and too surely recognized, image of familiar suffering is felt at once to be real where all else had been false; and the historian of the gestures of fever and words of delirium can count on the applause of a gratified audience as surely as the dramatist who introduces on the stage of his flagging action a carriage that can be driven or a fountain that will flow. But the masters of strong imagination disdain such work, and those of deep sensibility shrink from it.* Only under conditions of personal weakness, presently to be noted, would Scott comply with the cravings of his lower audience in scenes of terror like the death of Front-de-Bœuf. But he never once withdrew the sacred curtain of the sick-chamber, nor permitted the

---

* Nell, in *The Old Curiosity Shop*, was simply killed for the market, as a butcher kills a lamb (see Forster's *Life*), and Paul was written under the same conditions of illness which affected Scott—a part of the ominous palsies, grasping alike author and subject both in *Dombey* and *Little Dorrit*. [Ruskin's note.]

disgrace of wanton tears round the humiliation of strength, or the wreck of beauty. . . .

The mean anxieties, moral humiliations, and mercilessly demanded brain-toil, which killed him, show their sepul-chral grasp for many and many a year before their final victory; and the states of more or less dulled, distorted, and polluted imagination which culminate in *Castle Dangerous* cast a Stygian hue over *St. Ronan's Well, The Fair Maid of Perth,* and *Anne of Geierstein,* which lowers them, the first altogether, the other two at frequent intervals, into fellowship with the normal disease which festers throughout the whole body of our lower fictitious literature.

Fictitious! I use the ambiguous word deliberately; for it is impossible to distinguish in these tales of the prison-house how far their vice and gloom are thrown into their manufacture only to meet a vile demand, and how far they are an integral condition of thought in the minds of men trained from their youth up in the knowledge of Londinian and Parisian misery. The speciality of the plague is a delight in the exposition of the relations between guilt and decrepi-tude; and I call the results of it literature "of the prison-house," because the thwarted habits of body and mind, which are the punishment of reckless crowding in cities, become, in the issue of that punishment, frightful subjects of exclusive interest to themselves; and the art of fiction in which they finally delight is only the more studied arrange-ment and illustration, by coloured firelights, of the daily bulletins of their own wretchedness, in the prison calendar, the police news, and the hospital report. . . .

But the effectual head of the whole cretinous school is the renowned novel in which the hunch-backed lover watches the execution of his mistress from the tower of Notre-Dame; and its strength passes gradually away into the anatomical preparations, for the general market, of novels like *Poor Miss Finch,** in which the heroine is blind, the hero epileptic, and the obnoxious brother is found dead with his hands dropped off, in the Arctic regions.

* By Wilkie Collins, published in 1872.

This literature of the Prison-house, understanding by the word not only the cell of Newgate, but also and even more definitely the cell of the Hôtel-Dieu, the Hôpital des Fous, and the grated corridor with the dripping slabs of the Morgue, having its central root thus in the Île de Paris —or historically and pre-eminently the "Cité de Paris"— is, when understood deeply, the precise counter-corruption of the religion of the Sainte Chapelle, just as the worst forms of bodily and mental ruin are the corruption of love. I have therefore called it "Fiction mécroyante," with literal accuracy and precision: according to the explanation of the word, which the reader may find in any good French dictionary, and round its Arctic pole in the Morgue, he may gather into one Caina of gelid putrescence the entire product of modern infidel imagination, amusing itself with destruction of the body, and busying itself with aberration of the mind.

Aberration, palsy, or plague, observe, as distinguished from normal evil, just as the venom of rabies or cholera differs from that of a wasp or a viper. The life of the insect and serpent deserves, or at least permits, our thoughts; not so the stages of agony in the fury-driven hound. There is some excuse, indeed, for the pathologic labour of the modern novelist in the fact that he cannot easily, in a city population, find a healthy mind to vivisect: but the greater part of such amateur surgery is the struggle, in an epoch of wild literary competition, to obtain novelty of material. The varieties of aspect and colour in healthy fruit, be it sweet or sour, may be within certain limits described exhaustively. Not so the blotches of its conceivable blight: and while the symmetries of integral human character can only be traced by harmonious and tender skill, like the branches of a living tree, the faults and gaps of one gnawed away by corroding accident can be shuffled into senseless change like the wards of a Chubb lock.*

* An unpickable, tumbler lock, named after its inventor.

THE STORM-CLOUD
OF THE NINETEENTH CENTURY

Lecture I*

Let me first assure my audience that I have no *arrière pensée* in the title chosen for this lecture. I might, indeed, have meant, and it would have been only too like me to mean, any number of things by such a title;—but, to-night, I mean simply what I have said, and propose to bring to your notice a series of cloud phenomena, which, so far as I can weigh existing evidence, are peculiar to our own times; yet which have not hitherto received any special notice or description from meteorologists.

So far as the existing evidence, I say, of former literature can be interpreted, the storm-cloud—or more accurately plague-cloud, for it is not always stormy—which I am about to describe to you, never was seen but by now living, or

* Delivered at the London Institution on February 4, 1884. A week later, in the final lecture, Ruskin told his audience that "had the weather when I was young been such as it is now, no book such as *Modern Painters* ever would or *could* have been written; for every argument, and every sentiment in that book, was founded on the personal experience of the beauty and blessing of nature, all spring and summer long; and on the then demonstrable fact that over a great portion of the world's surface the air and the earth were fitted to the education of the spirit of man as closely as a schoolboy's primer is to his labour, and as gloriously as a lover's mistress is to his eyes.

"That harmony is now broken, and broken the world round: fragments, indeed, of what existed still exist, and hours of what is past still return; but month by month the darkness gains upon the day, and the ashes of the Antipodes glare through the night."

The image of the glaring ashes alludes to the lurid and spectacular sunsets of the previous autumn, shortly after the explosion of the island of Krakatau.

lately living eyes. It is not yet twenty years that this—I may well call it, wonderful—cloud has been, in its essence, recognizable. There is no description of it, so far as I have read, by any ancient observer. Neither Homer nor Virgil, neither Aristophanes nor Horace, acknowledge any such clouds among those compelled by Jove. Chaucer has no word of them, nor Dante; Milton none, nor Thomson. In modern times, Scott, Wordsworth, and Byron are alike unconscious of them; and the most observant and descriptive of scientific men, De Saussure,* is utterly silent concerning them. Taking up the traditions of air from the year before Scott's death, I am able, by my own constant and close observation, to certify you that in the forty following years (1831 to 1871 approximately—for the phenomena in question came on gradually)—no such clouds as these are, and are now often for months without intermission, were ever seen in the skies of England, France, or Italy.

In those old days, when weather was fine, it was luxuriously fine; when it was bad—it was often abominably bad, but it had its fit of temper and was done with it—it didn't sulk for three months without letting you see the sun,—nor send you one cyclone inside out, every Saturday afternoon, and another outside in, every Monday morning.

In fine weather the sky was either blue or clear in its light; the clouds, either white or golden, adding to, not abating, the lustre of the sky. In wet weather, there were two different species of clouds,—those of beneficent rain, which for distinction's sake I will call the non-electric rain-cloud, and those of storm, usually charged highly with electricity. The beneficent rain-cloud was indeed often extremely dull and grey for days together, but gracious nevertheless, felt to be doing good, and often to be delightful after drought; capable also of the most exquisite colouring, under certain conditions; and continually traversed in clear-

* Horace Bénédict de Saussure, Ruskin's "master" in geology and the author of *Voyages dans les Alpes* (1779–96).

ing by the rainbow:—and, secondly, the storm-cloud, always majestic, often dazzlingly beautiful, and felt also to be beneficent in its own way, affecting the mass of the air with vital agitation, and purging it from the impurity of all morbific elements.

In the entire system of the Firmament, thus seen and understood, there appeared to be, to all the thinkers of those ages, the incontrovertible and unmistakable evidence of a Divine Power in creation, which had fitted, as the air for human breath, so the clouds for human sight and nourishment;—the Father who was in heaven feeding day by day the souls of His children with marvels, and satisfying them with bread, and so filling their hearts with food and gladness. . . .

The first time I recognized the clouds brought by the plague-wind as distinct in character was in walking back from Oxford, after a hard day's work, to Abingdon, in the early spring of 1871: it would take too long to give you any account this evening of the particulars which drew my attention to them; but during the following months I had too frequent opportunities of verifying my first thoughts of them, and on the first of July in that year wrote the description of them which begins the *Fors Clavigera* of August, thus:—

"*It is the first of July, and I sit down to write by the dismallest light that ever yet I wrote by; namely, the light of this midsummer morning, in mid-England (Matlock, Derbyshire), in the year 1871.*

"*For the sky is covered with grey cloud;—not rain-cloud, but a dry black veil, which no ray of sunshine can pierce; partly diffused in mist, feeble mist, enough to make distant objects unintelligible, yet without any substance, or wreathing, or colour of its own. And everywhere the leaves of the trees are shaking fitfully, as they do before a thunderstorm; only not violently, but enough to show the passing to and fro of a strange, bitter, blighting wind. Dismal enough, had it been the first morning of its kind that summer had sent. But during all this spring, in London, and at Oxford, through meagre March, through changelessly sullen April, through despondent May, and darkened June, morning after morning has come grey-shrouded thus.*

"And it is a new thing to me, and a very dreadful one. I am fifty years old, and more; and since I was five, have gleaned the best hours of my life in the sun of spring and summer mornings; and I never saw such as these, till now.

"And the scientific men are busy as ants, examining the sun and the moon, and the seven stars, and can tell me all about them, I believe, by this time; and how they move, and what they are made of.

"And I do not care, for my part, two copper spangles how they move, nor what they are made of. I can't move them any other way than they go, nor make them of anything else, better than they are made. But I would care much and give much, if I could be told where this bitter wind comes from, and what it is made of.

"For, perhaps, with forethought, and fine laboratory science, one might make it of something else.

"It looks partly as if it were made of poisonous smoke; very possibly it may be: there are at least two hundred furnace chimneys in a square of two miles on every side of me. But mere smoke would not blow to and fro in that wild way. It looks more to me as if it were made of dead men's souls—such of them as are not gone yet where they have to go, and may be flitting hither and thither, doubting, themselves, of the fittest place for them.

"You know, if there are such things as souls, and if ever any of them haunt places where they have been hurt, there must be many above us, just now, displeased enough!"

The last sentence refers of course to the battles of the Franco-German campaign, which was especially horrible to me, in its digging, as the Germans should have known, a moat flooded with waters of death between the two nations for a century to come.

Since that Midsummer day, my attention, however otherwise occupied, has never relaxed in its record of the phenomena characteristic of the plague-wind; and I now define for you, as briefly as possible, the essential signs of it.

(1.) It is a wind of darkness,—all the former conditions of tormenting winds, whether from the north or east, were more or less capable of co-existing with sunlight, and often with steady and bright sunlight; but whenever, and wherever the plague-wind blows, be it but for ten minutes, the sky is darkened instantly.

(2.) It is a malignant *quality* of wind, unconnected with any one quarter of the compass; it blows indifferently from all, attaching its own bitterness and malice to the worst characters of the proper winds of each quarter. It will blow either with drenching rain, or dry rage, from the south,—with ruinous blasts from the west,—with bitterest chills from the north,—and with venomous blight from the east.

Its own favourite quarter, however, is the south-west, so that it is distinguished in its malignity equally from the Bise of Provence, which is a north wind always, and from our own old friend, the east.

(3.) It always blows *tremulously*, making the leaves of the trees shudder as if they were all aspens, but with a peculiar fitfulness which gives them—and I watch them this moment as I write—an expression of anger as well as of fear and distress. You may see the kind of quivering, and hear the ominous whimpering, in the gusts that precede a great thunderstorm; but plague-wind is more panic-struck, and feverish; and its sound is a hiss instead of a wail.

When I was last at Avallon, in South France, I went to see *Faust* played at the little country theatre: it was done with scarcely any means of pictorial effect, except a few old curtains, and a blue light or two. But the night on the Brocken was nevertheless extremely appalling to me,—a strange ghastliness being obtained in some of the witch scenes merely by fine management of gesture and drapery; and in the phantom scenes, by the half-palsied, half-furious, faltering or fluttering past of phantoms stumbling as into graves; as if of not only soulless, but senseless, Dead, moving with the very action, the rage, the decrepitude, and the trembling of the plague-wind.

(4.) Not only tremulous at every moment, it is also *intermittent* with a rapidity quite unexampled in former weather. There are, indeed, days—and weeks, on which it blows without cessation, and is as inevitable as the Gulf Stream; but also there are days when it is contending with healthy weather, and on such days it will remit for half an hour, and the sun will begin to show itself, and then the wind will come back and cover the whole sky with clouds in ten minutes; and so on, every half-hour, through the whole day; so that it is often impossible to go on with any kind of drawing in colour, the light being never for two seconds the same from morning till evening.

(5.) It degrades, while it intensifies, ordinary storm; but before I read you any description of its efforts in this kind, I must correct an impression which has got abroad through the papers, that I speak as if the plague-wind blew now always, and there were no more any natural weather. On the contrary, the winter of 1878–9 was one of the most healthy and lovely I ever saw ice in;—Coniston lake shone under the calm clear frost in one marble field, as strong as the floor of Milan Cathedral, half a mile across and four miles down; and the first entries in my diary which I read you shall be from the 22nd to 26th June, 1876, of perfectly lovely and natural weather: . . .

"*Monday, 26th June,* 1876.

Yesterday an entirely perfect summer light on the Old Man; Lancaster Bay all clear; Ingleborough and the great Pennine fault as on a map. Divine beauty of western colour on thyme and rose,—then twilight of clearest *warm* amber far into night, of *pale* amber all night long; hills dark-clear against it.

"And so it continued, only growing more intense in blue and sunlight, all day. After breakfast, I came in from the well under strawberry bed, to say I had never seen anything like it, so pure or intense, in Italy; and so it went glowing on, cloudless, with soft north wind, all day."

"16th July.

"The sunset almost too bright *through the blinds* for me to read Humboldt at tea by,—finally, new moon like a lime-light, reflected on breeze-struck water; traces, across dark calm, of reflected hills."

These extracts are, I hope, enough to guard you against the absurdity of supposing that it only means that I am myself soured, or doting, in my old age, and always in an ill humour. Depend upon it, when old men are worth any-thing, they are better-humoured than young ones; and have learned to see what good there is, and pleasantness, in the world they are likely so soon to have orders to quit.

Now then—take the following sequences of accurate de-scription of thunderstorm, *with* plague-wind. . . .

"*Brantwood, 13th August,* 1879.

"The most terrific and horrible thunderstorm, this morn-ing, I ever remember. It waked me at six, or a little before —then rolling incessantly, like railway luggage trains, quite ghastly in its mockery of them—the air one loathsome mass of sultry and foul fog, like smoke; scarcely raining at all, but increasing to heavier rollings, with flashes quivering vaguely through all the air, and at last terrific double streams of reddish-violent fire, not forked or zigzag, but rippled rivulets—two at the same instant some twenty to thirty degrees apart, and lasting on the eye at least half a second, with grand artillery-peals following; not rattling crashes, or irregular cracklings, but delivered volleys. It lasted an hour, then passed off, clearing a little, without rain to speak of,—not a glimpse of blue,—and now, half-past seven, seems settling down again into Manchester devil's darkness.

"Quarter to eight, morning.—Thunder returned, all the air collapsed into one black fog, the hills invisible, and scarcely visible the opposite shore; heavy rain in short fits, and frequent though less formidable, flashes, and shorter thunder. While I have written this sentence the cloud has again dissolved itself, like a nasty solution in a bottle, with miraculous and unnatural rapidity, and the hills are in sight again; a double-forked flash—rippled, I mean, like the others—starts into its frightful ladder of light between me and Wetherlam, as I raise my eyes. All black above, a rugged spray cloud on the Eaglet. (The 'Eaglet' is my own name for the bold and elevated crag to the west of the little lake above Coniston mines. It had no name among the country people, and is one of the most conspicuous features of the mountain chain, as seen from Brantwood.)

"Half-past eight.—Three times light and three times dark since last I wrote, and the darkness seeming each time as it settles more loathsome, at last stopping my reading in mere blindness. One lurid gleam of white cumulus in upper lead-blue sky, seen for half a minute through the sulphurous chimney-pot vomit of blackguardly cloud beneath, where its rags were thinnest."

"Thursday, 22nd Feb. 1883.

"Yesterday a fearfully dark mist all afternoon, with steady, south plague-wind of the bitterest, nastiest, poisonous blight, and fretful flutter. I could scarcely stay in the wood for the horror of it. To-day, really rather bright blue, and bright semi-cumuli, with the frantic Old Man blowing sheaves of lancets and chisels across the lake—not in strength enough, or whirl enough, to raise it in spray, but tracing every squall's outline in black on the silver grey waves, and whistling meanly, and as if on a flute made of a file."

"Sunday, 17th August, 1879.

"Raining in foul drizzle, slow and steady; sky pitch-dark, and I just get a little light by sitting in the bow-window; diabolic clouds over everything: and looking over my kitchen garden yesterday, I found it one miserable mass of weeds gone to seed, the roses in the higher garden putrefied into brown sponges, feeling like dead snails; and the half-ripe strawberries all rotten at the stalks."

(6.) And now I come to the most important sign of the plague-wind and the plague-cloud: that in bringing on their peculiar darkness, they *blanch* the sun instead of reddening it. And here I must note briefly to you the uselessness of observation by instruments, or machines, instead of eyes. In the first year when I had begun to notice the specialty of the plague-wind, I went of course to the Oxford observatory to consult its registrars. They have their anemometer always on the twirl, and can tell you the force, or at least the pace, of a gale, by day or night. But the anemometer can only record for you how often it has been driven round, not at all whether it went round *steadily*, or went round *trembling*. And on that point depends the entire question whether it is a plague breeze or a healthy one: and what's the use of telling you whether the wind's strong or not, when it can't tell you whether it's a strong medicine, or a strong poison? . . .

Blanched Sun,—blighted grass—blinded man.—If, in conclusion, you ask me for any conceivable cause or meaning of these things—I can tell you none, according to your modern beliefs; but I can tell you what meaning it would have borne to the men of old time. Remember, for the last twenty years, England, and all foreign nations, either tempting her, or following her, have blasphemed the name of God deliberately and openly; and have done iniquity by proclamation, every man doing as much injustice to his brother as it is in his power to do. Of states in such moral gloom every seer of old predicted the physical gloom, saying, "The light shall be darkened in the heavens thereof, and the stars shall withdraw their shining." All Greek, all Christian, all Jewish prophecy insists on the same truth through a thousand myths; but of all the chief, to former thought, was the fable of the Jewish warrior and prophet, for whom the sun hasted not to go down, with which I leave you to compare at leisure the physical result of your own wars and prophecies, as declared by your own elect journal not fourteen days ago,—that the Empire of England, on which formerly the sun never set, has become one on which he never rises.*

What is best to be done, do you ask me? The answer is plain. Whether you can affect the signs of the sky or not, you *can* the signs of the times. Whether you can bring the *sun* back or not, you can assuredly bring back your own cheerfulness, and your own honesty. You may not be able to say to the winds, "Peace; be still," but you can cease from the insolence of your own lips, and the troubling of your own passions. And all *that* it would be extremely well to do, even though the day *were* coming when the sun should be as darkness, and the moon as blood. But, the paths of rectitude and piety once regained, who shall say that the promise of old time would not be found to hold for us also?—"Bring ye all the tithes into my storehouse, and prove me now herewith, saith the Lord God, if I will not open you the windows of heaven, and pour you out a blessing, that there shall not be room enough to receive it."

* On January 2, the *Pall Mall Gazette* reported that the year in London had ended with a totally sunless week. In the month preceding Ruskin's lecture, the sun shone for an average of less than an hour a day.

Self

In *Fors Clavigera* Ruskin had interspersed autobiographical reminiscences of great calm and clarity among passages
of ferocious invective. In *The Storm-Cloud of the Nineteenth Century* he purged the unspent portion of his wrath
in a raging, apocalyptic denunciation of the whole century, from its fouled skies to its festering cities. Lecturing
on *The Storm-Cloud* was the act of exorcism which enabled
him to write *Præterita*. Although the cloud did not pass
from Ruskin's life, it lifted from his writing the moment he
turned to the past. Thereafter he mentioned only in his
letters and diaries the wasted, malevolent nature he perceived everywhere in the present. The great invocations in
Præterita to the skies and mountains mark his return to
the sacred nature he had worshiped in *Modern Painters*
and could again perceive with the ecstatic vision of his
youth.

Præterita was published at irregular intervals between
1885 and 1889, when a final siege of madness left Ruskin
capable of little more than signing his name. These last
years of consciousness were the bleakest of his life; yet they
produced the most charming autobiography in English and
the only book Ruskin wrote with the intention of giving
pleasure. He succeeded largely because of what he chose to
omit* or was later compelled to leave unwritten. As origi-

* The cardinal omission is Ruskin's marriage, which he passes over
in total silence. See the Preface to *Præterita*, below.

nally planned, the book was to have traced the course of his life until the death of Rose La Touche in 1875. In its final form, the last event is the death of his father in 1864. We catch no glimpse of Ruskin's embattled, embittered years of social criticism or the still darker years of his decline. Rose appears at the very end of *Præterita,* but only as a child who once walked with him in the garden of Denmark Hill. One never learns of the torment of their progressive estrangement, nor of her premature death, fever-wracked and insane. As the past encroached too painfully on the present, he lost control of his material and had to abandon the book.

Ruskin once described *Præterita* as "the 'natural' me— only . . . peeled carefully." He felt no compulsion to confess what he took no pleasure in recalling. His own unhurried delight—expansive, immediate, unbroken—in the people and places that had once delighted him is the heart of the book. Quite naturally, Ruskin himself was one of the people he found most interesting. No writer was more self-absorbed than he, but none ever had a more fascinating subject. To use his own phrase, *Præterita* describes the effect on his mind of meeting himself, by turning back, face to face. His egoism was unabashed yet uncannily objective, at once self-obsessed and ironically detached.

To pass from *Fors* or *The Storm-Cloud* to *Præterita* is to enter another world, in which pain has yielded to understanding, chaos to order, passion to peace. The tone of Ruskin's early writing is lyrical; that of his middle period is tragic; but his last book, like Shakespeare's last plays, exists in the uncharted realm beyond tragedy. The felicity of *Præterita* was, paradoxically, a product of the very madness which forced Ruskin to abandon the book. By alienating him from the present, his illnesses brought the past into serene and crystalline focus, giving him the detachment he needed in order to write engagingly about a child who was whipped whenever it cried.

One feels an uncanny closeness to the objects and events Ruskin describes in *Præterita,* together with his own remoteness from whatever anguish they aroused. The recall is total, yet totally unembittered. He sensed nothing strange in his enforced isolation from other children, the austerity of his nursery, or the unbending aloofness of his parents. During the day he stared at things with rapturous and riveted attention. In the evenings he sat recessed like "an Idol in a Niche" at his own table in the drawing room, while his mother knitted and his father read aloud. No household was ever more quietly self-engrossed, and none could have drawn out his eccentric genius more fully.

The very lack of distractions, including the distraction even of love, forced Ruskin to develop his analytic gifts almost from infancy. Sight and insight became a single instinctive act, the one unfailing pleasure of his life. It was perforce a solitary pleasure, and hence *Prœterita* is filled with things stared at in the privacy of his visual ecstasy. He led the most isolated of lives, yet was the most urgently communicative of writers, escaping through his words the solitude to which his eyes confined him.

To see clearly, he wrote in *Modern Painters,* is poetry, prophecy, and religion all in one. Preserving what he had seen was a sacred duty, and his notebooks and sketches were the reliquaries of his experience. With their aid he could recall not a memory of a memory but the terror or delight, taste or touch, of first contact. This clarity of recall so attracted Proust to *Prœterita* that he came to know it by heart. Proust also discovered a technique of composition, dependent upon memory, which Ruskin had employed before but never so effectively. The elusive unity of *Prœterita* stems from a series of linked images—the springs of the River Wandel, the crystal waters of the River Tay—which function like a recurrent musical phrase. *Prœterita* is a tissue of these intertwined motifs, at times scarcely glimpsed and at times elaborated with *"une vision au ralenti, presque microscopique,"* to use the phrase André Maurois applied both to Proust and Ruskin.

Although the book was written in lucid intervals between

seizures of madness, only at the end of Volume II does one
sense that Ruskin's mind was failing. He suspended publication for six months and in May of 1888 issued the superb
opening chapter of the final volume, "The Grande Chartreuse." Ruskin's account of his unconversion at the end
of the chapter is one of the most exquisitely written passages
in all of *Præterita*. Again one is struck by the resilience of
a mind which could triumph over such frequent and violent
derangement.

But Ruskin could no longer evade the coming of the
night wherein no man can work. He was already living a
posthumous existence when he began the last chapter,
"Joanna's Care," in the spring of 1889. It was intended as
a thank offering to Joan Severn, his Scottish cousin who at
the age of seventeen came to live at Denmark Hill and later
nursed him through his illnesses, bringing up her children
in the shadow of his madness. But he could not carry the
story beyond her arrival at the Ruskin household. The narrative began to move in reverse as the associations evoked by
her native Scotland led him helplessly into a long digression
on the landscape of Scott's novels.

Ruskin's hand had become so unsteady that he was forced
to dictate most of "Joanna's Care" to Mrs. Severn. As she
recorded his infinitely grateful but confused words, he saw
by his side not a middle-aged matron but "my little
Joanie." And in place of the dying Rose of the 1870s, his
memory offered him the fairer image of a young girl in his
garden, where he had once known "the peace, and hope,
and loveliness of . . . Elysian walks with Joanie, and Paradisiacal with Rosie, under the peach-blossom branches by
the little glittering stream which I had paved with crystal
for them. . . . 'Eden-land' Rosie calls it." *Calls* rather than
called because time no longer separated his recollection from
her words themselves. In the closing paragraphs of *Præterita*
Ruskin had finally recaptured the past. But it was a barren
victory, for at the moment of achievement his mind became
a blank, and so remained until his death in 1900.

It is surprising that Ruskin could have written *Præterita* at all; it is astonishing that he wrote so great a book under such great adversity. His life was a long, unavailing struggle to preserve his mental balance. In his works, however, his sanity triumphs over his sickness and his words retain their life. Reading *Modern Painters* still gives one new eyes; reading *Fors Clavigera* enlarges one's insight into consciousness; and the message of *Unto This Last*—"the message that ye have heard from the beginning, that we love one another"— appears insane only in a world that is itself insane.

—J. D. R.

PRAETERITA

Preface

I have written these sketches of effort and incident in former years for my friends; and for those of the public who have been pleased by my books.

I have written them therefore, frankly, garrulously, and at ease; speaking, of what it gives me joy to remember, at any length I like—sometimes very carefully of what I think it may be useful for others to know; and passing in total silence things which I have no pleasure in reviewing, and which the reader would find no help in the account of. My described life has thus become more amusing than I expected to myself, as I summoned its long past scenes for present scrutiny:—its main methods of study, and principles of work, I feel justified in commending to other students; and very certainly any habitual readers of my books will understand them better, for having knowledge as complete as I can give them of the personal character which, without endeavour to conceal, I yet have never taken pains to display, and even, now and then, felt some freakish pleasure in exposing to the chance of misinterpretation.

I write these few prefatory words on my father's birthday, in what was once my nursery in his old house,—to which he brought my mother and me, sixty-two years since, I being then four years old. What would otherwise in the following pages have been little more than an old man's recreation in gathering visionary flowers in fields of youth, has taken, as I wrote, the nobler aspect of a dutiful offering at the grave of parents who trained my childhood to all the good it could attain, and whose memory makes declining life cheerful in the hope of being soon again with them.

HERNE HILL, 10*th May*, 1885.

*The Springs of Wandel**

I am, and my father was before me, a violent Tory of the old school;—Walter Scott's school, that is to say, and Homer's. I name these two out of the numberless great Tory writers, because they were my own two masters. I had Walter Scott's novels, and the *Iliad* (Pope's translation), for constant reading when I was a child, on week-days: on Sunday, their effect was tempered by *Robinson Crusoe* and the *Pilgrim's Progress;* my mother having it deeply in her heart to make an evangelical clergyman of me. Fortunately, I had an aunt more evangelical than my mother; and my aunt gave me cold mutton for Sunday's dinner, which—as I much preferred it hot—greatly diminished the influence of the *Pilgrim's Progress;* and the end of the matter was, that I got all the noble imaginative teaching of Defoe and Bunyan, and yet—am not an evangelical clergyman.

I had, however, still better teaching than theirs, and that compulsorily, and every day of the week.

Walter Scott and Pope's Homer were reading of my own election, and my mother forced me, by steady daily toil, to learn long chapters of the Bible by heart; as well as to read it every syllable through, aloud, hard names and all, from Genesis to the Apocalypse, about once a year: and to that discipline—patient, accurate, and resolute—I owe, not only a knowledge of the book, which I find occasionally service-able, but much of my general power of taking pains, and the best part of my taste in literature. From Walter Scott's

* Ruskin reprinted the major part of the first two chapters, with slight revision, from *Fors Clavigera*. However, over nine-tenths of *Præterita* consists of new material written between 1885 and 1889.

novels I might easily, as I grew older, have fallen to other people's novels; and Pope might, perhaps, have led me to take Johnson's English, or Gibbon's, as types of language; but, once knowing the 32nd of Deuteronomy, the 119th Psalm, the 15th of 1st Corinthians, the Sermon on the Mount, and most of the Apocalypse, every syllable by heart, and having always a way of thinking with myself what words meant, it was not possible for me, even in the foolishest times of youth, to write entirely superficial or formal English; and the affectation of trying to write like Hooker and George Herbert was the most innocent I could have fallen into.

From my own chosen masters, then, Scott and Homer, I learned the Toryism which my best after-thought has only served to confirm.

That is to say, a most sincere love of kings, and dislike of everybody who attempted to disobey them. Only, both by Homer and Scott, I was taught strange ideas about kings, which I find for the present much obsolete; for, I perceived that both the author of the *Iliad* and the author of *Waverley* made their kings, or king-loving persons, do harder work than anybody else. Tydides or Idomeneus always killed twenty Trojans to other people's one, and Redgauntlet speared more salmon than any of the Solway fishermen; and —which was particularly a subject of admiration to me—I observed that they not only did more, but in proportion to their doings *got* less, than other people—nay, that the best of them were even ready to govern for nothing! and let their followers divide any quantity of spoil or profit. Of late it has seemed to me that the idea of a king has become exactly the contrary of this, and that it has been supposed the duty of superior persons generally to govern less, and get more, than anybody else. So that it was, perhaps, quite as well that in those early days my contemplation of existent kingship was a very distant one.

The aunt who gave me cold mutton on Sundays was my father's sister: she lived at Bridge-end, in the town of Perth, and had a garden full of gooseberry-bushes, sloping down to the Tay, with a door opening to the water, which ran past it, clear-brown over the pebbles three or four feet deep; swift-eddying,—an infinite thing for a child to look down into.

My father began business as a wine-merchant, with no capital, and a considerable amount of debts bequeathed him by my grandfather.* He accepted the bequest, and paid them all before he began to lay by anything for himself,—for which his best friends called him a fool, and I, without expressing any opinion as to his wisdom, which I knew in such matters to be at least equal to mine, have written on the granite slab over his grave that he was "an entirely honest merchant." As days went on he was able to take a house in Hunter Street, Brunswick Square, No. 54, (the windows of it, fortunately for me, commanded a view of a marvellous iron post, out of which the water-carts were filled through beautiful litle trapdoors, by pipes like boa-constrictors; and I was never weary of contemplating that mystery, and the delicious dripping consequent); and as years went on, and I came to be four or five years old, he could command a postchaise and pair for two months in the summer, by help of which, with my mother and me, he went the round of his country customers (who liked to see the principal of the house his own traveller); so that, at a jogtrot pace, and through the panoramic opening of the four windows of a postchaise, made more panoramic still to me because my seat was a little bracket in front, (for we used to hire the chaise regularly for the two months out of Long Acre, and so could have it bracketed and pocketed as we liked,) I saw all the high-roads, and most of the cross ones, of England and Wales; and great part of lowland Scotland, as far as Perth, where every other year we spent the whole summer: and I used to read the *Abbot* at Kinross, and the *Monastery* in Glen Farg, which I confused with "Glen-

* John Thomas Ruskin, who had gone mad and taken his own life in 1817, a year before Ruskin's parents—first cousins—were married.

dearg," and thought that the White Lady had as certainly lived by the streamlet in that glen of the Ochils, as the Queen of Scots in the island of Loch Leven.

To my farther great benefit, as I grew older, I thus saw nearly all the noblemen's houses in England; in reverent and healthy delight of uncovetous admiration,—perceiving, as soon as I could perceive any political truth at all, that it was probably much happier to live in a small house, and have Warwick Castle to be astonished at, than to live in Warwick Castle and have nothing to be astonished at; but that, at all events, it would not make Brunswick Square in the least more pleasantly habitable, to pull Warwick Castle down. And at this day, though I have kind invitations enough to visit America, I could not, even for a couple of months, live in a country so miserable as to possess no castles.

Nevertheless, having formed my notion of kinghood chiefly from the FitzJames of the *Lady of the Lake,* and of noblesse from the Douglas there, and the Douglas in *Marmion,* a painful wonder soon arose in my child-mind, why the castles should now be always empty. Tantallon was there; but no Archibald of Angus:—Stirling, but no Knight of Snowdoun. The galleries and gardens of England were beautiful to see—but his Lordship and her Ladyship were always in town, said the housekeepers and gardeners. Deep yearning took hold of me for a kind of "Restoration," which I began slowly to feel that Charles the Second had not altogether effected, though I always wore a gilded oak-apple very piously in my button-hole on the 29th of May. It seemed to me that Charles the Second's Restoration had been, as compared with the Restoration I wanted, much as that gilded oak-apple to a real apple. And as I grew wiser, the desire for sweet pippins instead of bitter ones, and Living Kings instead of dead ones, appeared to me rational as well as romantic; and gradually it has become the main purpose of my life to grow pippins, and its chief hope, to see Kings.

I have never been able to trace these prejudices to any royalty of descent: of my father's ancestors I know nothing, nor of my mother's more than that my maternal grandmother was the landlady of the Old King's Head in Market Street, Croydon; and I wish she were alive again, and I could paint her Simone Memmi's King's Head, for a sign.

My maternal grandfather was, as I have said, a sailor, who used to embark, like Robinson Crusoe, at Yarmouth, and come back at rare intervals, making himself very delightful at home. I have an idea he had something to do with the herring business, but am not clear on that point; my mother never being much communicative concerning it. He spoiled her, and her (younger) sister, with all his heart, when he was at home; unless there appeared any tendency to equivocation, or imaginative statements, on the part of the children, which were always unforgiveable. My mother being once perceived by him to have distinctly told him a lie, he sent the servant out forthwith to buy an entire bundle of new broom twigs to whip her with. "They did not hurt me so much as one" (twig) "would have done," said my mother, "but I *thought* a good deal of it."

My maternal grandfather was killed at two-and-thirty, by trying to ride, instead of walk, into Croydon; he got his leg crushed by his horse against a wall; and died of the hurt's mortifying. My mother was then seven or eight years old, and, with her sister, was sent to quite a fashionable (for Croydon) day-school, Mrs. Rice's: where my mother was taught evangelical principles, and became the pattern girl and best needlewoman in the school; and where my aunt absolutely refused evangelical principles, and became the plague and pet of it.

My mother, being a girl of great power, with not a little pride, grew more and more exemplary in her entirely conscientious career, much laughed at, though much beloved, by her sister; who had more wit, less pride, and no conscience. At last my mother, formed into a consummate housewife, was sent for to Scotland to take care of my paternal grandfather's house; who was gradually ruining himself; and who at last effectually ruined, and killed, himself. My father came up to London; was a clerk in a merchant's house for nine years, without a holiday; then began business on his own account; paid his father's debts; and married his exemplary Croydon cousin.

Meantime my aunt had remained in Croydon, and married a baker. By the time I was four years old, and beginning to recollect things,—my father rapidly taking higher commercial position in London,—there was traceable—though to me, as a child, wholly incomprehensible,—just the least possible shade of shyness on the part of Hunter Street, Brunswick Square, towards Market Street, Croydon. But whenever my father was ill,—and hard work and sorrow had already set their mark on him,—we all went down to Croydon to be petted by my homely aunt; and walk on Duppas Hill, and on the heather of Addington.

My aunt lived in the little house still standing—or which was so four months ago—the fashionablest in Market Street, having actually two windows over the shop, in the second story; but I never troubled myself about that superior part of the mansion, unless my father happened to be making drawings in Indian ink, when I would sit reverently by and watch; my chosen domains being, at all other times, the shop, the bakehouse, and the stones round the spring of crystal water at the back door (long since let down into the modern sewer); and my chief companion, my aunt's dog, Towzer, whom she had taken pity on when he was a snappish, starved vagrant; and made a brave and affectionate dog of: which was the kind of thing she did for every living creature that came in her way, all her life long.

Contented, by help of these occasional glimpses of the rivers of Paradise, I lived until I was more than four years old in Hunter Street, Brunswick Square, the greater part of the year; for a few weeks in the summer breathing country air by taking lodgings in small cottages (real cottages, not villas, so-called) either about Hampstead, or at Dulwich, at

"Mrs. Ridley's," the last of a row in a lane which led out into the Dulwich fields on one side, and was itself full of buttercups in spring, and blackberries in autumn. But my chief remaining impressions of those days are attached to Hunter Street. My mother's general principles of first treatment were, to guard me with steady watchfulness from all avoidable pain or danger; and, for the rest, to let me amuse myself as I liked, provided I was neither fretful nor troublesome. But the law was, that I should find my own amusement. No toys of any kind were at first allowed;—and the pity of my Croydon aunt for my monastic poverty in this respect was boundless. On one of my birthdays, thinking to overcome my mother's resolution by splendour of temptation, she bought the most radiant Punch and Judy she could find in all the Soho bazaar—as big as a real Punch and Judy, all dressed in scarlet and gold, and that would dance, tied to the leg of a chair. I must have been greatly impressed, for I remember well the look of the two figures, as my aunt herself exhibited their virtues. My mother was obliged to accept them; but afterwards quietly told me it was not right that I should have them; and I never saw them again.

Nor did I painfully wish, what I was never permitted for an instant to hope, or even imagine, the possession of such things as one saw in toy-shops. I had a bunch of keys to play with, as long as I was capable only of pleasure in what glittered and jingled; as I grew older, I had a cart, and a ball; and when I was five or six years old, two boxes of well-cut wooden bricks. With these modest, but, I still think, entirely sufficient possessions, and being always summarily whipped if I cried, did not do as I was bid, or tumbled on the stairs, I soon attained serene and secure methods of life and motion; and could pass my days contentedly in tracing the squares and comparing the colours of my carpet;—examining the knots in the wood of the floor, or counting the bricks in the opposite houses; with rapturous intervals of excitement during the filling of the water-cart, through its leathern pipe, from the dripping iron post at the pavement edge; or the still more admirable proceedings of the turn-cock, when he turned and turned till a fountain sprang up in the middle of the street. But the carpet, and what patterns I could find in bed-covers, dresses, or wall-papers to be examined, were my chief resources, and my attention to the particulars in these was soon so accurate, that when at three and a half I was taken to have my portrait painted by Mr. Northcote, I had not been ten minutes alone with him before I asked him why there were holes in his carpet. The portrait in question represents a very pretty child with yellow hair, dressed in a white frock like a girl, with a broad light-blue sash and blue shoes to match; the feet of the child wholesomely large in proportion to its body; and the shoes still more wholesomely large in proportion to the feet.

These articles of my daily dress were all sent to the old painter for perfect realization; but they appear in the picture more remarkable than they were in my nursery, because I am represented as running in a field at the edge of a wood with the trunks of its trees striped across in the manner of Sir Joshua Reynolds; while two rounded hills, as blue as my shoes, appear in the distance, which were put in by the painter at my own request; for I had already been once, if not twice, taken to Scotland; and my Scottish nurse having always sung to me as we approached the Tweed or Esk,—

> "For Scotland, my darling, lies full in thy view,
>   With her barefooted lassies, and mountains so blue,"

the idea of distant hills was connected in my mind with approach to the extreme felicities of life, in my Scottish aunt's garden of gooseberry bushes, sloping to the Tay. But that, when old Mr. Northcote asked me (little thinking, I fancy, to get any answer so explicit) what I would like to have in the distance of my picture, I should have said "blue hills" instead of "gooseberry bushes," appears to me—and I think without any morbid tendency to think over-much

of myself—a fact sufficiently curious, and not without promise, in a child of that age.

I think it should be related also that having, as aforesaid,
been steadily whipped if I was troublesome, my formed
habit of serenity was greatly pleasing to the old painter;
for I sat contentedly motionless, counting the holes in his
carpet, or watching him squeeze his paint out of its blad-
ders,—a beautiful operation, indeed, to my thinking;—but
I do not remember taking any interest in Mr. Northcote's
application of the pigments to the canvas; my ideas of delightful art, in that respect, involving indispensably the
possession of a large pot, filled with paint of the brightest
green, and of a brush which would come out of it soppy.
But my quietude was so pleasing to the old man that he
begged my father and mother to let me sit to him for the
face of a child which he was painting in a classical subject;
where I was accordingly represented as reclining on a leopard skin, and having a thorn taken out of my foot by a wild
man of the woods.

In all these particulars, I think the treatment, or accidental conditions, of my childhood, entirely right, for a
child of my temperament: but the mode of my introduction
to literature appears to me questionable, and I am not prepared to carry it out in St. George's schools, without much
modification. I absolutely declined to learn to read by
syllables; but would get an entire sentence by heart with
great facility, and point with accuracy to every word in the
page as I repeated it. As, however, when the words were
once displaced, I had no more to say, my mother gave up,
for the time, the endeavour to teach me to read, hoping
only that I might consent, in process of years, to adopt the
popular system of syllabic study. But I went on to amuse
myself, in my own way, learnt whole words at a time, as I
did patterns; and at five years old was sending for my "second volumes" to the circulating library.

This effort to learn the words in their collective aspect,
was assisted by my real admiration of the look of printed

type, which I began to copy for my pleasure, as other children draw dogs and horses. The following inscription, facsimile'd from the fly-leaf of my *Seven Champions of Christendom* (judging from the independent views taken in it of the character of the letter L, and the relative elevation of G,) I believe to be an extremely early art study of this class; and as by the will of Fors, the first lines of the

note, written after an interval of fifty years, underneath my copy of it, in direction to Mr. Burgess, presented some notable points of correspondence with it, I thought it well he should engrave them together, as they stood.

My mother had, as she afterwards told me, solemnly "devoted me to God" before I was born; in imitation of Hannah.

Very good women are remarkably apt to make away with their children prematurely, in this manner: the real meaning of the pious act being, that, as the sons of Zebedee are not (or at least they hope not), to sit on the right and left of Christ, in His kingdom, their own sons may perhaps, they think, in time be advanced to that respectable position in eternal life; especially if they ask Christ very humbly for it every day: and they always forget in the most naïve way that the position is not His to give!

"Devoting me to God," meant, as far as my mother knew herself what she meant, that she would try to send me to college, and make a clergyman of me: and I was accordingly bred for "the Church." My father, who—rest be to his soul —had the exceedingly bad habit of yielding to my mother in large things and taking his own way in little ones, allowed me, without saying a word, to be thus withdrawn from the sherry trade as an unclean thing; not without some pardonable participation in my mother's ultimate views for me. For, many and many a year afterwards, I remember, while he was speaking to one of our artist friends, who admired Raphael, and greatly regretted my endeavours to interfere with that popular taste,—while my father and he were condoling with each other on my having been impudent enough to think I could tell the public about Turner and Raphael,—instead of contenting myself, as I ought, with explaining the way of their souls' salvation to them— and what an amiable clergyman was lost in me,—"Yes," said my father, with tears in his eyes—(true and tender tears, as ever father shed,) "he would have been a Bishop."

Luckily for me, my mother, under these distinct impressions of her own duty, and with such latent hopes of my future eminence, took me very early to church;—where, in spite of my quiet habits, and my mother's golden vinaigrette, always indulged to me there, and there only, with its lid unclasped that I might see the wreathed open pattern above the sponge, I found the bottom of the pew so extremely dull a place to keep quiet in, (my best storybooks being also taken away from me in the morning,) that, as I have somewhere said before, the horror of Sunday used even to cast its prescient gloom as far back in the week as Friday —and all the glory of Monday, with church seven days removed again, was no equivalent for it.

Notwithstanding, I arrived at some abstract in my own mind of the Rev. Mr. Howell's sermons; and occasionally, in imitation of him, preached a sermon at home over the red sofa cushions;—this performance being always called for by my mother's dearest friends, as the great accomplishment of my childhood. The sermon was, I believe, some eleven words long; very exemplary, it seems to me, in that respect—and I still think must have been the purest gospel, for I know it began with, "People, be good."

We seldom had company, even on week days; and I was never allowed to come down to dessert, until much later in life—when I was able to crack nuts neatly. I was then permitted to come down to crack other people's nuts for them —(I hope they liked the ministration)—but never to have any myself; nor anything else of dainty kind, either then or at other times. Once at Hunter Street, I recollect my mother giving me three raisins, in the forenoon, out of the store cabinet; and I remember perfectly the first time I tasted custard, in our lodgings in Norfolk Street—where we had gone while the house was being painted, or cleaned, or something. My father was dining in the front room, and did not finish his custard; and my mother brought me the bottom of it into the back room.

But for the reader's better understanding of such further progress of my poor little life as I may trespass on his patience in describing, it is now needful that I give some account of my father's mercantile position in London.

The firm of which he was head partner may be yet remembered by some of the older city houses, as carrying on their business in a small counting-house on the first floor of narrow premises, in as narrow a thoroughfare of East London,—Billiter Street, the principal traverse from Leadenhall Street into Fenchurch Street.

The names of the three partners were given in full on their brass plate under the counting-house bell,—Ruskin, Telford, and Domecq.

Mr. Domecq's name should have been the first, by rights, for my father and Mr. Telford were only his agents. He was the sole proprietor of the estate which was the main capital of the firm,—the vineyard of Macharnudo, the most precious hillside, for growth of white wine, in the Spanish peninsula. The quality of the Macharnudo vintage essentially fixed the standard of Xeres "sack," or "dry"—secco—sherris, or sherry, from the days of Henry the Fifth to our own;—the unalterable and unrivalled chalk-marl of it putting a strength into the grape which age can only enrich and darken,—never impair.

Mr. Peter Domecq was, I believe, Spanish born; and partly French, partly English bred; a man of strictest honour, and kindly disposition; how descended, I do not know; how he became possessor of his vineyard, I do not know; what position he held, when young, in the firm of Gordon, Murphy, and Company, I do not know; but in their house he watched their head clerk, my father, during his nine years of duty, and when the house broke up, asked him to be his own agent in England. My father saw that he could fully trust Mr. Domecq's honour, and feeling;—but not so fully either his sense, or his industry; and insisted, though taking only his agent's commission, on being both nominally, and practically, the head-partner of the firm.

Mr. Domecq lived chiefly in Paris; rarely visiting his Spanish estate, but having perfect knowledge of the proper processes of its cultivation, and authority over its labourers almost like a chief's over his clan. He kept the wines at the highest possible standard; and allowed my father to manage all matters concerning their sale, as he thought best. The second partner, Mr. Henry Telford, brought into the business what capital was necessary for its London branch. The premises in Billiter Street belonged to him; and he had a pleasant country house at Widmore, near Bromley; a quite far-away Kentish village in those days.

He was a perfect type of an English country gentleman of moderate fortune; unmarried, living with three unmarried sisters,—who, in the refinement of their highly educated, unpretending, benevolent, and felicitous lives, remain in my memory more like the figures in a beautiful story than realities. Neither in story, nor in reality, have I ever again heard of, or seen, anything like Mr. Henry Telford;—so gentle, so humble, so affectionate, so clear in common sense, so fond of horses,—and so entirely incapable of doing, thinking, or saying, anything that had the slightest taint in it of the racecourse or the stable.

Yet I believe he never missed any great race; passed the greater part of his life on horseback; and hunted during the whole Leicestershire season; but never made a bet, never had a serious fall, and never hurt a horse. Between him and my father there was absolute confidence, and the utmost friendship that could exist without community of pursuit. My father was greatly proud of Mr. Telford's standing among the country gentlemen; and Mr. Telford was affectionately respectful to my father's steady industry and infallible commercial instinct. Mr. Telford's actual part in the conduct of the business was limited to attendance in the counting-house during two months at Midsummer, when my father took his holiday, and sometimes for a month at the beginning of the year, when he travelled for orders. At these times Mr. Telford rode into London daily from Widmore, signed what letters and bills needed signature, read the papers, and rode home again; any matters needing deliberation were referred to my father, or awaited his return. All the family at Widmore would have been limitlessly kind to my mother and me, if they had been permitted any opportunity; but my mother always felt, in cultivated society,—and was too proud to feel with patience,—the defects of her own early education; and therefore (which was the true and fatal sign of such defect) never familiarly visited any one whom she did not feel to be, in some sort, her inferior.

Nevertheless, Mr. Telford had a singularly important influence in my education. By, I believe, his sisters' advice, he gave me, as soon as it was published, the illustrated edition of Rogers's *Italy*. This book was the first means I had of looking carefully at Turner's work: and I might, not without some appearance of reason, attribute to the gift the entire direction of my life's energies. But it is the great error of thoughtless biographers to attribute to the accident which introduces some new phase of character, all the circumstances of character which gave the accident importance. The essential point to be noted, and accounted for, was that I could understand Turner's work, when I saw it;—not by what chance, or in what year, it was first seen. Poor Mr. Telford, nevertheless, was always held by papa and mamma primarily responsible for my Turner insanities.

In a more direct, though less intended way, his help to me was important. For, before my father thought it right to hire a carriage for the above-mentioned Midsummer holiday, Mr. Telford always lent us his own travelling chariot.

Now the old English chariot is the most luxurious of travelling carriages, for two persons, or even for two persons and so much of third personage as I possessed at three years old. The one in question was hung high, so that we could see well over stone dykes and average hedges out of it; such elevation being attained by the old-fashioned folding steps, with a lovely padded cushion fitting into the recess of the door,—steps which it was one of my chief travelling delights to see the hostlers fold up and down; though my delight was painfully alloyed by envious ambition to be allowed to do it myself:—but I never was,—lest I should pinch my fingers.

The "dickey,"—(to think that I should never till this moment have asked myself the derivation of that word, and now be unable to get at it!)—being, typically, that commanding seat in her Majesty's mail, occupied by the Guard; and classical, even in modern literature, as the scene of Mr. Bob Sawyer's arrangements with Sam,—was thrown far back in Mr. Telford's chariot, so as to give perfectly comfortable room for the legs (if one chose to travel outside on fine days), and to afford beneath it spacious area to the boot, a storehouse of rearward miscellaneous luggage. Over which—with all the rest of forward and superficial luggage —my nurse Anne presided, both as guard and packer; unrivalled, she, in the flatness and precision of her in-laying of dresses, as in turning of pancakes; the fine precision, observe, meaning also the easy wit and invention of her art; for, no more in packing a trunk than commanding a campaign, is precision possible without foresight.

Among the people whom one must miss out of one's life, dead, or worse than dead, by the time one is past fifty, I can only say for my own part, that the one I practically and truly miss most next to father and mother, (and putting losses of imaginary good out of the question,) is this Anne, my father's nurse, and mine. She was one of our "many," (our many being always but few,) and from her girlhood to her old age, the entire ability of her life was given to serving us. She had a natural gift and speciality for doing disagreeable things; above all, the service of a sick room; so that she was never quite in her glory unless some of us were ill. She had also some parallel speciality for *saying* disagreeable things; and might be relied upon to give the extremely darkest view of any subject, before proceeding to ameliorative action upon it. And she had a very creditable and republican aversion to doing immediately, or in set terms, as she was bid; so that when my mother and she got old together, and my mother became very imperative and particular about having her teacup set on one side of her little round table, Anne would observantly and punctiliously put it always on the other; which caused my mother to state to me, every morning after breakfast, gravely, that if ever a woman in this world was possessed by the Devil, Anne was that woman. But in spite of these momentary and petulant aspirations to liberality and independence of character, poor Anne remained very servile in soul all her days; and was altogether occupied, from the age of fifteen to seventy-two, in doing other people's wills instead of her own, and seeking other people's good instead of her own: nor did I ever hear on any occasion of her doing harm to a human being, except by saving two hundred and some odd pounds for her relations; in consequence of which some of them, after her funeral, did not speak to the rest for several months.

The dickey then aforesaid, being indispensable for our guard Anne, was made wide enough for two, that my father might go outside also when the scenery and day were fine. The entire equipage was not a light one of its kind; but, the luggage being carefully limited, went gaily behind good horses on the then perfectly smooth mail roads; and posting, in those days, being universal, so that at the leading inns in every country town, the cry "Horses out!" down the yard, as one drove up, was answered, often instantly, always within five minutes, by the merry trot through the archway of the booted and bright-jacketed rider, with his caparisoned pair,—there was no driver's seat in front: and the four large, admirably fitting and sliding windows, admitting no drop of rain when they were up, and never sticking as they were let down, formed one large moving oriel, out of which one saw the country round, to the full half of the horizon. My own prospect was more extended still, for my seat was the little box containing my clothes, strongly made, with a cushion on one end of it; set upright in front (and well forward), between my father and mother. I was thus not the least in their way, and my horizon of sight the widest possible. When no object of particular interest presented itself, I trotted, keeping time with the postboy on my trunk cushion for a saddle, and whipped my father's legs for horses; at first theoretically only, with dexterous motion of wrist; but ultimately in a quite practical and efficient manner, my father having presented me with a silver-mounted postillion's whip.

The Midsummer holiday, for better enjoyment of which Mr. Telford provided us with these luxuries, began usually on the fifteenth of May, or thereabouts;—my father's birthday was the tenth; on that day I was always allowed to gather the gooseberries for his first gooseberry pie of the year, from the tree between the buttresses on the north wall of the Herne Hill garden; so that we could not leave before that *festa*. The holiday itself consisted in a tour for orders through half the English counties; and a visit (if the counties lay northward) to my aunt in Scotland.

The mode of journeying was as fixed as that of our home life. We went from forty to fifty miles a day, starting always early enough in the morning to arrive comfortably to four o'clock dinner. Generally, therefore, getting off at six o'clock, a stage or two were done before breakfast, with the dew on the grass, and first scent from the hawthorns; if in the course of the midday drive there were any gentleman's house to be seen,—or, better still, a lord's—or, best of all, a duke's,—my father baited the horses, and took my mother and me reverently through the state rooms; always speaking a little under our breath to the housekeeper, major-domo, or other authority in charge; and gleaning worshipfully what fragmentary illustrations of the history and domestic ways of the family might fall from their lips.

In analyzing above, page 464, the effect on my mind of all this, I have perhaps a little antedated the supposed resultant impression that it was probably happier to live in a small house than a large one. But assuredly, while I never to this day pass a lattice-windowed cottage without wishing to be its cottager, I never yet saw the castle which I envied to its lord; and although, in the course of these many worshipful pilgrimages, I gathered curiously extensive knowledge, both of art and natural scenery, afterwards infinitely useful, it is evident to me in retrospect that my own character and affections were little altered by them; and that the personal feeling and native instinct of me had been fastened, irrevocably, long before, to things modest, humble, and pure in peace, under the low red roofs of Croydon, and by the cress-set rivulets in which the sand danced and minnows darted above the Springs of Wandel.   [Vol. I, Chap. 1]

Herne-Hill Almond Blossoms

When I was about four years old my father found himself able to buy the lease of a house on Herne Hill, a rustic eminence four miles south of the "Standard in Cornhill"; of which the leafy seclusion remains, in all essential points of character, unchanged to this day: certain Gothic splendours, lately indulged in by our wealthier neighbours, being the only serious innovations; and these are so graciously concealed by the fine trees of their grounds, that the passing viator remains unappalled by them; and I can still walk up and down the piece of road between the Fox tavern and the Herne Hill station, imagining myself four years old.

Our house was the northernmost of a group which stand accurately on the top or dome of the hill, where the ground is for a small space level, as the snows are, (I understand,) on the dome of Mont Blanc; presently falling, however, in what may be, in the London clay formation, considered a precipitous slope, to our valley of Chamouni (or of Dulwich) on the east; and with a softer descent into Cold Harbour-lane on the west: on the south, no less beautifully declining to the dale of the Effra, (doubtless shortened from Effrena, signifying the "Unbridled" river; recently, I regret to say, bricked over for the convenience of Mr. Biffin, chemist, and others); while on the north, prolonged indeed with slight depression some half mile or so, and receiving, in the parish of Lambeth, the chivalric title of "Champion Hill," it plunges down at last to efface itself in the plains of Peckham, and the rural barbarism of Goose Green.

The group, of which our house was the quarter, consisted of two precisely similar partner-couples of houses, gardens and all to match; still the two highest blocks of buildings seen from Norwood on the crest of the ridge; so that the house itself, three-storied, with garrets above, commanded, in those comparatively smokeless days, a very notable view from its garret windows, of the Norwood hills on one side, and the winter sunrise over them; and of the valley of the Thames on the other, with Windsor telescopically clear in the distance, and Harrow, conspicuous always in fine weather to open vision against the summer sunset. It had front and back garden in sufficient proportion to its size; the front, richly set with old evergreens, and well-grown lilac and laburnum; the back, seventy yards long by twenty wide, renowned over all the hill for its pears and apples, which had been chosen with extreme care by our predecessor, (shame on me to forget the name of a man to whom I owe so much!)—and possessing also a strong old mulberry tree, a tall white-heart cherry tree, a black Kentish one, and an almost unbroken hedge, all round, of alternate gooseberry and currant bush; decked, in due season, (for the ground was wholly beneficent,) with magical splendour of abundant fruit: fresh green, soft amber, and rough-bristled crimson bending the spinous branches; clustered pearl and pendant ruby joyfully discoverable under the large leaves that looked like vine.

The differences of primal importance which I observed between the nature of this garden, and that of Eden, as I had imagined it, were, that, in this one, *all* the fruit was forbidden; and there were no companionable beasts: in other respects the little domain answered every purpose of Paradise to me; and the climate, in that cycle of our years, allowed me to pass most of my life in it. My mother never gave me more to learn than she knew I could easily get learnt, if I set myself honestly to work, by twelve o'clock. She never allowed anything to disturb me when my task was set; if it was not said rightly by twelve o'clock, I was kept in till I knew it, and in general, even when Latin Grammar came to supplement the Psalms, I was my own master for at least an hour before half-past one dinner, and for the rest of the afternoon.

My mother, herself finding her chief personal pleasure in her flowers, was often planting or pruning beside me, at least if I chose to stay beside *her*. I never thought of doing anything behind her back which I would not have done before her face; and her presence was therefore no restraint to me; but, also, no particular pleasure, for, from having always been left so much alone, I had generally my own little affairs to see after; and, on the whole, by the time I was seven years old, was already getting too independent, mentally, even of my father and mother; and, having nobody else to be dependent upon, began to lead a very small, perky, contented, conceited, Cock-Robinson-Crusoe sort of life, in the central point which it appeared to me, (as it must naturally appear to geometrical animals,) that I occupied in the universe.

This was partly the fault of my father's modesty; and partly of his pride. He had so much more confidence in my mother's judgment as to such matters than in his own, that he never ventured even to help, much less to cross her, in the conduct of my education; on the other hand, in the fixed purpose of making an ecclesiastical gentleman of me, with the superfinest of manners, and access to the highest circles of fleshly and spiritual society, the visits to Croydon, where I entirely loved my aunt, and young baker-cousins, became rarer and more rare: the society of our neighbours on the hill could not be had without breaking up our regular and sweetly selfish manner of living; and on the whole, I had nothing animate to care for, in a childish way, but myself, some nests of ants, which the gardener would never leave undisturbed for me, and a sociable bird or two; though I never had the sense or perseverance to make one really tame. But that was partly because, if ever I managed to bring one to be the least trustful of me, the cats got it.

Under these circumstances, what powers of imagination I possessed, either fastened themselves on inanimate things —the sky, the leaves, and pebbles, observable within the walls of Eden,—or caught at any opportunity of flight into regions of romance, compatible with the objective realities of existence in the nineteenth century, within a mile and a quarter of Camberwell Green.

Herein my father, happily, though with no definite intention other than of pleasing me, when he found he could do so without infringing any of my mother's rules, became my guide. I was particularly fond of watching him shave; and was always allowed to come into his room in the morning (under the one in which I am now writing), to be the motionless witness of that operation. Over his dressing-table hung one of his own water-colour drawings, made under the teaching of the elder Nasmyth; I believe, at the High School of Edinburgh. It was done in the early manner of tinting, which, just about the time when my father was at the High School, Dr. Monro was teaching Turner; namely, in grey under-tints of Prussian blue and British ink, washed with warm colour afterwards on the lights. It represented Conway Castle, with its Frith, and, in the foreground, a cottage, a fisherman, and a boat at the water's edge.

When my father had finished shaving, he always told me a story about this picture. The custom began without any initial purpose of his, in consequence of my troublesome curiosity whether the fisherman lived in the cottage, and where he was going to in the boat. It being settled, for peace' sake, that he *did* live in the cottage, and was going in the boat to fish near the castle, the plot of the drama afterwards gradually thickened; and became, I believe, involved with that of the tragedy of *Douglas*, and of the *Castle Spectre,* in both of which pieces my father had performed in private theatricals, before my mother, and a select Edinburgh audience, when he was a boy of sixteen, and she, at grave twenty, a model housekeeper, and very scornful and religiously suspicious of theatricals. But she was never weary of telling me, in later years, how beautiful my father looked in his Highland dress, with the high black feathers.

In the afternoons, when my father returned (always

punctually) from his business, he dined, at half-past four, in the front parlour, my mother sitting beside him to hear the events of the day, and give counsel and encouragement with respect to the same;—chiefly the last, for my father was apt to be vexed if orders for sherry fell the least short of their due standard, even for a day or two. I was never present at this time, however, and only avouch what I relate by heresay and probable conjecture; for between four and six it would have been a grave misdemeanour in me if I so much as approached the parlour door. After that, in summer time, we were all in the garden as long as the day lasted; tea under the white-heart cherry tree; or in winter and rough weather, at six o'clock in the drawing-room,—I having my cup of milk, and slice of bread-and-butter, in a little recess, with a table in front of it, wholly sacred to me; and in which I remained in the evenings as an Idol in a niche, while my mother knitted, and my father read to her, —and to me, so far as I chose to listen.

The series of the Waverley novels, then drawing towards its close, was still the chief source of delight in all households caring for literature; and I can no more recollect the time when I did not know them than when I did not know the Bible; but I have still a vivid remembrance of my father's intense expression of sorrow mixed with scorn, as he threw down *Count Robert of Paris*, after reading three or four pages; and knew that the life of Scott was ended: the scorn being a very complex and bitter feeling in him,— partly, indeed, of the book itself, but chiefly of the wretches who were tormenting and selling the wrecked intellect, and not a little, deep down, of the subtle dishonesty which had essentially caused the ruin. My father never could forgive Scott his concealment of the Ballantyne partnership.

Such being the salutary pleasures of Herne Hill, I have next with deeper gratitude to chronicle what I owe to my mother for the resolutely consistent lessons which so exercised me in the Scriptures as to make every word of them familiar to my ear in habitual music,—yet in that familiarity reverenced, as transcending all thought, and ordaining all conduct.

This she effected, not by her own sayings or personal authority; but simply by compelling me to read the book thoroughly, for myself. As soon as I was able to read with fluency, she began a course of Bible work with me, which never ceased till I went to Oxford. She read alternate verses with me, watching, at first, every intonation of my voice, and correcting the false ones, till she made me understand the verse, if within my reach, rightly, and energetically. It might be beyond me altogether; that she did not care about; but she made sure that as soon as I got hold of it at all, I should get hold of it by the right end.

In this way she began with the first verse of Genesis, and went straight through, to the last verse of the Apocalypse; hard names, numbers, Levitical law, and all; and began again at Genesis the next day. If a name was hard, the better the exercise in pronunciation,—if a chapter was tiresome, the better lesson in patience,—if loathsome, the better lesson in faith that there was some use in its being so outspoken. After our chapters, (from two to three a day, according to their length, the first thing after breakfast, and no interruption from servants allowed,—none from visitors, who either joined in the reading or had to stay upstairs,— and none from any visitings or excursions, except real travelling,) I had to learn a few verses by heart, or repeat, to make sure I had not lost, something of what was already known; and, with the chapters thus gradually possessed from the first word to the last, I had to learn the whole body of the fine old Scottish paraphrases, which are good, melodious, and forceful verse; and to which, together with the Bible itself, I owe the first cultivation of my ear in sound.

It is strange that of all the pieces of the Bible which my mother thus taught me, that which cost me most to learn, and which was, to my child's mind, chiefly repulsive—the 119th Psalm—has now become of all the most precious to

me, in its overflowing and glorious passion of love for the
Law of God, in opposition to the abuse of it by modern
preachers of what they imagine to be His gospel.

But it is only by deliberate effort that I recall the long
morning hours of toil, as regular as sunrise,—toil on both
sides equal—by which, year after year, my mother forced
me to learn these paraphrases, and chapters, (the eighth of
1st Kings being one—try it, good reader, in a leisure hour!)
allowing not so much as a syllable to be missed or misplaced;
while every sentence was required to be said over and over
again till she was satisfied with the accent of it. I recollect
a struggle between us of about three weeks, concerning the
accent of the "of" in the lines

> *"Shall any following spring revive*
> *The ashes of the urn?"*—

I insisting, partly in childish obstinacy, and partly in true
instinct for rhythm, (being wholly careless on the subject
both of urns and their contents,) on reciting it with an ac-
cented *of*. It was not, I say, till after three weeks' labour,
that my mother got the accent lightened on the "of" and
laid on the ashes, to her mind. But had it taken three years
she would have done it, having once undertaken to do it.
And, assuredly, had she not done it,—well, there's no knowing what would have happened; but I'm very thankful she
did.

I have just opened my oldest (in use) Bible,—a small,
closely, and very neatly printed volume it is, printed in
Edinburgh by Sir D. Hunter Blair and J. Bruce, Printers to
the King's Most Excellent Majesty, in 1816. Yellow, now,
with age; and flexible, but not unclean, with much use;
except that the lower corners of the pages at 8th of 1st
Kings, and 32nd Deuteronomy, are worn somewhat thin and
dark, the learning of these two chapters having cost me
much pains. My mother's list of the chapters with which,
thus learned, she established my soul in life, has just fallen
out of it. I will take what indulgence the incurious reader

can give me, for printing the list thus accidentally occurrent:—

Exodus	chapters	15th and 20th.
2 Samuel	"	1st, from 17th verse to the end.
1 Kings	"	8th.
Psalms	"	23rd, 32nd, 90th, 91st, 103rd, 112th, 119th, 139th.
Proverbs	"	2nd, 3rd, 8th, 12th.
Isaiah	"	58th.
Matthew	"	5th, 6th, 7th.
Acts	"	26th.
1 Corinthians	"	13th, 15th.
James	"	4th.
Revelation	"	5th, 6th.

And truly, though I have picked up the elements of a little further knowledge—in mathematics, meteorology, and the like, in after life,—and owe not a little to the teaching of many people, this maternal installation of my mind in that property of chapters I count very confidently the most precious, and, on the whole, the one *essential* part of all my education.

And it is perhaps already time to mark what advantage and mischief, by the chances of life up to seven years old, had been irrevocably determined for me.

I will first count my blessings (as a not unwise friend once recommended me to do, continually; whereas I have a bad trick of always numbering the thorns in my fingers and not the bones in them).

And for the best and truest beginning of all blessings, I had been taught the perfect meaning of Peace, in thought, act, and word.

I never had heard my father's or mother's voice once raised in any question with each other; nor seen an angry, or even slightly hurt or offended, glance in the eyes of either. I had never heard a servant scolded; nor even suddenly, passionately, or in any severe manner, blamed. I had never seen a moment's trouble or disorder in any household matter; nor anything whatever either done in a hurry, or undone in due time. I had no conception of such a feeling as anxiety; my father's occasional vexation in the afternoons, when he had only got an order for twelve butts after expecting one for fifteen, as I have just stated, was never manifested to *me;* and itself related only to the question whether his name would be a step higher or lower in the year's list of sherry exporters; for he never spent more than half his income, and therefore found himself little incommoded by occasional variations in the total of it. I had never done any wrong that I knew of—beyond occasionally delaying the commitment to heart of some improving sentence, that I might watch a wasp on the window pane, or a bird in the cherry tree; and I had never seen any grief.

Next to this quite priceless gift of Peace, I had received the perfect understanding of the natures of Obedience and Faith. I obeyed word, or lifted finger, of father or mother, simply as a ship her helm; not only without idea of resistance, but receiving the direction as a part of my own life and force, and helpful law, as necessary to me in every moral action as the law of gravity in leaping. And my practice in Faith was soon complete: nothing was ever promised me that was not given; nothing ever threatened me that was not inflicted, and nothing ever told me that was not true.

Peace, obedience, faith; these three for chief good; next to these, the habit of fixed attention with both eyes and mind—on which I will not further enlarge at this moment, this being the main practical faculty of my life, causing Mazzini to say of me, in conversation authentically reported, a year or two before his death, that I had "the most analytic mind in Europe." An opinion in which, so far as I am acquainted with Europe, I am myself entirely disposed to concur.

Lastly, an extreme perfection in palate and all other bodily senses, given by the utter prohibition of cake, wine, comfits, or, except in carefullest restriction, fruit; and by fine preparation of what food was given me. Such I esteem the main blessings of my childhood;—next, let me count the equally dominant calamities.

First, that I had nothing to love.

My parents were—in a sort—visible powers of nature to me, no more loved than the sun and the moon: only I should have been annoyed and puzzled if either of them had gone out; (how much, now, when both are darkened!)—still less did I love God; not that I had any quarrel with Him, or fear of Him; but simply found what people told me was His service, disagreeable; and what people told me was His book, not entertaining. I had no companions to quarrel with, neither; nobody to assist, and nobody to thank. Not a servant was ever allowed to do anything for me, but what it was their duty to do; and why should I have been grateful to the cook for cooking, or the gardener for gardening,—when the one dared not give me a baked potato without asking leave, and the other would not let my ants' nests alone, because they made the walks untidy? The evil consequence of all this was not, however, what might perhaps have been expected, that I grew up selfish or unaffectionate; but that, when affection did come, it came with violence utterly rampant and unmanageable, at least by me, who never before had anything to manage.

For (second of chief calamities) I had nothing to endure. Danger or pain of any kind I knew not: my strength was never exercised, my patience never tried, and my courage never fortified. Not that I was ever afraid of anything,—either ghosts, thunder, or beasts; and one of the nearest approaches to insubordination which I was ever tempted into as a child, was in passionate effort to get leave to play with the lion's cubs in Wombwell's menagerie.

Thirdly. I was taught no precision nor etiquette of manners; it was enough if, in the little society we saw, I remained unobtrusive, and replied to a question without shyness: but the shyness came later, and increased as I grew conscious of the rudeness arising from the want of social discipline, and found it impossible to acquire, in advanced life, dexterity in any bodily exercise, skill in any pleasing accomplishment, or ease and tact in ordinary behaviour.

Lastly, and chief of evils. My judgment of right and wrong, and powers of independent action, were left entirely undeveloped; because the bridle and blinkers were never taken off me. Children should have their times of being off duty, like soldiers; and when once the obedience, if required, is certain, the little creature should be very early put for periods of practice in complete command of itself; set on the barebacked horse of its own will, and left to break it by its own strength. But the ceaseless authority exercised over my youth left me, when cast out at last into the world, unable for some time to do more than drift with its vortices.

My present verdict, therefore, on the general tenor of my education at that time, must be, that it was at once too formal and too luxurious; leaving my character, at the most important moment for its construction, cramped indeed, but not disciplined; and only by protection innocent, instead of by practice virtuous. My mother saw this herself, and but too clearly, in later years; and whenever I did anything wrong, stupid, or hard-hearted,—(and I have done many things that were all three,)—always said, "It is because you were too much indulged." . . .   [Vol. I, Chap. 2]

Schaffhausen and Milan

The visit to the field of Waterloo, spoken of by chance in [a previous] chapter, must have been when I was five years old,—on the occasion of papa and mamma's taking a fancy to see Paris in its festivities following the coronation of Charles X. We stayed several weeks in Paris, in a quiet family inn, and then some days at Brussels,—but I have no memory whatever of intermediate stages. It seems to me, on revision of those matin times, that I was very slow in receiving impressions, and needed to stop two or three days at least in a place, before I began to get a notion of it; but the notion, once got, was, as far as it went, always right; and since I had no occasion afterwards to modify it, other impressions fell away from that principal one, and disappeared altogether. Hence what people call my preju-diced views of things,—which are, in fact, the exact con-trary, namely, post-judiced. (I do not mean to introduce this word for general service, but it saves time and print just now.)

Another character of my perceptions I find curiously steady—that I was only interested by things near me, or at least clearly visible and present. I suppose this is so with children generally; but it remained—and remains—a part of my grown-up temper. In this visit to Paris, I was ex-tremely taken up with the soft red cushions of the arm-chairs, which it took one half-an-hour to subside into after sitting down,—with the exquisitely polished floor of the salon, and the good-natured French "Boots" (more properly "Brushes"), who skated over it in the morning till it became as reflective as a mahogany table,—with the pretty court full of flowers and shrubs in beds and tubs between our rez-de-chaussée windows and the outer gate,—with a nice black servant belonging to another family, who used to catch the house-cat for me; and with an equally good-natured fille de chambre, who used to catch it back again, for fear I should tease it, (her experience of English boy-children having made her dubious of my intentions);—all these things and people I remember,—and the Tuileries garden, and the "Tivoli" gardens, where my father took me up and down a "Russian mountain," and I saw fireworks of the finest. But I remember nothing of the Seine, nor of Notre Dame, nor of anything in or even out of the town, except the wind-mills on Mont Martre. . . .

And now, I must get on, and come to the real first sights of several things.

I said that, for our English tours, Mr. Telford usually

lent us his chariot. But for Switzerland, now taking Mary,* we needed stronger wheels and more room; and for this, and all following tours abroad, the first preparation and the beginning of delight was the choosing a carriage to our fancy, from the hireable reserves at Mr. Hopkinson's, of Long Acre.

The poor modern slaves and simpletons who let themselves be dragged like cattle, or felled timber, through the countries they imagine themselves visiting, can have no conception whatever of the complex joys, and ingenious hopes, connected with the choice and arrangement of the travelling carriage in old times. The mechanical questions first, of strength—easy rolling—steady and safe poise of persons and luggage; the general stateliness of effect to be obtained for the abashing of plebeian beholders; the cunning design and distribution of store-cellars under the seats, secret drawers under front windows, invisible pockets under padded lining, safe from dust, and accessible only by insidious slits, or necromantic valves like Aladdin's trap-door; the fitting of cushions where they would not slip, the rounding of corners for more delicate repose; the prudent attachments and springs of blinds; the perfect fitting of windows, on which one-half the comfort of a travelling carriage really depends; and the adaptation of all these concentrated luxuries to the probabilities of who would sit where, in the little apartment which was to be virtually one's home for five or six months;—all this was an imaginary journey in itself, with every pleasure, and none of the discomfort, of practical travelling.

On the grand occasion of our first continental journey— which was meant to be half a year long—the carriage was chosen with, or in addition fitted with, a front seat outside for my father and Mary, a dickey, unusually large, for Anne and the courier, and four inside seats, though those in front

* Ruskin's orphaned cousin, four years his senior, who came to live at Herne Hill in 1829.

very small, that papa and Mary might be received inside in stress of weather. I recollect, when we had finally settled which carriage we would have, the polite Mr. Hopkinson, advised of my dawning literary reputation, asking me (to the joy of my father) if I could translate the motto of the former possessor, under his painted arms,—"*Vix ea nostra voco,*"*—which I accomplishing successfully, farther wittily observed that however by right belonging to the former possessor, the motto was with greater propriety applicable to *us.*

For a family carriage of this solid construction, with its luggage, and load of six or more persons, four horses were of course necessary to get any sufficient way on it; and half-a-dozen such teams were kept at every post-house. The modern reader may perhaps have as much difficulty in realizing these savagely and clumsily locomotive periods, though so recent, as any aspects of migratory Saxon or Goth; and may not think me vainly garrulous in their description.

The French horses, and more or less those on all the great lines of European travelling, were properly stout trotting cart-horses, well up to their work and over it; untrimmed, long-tailed, good-humouredly licentious, whinnying and frolicking with each other when they had a chance; sagaciously steady to work; obedient to the voice mostly, to the rein only for more explicitness; never touched by the whip, which was used merely to express the driver's exultation in himself and them,—signal obstructive vehicles in front out of the way, and advise all the inhabitants of the villages and towns traversed on the day's journey, that persons of distinction were honouring them by their transitory presence. If everything was right, the four horses were driven by one postillion riding the shaft horse; but if the horses were young, or the riders unpractised, there was a postillion for the leaders also. As a rule, there were four steady horses and a good driver, rarely drunk, often very young, the

* "I scarcely call these things mine" (Ovid's *Metamorphoses*, xiii: 140).

men of stronger build being more useful for other work, and any clever young rider able to manage the well-trained and merry-minded beasts, besides being lighter on their backs. Half the weight of the cavalier, in such cases, was in his boots, which were often brought out slung from the saddle like two buckets, the postillion, after the horses were harnessed, walking along the pole and getting into them.

Scarcely less official, for a travelling carriage of good class, than its postillions, was the courier, or properly, avant-courier, whose primary office it was to ride in advance at a steady gallop, and order the horses at each post-house to be harnessed and ready waiting, so that no time might be lost between stages. His higher function was to make all bargains and pay all bills, so as to save the family unbecoming cares and mean anxieties, besides the trouble and disgrace of trying to speak French or any other foreign language. He, farther, knew the good inns in each town, and all the good rooms in each inn, so that he could write beforehand to secure those suited to his family. He was also, if an intelligent man and high-class courier, well acquainted with the proper sights to be seen in each town, and with all the occult means to be used for getting sight of those that weren't to be seen by the vulgar. Murray, the reader will remember, did not exist in those days; the courier was a private Murray, who knew, if he had any wit, not the things to be seen only, but those you would yourself best like to see, and gave instructions to your valet-de-place accordingly, interfering only as a higher power in cases of difficulty needing to be overcome by money or tact. He invariably attended the ladies in their shopping expeditions, took them to the fashionable shops, and arranged as he thought proper the prices of articles. Lastly, he knew, of course, all the other high-class couriers on the road, and told you, if you wished to know, all the people of consideration who chanced to be with you in the inn.

My father would have considered it an insolent and revolutionary trespass on the privileges of the nobility to have mounted his courier to ride in advance of us; besides that, wisely liberal of his money for comfort and pleasure, he never would have paid the cost of an extra horse for show. The horses were, therefore, ordered in advance, when possible, by the postillions of any preceding carriage (or, otherwise, we did not mind waiting till they were harnessed), and we carried our courier behind us in the dickey with Anne, being in all his other functions and accomplishments an indispensable luxury to us. Indispensable, first, because none of us could speak anything but French, and that only enough to ask our way in; for all specialties of bargaining, or details of information, we were helpless, even in France, —and might as well have been migratory sheep, or geese, in Switzerland or Italy. Indispensable, secondly, to my father's peace of mind, because, with perfect liberality of temper, he had a great dislike to being over-reached. He perfectly well knew that his courier would have his commission, and allowed it without question; but he knew also that his courier would not be cheated by other people, and was content in his representative. Not for ostentation, but for real enjoyment and change of sensation from his suburban life, my father liked large rooms; and my mother, in mere continuance of her ordinary and essential habits, liked clean ones; clean, and large, means a good inn and a first floor. Also my father liked a view from his windows, and reasonably said, "Why should we travel to see less than we may?" —so that meant first floor *front*. Also my father liked delicate cookery, just because he was one of the smallest and rarest eaters; and my mother liked good meat. That meant, dinner without limiting price, in reason. Also, though my father never went into society, he all the more enjoyed getting a glimpse, reverentially, of fashionable people—I mean, people of rank—he scorned fashion,—and it was a great thing to him to feel that Lord and Lady —— were on the opposite landing, and that, at any moment, he might conceivably meet and pass them on the stairs. Salvador, duly advised, or penetratively perceptive of these dispositions of my father, entirely pleasing and admirable to the courier mind, had carte-blanche in all administrative functions and bargains. We found our pleasant rooms always ready, our good horses always waiting, everybody took their hats off when we arrived and departed. Salvador presented his accounts weekly, and they were settled without a word of demur.

To all these conditions of luxury and felicity, can the modern steam-puffed tourist conceive the added ruling and culminating one—that we were never in a hurry? coupled with the correlative power of always starting at the hour we chose, and that if we weren't ready, the horses would wait? As a rule, we breakfasted at our own home time—eight; the horses were pawing and neighing at the door (under the archway, I should have said) by nine. Between nine and three,—reckoning seven miles an hour, including stoppages, for minimum pace,—we had done our forty to fifty miles of journey, sate down to dinner at four,—and I had two hours of delicious exploring by myself in the evening; ordered in punctually at seven to tea, and finishing my sketches till half-past nine,—bed-time.

On longer days of journey we started at six, and did twenty miles before breakfast, coming in for four o'clock dinner as usual. In a quite long day we made a second stop, dining at any nice village hostelry, and coming in for late tea, after doing our eighty or ninety miles. But these pushes were seldom made unless to get to some pleasant cathedral town for Sunday, or pleasant Alpine village. We never travelled on Sunday; my father and I nearly always went— as philosophers—to mass, in the morning, and my mother, in pure good-nature to us, (I scarcely ever saw in her a trace of feminine curiosity,) would join with us in some such profanity as a drive on the Corso, or the like, in the afternoon. But we all, even my father, liked a walk in the fields better, round an Alpine châlet village.

[In Chapter IV] I threatened more accurate note of my

first impressions of Switzerland and Italy in 1833. Of customary Calais I have something to say later on,—here I note
only our going up Rhine to Strasburg, where, with all its
miracles of building, I was already wise enough to feel the
cathedral stiff and iron-worky; but was greatly excited and
impressed by the high roofs and rich fronts of the wooden
houses, in their sudden indication of nearness to Switzerland; and especially by finding the scene so admirably expressed by Prout in the 36th plate of his *Flanders and
Germany*, still uninjured. And then, with Salvador was held
council in the inn-parlour of Strasburg, whether—it was
then the Friday afternoon—we should push on to-morrow
for our Sunday's rest to Basle, or to Schaffhausen.

How much depended—if ever anything "depends" on anything else,—on the issue of that debate! Salvador inclined to
the straight and level Rhine-side road, with the luxury of
the "Three Kings," attainable by sunset. But at Basle, it had
to be admitted, there were no Alps in sight, no cataract
within hearing, and Salvador honourably laid before us the
splendid alternative possibility of reaching, by traverse of
the hilly road of the Black Forest, the gates of Schaffhausen
itself, before they closed for the night.

The Black Forest! The fall of Schaffhausen! The chain
of the Alps! within one's grasp for Sunday! What a Sunday,
instead of customary Walworth and the Dulwich fields!
My impassioned petition at last carried it, and the earliest
morning saw us trotting over the bridge of boats to Kehl,
and in the eastern light I well remember watching the line
of the Black Forest hills enlarge and rise, as we crossed the
plain of the Rhine. "Gates of the hills"; opening for me to
a new life—to cease no more; except at the Gates of the
Hills whence one returns not.

And so, we reached the base of the Schwarzwald, and entered an ascending dingle; and scarcely, I think, a quarter
of an hour after entering, saw our first "Swiss cottage."
How much it meant to all of us,—how much prophesied to

me, no modern traveller could the least conceive, if I spent days in trying to tell him. A sort of triumphant shriek—like all the railway whistles going off at once at Clapham Junction—has gone up from the Fooldom of Europe at the destruction of the myth of William Tell. To us, every word of it was true—but mythically luminous with more than mortal truth; and here, under the black woods, glowed the visible, beautiful, tangible testimony to it in the purple larch timber, carved to exquisiteness by the joy of peasant life, continuous, motionless there in the pine shadow on its ancestral turf,—unassailed and unassailing, in the blessedness of righteous poverty, of religious peace.

The myth of William Tell is destroyed forsooth? and you have tunnelled Gothard, and filled, it may be, the Bay of Uri;—and it was all for you and your sake that the grapes dropped blood from the press of St. Jacob, and the pine club struck down horse and helm in Morgarten Glen?*

Difficult enough for you to imagine, that old travellers' time when Switzerland was yet the land of the Swiss, and the Alps had never been trod by foot of man. Steam, never heard of yet, but for short fair weather crossing at sea (were there paddle-packets across Atlantic? I forget). Any way, the roads by land were safe; and entered once into this mountain Paradise, we wound on through its balmy glens, past cottage after cottage on their lawns, still glistering in the dew.

The road got into more barren heights by the mid-day, the hills arduous; once or twice we had to wait for horses, and we were still twenty miles from Schaffhausen at sunset; it was past midnight when we reached her closed gates. The disturbed porter had the grace to open them—not quite wide enough; we carried away one of our lamps in collision with the slanting bar as we drove through the arch. How much happier the privilege of dreamily entering a mediæval

* Allusions to the battles in which the Swiss Confederation defeated the Austrians at Morgarten (1315) and the French at St. Jacob (1444).

city, though with the loss of a lamp, than the free ingress of being jammed between a dray and a tramcar at a railroad station!

It is strange that I but dimly recollect the following morning; I fancy we must have gone to some sort of church or other; and certainly, part of the day went in admiring the bow-windows projecting into the clean streets. None of us seem to have thought the Alps would be visible without profane exertion in climbing hills. We dined at four, as usual, and the evening being entirely fine, went out to walk, all of us,—my father and mother and Mary and I.

We must have still spent some time in town-seeing, for it was drawing towards sunset, when we got up to some sort of garden promenade—west of the town, I believe; and high above the Rhine, so as to command the open country across it to the south and west. At which open country of low undulation, far into blue,—gazing as at one of our own distances from Malvern of Worcestershire, or Dorking of Kent, —suddenly—behold—beyond!

There was no thought in any of us for a moment of their being clouds. They were clear as crystal, sharp on the pure horizon sky, and already tinged with rose by the sinking sun. Infinitely beyond all that we had ever thought or dreamed,—the seen walls of lost Eden could not have been more beautiful to us; not more awful, round heaven, the walls of sacred Death.

It is not possible to imagine, in any time of the world, a more blessed entrance into life, for a child of such a temperament as mine. True, the temperament belonged to the age: a very few years,—within the hundred,—before that, no child could have been born to care for mountains, or for the men that lived among them, in that way. Till Rousseau's time, there had been no "sentimental" love of nature; and till Scott's, no such apprehensive love of "all sorts and conditions of men," not in the soul merely, but in the flesh. St. Bernard of La Fontaine, looking out to

Mont Blanc with his child's eyes, sees above Mont Blanc the Madonna; St. Bernard of Talloires, not the Lake of Annecy, but the dead between Martigny and Aosta. But for me, the Alps and their people were alike beautiful in their snow, and their humanity; and I wanted, neither for them nor myself, sight of any thrones in heaven but the rocks, or of any spirits in heaven but the clouds.

Thus, in perfect health of life and fire of heart, not wanting to be anything but the boy I was, not wanting to have anything more than I had; knowing of sorrow only just so much as to make life serious to me, not enough to slacken in the least its sinews; and with so much of science mixed with feeling as to make the sight of the Alps not only the revelation of the beauty of the earth, but the opening of the first page of its volume,—I went down that evening from the garden-terrace of Schaffhausen with my destiny fixed in all of it that was to be sacred and useful. To that terrace, and the shore of the Lake of Geneva, my heart and faith return to this day, in every impulse that is yet nobly alive in them, and every thought that has in it help or peace.

The morning after that Sunday's eve at Schaffhausen was also cloudless, and we drove early to the falls, seeing again the chain of the Alps by morning light, and learning, at Lauffen, what an Alpine river was. Coming out of the gorge of Balsthal, I got another ever memorable sight of the chain of the Alps, and these distant views, never seen by the modern traveller, taught me, and made me feel, more than the close marvels of Thun and Interlachen. It was again fortunate that we took the grandest pass into Italy,—that the first ravine of the main Alps I saw was the Via Mala, and the first lake of Italy, Como.

We took boat on the little recessed lake of Chiavenna, and rowed down the whole way of waters, passing another Sunday at Cadenabbia, and then, from villa to villa, across the lake, and across to Como, and so to Milan by Monza.

It was then full, though early, summer time; and the first

impression of Italy always ought to be in her summer. It was also well that, though my heart was with the Swiss cottager, the artificial taste in me had been mainly formed by Turner's rendering of those very scenes, in Rogers's *Italy*. The "Lake of Como," the two moonlight villas, and the "Farewell," had prepared me for all that was beautiful and right in the terraced gardens, proportioned arcades, and white spaces of sunny wall, which have in general no honest charm for the English mind. But to me, they were almost native through Turner,—familiar at once, and revered. I had no idea then of the Renaissance evil in them; they were associated only with what I had been told of the "divine art" of Raphael and Leonardo, and, by my ignorance of dates, associated with the stories of Shakespeare. Portia's villa,—Juliet's palace,—I thought to have been like these. . . .

Again, most fortunately, the weather was clear and cloudless all day long, and as the sun drew westward, we were able to drive to the Corso, where, at that time, the higher Milanese were happy and proud as ours in their park, and whence, no railway station intervening, the whole chain of the Alps was visible on one side, and the beautiful city with its dominant frost-crystalline Duomo on the other. Then the drive home in the open carriage through the quiet twilight, up the long streets, and round the base of the Duomo, the smooth pavement under the wheels adding with its silentness to the sense of dream wonder in it all,—the perfect air in absolute calm, the just seen majesty of encompassing Alps, the perfectness—so it seemed to me—and purity, of the sweet, stately, stainless marble against the sky. What more, what else, could be asked of seemingly immutable good in this mutable world?

I wish in general to avoid interference with the reader's judgment on the matters which I endeavour serenely to narrate; but may, I think, here be pardoned for observing to him the advantage, in a certain way, of the contemplative abstraction from the world which, during this early continental travelling, was partly enforced by our ignorance, and partly secured by our love of comfort. There is something peculiarly delightful—nay, delightful inconceivably by the modern German-plated and French-polished tourist, in passing through the streets of a foreign city without understanding a word that anybody says! One's ear for all sound of voices then becomes entirely impartial; one is not diverted by the meaning of syllables from recognizing the absolute guttural, liquid, or honeyed quality of them: while the gesture of the body and the expression of the face have the same value for you that they have in a pantomime; every scene becomes a melodious opera to you, or a picturesquely inarticulate Punch. Consider, also, the gain in so consistent tranquillity. Most young people nowadays, or even lively old ones, travel more in search of adventures than of information. One of my most valued records of recent wandering is a series of sketches by an amiable and extremely clever girl, of the things that happened to her people and herself every day that they were abroad. Here it is brother Harry, and there it is mamma, and now paterfamilias, and now her little graceful self, and anon her merry or remonstrant sisterhood, who meet with enchanting hardships, and enviable misadventures; bind themselves with fetters of friendship, and glance into sparklings of amourette, with any sort of people in conical hats and fringy caps: and it is all very delightful and condescending; and, of course, things are learnt about the country that way which can be learned in no other way, but only about that ·part of it which interests itself in you, or which you have pleasure in being acquainted with. Virtually, you are thinking of yourself all the time; you necessarily talk to the cheerful people, not to the sad ones; and your head is for the most part vividly taken up with very little things. I don't say that our isolation was meritorious, or that people in general should know no language but their own. Yet the meek ignorance has these advantages. We did not travel for adventures, nor for company, but to see with our eyes, and to measure with our hearts. If you have sympathy, the aspect of humanity is more true to the depths of it than its words; and even in my own land, the things in which I have been least deceived are those which I have learned as their Spectator. [Vol. I, Chap. 6]

Papa and Mamma

It is time now to explain, with such clue as I have found to them, the somewhat peculiar character and genius of both my parents; the influence of which was more important upon me, then, and far on into life, than any external conditions, either of friendship or tutorship, whether at the University, or in the world.

It was, in the first place, a matter of essential weight in the determination of subsequent lines, not only of labour but of thought, that while my father, as before told, gave me the best example of emotional reading,—*reading,* observe, proper; not recitation, which he disdained, and I disliked,—my mother was both able to teach me, and resolved that I should learn, absolute accuracy of diction and precision of accent in prose; and made me know, as soon as I could speak plain, what I have in all later years tried to enforce on my readers, that accuracy of diction means accuracy of sensation, and precision of accent, precision of feeling. Trained, herself in girlhood, only at Mrs. Rice's country school, my mother had there learned severely right principles of truth, charity, and housewifery, with punctilious respect for the purity of that English which in her home surroundings she perceived to be by no means as undefiled as the ripples of Wandel. She was the daughter, as aforesaid, of the early widowed landlady of the King's Head Inn and Tavern, which still exists, or existed a year or two since, presenting its side to Croydon market-place, its front and entrance door to the narrow alley which descends, steep for pedestrians, impassable to carriages, from the High Street to the lower town.

Thus native to the customs and dialect of Croydon Agora, my mother, as I now read her, must have been an extremely intelligent, admirably practical, and naïvely ambitious girl; keeping, without contention, the headship of her class, and availing herself with steady discretion of every advantage the country school and its modest mistress could offer her. I never in her after-life heard her speak with regret, and seldom without respectful praise, of any part of the discipline of Mrs. Rice.

I do not know for what reason, or under what conditions, my mother went to live with my Scottish grandfather and grandmother, first at Edinburgh, and then at the house of Bower's Well, on the slope of the Hill of Kinnoul, above Perth. I was stupidly and heartlessly careless of the past history of my family as long as I could have learnt it; not till after my mother's death did I begin to desire to know what I could never more be told.

But certainly the change, for her, was into a higher sphere of society,—that of real, though sometimes eccentric, and frequently poor, gentlemen and gentlewomen. She must then have been rapidly growing into a tall, handsome, and very finely made girl, with a beautiful mild firmness of expression; a faultless and accomplished housekeeper, and a natural, essential, unassailable, yet inoffensive, prude. I never heard a single word of any sentiment, accident, admiration, or affection disturbing the serene tenor of her Scottish stewardship; yet I noticed that she never spoke without some slight shyness before my father. . . .

When my mother was thus, at twenty, in a Desdemona-like prime of womanhood, intent on highest moral philosophy,—"though still the house affairs would draw her thence" —my father was a dark-eyed, brilliantly active, and sensitive youth of sixteen. Margaret became to him an absolutely respected and admired—mildly liked—governess and confidante. Her sympathy was necessary to him in all his flashingly transient amours; her advice in all domestic business or sorrow, and her encouragement in all his plans of life.

These were already determined for commerce;—yet not to the abandonment of liberal study. He had learned Latin thoroughly, though with no large range of reading, under the noble traditions of Adam at the High School of Edinburgh: while, by the then living and universal influence of Sir Walter, every scene of his native city was exalted in his imagination by the purest poetry, and the proudest history, that ever hallowed or haunted the streets and rocks of a brightly inhabited capital. . . .

Their frank, cousinly relation went on, however, without a thought on either side of any closer ties, until my father, at two or three and twenty, after various apprenticeship in London, was going finally to London to begin his career in his own business. By that time he had made up his mind that Margaret, though not the least an ideal heroine to him, was quite the best sort of person he could have for a wife, the rather as they were already so well used to each other; and in a quiet, but enough resolute way, asked her if she were of the same mind, and would wait until he had an independence to offer her. His early tutress consented with frankly confessed joy, not indeed in the Agnes Wickfield way, "I have loved you all my life," but feeling and admitting that it was great delight to be allowed to love him now. The relations between Grace Nugent and Lord Colambre in Miss Edgeworth's *Absentee* extremely resemble those between my father and mother, except that Lord Colambre is a more eager lover. My father chose his wife much with the same kind of serenity and decision with which afterwards he chose his clerks.

A time of active and hopeful contentment for both the young people followed, my mother being perhaps the more deeply in love, while John depended more absolutely on her sympathy and wise friendship than is at all usual with young men of the present day in their relations with admired young ladies. But neither of them ever permitted their feelings to degenerate into fretful or impatient passion. My mother showed her affection chiefly in steady endeavour to cultivate her powers of mind, and form her manners, so as to fit herself to be the undespised companion of a man whom she considered much her superior: my father in unremitting attention to the business on the success of which his marriage depended: and in a methodical regularity of conduct and correspondence which never left his mistress a moment of avoidable anxiety, or gave her motive for any serious displeasure.

On these terms the engagement lasted nine years; at the end of which time, my grandfather's debts having been all paid, and my father established in a business gradually increasing, and liable to no grave contingency, the now not very young people were married in Perth one evening after supper, the servants of the house having no suspicion of the event until John and Margaret drove away together next morning to Edinburgh.*. . .

Of our neighbours on Herne Hill we saw nothing, with one exception only, afterwards to be noticed. They were for the most part well-to-do London tradesmen of the better class, who had little sympathy with my mother's old-fashioned ways, and none with my father's romantic sentiment.

There was probably the farther reason for our declining the intimacy of our immediate neighbours, that most of them were far more wealthy than we, and inclined to demonstrate their wealth by the magnificence of their establishments. My parents lived with strict economy, kept only female servants, used only tallow candles in plated candlesticks, were content with the leasehold territory of their front and back gardens,—scarce an acre altogether,—and kept neither horse nor carriage. Our shop-keeping neighbours, on the contrary, had usually great cortège of footmen and glitter of plate, extensive pleasure grounds, costly hot-houses, and carriages driven by coachmen in wigs. It may be perhaps doubted by some of my readers whether the coldness of acquaintanceship was altogether on our side;

* In February 1818. She was 37, and he 33.

but assuredly my father was too proud to join entertainments for which he could give no like return, and my mother did not care to leave her card on foot at the doors of ladies who dashed up to hers in their barouche.

Protected by these monastic severities and aristocratic dignities from the snares and disturbances of the outer world, the routine of my childish days became fixed, as of the sunrise and sunset to a nestling. It may seem singular to many of my readers that I remember with most pleasure the time when it was most regular and most solitary. . . . And although I have dwelt with thankfulness on the many joys and advantages of these secluded years, the vigilant reader will not, I hope, have interpreted the accounts rendered of them into general praise of a like home education in the environs of London. But one farther good there was in it, hitherto unspoken; that great part of my acute perception and deep feeling of the beauty of architecture and scenery abroad, was owing to the well-formed habit of narrowing myself to happiness within the four brick walls of our fifty by one hundred yards of garden; and accepting with resignation the aesthetic external surroundings of a London suburb, and, yet more, of a London chapel. For Dr. Andrews' was the Londonian chapel in its perfect type, definable as accurately as a Roman basilica,—an oblong, flat-ceiled barn, lighted by windows with semi-circular heads, brick-arched, filled by small-paned glass held by iron bars, like fine threaded halves of cobwebs; galleries propped on iron pipes, up both sides; pews, well shut in, each of them, by partitions of plain deal, and neatly brass-latched deal doors, filling the barn floor, all but its two lateral straw-matted passages; pulpit, sublimely isolated, central from sides and clear of altar rails at end; a stout, four-legged box of well-grained wainscot, high as the level of front galleries, and decorated with a cushion of crimson velvet, padded six inches thick, with gold tassels at the corners; which was a great resource to me when I was tired of the sermon, because I liked watching the rich colour of the folds and creases that came in it when the clergyman thumped it.

Imagine the change between one Sunday and the next,—
from the morning service in this building, attended by the
families of the small shopkeepers of the Walworth Road,
in their Sunday trimmings; (our plumber's wife, fat, good,
sensible Mrs. Goad, sat in the next pew in front of us,
sternly sensitive to the interruption of her devotion by our
late arrivals); fancy the change from this, to high mass in
Rouen Cathedral, its nave filled by the white-capped peas-
antry of half Normandy!   [Vol. I, Chap. 7]

The Col de la Faucille

About the moment in the forenoon when the modern fashionable traveller, intent on Paris, Nice, and Monaco, and
started by the morning mail from Charing Cross, has a little
recovered himself from the qualms of his crossing, and the
irritation of fighting for seats at Boulogne, and begins to
look at his watch to see how near he is to the buffet of
Amiens, he is apt to be baulked and worried by the train's
useless stop at one inconsiderable station, lettered ABBE-
VILLE. As the carriage gets in motion again, he may see, if
he cares to lift his eyes for an instant from his newspaper,
two square towers, with a curiously attached bit of traceried
arch, dominant over the poplars and osiers of the marshy
level he is traversing. Such glimpse is probably all he will
ever wish to get of them; and I scarcely know how far I can
make even the most sympathetic reader understand their
power over my own life.

The country town in which they are central,—once, like
Croyland, a mere monk's and peasant's refuge (so for some
time called "Refuge"),—among the swamps of Somme, received about the year 650 the name of "Abbatis Villa,"—
"Abbot's-ford," I had like to have written: house and village, I suppose we may rightly say,—as the chief dependence
of the great monastery founded by St. Riquier at his native
place, on the hillside five miles east of the present town.
Concerning which saint I translate from the *Dict^{re} des*

Sciences Eccles^{ques}, what it may perhaps be well for the reader, in present political junctures, to remember for more weighty reasons than any arising out of such interest as he may take in my poor little nascent personality:—

"St. Riquier, in Latin 'Sanctus Richarius,' born in the village of Centula, at two leagues from Abbeville, was so touched by the piety of two holy priests of Ireland, whom he had hospitably received, that he also embraced 'la pénitence.' Being ordained priest, he devoted himself to preaching, and so passed into England. Then, returning into Ponthieu, he became, by God's help, powerful in work and word in leading the people to repentance. He preached at the court of Dagobert, and, a little while after that prince's death, founded the monastery which bore his name, and another, called Forest-Montier, in the wood of Crécy, where he ended his life and penitence.". . .

In the year when the above quoted history of Abbeville was written (say 1600 for surety), the town, then familiarly called "Faithful Abbeville," contained 40,000 souls, "living in great unity among themselves, of a marvellous frankness, fearing to do wrong to their neighbour, the women modest, honest, full of faith and charity, and adorned with a goodness and beauty *toute innocente*. . . ." Moreover, the town contained, besides the great church of St. Vulfran, thirteen parish churches, six monasteries, eight nunneries, and five hospitals, among which churches I am especially bound to name that of St. George, begun by our own Edward in 1368, on the 10th of January; transferred and reconsecrated in 1469 by the Bishop of Bethlehem, and enlarged by the *marguilliers* in 1536, "because the congregation had so increased that numbers had to remain outside on days of solemnity."

These reconstructions took place with so great ease and rapidity at Abbeville, owing partly to the number of its unanimous workmen, partly to the easily workable quality of the stone they used, and partly to the uncertainty of a foundation always on piles, that there is now scarce vestige left of any building prior to the fifteenth century. St. Vulfran itself, with St. Riquier, and all that remain of the parish churches (four only, now, I believe, besides St. Vulfran), are of the same flamboyant Gothic,—walls and towers alike coeval with the gabled timber houses of which the busier streets chiefly consisted when first I saw them.

I must here, in advance, tell the general reader that there have been, in sum, three centres of my life's thought: Rouen, Geneva, and Pisa. All that I did at Venice was bye-work, because her history had been falsely written before, and not even by any of her own people understood; and because, in the world of painting, Tintoret was virtually unseen, Veronese unfelt, Carpaccio not so much as named, when I began to study them; something also was due to my love of gliding about in gondolas. But Rouen, Geneva, and Pisa have been tutresses of all I know, and were mistresses of all I did, from the first moments I entered their gates.

In this journey of 1835 I first saw Rouen and Venice— Pisa not till 1840; nor could I understand the full power of any of those great scenes till much later. But for Abbeville, which is the preface and interpretation of Rouen, I was ready on that 5th of June, and felt that here was entrance for me into immediately healthy labour and joy.

For here I saw that art (of its local kind), religion, and present human life, were yet in perfect harmony. There were no dead six days and dismal seventh in those sculptured churches; there was no beadle to lock me out of them, or pew-shutter to shut me in. I might haunt them, fancying myself a ghost; peep round their pillars, like Rob Roy; kneel in them, and scandalize nobody; draw in them, and disturb none. Outside, the faithful old town gathered itself, and nestled under their buttresses like a brood beneath the mother's wings; the quiet, uninjurious aristocracy of the newer town opened into silent streets, between self-possessed and hidden dignities of dwelling, each with its courtyard and richly trellised garden. The commercial square, with

510 THE GENIUS OF JOHN RUSKIN

the main street of traverse, consisted of uncompetitive shops, such as were needful, of the native wares: cloth and hosiery spun, woven, and knitted within the walls; cheese of neighbouring Neufchâtel; fruit of their own gardens, bread from the fields above the green coteaux; meat of their herds, untainted by American tin; smith's work of sufficient scythe and ploughshare, hammered on the open anvil; groceries dainty, the coffee generally roasting odoriferously in the street, before the door; for the modistes,—well, perhaps a bonnet or two from Paris, the rest, wholesome dress for peasant and dame of Ponthieu. Above the prosperous, serenely busy and beneficent shop, the old dwelling-house of its ancestral masters; pleasantly carved, proudly roofed, keeping its place, and order, and recognized function, unfailing, unenlarging, for centuries. Round all, the breezy ramparts, with their long waving avenues; through all, in variously circuiting cleanness and sweetness of navigable river and active millstream, the green chalk-water of the Somme.

My most intense happinesses have of course been among mountains. But for cheerful, unalloyed, unwearying pleasure, the getting in sight of Abbeville on a fine summer afternoon, jumping out in the courtyard of the Hotel de l'Europe, and rushing down the street to see St. Wulfran again before the sun was off the towers, are things to cherish the past for,—to the end. . . .

We used always to drive out of the yard of La Cloche at Dijon in early morning—seven, after joyful breakfast at half-past six. The small saloon on the first floor to the front had a bedroom across the passage at the west end of it, whose windows commanded the cathedral towers over a low roof on the opposite side of the street. This was always mine, and its bed was in an alcove at the back, separated only by a lath partition from an extremely narrow passage leading from the outer gallery to Anne's room. It was a delight for Anne to which I think she looked forward all across France, to open a little hidden door from this passage, at the back of the alcove exactly above my pillow, and surprise, or wake, me in the morning.

I think I only remember once starting in rain. Usually the morning sun shone through the misty spray and far-thrown diamonds of the fountain in the south-eastern sub-urb, and threw long poplar shadows across the road to Genlis.

Genlis, Auxonne, Dôle, Mont-sous-Vaudrey—three stages of 12 or 14 kilometres each, two of 18; in all about 70 kilometres = 42 miles, from Dijon gate to Jura foot—we went straight for the hills always, lunching on French plums and bread. . . .

The old Hotel de la Poste at Champagnole stood just above the bridge of Ain, opposite the town, where the road got level again as it darted away towards Geneva. I think the year 1842 was the first in which we lengthened the day from Dijon by the two stages beyond Poligny; but after-wards, the Hotel de la Poste at Champagnole became a kind of home to us: going out, we had so much delight there, and coming home, so many thoughts, that a great space of life seemed to be passed in its peace. No one was ever in the house but ourselves; if a family stopped every third day or so, it was enough to maintain the inn, which, besides, had its own farm; and those who did stop, rushed away for Geneva early in the morning. We, who were to sleep again at Morez, were in no hurry; and in returning always left Geneva on Friday, to get the Sunday at Cham-pagnole.

But my own great joy was in the early June evening, when we had arrived from Dijon, and I got out after the quickly dressed trout and cutlet for the first walk on rock and under pine.

With all my Tory prejudice (I mean, principle), I have to confess that one great joy of Swiss—above all, Jurassic

Swiss—ground to me, is in its effectual, not merely theoretic, *liberty*. Among the greater hills, one can't always go just where one chooses,—all around is the too far, or too steep,—one wants to get to this, and climb that, and can't do either; —but in Jura one can go every way, and be happy everywhere. Generally, if there was time, I used to climb the islet of crag to the north of the village, on which there are a few grey walls of ruined castle, and the yet traceable paths of its "pleasance," whence to look if the likeness of white cloud were still on the horizon. Still there, in the clear evening, and again and again, each year more marvellous to me; the Derniers Rochers, and *calotte* of Mont Blanc. Only those; that is to say, just as much as may be seen over the Dôme du Goûter from St. Martin's. But it looks as large from Champagnole as it does there—glowing in the last light like a harvest moon.

If there were not time to reach the castle rock, at least I could get into the woods above the Ain, and gather my first Alpine flowers. Again and again, I feel the duty of gratitude to the formalities and even vulgarities of Herne Hill, for making me to feel by contrast the divine wildness of Jura forest.

Then came the morning drive into the higher glen of the Ain, where the road began first to wind beside the falling stream. One never understands how those winding roads steal with their tranquil slope from height to height; it was but an hour's walking beside the carriage,—an hour passed like a minute; and one emerged on the high plain of St. Laurent, and the gentians began to gleam among the roadside grass, and the pines swept round the horizon with the dark infinitude of ocean.

All Switzerland was there in hope and sensation, and what was less than Switzerland was in some sort better, in its meek simplicity and healthy purity. The Jura cottage is not carved with the stately richness of the Bernese, nor set together with the antique strength of Uri. It is covered with thin slit fine shingles, side-roofed as it were to the ground for mere dryness' sake, a little crossing of laths here and there underneath the window its only ornament. It has no daintiness of garden nor wealth of farm about it,—is indeed little more than a delicately-built châlet, yet trim and domestic, mildly intelligent of things other than pastoral, watch-making and the like, though set in the midst of the meadows, the gentian at its door, the lily of the valley wild in the copses hard by.

My delight in these cottages, and in the sense of human industry and enjoyment through the whole scene, was at the root of all pleasure in its beauty; see the passage afterwards written in the *Seven Lamps* insisting on this as if it were general to human nature thus to admire through sympathy. I have noticed since, with sorrowful accuracy, how many people there are who, wherever they find themselves, think only "of their position." But the feeling which gave me so much happiness, both then and through life, differed also curiously, in its impersonal character, from that of many even of the best and kindest persons.

In the beginning of the Carlyle-Emerson correspondence, edited with too little comment by my dear friend Charles Norton, I find at page 18 this—to me entirely disputable, and to my thought, so far as undisputed, much blameable and pitiable, exclamation of my master's: "Not till we can think that here and there one is thinking of us, one is loving us, does this waste earth become a peopled garden." My training, as the reader has perhaps enough perceived, produced in me the precisely opposite sentiment. *My* times of happiness had always been when *nobody* was thinking of me; and the main discomfort and drawback to all proceedings and designs, the attention and interference of the public—represented by my mother and the gardener. The garden was no waste place to me, because I did not suppose myself an object of interest either to the ants or the butterflies; and the only qualification of the entire delight of my evening walk at Champagnole or St. Laurent was the sense that my father and mother *were* thinking of me, and would be frightened if I was five minutes late for tea.

I don't mean in the least that I could have done without them. They were, to me, much more than Carlyle's wife to him; and if Carlyle had written, instead of that he wanted Emerson to think of him in America, that he wanted his father and mother to be thinking of him at Ecclefechan, it had been well. But that the rest of the world was waste to him unless he had admirers in it, is a sorry state of sentiment enough; and I am somewhat tempted, for once, to admire the exactly opposite temper of my own solitude. My entire delight was in observing without being myself noticed,—if I could have been invisible, all the better. I was absolutely interested in men and their ways, as I was interested in marmots and chamois, in tomtits and trout. If only they would stay still and let me look at them, and not get into their holes and up their heights! The living inhabitation of the world—the grazing and nesting in it,—the spiritual power of the air, the rocks, the waters, to be in the midst of it, and rejoice and wonder at it, and help it if I could,—happier if it needed no help of mine,—this was the essential love *of Nature* in me, this the root of all that I have usefully become, and the light of all that I have rightly learned.

Whether we slept at St. Laurent or Morez, the morning of the next day was an eventful one. In ordinarily fine weather, the ascent from Morez to Les Rousses, walked most of the way, was mere enchantment; so also breakfast, and fringed-gentian gathering, at Les Rousses. Then came usually an hour of tortured watching the increase of the noon clouds; for, however early we had risen, it was impossible to reach the Col de la Faucille before two o'clock, or later if we had bad horses, and at two o'clock, if there are clouds above Jura, there will be assuredly clouds on the Alps.

It is worth notice, Saussure himself not having noticed it, that this main pass of Jura, unlike the great passes of the Alps, reaches its traverse-point very nearly under the highest summit of that part of the chain. The col, separating the source of the Bienne, which runs down to Morez and St. Claude, from that of the Valserine, which winds through the midst of Jura to the Rhone at Bellegarde, is a spur of the Dôle itself, under whose prolonged masses the road is then carried six miles farther, ascending very slightly to the Col de la Faucille, where the chain opens suddenly, and a sweep of the road, traversed in five minutes at a trot, opens the whole Lake of Geneva, and the chain of the Alps along a hundred miles of horizon.

I have never seen that view perfectly but once—in this year 1835; when I drew it carefully in my then fashion, and have been content to look back to it as the confirming sequel of the first view of the Alps from Schaffhausen. Very few travellers, even in old times, saw it at all; tired of the long posting journey from Paris, by the time they got to the col they were mostly thinking only of their dinners and rest at Geneva; the guide books said nothing about it; and though, for everybody, it was an inevitable task to ascend the Righi, nobody ever thought there was anything to be seen from the Dôle.

Both mountains have had enormous influence on my whole life;—the Dôle continually and calmly; the Righi at sorrowful intervals, as will be seen. But the Col de la Faucille, on that day of 1835, opened to me in distinct vision the Holy Land of my future work and true home in this world. My eyes had been opened, and my heart with them, to see and to possess royally such a kingdom! Far as the eye could reach—that land and its moving or pausing waters; Arve, and his gates of Cluse, and his glacier fountains; Rhone, and the infinitude of his sapphire lake,—his peace beneath the narcissus meads of Vevay—his cruelty beneath the promontories of Sierre. And all that rose against and melted into the sky, of mountain and mountain snow; and all that living plain, burning with human gladness—studded with white homes,—a milky way of star-dwellings cast across its sunlit blue.   [Vol. I, Chap. 9]

Quem Tu, Melpomene

... My mother, watching the naturalistic and methodic bent of me, was, I suppose, tranquil in the thought of my becoming another White of Selborne, or Vicar of Wakefield, victorious in Whistonian and every other controversy. My father perhaps conceived more cometic or meteoric career for me, but neither of them put the matter seriously in hand, however deeply laid up in heart: and I was allowed without remonstrance to go on measuring the blue of the sky, and watching the flight of the clouds, till I had forgotten most of the Latin I ever knew, and all the Greek, except Anacreon's ode to the rose.

Some little effort was made to pull me together in 1836 by sending me to hear Mr. Dale's lectures at King's College, where I explained to Mr. Dale, on meeting him one day in the court of entrance, that porticoes should not be carried on the top of arches; and considered myself exalted because I went in at the same door with boys who had square caps on. The lectures were on early English literature, of which, though I had never read a word of any before Pope, I thought myself already a much better judge than Mr. Dale. His quotation of "Knut the king came sailing by" stayed with me; and I think that was about all I learnt during the summer. For, as my adverse stars would have it, that year, my father's partner, Mr. Domecq, thought it might for once be expedient that he should himself pay a complimentary round of visits to his British customers, and asked if meanwhile he might leave his daughters at Herne Hill to see the lions at the Tower, and so on. How we got them all into Herne Hill corners and cupboards would be inexplicable but with a plan of the three stories! The arrangements were half Noah's ark, half Doll's house, but we got them all in: Clotilde, a graceful oval-faced blonde of fifteen; Cécile, a dark, finely-browed, beautifully-featured girl of thirteen; Elise, again fair, round-faced like an English girl, a treasure of good nature and good sense; Caroline, a delicately quaint

little thing of eleven. They had all been born abroad, Clotilde at Cadiz, and of course convent-bred; but lately accustomed to be much in society during vacation at Paris.
Deeper than any one dreamed, the sight of them in the
Champs Élysées had sealed itself in me,* for they were the
first well-bred and well-dressed girls I had ever seen—or at
least spoken to. I mean of course, by well-dressed, perfectly
simply dressed, with Parisian cutting and fitting. They were
all "bigoted"—as Protestants would say; quietly firm, as
they ought to say—Roman Catholics; spoke Spanish and
French with perfect grace, and English with broken precision: were all fairly sensible, Clotilde sternly and accurately so, Elise gaily and kindly, Cécile serenely, Caroline
keenly. A most curious galaxy, or southern cross, of uncon-
ceived stars, floating on a sudden into my obscure firmament
of London suburb.

How my parents could allow their young novice to be
cast into the fiery furnace of the outer world in this helpless
manner the reader may wonder, and only the Fates know;
but there was this excuse for them, that they had never seen
me the least interested or anxious about girls—never caring
to stay in the promenades at Cheltenham or Bath, or on the
parade at Dover; on the contrary, growling and mewing if
I was ever kept there, and off to the sea or the fields the
moment I got leave; and they had educated me in such extremely orthodox English Toryism and Evangelicalism that
they could not conceive their scientific, religious, and George
the Third revering youth, wavering in his constitutional
balance towards French Catholics. And I had never *said*
anything about the Champs Élysées! Virtually convent-bred
more closely than the maids themselves, without a single
sisterly or cousinly affection for refuge or lightning rod, and
having no athletic skill or pleasure to check my dreaming, I
was thrown, bound hand and foot, in my unaccomplished
simplicity, into the fiery furnace, or fiery cross, of these four
girls,—who of course reduced me to a mere heap of white

* The Ruskins had dined at the Paris home of the Domecqs in 1833,
when Ruskin was fourteen and first saw Adèle Clothilde.

ashes in four days. Four days, at the most, it took to reduce me to ashes, but the *Mercredi des cendres* lasted four years.

Anything more comic in the externals of it, anything more tragic in the essence, could not have been invented by the skilfullest designer in either kind. In my social behaviour and mind I was a curious combination of Mr. Traddles, Mr. Toots, and Mr. Winkle. I had the real fidelity and single-mindedness of Mr. Traddles, with the conversational abilities of Mr. Toots, and the heroic ambition of Mr. Winkle;— all these illuminated by imagination like Mr. Copperfield's, at his first Norwood dinner.

Clotilde (Adèle Clotilde in full, but her sisters called her Clotilde, after the queen-saint, and I Adèle, because it rhymed to shell, spell, and knell) was only made more resplendent by the circlet of her sisters' beauty; while my own shyness and unpresentableness were farther stiffened, or rather sanded, by a patriotic and Protestant conceit, which was tempered neither by politeness nor sympathy; so that, while in company I sate jealously miserable like a stock fish (in truth, I imagine, looking like nothing so much as a skate in an aquarium trying to get up the glass), on any blessed occasion of tête-à-tête I endeavoured to entertain my Spanish-born, Paris-bred, and Catholic-hearted mistress with my own views upon the subjects of the Spanish Armada, the Battle of Waterloo, and the doctrine of Transubstantiation.

To these modes of recommending myself, however, I did not fail to add what display I could make of the talents I supposed myself to possess. I wrote with great pains, and straining of my invention, a story about Naples (which I had never seen), and "the Bandit Leoni," whom I represented as typical of what my own sanguinary and adventurous disposition would have been had I been brought up a bandit; and "the Maiden Giuletta," in whom I portrayed all the perfections of my mistress. Our connection with Messrs. Smith & Elder enabled me to get this story printed in *Friendship's Offering;* and Adèle laughed over it in rippling ectasies of derision, of which I bore the pain bravely, for the sake of seeing her thoroughly amused.

I dared not address any sonnets straight to herself; but when she went back to Paris, wrote her a French letter seven quarto pages long, descriptive of the desolations and solitudes of Herne Hill since her departure. This letter, either Elise or Caroline wrote to tell me she had really read, and "laughed immensely at the French of." Both Caroline and Elise pitied me a little, and did not like to say she had also laughed at the contents.

The old people, meanwhile, saw little harm in all this. Mr. Domecq, who was extremely good-natured, and a good judge of character, rather liked me, because he saw that I was good-natured also, and had some seedling brains, which would come up in time: in the interests of the business he was perfectly ready to give me any of his daughters I liked, who could also be got to like me, but considered that the time was not come to talk of such things. My father was entirely of the same mind, besides being pleased at my getting a story printed in *Friendship's Offering*, glad that I saw something of girls with good manners, and in hopes that if I wrote poetry about them, it might be as good as the *Hours of Idleness*. My mother, who looked upon the idea of my marrying a Roman Catholic as too monstrous to be possible in the decrees of Heaven, and too preposterous to be even guarded against on earth, was rather annoyed at the whole business, as she would have been if one of her chimneys had begun smoking,—but had not the slightest notion her house was on fire. She saw more, however, than my father, into the depth of the feeling, but did not, in her motherly tenderness, like to grieve me by any serious check to it. She hoped, when the Domecqs went back to Paris, we might see no more of them, and that Adèle's influence and memory would pass away—with next winter's snow.

Under these indulgent circumstances,—bitterly ashamed of the figure I had made, but yet not a whit dashed back out of my daily swelling foam of furious conceit, supported as it was by real depth of feeling, and (note it well, good reader) by a true and glorious sense of the newly revealed miracle of human love, in its exaltation of the physical beauty of the world I had till then sought by its own light alone,—I set myself in that my seventeenth year, in a state of majestic imbecility, to write a tragedy on a Venetian subject, in which the sorrows of my soul were to be enshrined in immortal verse,—the fair heroine, Bianca, was to be endowed with the perfections of Desdemona and the brightness of Juliet,—and Venice and Love were to be described, as never had been thought of before. I may note in passing that on my first sight of the Ducal Palace, the year before, I had deliberately announced to my father and mother, and—it seemed to me stupidly incredulous—Mary, that I meant to make such a drawing of the Ducal Palace as never had been made before. This I proceeded to perform by collecting some hasty memoranda on the spot, and finishing my design elaborately out of my head at Treviso. The drawing still exists,—for a wonder, out of perspective, which I had now got too conceited to follow the rules of,—and with the diaper pattern of the red and white marbles represented as a bold panelling in relief. No figure disturbs the solemn tranquillity of the Riva, and the gondolas—each in the shape of a Turkish crescent standing on its back on the water—float about without the aid of gondoliers.

I remember nothing more of that year, 1836, than sitting under the mulberry tree in the back garden, writing my tragedy. I forget whether we went travelling or not, or what I did in the rest of the day. It is all now blank to me, except Venice, Bianca, and looking out over Shooter's Hill, where I could see the last turn of the road to Paris.*

[Vol. I, Chap. 10]

* In a later chapter of *Præterita* Ruskin returned to the subject of Adèle. One sentence from that chapter may be read as an epilogue to this one, and, indeed, to the whole tragic course of Ruskin's marriage and his subsequent attachment to Rose La Touche: "I wonder mightily now what sort of a creature I should have turned out, if at this time Love had been with me instead of against me; and instead of the distracting and useless pain, I had had the joy of approved love, and the untellable, incalculable motive of its sympathy and praise."

Fontainebleau

The year 1842 dawned for me, with many things in its morning cloud. In the early spring of it, a change came over
Turner's mind. He wanted to make some drawings to please
himself; but also to be paid for making them. He gave Mr.
Griffith fifteen sketches for choice of subject by any one who
would give him a commission. He got commissions for nine,
of which my father let me choose at first one, then was
coaxed and tricked into letting me have two. Turner got
orders, out of all the round world besides, for seven more.
With the sketches, four finished drawings were shown for
samples of the sort of thing Turner meant to make of them,
and for immediate purchase by anybody.

Among them was the "Splügen," which I had some hope
of obtaining by supplication, when my father, who was
travelling, came home. I waited dutifully till he should
come. In the meantime it was bought, with the loveliest
Lake Lucerne, by Mr. Munro of Novar.

The thing became to me grave matter for meditation. In
a story by Miss Edgeworth, the father would have come
home in the nick of time, effaced Mr. Munro as he hesitated
with the "Splügen" in his hand, and given the dutiful son
that, and another. I found, after meditation, that Miss Edgeworth's way was not the world's, nor Providence's. I perceived then, and conclusively, that if you do a foolish thing,
you suffer for it exactly the same, whether you do it piously
or not. I knew perfectly well that this drawing was the best
Swiss landscape yet painted by man; and that it was entirely
proper for *me* to have it, and inexpedient that anybody else
should. I ought to have secured it instantly, and begged my
father's pardon, tenderly. He would have been angry, and
surprised, and grieved; but loved me none the less, found in
the end I was right, and been entirely pleased. I should have
been very uncomfortable and penitent for a while, but loved
my father all the more for having hurt him, and, in the good

of the thing itself, finally satisfied and triumphant. As it was, the "Splügen" was a thorn in both our sides, all our lives. My father was always trying to get it; Mr. Munro, aided by dealers, always raising the price on him, till it got up from 80 to 400 guineas. Then we gave it up,—with unspeakable wear and tear of best feelings on both sides.

And how about "Thou shalt not covet," etc.? Good reader, if you ask this, please consult my philosophical works. Here, I can only tell you facts, whether of circumstance or law. It is a law that if you do a foolish thing you suffer for it, whatever your motive. I do not say the motive itself may not be rewarded or punished on its own merits. In this case, nothing but mischief, as far as I know, came of the whole matter.

In the meantime, bearing the disappointment as best I could, I rejoiced in the sight of the sketches, and the hope of the drawings that were to be. And they gave me much more to think of than my mischance. I saw that these sketches were straight impressions from nature,—not artificial designs, like the Carthages and Romes. And it began to occur to me that perhaps even in the artifice of Turner there might be more truth than I had understood. I was by this time very learned in *his* principles of composition; but it seemed to me that in these later subjects Nature herself was composing with him.

Considering of these matters, one day on the road to Norwood, I noticed a bit of ivy round a thorn stem, which seemed, even to my critical judgment, not ill "composed"; and proceeded to make a light and shade pencil study of it in my grey paper pocket-book, carefully, as if it had been a bit of sculpture, liking it more and more as I drew. When it was done, I saw that I had virtually lost all my time since I was twelve years old, because no one had ever told me to draw what was really there! All my time, I mean, given to drawing as an art; of course I had the records of places, but had never seen the beauty of anything, not even of a stone— how much less of a leaf!

I was neither so crushed nor so elated by the discovery as I ought to have been, but it ended the chrysalid days. Thenceforward my advance was steady, however slow.

This must have been in May, and a week or two afterwards I went up for my degree [at Oxford], but find no entry of it. I only went up for a pass, and still wrote Latin so badly that there was a chance of my *not* passing! but the examiners forgave it because the divinity, philosophy, and mathematics were all above the average; and they gave me a complimentary double-fourth.

When I was sure I had got through, I went out for a walk in the fields north of New College, (since turned into the Parks,) happy in the sense of recovered freedom, but extremely doubtful to what use I should put it. There I was, at two and twenty, with such and such powers, all second-rate except the analytic ones, which were as much in embryo as the rest, and which I had no means of measuring; such and such likings, hitherto indulged rather against conscience; and a dim sense of duty to myself, my parents, and a daily more vague shadow of Eternal Law.

What should I be, or do? my utterly indulgent father ready to let me do anything; with my room always luxuriously furnished in his house,—my expenses paid if I chose to travel. I was not heartless enough, yet, to choose to do that, alone. Perhaps it may deserve some dim praise that I never seriously thought of leaving my father and mother to explore foreign countries; and certainly the fear of grieving them was intermingled more or less with all my thoughts; but then, I did not much *want* to explore foreign countries. I had not the least love of adventure, but liked to have comfortable rooms always ordered, and a three-course dinner ready by four o'clock. Although no coward under circumstances of accidental danger, I extremely objected to any vestige of danger as a continuous element in one's life. I would not go to India for fear of tigers, nor to Russia for fear of bears, nor to Peru for fear of earthquakes; and finally, though I had no rightly glowing or grateful affection for either father or mother, yet as they could not well do without me, so also I found I was not altogether comfortable without *them*.

So for the present, we planned a summer-time in Switzerland, not of travelling, but chiefly stay in Chamouni, to give me mountain air, and the long coveted power of examining the Mont Blanc rocks accurately. My mother loved Chamouni nearly as much as I; but this plan was of severe self-denial to my father, who did not like snow, nor wooden-walled rooms.

But he gave up all his own likings for me, and let me plan the stages through France as I chose, by Rouen, Chartres, Fontainebleau, and Auxerre. A pencil-sketch or two at first show only want of faith in my old manner, and more endeavour for light and shade, futile enough. The flat cross-country between Chartres and Fontainebleau, with an oppressive sense of Paris to the north, fretted me wickedly; when we got to the Fountain of Fair Water I lay feverishly wakeful through the night, and was so heavy and ill in the morning that I could not safely travel, and fancied some bad sickness was coming on. However, towards twelve o'clock the inn people brought me a little basket of wild strawberries; and they refreshed me, and I put my sketch-book in pocket and trotted out, though still in an extremely languid and woe-begone condition; and getting into a cart-road among some young trees, where there was nothing to see but the blue sky through thin branches, lay lown on the bank by the roadside to see if I could sleep. But I couldn't, and the branches against the blue sky began to interest me, motionless as the branches of a tree of Jesse on a painted window.

Feeling gradually somewhat livelier, and that I wasn't going to die this time, and be buried in the sand, though I couldn't for the present walk any farther, I took out my book, and began to draw a little aspen tree, on the other side of the cart-road, carefully. . . .

Languidly, but not idly, I began to draw it; and as I drew, the languor passed away: the beautiful lines insisted on being traced,—without weariness. More and more beautiful they became, as each rose out of the rest, and took its place in the air. With wonder increasing every instant, I saw that they "composed" themselves, by finer laws than any known of men. At last, the tree was there, and everything that I had thought before about trees, nowhere.

The Norwood ivy had not abased me in that final manner, because one had always felt that ivy was an ornamental creature, and expected it to behave prettily, on occasion. But that all the trees of the wood (for I saw surely that my little aspen was only one of their millions) should be beautiful—more than Gothic tracery, more than Greek vase-imagery, more than the daintiest embroiderers of the East could embroider, or the artfullest painters of the West could limn,—this was indeed an end to all former thoughts with me, an insight into a new silvan world.

Not silvan only. The woods, which I had only looked on as wilderness, fulfilled I then saw, in their beauty, the same laws which guided the clouds, divided the light, and balanced the wave. "He hath made everything beautiful, in his time," became for me thenceforward the interpretation of the bond between the human mind and all visible things; and I returned along the wood-road feeling that it had led me far;—Farther than ever fancy had reached, or theodolite measured. . . .

We went home in 1842 by the Rhine and Flanders: and at Cologne and St. Quentin I made the last drawings ever executed in my old manner. That of the great square at Cologne was given to Osborne Gordon, and remains I believe with his sister, Mrs. Pritchard. The St. Quentin has vanished into space.

We returned once more to the house at Herne Hill, and the lovely drawings Turner had made for me, "Ehrenbreitstein" and "Lucerne," were first hung in its little front dining-room. But the Herne Hill days, and many joys with them, were now ended.

Perhaps my mother had sometimes—at Hampton Court,

or Chatsworth, or Isola-Bella—admitted into her quiet soul the idea that it might be nice to have a larger garden. Sometimes a gold-tasselled Oxford friend would come out from Cavendish or Grosvenor Square to see me; and there was only the little back room opposite the nursery for him to wash his hands in. As his bank-balance enlarged, even my father thought it possible that his country customers might be more impressed by enjoying their after-dinner sherry with more room for their legs. And, now that I was of age and B.A. and so on—did not *I* also want a larger house?

No, good reader; but ever since first I could drive a spade, I had wanted to dig a canal, and make locks on it, like Harry in *Harry and Lucy*. And in the field at the back of the Denmark Hill house, now, in this hour of all our weaknesses, offered in temptation, I saw my way to a canal with any number of locks down towards Dulwich.

It is very wonderful to me, looking back, to remember this, and how entirely boyish—and very young-boyish, too —I was still, in all instincts of personal delight: while yet, looking out of myself, I saw farther than Kings of Naples or Cardinals of Rome.

Yet there was much, and very closely balanced, debate, before the house was taken. My mother wisely, though sadly, said it was too late for her; she could not now manage a large garden: and my father, feeling his vanity had more than a word in the matter, besides all that might rightly be alleged of what was now convenient and becoming, hesitated painfully, as he had done about his first Copley Fielding.

But at last the lease of the larger house was bought: and everybody said how wise and proper; and my mother *did* like arranging the rows of pots in the big greenhouse; and the view from the breakfast-room into the field was really very lovely. And we bought three cows, and skimmed our own cream, and churned our own butter. And there was a stable, and a farmyard, and a haystack, and a pigstye, and a porter's lodge, where undesirable visitors could be stopped before startling us with a knock. But, for all these things, we never were so happy again. Never any more "at home."

At Champagnole, yes; and in Chamouni,—in La Cloche, at Dijon,—in Le Cygne, at Lucerne. All these places were of the old time. But though we had many happy days in the Denmark Hill house, none of our new ways ever were the same to us as the old: the basketfuls of peaches had not the flavour of the numbered dozen or score; nor were all the apples of the great orchard worth a single dishful of the Siberian crabs of Herne Hill.   [Vol. II, Chap. 4]

The Simplon

More and more deeply every hour, in retracing Alpine paths,—by my fireside,—the wonder grows on me, what Heaven made the Alps for, and gave the chamois its foot, and the gentian its blue,—yet gave no one the heart to love them. And in the Alps, why especially that mighty central pass was so divinely planned, yet no one to pass it but against their wills, till Napoleon came, and made a road over it.

Nor often, since, with any joy; though in truth there is no other such piece of beauty and power, full of human interest of the most strangely varied kind, in all the mountain scenery of the globe, as that traverse, with its two terminal cities, Geneva and Milan; its two lovely lakes of approach, Leman and Maggiore; its two tremendous valleys of vestibule, the Valais and Val d'Ossola; and its own, not desolate nor terrible, but wholly beautiful, upper region of rose and snow.

Of my early joy in Milan, I have already told; of Geneva, there is no telling, though I must now give what poor picture I may of the days we spent there, happy to young and old alike, again and again, in '33, '35, '42, and now, with full deliberation, in '44, knowing, and, in their repetitions twice, and thrice, and four times, magnifying, the well-remembered joys. And still I am more thankful, through every year of added life, that I was born in London, near enough to Geneva for me to reach it easily;—and yet a city so contrary to everything Genevoise as best to teach me what the wonders of the little canton were.

A little canton, four miles square, and which did not wish to be six miles square! A little town, composed of a cluster of water-mills, a street of penthouses, two wooden bridges, two dozen of stone houses on a little hill, and three or four perpendicular lanes up and down the hill. The four miles of acreage round, in grass, with modest gardens, and farm-dwelling houses; the people, pious, learned, and busy, to a man, to a woman—to a boy, to a girl, of them; progressing to and fro mostly on their feet, and only where they had business. And this bird's-nest of a place, to be the centre of religious and social thought, and of physical beauty, to all living Europe! That is to say, thinking and designing Europe,—France, Germany, and Italy. They, and their pieties, and their prides, their arts and their insanities, their wraths and slaughters, springing and flowering, building and forti-fying, foaming and thundering round this inconceivable point of patience: the most lovely spot, and the most nota-ble, without any possible dispute, of the European universe; yet the nations do not covet it, do not gravitate to it,—what is more wonderful, do not make a wilderness of it. They fight their battles at Chalons and Leipsic; they build their cotton mills on the Aire, and leave the Rhone running with a million of Aire power,—all pure. They build their pleas-ure houses on Thames shingle, and Seine mud, to look across to Lambeth, and—whatever *is* on the other side of the Seine. They found their military powers in the sand of Berlin, and leave this precipice-guarded plain in peace. And yet it rules them,—is the focus of thought to them, and of passion, of science, and of *contrat social;* of rational con-duct, and of decent—and other—manners. Saussure's school and Calvin's,—Rousseau's and Byron's,—Turner's,—

And of course, I was going to say, mine; but I didn't write all that last page to end so. Yet Geneva had better

have ended with educating me and the likes of me, instead
of the people who have hold of it now, with their polypous
knots of houses, communal with "London, Paris, and New
York."

Beneath which, and on the esplanades of the modern
casino, New York and London now live—no more the
Genevese. What their home once was, I must try to tell, as
I saw it.

First, it was a notable town for keeping all its poor,—
inside of it. In the very centre, where an English town has
its biggest square, and its Exchange on the model of the
Parthenon, built for the sake of the builder's commission
on the cost; there, on their little pile-propped island, and
by the steep lane-sides, lived the Genevoise poor; in their
garrets,—their laborious upper spinning or watch-wheel
cutting rooms,—their dark niches and angles of lane: mostly
busy; the infirm and old all seen to and cared for, their
porringers filled and their pallet-beds made, by household
care.

But, outside the ramparts, no more poor. A sputter, perhaps, southward, along the Savoy road; but in all the cham-
paign round, no mean rows of cubic lodgings with Doric
porches; no squalid fields of mud and thistles; no deserts
of abandoned brickfield and insolvent kitchen garden. On
the instant, outside Geneva gates, perfectly smooth, clean,
trim-hedged or prim-walled country roads; the main broad
one intent on far-away things, its signal-posts inscribed
"Route de Paris"; branching from it, right and left, a labyrinth of equally well-kept ways for fine carriage wheels, between the gentlemen's houses with their farms; each having
its own fifteen to twenty to fifty acres of mostly meadow,
rich-waving always (in my time for being there) with grass
and flowers, like a kaleidoscope. Stately plane trees, aspen
and walnut,—sometimes in avenue,—casting breezy, never
gloomy, shade round the dwelling-house. A *dwelling*-house
indeed, all the year round; no travelling from it to fairer
lands possible; no shutting up for seasons in town; hay-
time and fruit-time, school-time and play, for generation

after generation, within the cheerful white domicile with its green shutters and shingle roof,—pinnacled perhaps, humorously, at the corners, glittering on the edges with silvery tin. "Kept up" the whole place, and all the neighbours' places, not ostentatiously, but perfectly: enough gardeners to mow, enough vintagers to press, enough nurses to nurse; no foxes to hunt, no birds to shoot; but every household felicity possible to prudence and honour, felt and fulfilled from infancy to age. . . .

That was the way of things on the north side; on the south, the town is still, in the main buildings of it, as then; the group of officially aristocratic houses round the cathedral and college presenting the same inaccessible sort of family dignity that they do to-day; only, since then, the Geneva Liberals—— Well, I will not say what they have done; the main town stands still on its height of pebble-gravel, knit almost into rock; and still the upper terraces look across the variously mischievous Liberal works to the open southern country, rising in steady slope of garden, orchard, and vineyard—sprinkled with pretty farm-houses and bits of chateau, like a sea-shore with shells; rising always steeper and steeper, till the air gets rosy in the distance, then blue, and the great walnut-trees have become dots, and the farmsteads, minikin as if they were the fairy-finest of models made to be packed in a box; and then, instant— above vineyard, above farmstead, above field and wood, leaps up the Salève cliff, two thousand feet into the air.

I don't think anybody who goes to Geneva ever sees the Salève. For the most part, no English creature ever *does* see farther than over the way; and the Salève, unless you carefully peer into it, and make out what it is, pretends to be nothing,—a long, low swell like the South Downs, I fancy most people take it for, and look no more. Yet there are few rocks in the high Alps more awful than the "Angle" of the Salève, at its foot—seven Shakespeare's Cliffs set one on the top of another, and all of marble.

On the other side of the high town the houses stand closer, leaving yet space for a little sycamore-shaded walk, whence one looks down on the whole southern reach of lake, opening wide to the horizon, and edged there like the sea, but in the summer sunshine looking as if it was the one well of blue which the sunbeams drank to make the sky of. Beyond it, ghostly ranges of incredible mountains—the Dent d'Oche, and first cliffs towards Fribourg; to the west, the long wave of Jura, fading into the air above Neuchatel.

That was the view for full noon, when the lake was brightest and bluest. Then you fell down a perpendicular lane into the lower town again, and you went to Mr. Bautte's.

Virtually there was no other jeweller in Geneva, in the great times. There were some respectable, uncompetitive shops, not dazzling, in the main street; and smaller ones, with an average supply of miniature watches, that would go well for ten years; and uncostly, but honest, trinketry. But one went to Mr. Bautte's with awe, and of necessity, as one did to one's bankers. There was scarcely any external sign of Bautte whatever—a small brass plate at the side of a narrow arched door, into an alley—into a secluded alley—leading into a monastic courtyard, out of which—or rather out of the alley, where it opened to the court, you ascended a winding stair, wide enough for two only, and came to a green door, swinging, at the top of it; and there you paused to summon courage to enter.

A not large room, with a single counter at the further side. Nothing shown on the counter. Two confidential attendants behind it, and—it might possibly be Mr. Bautte!—or his son—or his partner—or anyhow the Ruling power—at his desk beside the back window. You told what you wanted: it was necessary to know your mind, and to be sure you *did* want it; there was no showing of things for temptation at Bautte's. You wanted a bracelet, a brooch, a watch—plain or enamelled. Choice of what was wanted was quietly given. There were no big stones, nor blinding galaxies of wealth. Entirely sound workmanship in the purest gold that could be worked; fine enamel for the most part, for colour, rather than jewels; and a certain Bauttesque subtlety of linked and wreathed design, which the experienced eye recognized when worn in Paris or London. Absolutely just and moderate price; wear,—to the end of your days. You came away with a sense of duty fulfilled, of treasure possessed, and of a new foundation to the respectability of your family.

You returned into the light of the open street with a blissful sense of a parcel being made up to be sent after you, and in the consequently calm expatiation of mind, went usually to watch the Rhone.

Bautte's was in the main street, out of which one caught glimpses, down the short cross ones, of the passing water; as at Sandgate, or the like fishing towns, one got peeps of the sea. With twenty steps you were beside it.

For all other rivers there is a surface, and an underneath, and a vaguely displeasing idea of the bottom. But the Rhone flows like one lambent jewel; its surface is nowhere, its ethereal self is everywhere, the iridescent rush and translucent strength of it blue to the shore, and radiant to the depth.

Fifteen feet thick, of not flowing, but flying water; not water, neither,—melted glacier, rather, one should call it; the force of the ice is with it, and the wreathing of the clouds, the gladness of the sky, and the continuance of Time.

Waves of clear sea are, indeed, lovely to watch, but they are always coming or gone, never in any taken shape to be seen for a second. But here was one mighty wave that was always itself, and every fluted swirl of it, constant as the wreathing of a shell. No wasting away of the fallen foam, no pause for gathering of power, no helpless ebb of discouraged recoil; but alike through bright day and lulling night, the never-pausing plunge, and never-fading flash, and never-hushing whisper, and, while the sun was up, the ever-answering glow of unearthly aquamarine, ultramarine, violet-blue, gentian-blue, peacock-blue, river-of-paradise blue, glass of a painted window melted in the sun, and the witch of the Alps flinging the spun tresses of it for ever from her snow.

[Vol. II, Chap. 5]

The Grande Chartreuse

There is no word, in the fragment of diary recording, in last *Præterita,* our brief visit to the Grande Chartreuse, of anything we saw or heard there that made impression upon any of us. Yet a word was said, of significance enough to alter the courses of religious thought in me, afterwards for ever.

I had been totally disappointed with the Monastery itself, with the pass of approach to it, with the mountains round it, and with the monk who showed us through it. The building was meanly designed and confusedly grouped; the road up to it nothing like so terrific as most roads in the Alps up to anywhere; the mountains round were simplest commonplace of Savoy cliff, with no peaks, no glaciers, no cascades, nor even any slopes of pine in extent of majesty. And the monk who showed us through the corridors had no cowl worth the wearing, no beard worth the wagging, no expression but of superciliousness without sagacity, and an ungraciously dull manner, showing that he was much tired of the place, more of himself, and altogether of my father and me.

Having followed him for a time about the passages of the scattered building, in which there was nothing to show, —not a picture, not a statue, not a bit of old glass, or well-wrought vestment or jewellery, nor any architectural feature in the least ingenious or lovely, we came to a pause at last in what I suppose was a type of a modern Carthusian's cell, wherein, leaning on the window sill, I said something in the style of *Modern Painters,* about the effect of the scene outside upon religious minds. Whereupon, with a curl of his lip, "We do not come here," said the monk, "to look at the mountains." Under which rebuke I bent my head silently, thinking however all the same, "What then, by all that's stupid, do you come here for at all?" . . .

The first impression from life of the secluded Sisterhoods

was given me at the Convent of St. Michael, on the summit of the isolated peak of lava at Le Puy, in Auvergne, in 1840. The hostess-sister who showed my father and me what it was permitted to see of chapel or interior buildings, was a cheerful, simple creature, pleased with us at once for our courtesy to her, and admiration of her mountain home, and belief in her sacred life. Protestant visitors being then rare in Auvergne, and still more, reverent and gentle ones, she gave her pretty curiosity free sway; and inquired earnestly of us, what sort of creatures we were,—how far we believed in God, or tried to be good, or hoped to go to heaven? And our responses under this catechism being in their sum more pleasing to her than she had expected, and manifesting, to her extreme joy and wonder, a Christian spirit, so far as she could judge, in harmony with all she had been herself taught, she proceeded to cross-examine us on closer points of Divinity, to find out, if she could, why we were, or unnecessarily called ourselves, anything else than Catholic? The one flaw in our faith which at last her charity fastened on, was that we were not *sure* of our salvation in Christ, but only hoped to get into heaven,—and were not at all, by that dim hope, relieved from terror of death, when at any time it should come. Whereupon she launched involuntarily into an eager and beautiful little sermon, to every word of which her own perfectly happy and innocent face gave vivid power, and assurance of sincerity,—how "we needed to be *sure* of our safety in Christ, and that every one might be so who came to Him and prayed to Him; and that all good Catholics were as sure of heaven as if they were already there;" and so dismissed us at the gate with true pity, and beseeching that we would prove the goodness of God, and be in peace. Which exhortation of hers I have never forgotten; only it has always seemed to me that there was no entering into that rest of hers but by living on the top of some St. Michael's rock too, which it did not seem to me I was meant to do, by any means.

But in here recording the impression made on my father

and me, I must refer to what I said above of our common feeling of being, both of us, as compared with my mother, reprobate and worldly characters, despising our birthright like Esau, or cast out, for our mocking ways, like Ishmael. For my father never ventured to give me a religious lesson; and though he went to church with a resigned countenance, I knew very well that he liked going just as little as I did. . . .

This breaking down of my Puritan faith, being the matter probably most important to many readers of my later books, shall be traced in this chapter to the sorrowful end. . . . And here I must trace, as simply and rapidly as may be, the story of my relations with the Working Men's College.

I knew of its masters only the Principal, F. D. Maurice, and my own friend Rossetti. It is to be remembered of Rossetti with loving honour, that he was the only one of our modern painters who taught disciples for love of them. He was really not an Englishman, but a great Italian tormented in the Inferno of London; doing the best he could, and teaching the best he could; but the "could" shortened by the strength of his animal passions, without any trained control, or guiding faith. Of him, more hereafter.

I loved Frederick Maurice, as every one did who came near him; and have no doubt he did all that was in him to do of good in his day. Which could by no means be said either of Rossetti or of me: but Maurice was by nature puzzle-headed, and, though in a beautiful manner, *wrong*-headed; while his clear conscience and keen affections made him egotistic, and in his Bible-reading, as insolent as any infidel of them all. I only went once to a Bible-lesson of his; and the meeting was significant, and conclusive.

The subject of lesson, Jael's slaying of Sisera. Concerning which, Maurice, taking an enlightened modern view of what was fit and not, discoursed in passionate indignation; and warned his class, in the most positive and solemn manner, that such dreadful deeds could only have been done in cold blood in the Dark Biblical ages; and that no religious and patriotic Englishwoman ought ever to think of imitating Jael by nailing a Russian's or Prussian's skull to the ground, —especially after giving him butter in a lordly dish. At the close of the instruction, through which I sate silent, I ventured to inquire, why then had Deborah the prophetess declared of Jael, "Blessed above women shall the wife of Heber the Kenite be"? On which Maurice, with startled and flashing eyes, burst into partly scornful, partly alarmed, denunciation of Deborah the prophetess, as a mere blazing Amazon; and of her Song as a merely rhythmic storm of battle-rage, no more to be listened to with edification or faith than the Norman's sword-song at the battle of Hastings.

Whereupon there remained nothing for *me*,—to whom the Song of Deborah was as sacred as the Magnificat,—but total collapse in sorrow and astonishment; the eyes of all the class being also bent on me in amazed reprobation of my benighted views, and unchristian sentiments. And I got away how I could, but never went back. . . .

Somewhat before the date of my farewell to Maurician free-thinking, I had come into still more definite collision with the Puritan dogmata which forbid thinking at all, in a séance to which I was invited, shyly, by my friend Macdonald,—fashionable séance of Evangelical doctrine, at the Earl of Ducie's; presided over by Mr. Molyneux, then a divine of celebrity in that sect; who sate with one leg over his other knee in the attitude always given to Herod at the massacre of the Innocents in mediæval sculpture; and discoursed in tones of consummate assurance and satisfaction, and to the entire comfort and consent of his Belgravian audience, on the beautiful parable of the Prodigal Son. Which, or how many, of his hearers he meant to describe as having personally lived on husks, and devoured their fathers' property, did not of course appear; but that something of the sort was necessary to the completeness of the joy in heaven over them, now in Belgrave Square, at the feet—or one foot —of Mr. Molyneux, could not be questioned.

Waiting my time, till the raptures of the converted company had begun to flag a little, I ventured, from a back seat, to inquire of Mr. Molyneux what we were to learn from the example of the *other* son, not prodigal, who was, his father said of him, "ever with me, and all that I have, thine"? A sudden horror, and unanimous feeling of the serpent having, somehow, got over the wall into their Garden of Eden, fell on the whole company; and some of them, I thought, looked at the candles, as if they expected them to burn blue. After a pause of a minute, gathering himself into an expression of pity and indulgence, withholding latent thunder, Mr. Molyneux explained to me that the home-staying son was merely a picturesque figure introduced to fill the background of the parable agreeably, and contained no instruction or example for the well-disposed scriptural student, but, on the contrary, rather a snare for the unwary, and a temptation to self-righteousness,—which was, of all sins, the most offensive to God.

Under the fulmination of which answer I retired, as from Maurice's, from the séance in silence; nor ever attended another of the kind from that day to this.

But neither the Puritanism of Belgravia, nor Liberalism of Red Lion Square, interested, or offended, me, otherwise than as the grotesque conditions of variously typhoid or smoke-dried London life. To my old Scotch shepherd Puritanism, and the correspondent forms of noble French Protestantism, I never for an instant failed in dutiful affection and honour. From John Bunyan and Isaac Ambrose, I had received the religion by which I still myself lived, as far as I had spiritual life at all; and I had again and again proof enough of its truth, within limits, to have served me for all my own need, either in this world or the next. But my ordained business, and mental gifts, were outside of those limits. I saw, as clearly as I saw the sky and its stars, that music in Scotland was not to be studied under a Free

Church precentor, nor indeed under any disciples of John Knox, but of Signior David; that, similarly, painting in England was not to be admired in the illuminations of Watts's hymns; nor architecture in the design of Mr. Irons's chapel in the Grove. And here I must take up a thread of my mental history, as yet unfastened.

I have spoken several times of the effect given cheaply to my drawings of architecture by dexterous dots and flourishes, doing duty for ornament. Already, in 1845, I had begun to distinguish Corinthian from Norman capitals, and in 1848, drew the niches and sculpture of French Gothic with precision and patience. But I had never cared for ornamental design until in 1850 or '51 I chanced, at a bookseller's in a back alley, on a little fourteenth-century Hours of the Virgin, not of refined work, but extremely rich, grotesque, and full of pure colour.

The new worlds which every leaf of this book opened to me, and the joy I had, counting their letters and unravelling their arabesques as if they had all been of beaten gold,—as many of them indeed were,—cannot be told, any more than—everything else, of good, that I wanted to tell. Not that the worlds thus opening were themselves new, but only the possession of any part in them; for long and long ago I had gazed at the illuminated missals in noblemen's houses (see above, p. 464), with a wonder and sympathy deeper than I can give now; my love of toil, and of treasure, alike getting their thirst gratified in them. For again and again I must repeat it, my nature is a worker's and a miser's; and I rejoiced, and rejoice still, in the mere quantity of chiselling in marble, and stitches in embroidery; and was never tired of numbering sacks of gold and caskets of jewels in the *Arabian Nights:* and though I am generous too, and love giving, yet my notion of charity is not at all dividing my last crust with a beggar, but riding through a town like a Commander of the Faithful, having any quantity of sequins and ducats in saddle-bags (where cavalry officers have holsters for their pistols), and throwing them round in radiant showers and hailing handfuls; with more bags to brace on when those were empty.

But now that I had a missal of my own, and could touch its leaves and turn, and even here and there understand the Latin of it, no girl of seven years old with a new doll is prouder or happier: but the feeling was something between the girl's with her doll, and Aladdin's in a new Spirit-slave to build palaces for him with jewel windows. For truly a well-illuminated missal is a fairy cathedral full of painted windows, bound together to carry in one's pocket, with the music and the blessing of all its prayers besides.

And then followed, of course, the discovery that all beautiful prayers were Catholic,—all wise interpretations of the Bible Catholic;—and every manner of Protestant written services whatsoever either insolently altered corruptions, or washed-out and ground-down rags and débris of the great Catholic collects, litanies, and songs of praise.

"But why did not you become a Catholic at once, then?"

It might as well be asked, Why did not I become a fire-worshipper? I *could* become nothing but what I was, or was growing into. I no more believed in the living Pope than I did in the living Khan of Tartary. I saw indeed that twelfth-century psalters were lovely and right, and that presbyterian prayers against time, by people who never expected to be any the better for them, were unlovely and wrong. But I had never read the Koran, nor Confucius, nor Plato, nor Hesiod, and was only just beginning to understand my Virgil and Horace. How I ever came to understand *them* is a new story, which must be for next chapter: meantime let me finish the confessions of this one in the tale of my final apostasy from Puritan doctrine. . . .

I have registered the year 1858 as the next, after 1845, in which I had complete guidance of myself. Couttet met me at Basle, and I went on to Rheinfelden with great joy, and stayed to draw town and bridges completely (two of the studies are engraved in *Modern Painters*).

I think it was the second Sunday there, and no English

church. I had read the service with George,* and gone out afterwards alone for a walk up a lovely dingle on the Black Forest side of the Rhine, where every pretty cottage was inscribed, in fair old German characters, with the date of its building, the names of the married pair who had built it, and a prayer that, with God's blessing, their habitation of it, and its possession by their children, might be in right-eousness and peace. Not in these set terms, of course, on every house, but in variously quaint verses or mottoes, meaning always as much as this.

Very happy in my Sunday walk, I gathered what wild flowers were in their first springing, and came home with a many-coloured cluster, in which the dark-purple orchis was chief. I had never examined its structure before, and by this afternoon sunlight did so with care; also it seemed to me wholly right to describe it as I examined; and to draw the outlines as I described, though with a dimly alarmed consciousness of its being a new fact in existence for me, that I should draw on Sunday.

Which thenceforward I continued to do, if it seemed to me there was due occasion. Nevertheless, come to pass how it might, the real new fact in existence for me was that my drawings did not prosper that year, and, in deepest sense, never prospered again. They might not have prospered in the course of things,—and indeed, could not without better guidance than my own; nevertheless, the crisis of change is marked at Rheinfelden by my having made there two really pretty colour-vignettes, which, had I only gone on doing the like of, the journey would have been visibly successful in everybody's sight. Whereas, what actually followed those vignettes at Rheinfelden was a too ambitious attempt at the cliffs of the Bay of Uri, which crushed the strength down in me; and next, a persistently furious one to draw the entire town, three fortresses, and surrounding mountains of Bel-linzona, gradually taming and contracting itself into a

* Ruskin's valet, John Hobbs, called "George" to avoid confusion in a household with a surfeit of Johns.

meekly obstinate resolve that at least I would draw every stone of the roof right in *one* tower of the vineyards,— "cette baraque," as Couttet called it.

I *did* draw every stone, nearly right, at last in that single roof; and meantime read the *Plutus* of Aristophanes, three or four times over in two months, with long walks every afternoon, besides. Total result on 1st of August—general desolation, and disgust with Bellinzona,—cette baraque,— and most of all with myself, for not yet knowing Greek enough to translate the *Plutus*. In this state of mind, a fit took me of hunger for city life again, military bands, nicely-dressed people, and shops with something inside. And I emphasized Couttet's disapproval of the whole tour, by announcing to him suddenly that I was going, of all places in the world, to Turin!

I had still some purpose, even in this libertinage, namely, to outline the Alpine chain from Monte Viso to Monte Rosa. Its base was within a drive; and there were Veroneses in the Royal gallery, for wet days. The luxury of the Hôtel de l'Europe was extremely pleasant after brick floors and bad dinners at Bellinzona;—there was a quiet little opera-house, where it was always a kindness to the singers to attend to the stage business; finally, any quantity of marching and manœuvring by the best troops in Italy, with perfect military bands, beautifully tossing plumes, and pretty ladies looking on. So I settled at Turin for the autumn.

There, one Sunday morning, I made my way in the south suburb to a little chapel which, by a dusty roadside, gathered to its unobserved door the few sheep of the old Waldensian faith who had wandered from their own pastures under Monte Viso into the worldly capital of Piedmont.

The assembled congregation numbered in all some three or four and twenty, of whom fifteen or sixteen were grey-haired women. Their solitary and clerkless preacher, a somewhat stunted figure in a plain black coat, with a cracked voice, after leading them through the languid forms of prayer which are all that in truth are possible to people

whose present life is dull and its terrestrial future unchange-
able, put his utmost zeal into a consolatory discourse on the
wickedness of the wide world, more especially of the plain
of Piedmont and city of Turin, and on the exclusive favour
with God, enjoyed by the between nineteen and twenty-
four elect members of his congregation, in the streets of
Admah and Zeboim.

Myself neither cheered nor greatly alarmed by this doctrine, I walked back into the condemned city, and up into
the gallery where Paul Veronese's Solomon and the Queen
of Sheba glowed in full afternoon light. The gallery windows being open, there came in with the warm air, floating
swells and falls of military music, from the courtyard before
the palace, which seemed to me more devotional, in their
perfect art, tune, and discipline, than anything I remembered of evangelical hymns. And as the perfect colour and
sound gradually asserted their power on me, they seemed
finally to fasten me in the old article of Jewish faith, that
things done delightfully and rightly were always done by the
help and in the Spirit of God.

Of course that hour's meditation in the gallery of Turin
only concluded the courses of thought which had been
leading me to such end through many years. There was no
sudden conversion possible to me, either by preacher, picture, or dulcimer. But, that day, my evangelical beliefs were
put away, to be debated of no more.   [Vol. III, Chap. 1]

L'Esterelle

Soon after I returned home, in the eventful year 1858, a
lady wrote to me from—somewhere near Green Street, W.,
—saying, as people sometimes did, in those days, that she
saw I was the only sound teacher in Art; but this farther,
very seriously, that she wanted her children—two girls and
a boy—taught the beginnings of Art rightly; especially the
younger girl, in whom she thought I might find some power

worth developing:—would I come and see her? I thought
I should rather like to; so I went, to near Green Street; and
found the mother—the sort of person I expected, but a
good deal more than I expected and in all sorts of ways.
Extremely pretty still, herself, nor at all too old to learn
many things; but mainly anxious for her children. Emily,
the elder daughter, wasn't in; but Rosie was,—should she
be sent for to the nursery? Yes, I said, if it wouldn't tease the
child, she might be sent for. So presently the drawing-room
door opened, and Rosie came in, quietly taking stock of
me with her blue eyes as she walked across the room; gave
me her hand, as a good dog gives its paw, and then stood
a little back. Nine years old, on 3rd January, 1858, thus
now rising towards ten; neither tall nor short for her age;
a little stiff in her way of standing. The eyes rather deep
blue at that time, and fuller and softer than afterwards. Lips
perfectly lovely in profile;—a little too wide; and hard in
edge, seen in front; the rest of the features what a fair, well-
bred Irish girl's usually are; the hair, perhaps, more graceful in short curl round the forehead, and softer than one
sees often, in the close-bound tresses above the neck.

I thought it likely she *might* be taught to draw a little, if
she would take time; I did not expect her to take *pains*, and
told her mother so, at once. Rosie says never a word, but we
continue to take stock of each other. "I thought you *so*
ugly," she told me, afterwards. She didn't quite mean that;
but only, her mother having talked much of my "greatness"
to her, she had expected me to be something like Garibaldi,
or the Elgin Theseus; and was extremely disappointed.

I expressed myself as ready to try what I could make of
Rosie; only I couldn't come every other day all the way
in to Green Street. Mamma asked what sort of a road there
was to Denmark Hill? I explained the simplicity and beauty
of its ramifications round the "Elephant and Castle," and
how one was quite in the country as soon as one got past
the triangular field at Champion Hill. And the wildernesses
of the Obelisk having been mapped out, and determined to

be passable, the day was really appointed for first lesson at Denmark Hill—and Emily came with her sister.

Emily was a perfectly sweet, serene, delicately-chiselled marble nymph of fourteen, softly dark-eyed, rightly tender and graceful in all she did and said. I never saw such a faculty for the arrangement of things beautifully, in any other human being. If she took up a handful of flowers, they fell out of her hand in wreathed jewellery of colour and form, as if they had been sown, and had blossomed, to live together so, and no otherwise. Her mother had the same gift, but in its more witty, thoughtful, and scientific range; in Emily it was pure wild instinct. For an Irish girl, she was not witty, for she could not make a mistake; one never laughed at what she said, but the room was brighter for it. To Rose and me she soon became no more Emily, but "Wisie," named after my dead Wisie.* All the children, and their father, loved animals;—my first sight of papa was as he caressed a green popinjay which was almost hiding itself in his waistcoat. Emily's pony, Swallow, and Rosie's dog, Bruno, will have their day in these memoirs; but Emily's "Bully" was the perfectest pet of all;—he used to pass half his day in the air, above her head, or behind her shoulders, holding a little tress of her long hair as far out as he could, on the wing.

That first day, when they came to Denmark Hill, there was much for them to see;—my mother, to begin with, and she also had to see them; on both sides the sight was thought good. Then there were thirty Turners, including the great Rialto; half-a-dozen Hunts; a beautiful Tintoret; my minerals in the study; the loaded apple trees in the orchard; the glowing peaches on the old red garden wall. The lesson lost itself that day in pomiferous talk, with rustic interludes in the stables and pigsty. The pigs especially, it was observed, were highly educated, and spoke excellent Irish. . . .

Having Turner's mountain drawings of his best time

* Ruskin's pet white spitz, who "ran like a hare and leaped like a horse."

beside us, and any quantity of convolvuluses, hollyhocks, plums, peaches, and apples, to bring in from the garden, the afternoon hours went fast; but so much more in talk than work, that I soon found, if either triangles or bind-weeds were to come to anything, it must be under the governess's superintendence, not mamma's: and that I should have to make my way to Green Street, and up to the school-room, after all, on at least two out of three of the lesson days. Both the children, to my extreme satisfaction, approved of this arrangement, and the final order was that whenever I happened to go through Green Street, I should pay them a visit in the nursery. Somehow, from that time, most of my London avocations led me through Green Street.

It chanced above all things well for me that their governess was a woman of great sense and power, whom the children entirely loved, and under whom mamma put herself, in the schoolroom, no less meekly than they; partly in play, but really also a little subdued by the clear insight of the fearlessly frank preceptress into her own faults. I cannot call them "foibles," for her native wit and strength of character admitted none.

Rosie had shortly expressed her sense of her governess's niceness by calling her "Bun"; and I had not been long free of the schoolroom before she wanted a name for me also, significant of like approval. After some deliberation, she christened me "Crumpet"; then, impressed by seeing my gentleness to beggars, canonized me as "Saint Crumpet," or, shortly and practically, "St. C.,"—which I remained ever afterwards; only Emily said one day to her sister that the C. did in truth stand for "Chrysostom."

The drawing, and very soon painting, lessons went on meantime quite effectively, both the girls working with quick intelligence and perfect feeling; so that I was soon able, with their mother's strong help, to make them understand the essential qualities both of good painting and sculpture. Rose went on into geology; but only far enough to find another play-name for me—"Archigosaurus." This was meant partly to indicate my scientific knowledge of Depths and Ages; partly to admit me more into family relations, her mother having been named, by her cleverest and fondest friend, "Lacerta,"—to signify that she had the grace and wisdom of the serpent, without its poison.

And things went on,—as good girls will know how, through all that winter;—in the spring, the Fates brought the first whirlpool into the current of them, in that (I forget exactly why) it was resolved that they should live by the Cascine of Florence in the spring, and on the Lung' Arno, instead of in the Park by the Serpentine. But there was the comfort for me that Rosie was really a little sorry to go away; and that she understood in the most curious way how sorry *I* was.

Some wise, and prettily mannered, people have told me I shouldn't say anything about Rosie at all. But I am too old now to take advice. . . .   [Vol. III, Chap. 3]

Joanna's Care

The mischances which have delayed the sequence of *Præterita* must modify somewhat also its intended order. I leave Rosie's letter* to tell what it can of the beginning of happiest days; but omit, for a little while, the further record of them,—of the shadows which gathered around them, and increased, in my father's illness; and of the lightning which struck him down in death—so sudden, that I find it extremely difficult, in looking back, to realize the state of mind in which it left either my mother or me. My own principal feeling was certainly anxiety for her, who had been for so many years in every thought dependent on my father's wishes, and withdrawn from all other social

---

* Ruskin had closed the previous chapter by reprinting in full Rose's first letter to him, lest it "moulder away, when I can read it no more, lost to all loving hearts." This was very likely the same letter which for years he carried between plates of fine gold in his breast pocket.

pleasure as long as she could be *his* companion. I scarcely felt the power I had over her, myself; and was at first amazed to find my own life suddenly becoming to her another ideal; and that new hope and pride were possible to her, in seeing me take command of my father's fortune, and permitted by him, from his grave, to carry out the theories I had formed for my political work, with unrestricted and deliberate energy.

My mother's perfect health of mind, and vital religious faith, enabled her to take all the good that was left to her, in the world, while she looked in secure patience for the heavenly future: but there was immediate need for some companionship which might lighten the burden of the days to her.

I have never yet spoken of the members of my grandmother's family, who either remained in Galloway, or were associated with my early days in London. Quite one of the dearest of them at this time, was Mrs. Agnew, born Catherine Tweddale, and named Catherine after her aunt, my father's mother. She had now for some years been living in widowhood; her little daughter, Joan, only five years old when her father died, having grown up in their pretty old house at Wigtown, in the simplicity of entirely natural and contented life. . . .

And so it chanced, providentially, that at this moment, when my mother's thoughts dwelt constantly on the past, there should be this child near us,—still truly a child, in her powers of innocent pleasure, but already so accustomed to sorrow, that there was nothing that could farther depress her in my mother's solitude. I have not time to tell of the pretty little ways in which it came about, but they all ended in my driving to No. 1, Cambridge Street, on the 19th April 1864: where her uncle (my cousin, John Tweddale) brought her up to the drawing-room to me, saying, "This is Joan."

I had seen her three years before, but not long enough to remember her distinctly: only I had a notion that she

would be "nice," and saw at once that she *was* entirely
nice, both in my mother's way, and mine; being now seventeen years and some—well, for example of accuracy and
conscience—forty-five days, old. And I very thankfully took
her hand out of her uncle's, and received her in trust, saying
—I do not remember just what,—but certainly *feeling* much
more strongly than either her uncle or she did, that the
gift, both to my mother and me, was one which we should
not easily bear to be again withdrawn. I put her into my
father's carriage at the door, and drove her out to Denmark
Hill. . . .

I draw back to my own home, twenty years ago, permitted to thank Heaven once more for the peace, and
hope, and loveliness of it, and the Elysian walks with Joanie,
and Paradisiacal with Rosie, under the peach-blossom
branches by the little glittering stream which I had paved
with crystal for them. I had built behind the highest cluster
of laurels a reservoir, from which, on sunny afternoons, I
could let a quite rippling film of water run for a couple
of hours down behind the hayfield, where the grass in
spring still grew fresh and deep. There used to be always
a corncrake or two in it. Twilight after twilight I have
hunted that bird, and never once got glimpse of it: the
voice was always at the other side of the field, or in the
inscrutable air or earth. And the little stream had its falls,
and pools, and imaginary lakes. Here and there it laid for
itself lines of graceful sand; there and here it lost itself under beads of chalcedony. It wasn't the Liffey, nor the Nith,
nor the Wandel; but the two girls were surely a little cruel
to call it "The Gutter"! Happiest times, for all of us, that
ever were to be; not but that Joanie and her Arthur* are
giddy enough, both of them yet, with their five little ones,
but they have been sorely anxious about me, and I have been

* Joan married Arthur Severn, the son of the painter Joseph Severn,
who had nursed the dying Keats in Rome and later became a friend of
the Ruskins.

sorrowful enough for myself, since ever I lost sight of that peach-blossom avenue. "Eden-land" Rosie calls it sometimes in her letters. Whether its tiny river were of the waters of Abana, or Euphrates, or Thamesis, I know not, but they were sweeter to my thirst than the fountains of Trevi or Branda.

How things bind and blend themselves together! The last time I saw the Fountain of Trevi, it was from Arthur's father's room—Joseph Severn's, where we both took Joanie to see him in 1872, and the old man made a sweet drawing of his pretty daughter-in-law, now in her schoolroom; he himself then eager in finishing his last picture of the Marriage in Cana, which he had caused to take place under a vine trellis, and delighted himself by painting the crystal and ruby glittering of the changing rivulet of water out of the Greek vase, glowing into wine. Fonte Branda I last saw with Charles Norton, under the same arches where Dante saw it. We drank of it together, and walked together that evening on the hills above, where the fireflies among the scented thickets shone fitfully in the still undarkened air. *How* they shone! moving like fine-broken starlight through the purple leaves. How they shone! through the sunset that faded into thunderous night as I entered Siena three days before, the white edges of the mountainous clouds still lighted from the west, and the openly golden sky calm behind the Gate of Siena's heart, with its still golden words, "Cor magis tibi Sena pandit,* and the fireflies everywhere in sky and cloud rising and falling, mixed with the lightning, and more intense than the stars.

BRANTWOOD,
    June 19th, 1889.   [Vol. III, Chap. 4]

* The inscription over the north gate: "More than her gates, Siena opens her heart to you."

CHRONOLOGY

1819

Born in London on February 8, the only child of John James and Margaret Cox Ruskin, first cousins of Scottish ancestry. Father a prosperous sherry merchant and fancier of art; mother a pious evangelical whose fanatically disciplined Bible lessons Ruskin later described as "the one *essential* part" of his education.

1832

Given on thirteenth birthday a copy of Samuel Rogers's *Italy,* with vignettes by Turner; the gift awakens his enthusiasm for Turner and ultimately leads to the writing of *Modern Painters.*

1836

In Paris meets and falls in love with Adèle Domecq, the daughter of his father's partner; future marriage inconceivable because of her Catholicism. Writes pedestrian love poetry and a spirited but unpublished defense of Turner. Matriculates as a gentleman-commoner at Christ Church, Oxford.

1837

In residence at Oxford, accompanied by his mother, until 1840. Publishes *The Poetry of Architecture* in the *Architectural Magazine* (1837–38).

1840

Meets Turner. Learns of Adèle Domecq's marriage. Depressed and ill, leaves Oxford for protracted foreign tour with parents (1840–41).

1842

Takes A.B. at Oxford. Ruskins move from Herne Hill to larger home at Denmark Hill, London. At work on *Modern Painters I*.

1843

Publishes *Modern Painters I* anonymously (by "A Graduate of Oxford").

1845

First Continental tour without parents vastly widens his knowledge of Italian art; the new enthusiasm reflected in *Modern Painters II*.

1846

Publishes *Modern Painters II*.

1848

Marries Euphemia Chalmers Gray, a distant cousin ten years younger than he. Tours Normandy with wife and devotes self to study of Gothic architecture.

1849

Architectural studies in Venice, where he lives with his wife in 1849–50, 1851–52, delay completion of *Modern Painters*. Publishes *The Seven Lamps of Architecture* and begins *The Stones of Venice*.

1851

Friendship with Carlyle begins. Foundations of Ruskin's evangelicalism weaken as the "dreadful Hammers" of the geologists chip away at his faith. Publishes *The Stones of Venice*, Vol. I.

1852

Later social criticism foreshadowed by three radical letters to the *Times* which his father suppresses.

1853

Publishes *The Stones of Venice*, Vols. II and III.

1854

Marriage annulled on grounds of nonconsummation; the following year Effie Gray marries John Everett Millais, the Pre-Raphaelite painter. Ruskin begins lecturing on art at the newly founded Working Men's College.

1856

Publishes *Modern Painters III* and *IV*.

1857

Lectures at Manchester on *The Political Economy of Art*.

1858

Meets and soon falls tragically in love with Rose La Touche, a brilliant but strange child thirty years his junior. Experiences a religious "unconversion" at Turin.

1859

Lectures on "Modern Manufacture and Design," published the same year in *The Two Paths*.

1860

Completes the final volume of *Modern Painters*. While at Chamonix begins his great labor of social reform. Publishes four essays on political economy in the *Cornhill Magazine;* violent criticism curtails the essays, which he reprints in 1862 as *Unto This Last*.

1861

Depressed by the "unendurable solitude" of living at Denmark Hill, where his religious heresies strain his relationship with his mother and economic heresies alienate him from his father.

1862

Resumes attack on political economists in essays published in *Fraser's Magazine* (1862–63) and reprinted as *Munera Pulveris* (1872).

1864

Becomes independently wealthy upon the death of John James Ruskin. The tortured ambivalence of Ruskin's attitude toward his father now passes into guilty self-reproach. Lectures on "Traffic" (reprinted in *The Crown of Wild Olive*) and "Of Kings' Treasuries" (reprinted in *Sesame and Lilies*).

1865

Publishes *Sesame and Lilies*.

1866

Proposes marriage to Rose La Touche, who defers her answer. Their relationship clouded by Ruskin's religious unorthodoxy and Rose's morbid religious fervor. Allusions to Rose begin to appear in his books, notably in *Sesame and Lilies*. Publishes *The Crown of Wild Olive*.

1867

Publishes *Time and Tide*, letters on an ideal commonwealth; anxiety and depression apparent in autobiographical digressions of great allusiveness and power.

1868

Lectures in Dublin on "The Mystery of Life and Its Arts" (added to *Sesame and Lilies* in 1871).

1869

Publishes *The Queen of the Air*. Appointed first Slade Professor of Fine Art at Oxford.

1870

Publishes first series of Slade *Lectures on Art*.

1871

Publishes first installment of *Fors Clavigera*, issued monthly until 1878, then intermittently through 1884. Seriously ill at Matlock; writes in *Fors* of storm cloud and plague wind. Endows drawing mastership at Oxford; founds St. George's Fund with tithe of his fortune. Purchases Brantwood, on Coniston Lake, final home for the remainder of his life. Death of Margaret Ruskin at age of ninety. Period of social experiments (1871–74), including street-sweeping in London slums and road-mending on outskirts of Oxford.

1872

Publishes *Aratra Pentelici*, lectures on sculpture, and *The Eagle's Nest*, lectures on the relation of natural science to art. Rose becomes dangerously ill, mentally and physically; she finally refuses marriage until they meet " 'face to face' in that Kingdom where love will be perfected."

1874

Regains religious faith while at Assisi, living in sacristan's cell in Church of St. Francis. Frequently abroad in 1874–77; marked irritability and hyperesthetic responses to sounds and sights, evident in passages of pathological fury in *Mornings in Florence* (1875–77) and *St. Mark's Rest* (1877–84).

1875

Rose dies insane. Ruskin gives only one course of lectures at Oxford and none the following year.

1877

Attack on Whistler in July issue of *Fors* results in suit for libel; Ruskin fined a farthing's damages in 1878 and re-signs Slade Professorship.

1878

Suspends publication of *Fors* after first of seven attacks of madness recurring over next decade.

1880

Resumes *Fors*. Recovery evident in beautiful opening section of *The Bible of Amiens* (1880–85). Publishes *Fiction, Fair and Foul* in the *Nineteenth Century* (1880–81).

1883

Resumes Professorship at Oxford for a brief, disastrous tenure ending in 1885.

1884

Lectures at the London Institution on *The Storm-Cloud of the Nineteenth Century*.

1885

Publishes first two volumes of *Præterita*, 1885–88, remainder in 1889.

1889

Suffers his most damaging attack of madness in autumn; writes nothing thereafter and lives largely in mute retirement at Brantwood until death.

1900

Dies of influenza on January 20; buried in Coniston church-yard.

SELECT BIBLIOGRAPHY

This bibliography is new for this edition.

Abse, Joan. *John Ruskin: The Passionate Moralist.* New York: Knopf, 1981. (Little critical analysis, but a fine life.)

Anthony, Peter D. *John Ruskin's Labour: A Study of Ruskin's Social Theory.* Cambridge: Cambridge Univ. Press, 1983.

Arrowsmith, William. "Ruskin's Fireflies." In *The Ruskin Polygon,* ed. John Dixon Hunt and Faith M. Holland. Manchester: Manchester Univ. Press, 1982. (Excellent on *Praeterita.*)

Austin, Linda, M. *The Practical Ruskin: Economics and Audience in the Late Work.* Baltimore: Johns Hopkins Univ. Press, 1991.

Benson, Arthur Christopher. *Ruskin: A Study in Personality.* London: Smith Elder, 1911. (Uneven but often perceptive early study.)

Birch, Dinah. *Ruskin's Myths.* Oxford: Oxford Univ. Press, 1988. (Ruskin as interpreter of the moral iconography of Greek myth.)

Bloom, Harold, ed. *John Ruskin.* New York: Chelsea, 1986.

Bradley, John L., ed. *Ruskin: The Critical Heritage.* London: Routledge, 1984. (Criticism to 1900.)

Brooks, Michael W. *John Ruskin and Victorian Architecture.* New Brunswick: Rutgers Univ. Press, 1987. (Architecturally learned, literarily astute.)

Buckley, Jerome Hamilton. "The Moral Aesthetic." In *The Victorian Temper.* Cambridge: Harvard Univ. Press, 1951. (Excellent brief account of Ruskin's "deep if chaotic coherence.")

Bullen, J. B. "The Renaissance as Fall from Grace: John Ruskin." In *The Myth of the Renaissance in Nineteenth-Century Writing.* Oxford: Oxford Univ. Press, 1994. (Learned, subtle analysis of *Stones of Venice.*)

Clark, Sir Kenneth. *Ruskin at Oxford: An Inaugural Lecture Delivered Before the University of Oxford.* Oxford: Oxford Univ. Press, 1947. (Discerning praise.)

Clegg, Jeanne. *Ruskin and Venice.* London: Junction Books, 1981.

Collingwood, W. G. *The Life and Work of John Ruskin.* 2 vols. London: Methuen, 1893. (Early biography by one of Ruskin's disciples.)

Cook, E. T. *The Life of John Ruskin.* 2 vols. London: Allen, 1911. (Largely duplicated in Cook's introductions to the *Works.*)

Culler, A. Dwight. "Ruskin and Victorian Medievalism." In *The Victorian Mirror of History.* New Haven: Yale Univ. Press, 1985.

Dowling, Linda. "Ruskin's Law in Art." In *The Vulgarization of Art: The Victorians and Aesthetic Democracy*. Charlottesville: Univ. Press of Virginia, 1996. (Illuminating on "The Nature of Gothic" and Whistler vs. Ruskin.)

Ellmann, Richard. "Overtures to Wilde's *Salome*." In *Golden Codgers*. New York: Oxford Univ. Press, 1973. (Far-out, fascinating, on *Stones of Venice* as psycho-sexual drama.)

Emerson, Sheila. *Ruskin: The Genesis of Invention*. Cambridge: Cambridge Univ. Press, 1993. (Brilliantly illuminates continuities between Ruskin's juvenilia and all that follows.)

Evans, Joan. *John Ruskin*. London: Cape, 1954.

Fain, John T. *Ruskin and the Economists*. Nashville: Vanderbilt Univ. Press, 1956.

Fellows, Jay. *The Falling Distance: The Autobiographical Impulse in John Ruskin*. Baltimore: Johns Hopkins Univ. Press, 1975.

Finley, C. Stephen. *Nature's Covenant: Figures of Landscape in Ruskin*. University Park: Pennsylvania State Univ. Press, 1992. (Typological reading of Ruskin's landscapes as a "continual Gospel.")

Fitch, Raymond E. *The Poison Sky: Myth and Apocalypse in Ruskin*. Athens: Ohio Univ. Press, 1982. (Massive, impassioned, on Ruskin as ecological prophet.)

Fleishman, Avrom. "Ruskin's *Praeterita*: The Enclosed Garden." In *Figures of Autobiography*. Berkeley: Univ. of California Press, 1983.

Fontaney, Pierre. "Ruskin and Paradise Regained." *Victorian Studies* 12 (1969), 347–56. (On *Praeterita*.)

Garrigan, Kristine O. *Ruskin on Architecture: His Thought and Influence*. Madison: Univ. of Wisconsin Press, 1973. (Lively, intelligent, humane.)

Gordon, Susan Phelps, and Anthony L. Gully, eds. *John Ruskin and the Victorian Eye*. New York: 1993. (Sumptuously illustrated catalog, with essays by various hands.)

Harrison, Frederic. *John Ruskin*. New York: Macmillan, 1902. (Perceptive on Ruskin's style; otherwise, merely a popularization of his thought.)

Helsinger, Elizabeth K. *Ruskin and the Art of the Beholder*. Cambridge: Harvard Univ. Press, 1982. (Highly insightful on Ruskin as reader, seer, critic.)

———. "The Structure of Ruskin's *Praeterita*." In *Approaches to Victorian Autobiography*, ed. George P. Landow. Athens: Ohio Univ. Press, 1979. (A major essay.)

Henderson, Heather. "Revelation and Recurrence in Ruskin's *Praeterita*." In *The Victorian Self: Autobiography and Biblical Nar-*

rative. Ithaca: Cornell Univ. Press, 1989. (Apt title to a splendid reading.)

Hewison, Robert. *John Ruskin: The Argument of the Eye.* Princeton: Princeton Univ. Press, 1976. (Excellent on Ruskin's visual imagination.)

———, ed. *New Approaches to Ruskin: Thirteen Essays.* London: Routledge, 1981.

———. *Ruskin and Oxford: The Art of Education.* Oxford: Oxford Univ. Press, 1996. (Illustrated catalog with essay.)

Hilton, Tim. *John Ruskin: The Early Years 1819–1859.* New Haven: Yale Univ. Press, 1985.

Hobson, J. A. *John Ruskin: Social Reformer.* Boston: Dana Estes, 1898. (Dated; still useful.)

Hough, Graham. "Ruskin." In *The Last Romantics.* London: Duckworth, 1949. (Indispensable essay.)

Hunt, John Dixon. *The Wider Sea: A Life of John Ruskin.* New York: Viking, 1982. (Best modern biography.)

Hunt, John Dixon, and Faith M. Holland, eds. *The Ruskin Polygon: Essays on the Imagination of John Ruskin.* Manchester: Manchester Univ. Press, 1982.

Kempf, Wolfgang. *The Desire of My Eyes: The Life and Work of John Ruskin.* Transl. Jan Van Heurck. London: HarperCollins, 1991.

Ladd, Henry. *The Victorian Morality of Art: An Analysis of Ruskin's Esthetic.* Long & Smith, 1932.

Landow, George P. *Ruskin.* Oxford: Oxford Univ. Press, 1985. (Fine introduction.)

———. *The Aesthetic and Critical Theories of John Ruskin.* Princeton: Princeton Univ. Press, 1971. (Pioneering study of evangelical and typological roots of Ruskin's aesthetics.)

La Touche, Rose. *John Ruskin and Rose La Touche: Her Unpublished Diaries of 1861 and 1867.* Ed. and intr. Van Akin Burd. New York: Oxford Univ. Press, 1979.

Leon, Derrick. *Ruskin: The Great Victorian.* London: Routledge, 1949. (First draft of an important, massive biography unrevised at the author's death; especially useful on Ruskin's relations with Rose La Touche.)

Lutyens, Mary. *Millais and the Ruskins.* New York: Vanguard, 1968.

———, ed. *Young Mrs. Ruskin in Venice: Unpublished Letters . . . 1849–52.* New York: Vanguard, 1966. (The wife conspicuously absent from *Praeterita*).

Maurois, Andre. "Proust et Ruskin." *Essays and Studies by Members of the English Association* 17 (1931): 25–32. (Useful early account of Ruskin's influence on Proust and of their stylistic affinities.)

Merrill, Linda. *A Pot of Paint: Aesthetics on Trial in "Whistler v. Ruskin."* Washington, D.C.: Smithsonian Institution Press, 1992. (Definitive account of the celebrated trial.)

Miller, J. Hillis. "Prosopopeia and *Praeterita*." In *Nineteenth-Century Lives,* ed. Lawrence S. Lockridge et al. Cambridge: Cambridge Univ. Press, 1989. (Defies summary but rewards reading.)

Painter, George D. "Salvation through Ruskin." In *Proust: The Early Years.* Boston: Little, Brown, 1959.

Peltason, Timothy. "Ruskin's Finale: Vision and Imagination in *Praeterita.*" *ELH* 57 (1990): 665–84.

Peterson, Linda. "Ruskin's *Praeterita.*" In *Victorian Autobiography: The Tradition of Self-Interpretation.* New Haven: Yale Univ. Press, 1992. (Ruskin's rejection of typological narrative.)

Pritchett, V. S. "The Most Solitary Victorian." Review of *The Diaries of John Ruskin. New Statesman and Nation,* 20 October 1956: 489–90. (Brilliant, brief essay on Ruskin's "visual egotism.")

Proust, Marcel. *On Reading Ruskin: Prefaces to* La Bible d'Amiens *and* Sesame et les lys. Trans. and ed. Jean Autret et al. New Haven: Yale Univ. Press, 1987. (Extraordinary essays in which Proust, analyzing the quality of Ruskin's genius, comes to a sharpened consciousness of his own.)

Quennell, Peter. *John Ruskin: The Portrait of a Prophet.* New York: Viking Press, 1949.

Rhodes, Robert, and Del Ivan Janik, eds. *Studies in Ruskin: Essays in Honor of Van Akin Burd.* Athens: Ohio Univ. Press, 1982. (Several important essays.)

Rose, Phyllis. "Effie Gray and John Ruskin." In *Parallel Lives: Five Victorian Marriages.* New York: Knopf, 1983. (Eminently readable account of a disaster.)

Rosenberg, John D. *The Darkening Glass: A Portrait of Ruskin's Genius.* New York: Columbia Univ. Press, 1961. (Standard intellectual biography.)

———. "The Geopoetry of John Ruskin." *Études Anglaises* 22 (1969): 42–48.

———. "Ruskin's Benediction: A Reading of *Fors Clavigera.*" In *New Approaches to Ruskin,* ed. Robert Hewison. London: Routledge, 1981.

———. "Style and Sensibility in Ruskin's Prose." In *The Art of Victorian Prose,* ed. George Levine and William Madden. New York: Oxford Univ. Press, 1968.

Ruskin, John. *The Works of John Ruskin.* Ed. E. T. Cook and Alexander Wedderburn. 39 vols. London: George Allen, 1903–12. (Magisterial edition, superbly indexed, sumptuously illustrated with Ruskin's drawings; contains biographical notes and a complete bibliography through 1911.)

———. *The Diaries of John Ruskin.* Sel. and ed. Joan Evans and John Howard Whitehouse. 3 vols. Oxford: Clarendon Press, 1956–59. (The daily, spontaneous record of Ruskin's life from 1835–89.)

———. *The Brantwood Diary of John Ruskin.* Ed. Helen Gill Viljoen. New Haven: Yale Univ. Press, 1971. (Ruskin's diaries, superbly annotated, in the years of his mental breakdown.)

———. *Ruskin's Letters from Venice 1851–1852.* Ed. John Lewis Bradley. New Haven: Yale Univ. Press, 1955. (Rpt. Greenwood Press, 1978.) (Letters to Ruskin's parents; especially revealing of the deep religious doubt not yet evident in his published works.)

———. *The Correspondence of John Ruskin and Charles Eliot Norton.* Ed. John L. Bradley and Ian Ousby. New York: Cambridge Univ. Press, 1987. (Several of Ruskin's most revealing letters.)

———. *Christmas Story: John Ruskin's Venetian Letters of 1876–1877.* Ed. Van Akin Burd. Newark: Univ. of Delaware Press, 1990. (Ruskin, Rose La Touche, and the Spiritualists.)

———. *The Ruskin Family Letters: The Correspondence of John James Ruskin, His Wife, and Their Son, John, 1801–1843.* 2 vols. Ed. Van Akin Burd. Ithaca: Cornell Univ. Press, 1973. (Importantly modifies Ruskin's portrait of his parents in *Praeterita.*)

———. *The Correspondence of Thomas Carlyle and John Ruskin.* Ed. George Allen Cate. Stanford: Stanford Univ. Press, 1982.

———. *John Ruskin: Letters from the Continent, 1858.* Ed. John Hayman. Toronto: Univ. of Toronto Press, 1982. (The year of Ruskin's "unconversion" at Turin.)

———. *The Order of Release: The Story of John Ruskin, Effie Gray and John Everett Millais . . . Their Unpublished Letters.* Ed. Sir William James. London: John Murray, 1948. (Sharply biased but indispensable for the strange and sorry light it casts upon Ruskin's marriage and upon himself.)

———. *Ruskin in Italy: Letters to His Parents, 1845.* Ed. Harold I. Shapiro. Oxford: Clarendon Press, 1972. (The tour that shaped Ruskin's future career.)

———. *The Gulf of Years: Letters from John Ruskin to Kathleen Olander.* Ed. Rayner Unwin. London: Allen & Unwin, 1953. (The aged Ruskin's love letters to a young art student.)

———. *A Tour to the Lakes in Cumberland: John Ruskin's Diary for 1830.* Ed. James S. Dearden. Aldershot: Scholar Press, 1990.

Sawyer, Paul. *Ruskin's Poetic Argument: The Design of the Major Works.* Ithaca: Cornell Univ. Press, 1985. (Beautifully integrated study of the man, the mind, and the major works.)

Shaw, George Bernard. *Ruskin's Politics.* Ruskin Centenary Council, 1921. (Perverse but brilliant lecture on Ruskin as a Tory-Communist.)

Sherburne, James Clark. *John Ruskin, or the Ambiguities of Abundance: A Study in Social and Economic Criticism.* Cambridge: Harvard Univ. Press, 1972.

Spear, Jeffrey L. *Dreams of an English Eden: Ruskin and His Tradition in Social Criticism.* New York: Columbia Univ. Press, 1984.

Staley, Allen. *The Pre-Raphaelite Landscape.* Oxford, 1973. (Ruskin's influence.)

Stein, Richard L. *The Ritual of Interpretation: The Fine Arts as Literature in Ruskin, Rossetti, and Pater.* Cambridge: Harvard Univ. Press, 1975. (On *Modern Painters* and *The Stones of Venice.*)

Stein, Roger B. *John Ruskin and Aesthetic Thought in America, 1840–1900.* Cambridge: Harvard Univ. Press, 1967.

Stephen, Leslie. "John Ruskin." In *Studies of a Biographer,* 2d series, vol. 3. London: Duckworth, 1902. (Judicious appreciation.)

Tanner, Tony. "John Ruskin: This Sea-Dog of Towns." In *Venice Desired.* Cambridge: Harvard Univ. Press, 1992.

Townsend, Francis G. "John Ruskin." In *Victorian Prose: A Guide to Research,* ed. David J. DeLaura. New York: Modern Language Association, 1973. (Excellent survey through 1970.)

———. *Ruskin and the Landscape Feeling.* Urbana: Univ. of Illinois Press, 1951. (Ruskin's darkening sense of nature and the consequent waning of his love of art.)

Unrau, John. *Looking at Architecture with Ruskin.* London: Thames & Hudson, 1978. (Astute and engaging guide to Ruskin's architectural writings and drawings.)

Viljoen, Helen Gill. *Ruskin's Scottish Heritage: A Prelude.* Urbana: Univ. of Illinois Press, 1951. (The fullest account of Ruskin's ancestry and early influences; unfortunately, the "prelude" ends with Ruskin's birth.)

Walton, Paul H. *The Drawings of John Ruskin.* Oxford: Clarendon Press, 1972. (Reprint, New York: Hacker, 1985.) (Important, neglected aspect of Ruskin's creativity.)

Wheeler, Michael, ed. *Ruskin and Environment: The Storm-Cloud of the Nineteenth Century.* Manchester: Manchester Univ. Press, 1995. (Varied perspectives on a vital issue.)

Wheeler, Michael, and Nigel Whiteley, eds. *The Lamp of Memory: Ruskin, Tradition, and Architecture.* Manchester: Manchester Univ. Press, 1992. (Several important essays.)

Whistler, J. A. McNeill. *Whistler v. Ruskin: Art and Art Critics.* London: Chatto & Windus, 1878.

Wihl, Gary. *Ruskin and the Rhetoric of Infallibility.* New Haven: Yale Univ. Press, 1985. ("Epistemological cruxes" in *Modern Painters.*)

Wilenski, R. H. *John Ruskin: An Introduction to Further Study of His Life and Work.* London: Faber & Faber, 1933. (First modern study of Ruskin's mind worthy of its subject.)

Victorian Literature and Culture Series